Learn...
Carro... W9-DFB-234
1601 Washington Rd.
Westminster, MD 21157

WITHDRAWN

Third Edition

Literacy Development in the Early Years

Helping Children Read and Write

Lesley Mandel Morrow

Rutgers, The State University

Allyn and Bacon

Boston ◆ London ◆ Toronto ◆ Sydney ◆ Tokyo ◆ Singapore

Senior Editor: Virginia C. Lanigan
Series Editorial Assistant: Nihad M. Farooq
Executive Marketing Manager: Kathy Hunter
Editorial-Production Administrator: Deborah Brown
Editorial-Production Service: P. M. Gordon Associates
Composition Buyer: Linda Cox
Manufacturing Buyer: Megan Cochran
Cover Administrator: Suzanne Harbison

Copyright © 1997, 1993, 1990 by Allyn & Bacon
A Viacom Company
160 Gould Street
Needham Heights, MA 02194

Internet: www.abacon.com
America Online: Keyword: College Online

To Mary, Milton, Frank, and Stephanie
my very special parents,
my very special husband ,
and my very special daughter

All rights reserved. No part of the material protected by this copyright notice may be reproduced or utilized in any form or by any means, electronic or mechanical, including photocopying, recording, or by any information storage and retrieval system, without the written permission of the copyright owner.

Library of Congress Cataloging-in-Publication Data

Morrow, Lesley Mandel.
    Literacy development in the early years : helping children read and write / Lesley Mandel Morrow.—3rd ed.
      p. cm.
    Includes bibliographical references and index.
    ISBN 0–205–17442–6
    1. Language arts (Preschool)—United States. 2. Reading (Preschool)—United States. 3. Children—United States—Books and reading. I. Title.
LB1140.5.L3M66 1996
372.6'0973—dc20   96–10711
                                        CIP

Printed in the United States of America
10 9 8 7 6 5 4 3 2   01 00 99 98 97

Four line drawings, Morrow Literacy Center, floor plan of a classroom, a contract, and bookmaking directions: Pamela Cromey, Michael Gravois
Photographs: Lenore Arone, Susan Arone, Joyce Caponigro, Lori Harrje, Katherine Heiss, Pam Kelliher, Milton E. Mandel, Howard Manson, Franklin A. Morrow, Lesley Mandel Morrow, Andrea Shane

Contents

Chapter 1
Foundations of Early Literacy Development   1

Chapter 2
Observing and Assessing the Needs of Children: Multicultural and Special Learning Needs   31

Chapter 3
Family Literacy Partnerships: Home and School Working Together   53

Chapter 4
Language and Literacy Development   87

Chapter 5
How Young Children Learn to Read and Write: an Emergent Literacy Perspective   *125*

Chapter 6
Motivating Reading and Writing through the Use of Children's Literature   *151*

Chapter 7
Developing Concepts about Books and Comprehension of Text   191

Chapter 8
Developing Reading through Learning about Print   229

Chapter 9
Writing and Literacy Development   257

Chapter 10
Organizing and Managing the Learning Environment
for Literacy Development at School   299

Foreword

Dramatic changes in our understanding of early literacy development have occurred during the last decade. Where we once thought that children learned to speak and listen during their early years and later learned to read and write at school age of five or six years, we now know that they develop language-related abilities "all of a piece" (simultaneously) from the days of infancy onward.

During the last decade, we have also discovered that the conditions that promote first language learning are the same conditions that promote total literacy development. These conditions, created in the social context surrounding a child, involve immersion, approximation, opportunity to practice, feedback, and modeling (Cambourne, 1984).

Lesley Morrow demonstrates the value of immersing children in the language we want them to learn—that includes the language of literature as well as the language of daily living. She provides numerous examples of children's approximations of writing and reading as she establishes the necessity of giving them unlimited opportunities to practice. Further, she illustrates the ways adults provide feedback and models for young language learners as they attempt to read and write. Dr. Morrow takes a balanced perspective toward literacy instruction by selecting the best techniques from learning theory, such as constructivist ideas, to some more direct explicit instruction.

Children's literature, the area I know best, is central to Morrow's literacy environment. Literature serves as a model for language learning and provides strong motivation for learning to read and write. It is a springboard for all sorts of literacy-related activities. Most important, literature is a way of knowing. It is shaped around story—a primary act of human minds.

Dr. Lesley Morrow knows about children's literature, too. She recognizes the impact of fathers, mothers, siblings, babysitters, grandparents, and other caregivers reading to children and enjoying the wealth of books. She shows how reading to babies influences their grasp of language and story patterns that serve them well as they learn to read and write. She illustrates how children learn concepts about print, book handling, and conventions of stories as they interact with books. Morrow establishes that adults teach by example as they enjoy shared reading and shared writing with children. She shows the impact of having a literacy center in a classroom and the effects of storybook reading aloud by a teacher. She shows that when children know authors and illustrators as real people, they want to read their works and write in a manner similar to their idols. She states that storytelling is similar to reading aloud in its impact on children.

Speaking from her own experiences as a teacher, researcher, and parent, she charts a path that leads to successful literacy learning.

Lesley Morrow has taken a long view of literacy development in the early years, showing its historical roots, ideas that are valid today. She also knows and draws upon the trend-setting research of today's leaders because she is a member of that research community. She succinctly summarizes language theories and relates current research to shape sound practices. She has conducted much of the original research herself, testimony to the fact that she can bridge the gap between theory, research, and practice. Her examples are anchored in real classroom experiences—her own and those of other teachers with whom she works collaboratively. The examples have the ring of authenticity and add credibility to her argument.

Morrow's treatment of literacy development is on the cutting edge of current knowledge. She is well informed about her subject and makes connections among all aspects of literacy learning. She is a sensitive observer and writer as she lets children and teachers speak for themselves through their work.

Morrow states that few children learn to love books by themselves. Someone must lure them into the joys of the printed work and the wonderful world of stories. She shows us how to do that and enriches our lives and the lives of children through her work. Her contribution to the literary development of young children is a lasting one.

Bernice E. Cullinan
Professor of Early Childhood Education
and Elementary Education
New York University

Preface

Literacy Development in the Early Years, Third Edition, is for teachers, reading specialists, administrators, students in teacher education programs, and parents. It is appropriate for both graduate and undergraduate courses in early literacy, and it complements texts on the teaching of reading in the elementary school, child development, the early childhood curriculum, teaching language arts in the elementary school, and children's literature.

I wrote the book because of my special interest in literacy development in early childhood. I taught in preschools, kindergartens, the primary grades; was a reading specialist; and then went on to teach early childhood curriculum and literacy courses at the university level. My research has focused on instructional strategies in early literacy. A wealth of research information has been created in this area over the past several years. That research has generated new theory and given new strength to certain older theories of learning. It has implications for new instructional strategies and reinforces certain older practices that had little or no research to establish their validity. It describes a program that nurtures literacy development from birth to third grade.

Although the book is about early literacy, its content has strong ramifications for reading instruction in the elementary grades. The fundamental ideas presented in this volume are applicable for literacy instruction in elementary grade classrooms. As we all recognize, there is little in education that is radically new; what we know simply gets refined, reorganized, or verified. In many respects, some parts of this book may sound like some of the earliest volumes on early literacy.

This book does not offer a prescription. Formula programs stop teachers from thinking for themselves and therefore do not reflect the traditional ideals of American education. The ideas offered in this book have been tried and they have worked, but not all are appropriate for all teachers or all children. The good teacher functions most effectively with strategies he or she feels most comfortable with. The teacher needs to be a decision maker who thinks critically about the design of his or her literacy program and the selection of materials. Children should be included in some of the decision making. Children come to school with diverse cultural backgrounds, experiences, exposures to literacy, and abilities. Instructional programs can differ in different parts of the country, in different localities, and for different children in the same classroom.

Underlying this book is the merging of the art and the science of teaching. The science involves theories based on research findings that have generated instructional strategies. The book contains descriptions of strategies and steps for carrying them out. But, the scientific research does not necessarily take into account individual differences among teachers and children. The art of teaching concentrates on those human variables. The book provides a *balanced approach* to early literacy instruction. It discusses what research has found to be successful instructional strategies based on many learning theories. A blend of constructivist ideas with some explicit direct instruction approaches are presented so that teachers can decide what works best for the children they teach.

Chapter 1 provides a framework of theory and research, past and current, that has influenced strategies for developing early literacy.

Chapter 2 is new to the third edition of the book and deals with the important issues of assessment and children with special needs. Multicultural and special learning needs are also discussed. This chapter introduces these concepts to the reader. These practical strategies for assessment of children's growth in literacy are integrated throughout the book, as are concerns for individual differences, whether they be for multicultural needs or special learning problems.

Chapter 3 discusses the strong influence of the home on the development of literacy, especially in a child's earliest years. It discusses broad perspectives concerning family literacy such as integrated home/school programs, intergenerational programs, and sensitivity to cultural differences to provide programs that are not intrusive, but rather build on the strengths of the families being served.

Chapters 4 through 9 deal with areas of literacy development, oral language, reading, and writing. These chapters discuss theory, research, developmental trends, instructional strategies, and methods for assessment. The book views the development of literacy skills (reading, writing, and oral language) as concurrent and interrelated: the development of one enhances the development of the others. Furthermore, the theories, stages, acquisition, and strategies associated with each are similar, and it is difficult to separate them entirely. To make the volume more readable, however, I have treated the different areas of literacy in different chapters.

Chapter 10 discusses the preparation and management of the components, presented in the book, that are organized to create a successful program. This chapter emphasizes the interrelatedness of the areas of literacy and describes how they can be integrated into the entire school day within content areas. A separate chapter has not been devoted to addressing the needs of children with disabilities, or children from culturally diverse backgrounds. Instead, I integrated the concept—meeting individual needs—within all chapters throughout the book. Special attention to issues of individual differences is emphasized in Chapters 1, 2, 3, and 9.

Each chapter begins with questions to focus on while reading the text. Each chapter ends with suggested activities, questions, an idea for the classroom from the classroom, and case study activities to be used by preservice and inservice teachers. The appendixes list materials that teachers use in carrying out a successful program to develop early literacy. Key words dealing with early literacy development are defined in the glossary at the end of the book.

Acknowledgments

I want to thank many individuals who helped in the preparation of the first, second, and third editions of this book. Students who helped in the past were: Patricia Addonizio, Mary Belchik, Susan Burks, Kathleen Cunningham, Katie Farrell, Donna Fino Nagi, Mary Ann Gavin, Laura Babarca, Tricia Lyons, Melody Murray Olsen, Michele Preole, Mary Joyce Santoloci, Sari Schnipper, and Karen Szabo. Students who helped with this edition include: Patricia DeWitt, Erica Erlanger, Michael Gravois, Katherine Heiss, Pamela Kelliher, Lisa Lozak, Stacey Rog, Monica Saraiya, and Connie Zauderer.

Thank you to the teachers and administrators who helped in the past and in this present volume: Maxine Bell, Karen Buda, Pat Burton, Barbara Callister, Tom DelCasale, Fran Diamente, Arlene Hall, David Harris, Lori Harrje, Noreen Johnson, Sheryl King, Penelope Lattimer, Gail Martinez, Nancy Mason, Joyce McGee, Carna Meechem, Dennis Monaghan, Stephanie Moretti, Joyce Ng, Ellen O'Connor, Lucy Oman, Barbara Oxfeld, Mary Payton, Tammye Pelovitz, Cynthia Peters, John Quintaglie, Robert Rosado, Sonia Satterwhite, Joyce Schenkman, Linda Schifflette, and Patty Thaxton.

Thank you to Andrea Shane, Milton Mandel, and Howard Manson for many of the photographs, and to Pamela Cromey and Michael Gravois for many of the illustrations.

Major portions of the appendixes were prepared by Patricia DeWitt, Erica Erlanger, Katherine Heiss, Pamela Kelliher, Tricia Lyons, Stacey Rog, and Mary Joyce Santoloci.

Thank you to Nancy Forsyth, Virginia Lanigan, Nihad Farooq, and Deborah Brown from Allyn and Bacon, and Mary McDonald from P. M. Gordon Associates for supporting the concept of a third edition of this book and for the guidance they offered during the revision process.

Thank you in particular to the children I have taught, my college students, and the excellent teachers I have observed, from whom I've learned so much. Thank you to the researchers in early literacy who have provided exciting information in the field. I consider this book a cooperative effort as a result of the contributions of so many in both direct and indirect ways.

Thank you to those who reviewed the third edition of the book including Toni Stiefer, South Eastern Oklahoma University; Carol R. Foster, Georgia State University; and Margaret Genision, Univeristy of Wisconsin; and to the many college professors, college students, teachers, and parents who purchased the book and demonstrated their support for the publication. The third edition was made possible by you.

Thank you to my parents, Mary and Milton Mandel, who provided a rich literacy environment for me; thank you to Frank Morrow, my companion and computer consultant; and thank you to Stephanie Morrow, my friend and daughter, for demonstrating the validity of many of the concepts expressed in the book.

L.M.M.

Chapter 1

Foundations of Early Literacy Development

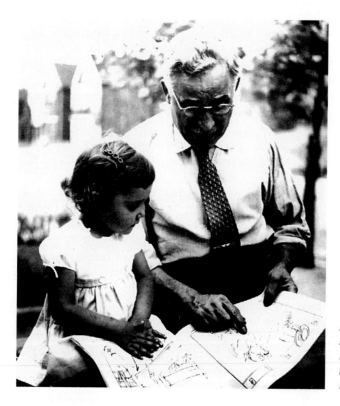

Learning requires a supportive environment that builds positive feelings about self and literacy activities.

What a dangerous activity reading is: teaching is. All this plastering of foreign stuff. Why plaster on at all when there's so much inside already? So much locked in? If only I could draw it out and use it as working material. And not draw it out either. If I had a light enough touch, it would just come out under its own volcanic power.

—Sylvia Ashton-Warner
Spinster

Questions To Focus On As You Read

◆ Which educators, theorists, philosophers, and psychologists influenced early childhood education, and what was each one's unique contribution to instructional strategies used in classrooms for young children?

◆ What knowledge about child development is important to literacy learning and why?

◆ What have been the different approaches to literacy learning from the early 1900s through the 1960s?

◆ How is the term *reading readiness* defined in relation to literacy instruction?

◆ What practical applications has the research on oral language, early reading and writing, and rich literacy environments at home had on early literacy instruction in the classroom?

◆ What concepts reflect the whole language orientation?

◆ What is meant by thematic unit instruction?

◆ What do we mean when we speak of a Balanced Perspective to Literacy Instruction?

1

Four-year-old Jonathan and his mother were driving in the car to do some errands. They approached the mall and Jonathan popped up in a loud voice and said, "Look Mommy, I can read those letters. M...A...C...Y...S. Those letters spell Sears." Jonathan's mother smiled and praised him. "That was great, Jon. You got every letter right. Now I'll read the sign for you; it says Macy's. This is another department store like Sears. You did some good thinking when you tried to read that word."

Not too long ago we would have laughed at Jonathan's remarks as cute but incorrect. Today we realize that he is demonstrating a great deal of literacy knowledge that needs to be recognized. First, he knows what letters are and can identify the ones in the sign. Next, he knows that letters spell words. He knows that words are read and have meaning. Although he did not read the word correctly, he made an informed guess. Jonathan was aware that this building was a department store, but he had never been to this one, so he called the new store by the name of the one with which he was already familiar. He was trying some of his literacy knowledge out on an adult who he knew was interested and willing to interact positively with him. His mother offered positive reinforcement for what he did know and support by modeling the correct response when he needed some help.

Babies begin to acquire information about literacy from the moment of birth. They continue to build on their knowledge of oral language, reading, and writing as they go through early childhood. Recently, a great deal of attention has been focused on literacy development in early childhood, an area somewhat neglected in the past. Teachers, parents, and administrators did not perceive preschoolers as readers or writers. They emphasized oral language development and preparation for reading. Because of increased research, thinking about early literacy has changed: very young children are now viewed as individuals with literacy skills. The literacy skills of preschoolers and kindergartners are not those of older children or adults, but youngsters do acquire literacy traits that must be acknowledged and that have implications for instructional practice.

Over the past few years, research on literacy development in early childhood has burgeoned. That research not only has introduced new information, it has also raised concerns about certain common practices in early childhood literacy instruction and an awareness of the need for change. Like a child's first words and first steps, learning to read and write should be an exciting, fulfilling, and rewarding experience. Unfortunately, it sometimes is not. This book draws on the newer research and blends it with theory and practice that have proved successful. It presents a program for developing literacy in children from birth to seven years. It is based on the following rationale (IRA, 1985):

1. Literacy learning begins in infancy.
2. Parents need to provide a rich literacy environment to help children acquire literacy skills.

3. School personnel must be aware that children come to school with prior knowledge of oral and written language.
4. Early reading and writing experiences at school should build upon that existing knowledge.
5. Learning requires a supportive environment that builds positive feelings about self as well as about literacy activities.
6. Adults must serve as models for literacy behavior, by demonstrating an interest in books and print.
7. During their literacy experiences, children must interact within a social context so that they can share information and learn from each other.
8. Early literacy experiences should be meaningful and concrete and should *actively* involve the child in problem solving and some explicit direct instruction.
9. A literacy development program should focus on utilizing functional experiences that include the use of oral language, listening, writing, and reading.
10. Differences in cultural and language backgrounds must be acknowledged and addressed.

This book incorporates the work of learning theorists, philosophers, educators, psychologists, and researchers who have described how young children learn. It builds on the implications their work holds for instruction and reflects a balanced approach toward literacy development in early childhood. Throughout, it emphasizes development of literacy through the teaching of language, listening, reading, and writing in coordination with other content areas across the curriculum. Though some of the chapters concentrate on language, reading, or writing, an important concern at all times is the integration of all four dimensions of literacy.

Literacy development early in life must focus on both learning and teaching. The teacher prepares an environment rich in literacy materials and activities from which children can choose; the children are encouraged to be actively involved in learning with other children, with materials, and with the teacher. A major focus of the book is how to provide an environment that will encourage children to take an interest in reading, to associate it with pleasure, and ultimately to read by choice.

Learning Theories That Have Shaped Practices

Several important philosophers, theorists, educators, and psychologists have addressed learning in early childhood, including the issue of appropriate educational practice. These ideas represent varying responses to the question of whether learning is primarily a matter of the *nature* or the *nurture* of the child.

Theory and Philosophy from the 1700s and 1800s

Rousseau Rousseau (1762) strongly suggested that a child's early education be natural. That is, children should not be forced to learn things for which they are not developmentally ready. Rousseau advocated abandoning the contrived imposition of instruction on children and instead allowing children to grow and learn with the freedom to be themselves. Education follows the child's own development and readiness for learning. According to Rousseau, children learn through curiosity; forcing education upon them interferes with their learning and development. He believed that individual children have ways of learning peculiar to themselves, ways that formal instruction should not tamper with. Rousseau's philosophy suggests that the role of the educator is to use strategies that mesh with the child's readiness to learn. Rousseau strongly emphasized as little intervention by an adult as possible. He believed a child's learning "unfolds" naturally.

Pestalozzi Pestalozzi (Rusk & Scotland, 1979) was influenced by Rousseau's emphasis on natural learning, but he added a dimension to it. He started his own school and developed principles for learning that combined natural elements with informal instruction. He found it unrealistic to expect children to learn totally on their own initiative. Although he felt that children may be able to teach themselves to read, for example, he also felt that it was necessary for teachers or parents to create the climate and conditions in which the reading process grows. The natural potential of a child develops, he believed, through sensory manipulative experiences, so he designed lessons that involved manipulating objects and learning about them through touch, smell, language, size, and shape.

Froebel Froebel's (1974) approach was similar in some ways to those of his predecessors. Like Rousseau, he believed that the adult responsible for the education of a child needs to be concerned with the child's natural unfolding. He also followed Pestalozzi's ideas and provided plans for instructing young children. But he is best known for emphasizing the importance of play in learning. He specified, however, that realizing the fullest benefits of playing-to-learn requires adult guidance and direction and a planned environment. Froebel saw the teacher as a designer of activities and experiences that facilitate learning. On this premise he designed a systematic curriculum for young children involving objects and materials that he called *gifts* and *occupations*. In handling and playing with these objects and materials, children not only use psychomotor skills but learn about shape, color, size, measurement, and comparison as well. It was Froebel who coined the word *kindergarten,* which means "children's garden." The phrase illustrates his basic philosophy that children, like plants, will grow to fruition only if they are tended and cared for. He often referred to the child as the seed being cared for by the gardener, or teacher.

Froebel was the first educator to design an organized curriculum for young children, and many of his strategies are evident in preschools and kindergartens today. Most significant among his strategies was his emphasis on guided play as a method for learning, the learning of certain concepts through manipulative materials that utilize the senses, and *circle time*—an opportunity to sing songs and learn new ideas through discussion.

Moving into the Twentieth Century

Dewey John Dewey's (1966) views in the twentieth century were not unlike Froebel's. His philosophy of early childhood education led to the concept of the child-centered curriculum or progressive education as it was often called. Dewey believed that the curriculum should be built around the interests of children. He agreed with Froebel that children learn best through play and in real life. He maintained that social interactions encourage learning and that interests are the vehicles for learning information and skills. He rejected the idea of teaching skills as an end unto themselves. He also believed that learning is maximized through the integration of content areas.

Froebel and Dewey have significantly influenced programs in American preschools and kindergartens throughout the twentieth century, and especially from the 1920s through the 1950s. During those decades, preschools and kindergartens typically had different areas for different activities. Shelves in a "block corner" held various sizes and shapes of blocks, small cars, trucks, and wooden figures of people. An art area contained easels with watercolors, crayons, paper, paste, scissors, construction paper, clay, and scraps of interesting materials such as fabric, plastic foam, and pipe cleaners for making collages. The dramatic-play corner was set up like a kitchen, with sink, oven, refrigerator, empty food boxes, table and chairs, telephone, mirror, dolls, and some clothing for dressing up. Still another area held manipulative toys that teach concepts about color, shape, and size. A science area revealed a water-play table, shells, interesting rocks, plants, a class animal, magnets, and magnifying glasses. The music area usually had a piano, rhythm instruments, and a record player. Sometimes there was a rug for children to sit on when they came to sing by the piano. One corner of the room had a shelf of children's literature and, depending on the teacher, soft pillows to lie on when looking at books.

The daily routine was similar in most of these settings. As children entered the classroom, they played with quiet toys. The teacher then called them to circle time to talk about the weather and the calendar. Conversation soon focused on a topic in social studies or science—animals or community helpers, for instance—with perhaps a song in keeping with the theme. Circle time was commonly followed by a long period called free play in which children could use the materials in the different areas of the room. There was minimal guidance during free play;

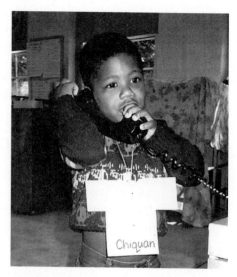

According to the concepts of Pestalozzi, Froebel, Dewey, Piaget, Vygotsky, and other philosophers and theorists, learning in early childhood will take place when youngsters have the opportunity to explore, experiment, play at real-life experiences, and manipulate materials. They need to do this sometimes by interacting with adults or other children and sometimes by working alone.

children could explore and experiment with the materials. A snack, sometimes followed by a rest period, was an integral part of the daily routine. The day might also include a special lesson in art, social studies, or science appropriate to the unit being studied. Outdoor play allowed children to run, climb, play in sand-boxes, and use riding toys. The teacher read a story daily, probably at the end of the day, often relating it to the topic being studied.

Reading and mathematics were not taught formally or as isolated skills. Instead, the teacher might ask a child to count out enough cookies for all the children in the class, to name the date on the calendar, or to compare the sizes of different children. There were no workbooks or commercial reading materials. Teachers led some informal activities that could eventually lead to reading, but they did not attempt to teach children to read. The letters of the alphabet might be found strung across the wall, the days of the week pointed out on a calendar, children's names written on their cubbies, and some other items in the room labeled with words. The general atmosphere was relaxed. The goal was to accustom children to school routines and make them comfortable in the school environment. The focus was on social, emotional, and physical development. There was no place in these programs for formal reading and writing instruction.

Montessori Maria Montessori (1965) departed from the educators and philosophers mentioned thus far. Although she believed in the use of the senses to promote learning, her emphasis on the senses was not based on the natural unfolding of the child, the child's interests, or play. Believing that children needed early, orderly, systematic training in mastering one skill after another, she supplied her teaching environment with materials for learning specific concepts in order to meet specific objectives. The materials provided the source of learning for the child. Children educated themselves by using these manipulatives, and because the materials were self-correcting, the children could determine their own errors and make corrections independently.

Montessori referred to this type of learning as *auto-education.* Like Froebel and Pestalozzi, she spoke of *sensitive periods,* when children are better able to learn certain things than at other times. It is the role of the parent or teacher to watch for these periods and take advantage of them by preparing the environment with appropriate materials and experiences for learning. In short, according to Montessori, the teacher is a guide who prepares an environment for learning. But unlike the educators already discussed, Montessori carefully designed learning materials to teach specific skills. In Montessori's curriculum, children's natural curiosity and their propensity for exploration are of less concern than their ability to work with specific materials to achieve a specific goal. Play is not as important as work because it might waste precious opportunities for goal achievement during sensitive periods for learning. Although some of her ideas are not relevant to the new thrust in early literacy, her emphasis on learning rather than teaching; her concerns about independent learning, sensitive periods for learning, and respect for the child; and her insistence on organization and a prepared environment hold implications for today's instruction.

Piaget   Piaget's theory (Piaget & Inhelder, 1969) of cognitive development has had a particularly strong impact on early childhood education. In describing the stages of cognitive development, he recognized that children at certain stages are capable of only certain types of intellectual endeavors. Trying to involve children in abstract experiences during the preoperational stages of their early childhood, for instance, is considered inappropriate. Piaget did not advocate Montessori's systematic approach, nor did he believe in maturation as a completely natural unfolding. He believed, rather, that a child acquires knowledge by interacting with the world. Educators who have applied his theories involve children in natural problem-solving situations where they can assimilate new experiences into their existing knowledge. Children are active participants in their own learning, constantly changing and reorganizing their own knowledge.

Piaget stressed that learning takes place when the child interacts with peers and adults in a social setting as they act upon the environment. Educators who have incorporated Piaget's theories in curricula for early childhood education have designed programs that look very much like what Pestalozzi or Froebel might have created: a setting with many real-life materials, including the opportunity to play, explore, and experiment. Piaget agreed that young children should use their curiosity, inquisitiveness, and spontaneity to help themselves learn. In addition, a Piagetian preschool curriculum emphasizes decision-making, problem solving, self-discipline, goal setting, planning one's own activities, and cooperating with teachers and peers in evaluating learning.

Vygotsky Vygotsky's (1981) general theory of intellectual development also has implications for learning in early childhood. Vygotsky believes that mental functions are acquired through social relationships. Children learn by internalizing activities conducted in the world around them. Children emulate behaviors and incorporate them into their existing structure of knowledge when they are exposed to new situations in which they can actively interact with others.

The learning theories of the individuals discussed have contributed to the way we look at literacy development in early childhood education. Their ideas are the basis for early literacy instruction as it is described in this book. Particularly applicable among their concepts are these:

1. Concern for a child's level of development—physical, social, emotional, and intellectual—when preparing a learning environment for that child
2. Concern for prepared environments in which learning can take place
3. Emphasis on learning rather than teaching
4. The learner's need for social interaction with supportive adults and other children
5. Focus on learning through real experiences in meaningful and natural settings rather than by imposed, contrived objectives or techniques
6. An awareness that children must actively participate in their own learning by engaging in manipulative experiences that are both functional and interesting

Practices in the Past

Judging from the professional literature of the early 1900s, little attention was paid to a child's literacy development before he or she entered school. Apparently it was generally assumed that literacy began with formal instruction in first grade. A strong influence on reading instruction came from developmental psychologists such as Gesell (1925) who advocated maturation as the most important factor in learning to read. Reading instruction was frowned on until the child was ready to read. Preschool and kindergarten teachers generally ignored or avoided reading instruction. But they did follow some of the teachings of Pestalozzi and Froebel. Typically, they read to children often; encouraged play, exploration, and problem solving; and led songs and discussions in circle times. Methods were child-centered, teaching units were interdisciplinary, and learning environments and instructional strategies were appropriate to the child's development.

Influenced by the climate of the times, Morphett and Washburne (1931) supported the postponement of reading instruction until a child was developmentally "old enough." Their study concluded that children with a mental age of six years six months made better progress on a test of reading achievement than younger children. But whereas many educators held fast to the concept of natural maturation as the precursor of literacy, others grew uncomfortable with simply waiting for children to become ready to read. They did not advocate formal reading instruction in early childhood, but they did begin to provide experiences that they believed would help children become ready for reading.

The growing popularity of testing during the 1930s and 1940s helped educators in this effort and affected the next several decades of early childhood reading instruction. Generally, the standardized tests served the prevailing concept of maturation by indicating if a child had reached the maturity he or she needed to be able to learn to read. The tests usually included sections on specific skills. Unfortunately, those skills came to be seen as elements on which to base experiences that would help children to become ready to read. The term **reading readiness** came into popular use during these decades and is still with us. Instead of waiting for a child's natural maturation to unfold, educators focused on nurturing that maturation through instruction in a set of skills identified as prerequisites for reading. The concept gained strength when publishers of basal readers capitalized on the idea of readiness skills and began to prepare materials for preschool and kindergarten that would make children ready to read. Skills associated with reading readiness include *auditory discrimination,* the ability to identify and differentiate familiar sounds, similar sounds, rhyming words, and the sounds of letters; *visual discrimination,* including color recognition, shape, and letter identification; *left to right eye progression* and *visual motor skills,* such as cutting on a line with scissors and coloring within the lines of a picture; and such *large motor abilities* as skipping, hopping, and walking on a line.

Early childhood literacy instruction based on the reading readiness model implies that one prepares for literacy by acquiring a set of prescribed skills. These skills are taught systematically on the assumption that all children are at a fairly similar level of development when they come to preschool or kindergarten. The system does not consider experiences or information that a child may already have about literacy, and it focuses on a set of skills perceived as those needed for learning to read. Activities in reading readiness programs are worksheet pencil and paper exercises. This approach follows a direct instruction approach for literacy development.

Research Brings Change

Research findings about literacy in early childhood have challenged the deep-rooted practices in reading readiness that have been evident since the 1950s. Teale (1982, p. 567) argues that the typical literacy curriculum with its progression from part to whole and its hierarchy of "skills" does not reflect the way children learn to read:

> The belief is that literacy development is a case of building competencies in certain cognitive operations with letters, words, sentences, and texts, competencies which can be applied in a variety of situations. A critical mistake here is that the motives,

goals, and conditions have been abstracted away from the activity in the belief that this enables the student to "get down to" working on the essential processes of reading and writing. But...these features are critical aspects of the reading and writing themselves. By organizing instruction which omits them, the teacher ignores how literacy is practiced (and therefore learned) and thereby creates a situation in which the teaching is an inappropriate model for the learning.

Teale's words are reminiscent of the days when reading readiness instruction flourished in kindergarten programs. Froebel's and Dewey's influences diminished because of the mandate for teaching skills. I questioned the relevance of some of the readiness activities for young children. The children were interested in looking at books, reading familiar words, and copying words that interested them. They approached the beginnings of literacy in ways that were meaningful, pleasurable, or functional. They carried out the reading readiness activities willingly, but it was obvious that they had no idea why they were doing them or how they were related to reading at all. This became even clearer to me in a conversation with Eric, who had chosen a worksheet identifying initial consonant sounds.

> *"I see you are practicing your reading, Eric," I said.*
> *He looked up at me and said "No, I'm not. I'm practicing my sounding."*
> *I then said, "Right, sounding is practicing reading."*
> *Eric looked up at me and said rather emphatically, "I'm not practicing reading, I am practicing sounding."*
> *"But Eric," I said, "sounding is a part of reading."*
> *Even more annoyed, Eric responded, "Now let's get this straight: reading is reading and sounding is sounding."*

That little interchange left a strong impression on me and launched my general questioning of the reading readiness program. In my observations of early childhood classrooms, I found that many teachers no longer scheduled play time. Block corners and dramatic-play areas disappeared from many rooms. Interdisciplinary units in social studies and science were replaced with units on skill instruction, such as learning the letter *t*. Classrooms were neither relaxed nor child-centered. Children spent most of their time working on one skill worksheet after another. Social, emotional, and physical development were no longer a major concern. We seemed to have gone from one extreme to another.

Influences for Change in Early Literacy Practices

Researchers investigating early childhood literacy development have brought about changes in theory and practice. Generally, they base learning and instructional strategies on what is known about cognitive development. They use varied research methodologies for data collection, including interviews, observations, videotapes, and case studies in diverse cultural, racial, and socioeconomic settings. The research is field-based, taking place in classrooms and homes rather than in laboratories as in the past.

Research on Oral Language Development

The first challenge to the attitudes rooted in the 1930s through the 1950s came in the 1960s and 1970s in studies of how children learn oral language. Although language acquisition is based somewhat on developmental maturity, much of the research concluded that children play an active role in their acquisition of language by constructing language. They imitate the language of adults and create their own when they do not have the conventional words they need to communicate their thoughts. Their first words are usually functional words, and they are motivated to continue generating language when their attempts are positively reinforced. Children who are constantly exposed to an environment rich in language and who interact with adults using language in a social context develop more facility with oral language than children lacking these opportunities (Bloom, 1972; Brown, 1973; Brown & Bellugi, 1964; Bruner, 1975; Cazden, 1972; Chomsky, 1965; Halliday, 1975; Lennenberg, 1967; McNeil, 1970; Menyuk, 1977). Findings from research on language acquisition motivated investigators to carry out similar studies of how reading and writing were acquired. Because reading and writing involve the use of language, many believed that the acquisition of oral language, reading, and writing might share some similarities.

Research about Literacy Development in the Home

Other studies investigated homes in which children learned to read without direct instruction before coming to school (Durkin 1966; Heath, 1980; Holdaway, 1979; Morrow, 1983; Ninio & Bruner, 1978; Taylor, 1983; Teale, 1984). Such homes provide rich reading environments that include books and other reading materials from which children are free to select. These family members serve as models of involvement in literacy activities. For example, they answer children's questions about books and print. They read to children frequently and reward them for participating in literacy activities. The description of homes in which children learn to read quite naturally has implications for early literacy instruction in schools.

The phrase *learning to read naturally* is a bit misleading. It paints a picture of a child suddenly picking up a book and reading it, with no instruction at all. Actually, a great deal is happening in homes where children learn to read "naturally," without formal instruction. These homes are rich in the supportive and interactive behaviors conducive to learning to read. Specific studies of home storybook readings have provided us with information on the kinds of interaction that encourage literacy development. Analyses of the recorded questions and comments of children during shared book experiences at home have given us information on what children already know about books and print and what they are interested in finding out (Flood, 1977; Heath, 1980; Morrow, 1988a; Ninio & Brunner, 1978; Roser & Martinez, 1985; Yaden, 1985). The results of these home studies hold strong implications for change in classroom instruction.

Research on the Development of Early Reading

In her research with preschool and kindergarten children, Yetta Goodman (1984) found that many already knew certain things necessary for reading. These children knew the difference between letter characters and pictures in books, how to handle a book, and how to turn pages. And they knew that books are sources of meaning through printed words. Her work also concerned children's awareness of environmental print in familiar contexts and suggested that literacy-rich environments can make learning to read as natural as language acquisition.

Other researchers have looked at the acquisition of reading in early childhood from a developmental point of view. They have studied children's knowledge and acquisition of the function, form, and structure of print (Clay, 1972; Ehri, 1979; Gibson & Levin, 1975; Mason, 1980, 1982; Mason & McCormick, 1981). The work of these researchers reinforces many of the ideas found in the studies of oral language and home literacy. These authors advocate early childhood reading instruction, but not instruction that emulates first-grade practice. Rather they suggest more informal strategies similar to those discovered in homes where children learned to read without direct instruction. They also encourage activities that enhance language development and experiences in problem solving, listening to stories, and writing stories.

Research on Early Writing Development

Another area of research in early childhood literacy is the burst of investigations on writing. Studies of children's first attempts to make marks on paper have made us aware that youngsters try to communicate in writing at a very early age. Through sample analysis of children's first attempts at writing, it is clear that they have an interest in writing, that they model adult writing behaviors, and that their scribbles, drawings, random letters, and invented spellings are early forms of writing (Clay, 1975). Many researchers now prefer to speak of reading and writing development as virtually one process. They view reading and writing as skills that build upon each other; when they are cultivated concurrently, each adds to proficiency in the other. Because it was traditionally perceived as developing after the ability to read, writing was an area that had been missing from the early childhood curriculum. Research in early childhood writing has changed attitudes and resulted in dramatic changes in classroom practice. Encouraging writing in preschool and kindergarten and praising children's first attempts to write have become standard practices in early childhood classrooms.

The research and theories reviewed here have enabled us to understand better the processes involved in becoming literate. Certain levels of maturity are required for a child to reach specific levels of ability. To acquire skill in oral language, writing, and reading, children need models to emulate and the freedom to create their own forms of reading, writing, and speaking. They must be positively reinforced and guided so that they will continue in their development.

We have come to realize that literacy development does not begin with formal instruction when children enter school. Children bring with them to school many concepts about literacy and certain competencies in oral language, writing, and reading. They have some command of their language and have internalized many of its rules and some of the processes for learning more about it. Many children know the difference between drawing and writing and can imitate writing in invented ways. Many children have developed reading vocabularies from such environmental print sources as road signs, food packages, and store displays. Children know that books are for reading and expect that they will be able to read books in the early stages of schooling. We cannot, therefore, rationally view literacy in early childhood as something achieved by drilling children in specific contrived skills. Rather, we need to build on children's existing knowledge of literacy and help their literacy evolve.

Research tells us that children learn best in situations that are meaningful and functional. Children have developed their levels of literacy in social and cultural contexts and through interaction with adults and other children. The instruction they receive should reflect to a certain extent the natural and meaningful way in which they have learned what they already know and be sensitive to a child's stage of development socially, emotionally, physically, and intellectu-

Tamika's early writing attempts consisting of a mixture of letterlike forms and some real letters, need to be encouraged and positively reinforced.

ally. However, some systematic presentation of skills is necessary as well. The chapters that follow address each of the areas involved in the process of becoming literate. They reflect both old and new ideas that have made us aware of changes needed in our approaches to early literacy instruction. Based on theory derived from research, they focus on oral language, writing, and reading and on how these are acquired. They also reflect the development of the child.

The Whole Language Movement

One cannot review theory, philosophies, and research that have influenced changes in early literacy practices without a discussion of whole language. It is difficult to describe the whole language orientation because it has been defined in so many different ways and, therefore, there is the risk of misinterpreting one theorist's perception or leaving out some idea related to the concept. In spite of this, the whole language orientation has had a strong impact on early literacy instruction and throughout the grades. Many of its beliefs are drawn from the theorists of the past discussed in this chapter.

Whole language advocates support the natural approaches to learning fostered by Rousseau, Pestalozzi, and Froebel. Pestalozzi and Froebel added other dimensions with their concern for active learning through sensory experiences with materials.

Dewey's progressive education contributed to the philosophy with its child-centered approach that integrated the learning of information and literacy skill development into content area themes that were of interest to children. The influence of Piaget and Vygotsky is certainly seen in whole language through its emphasis on active learning and the adult as a facilitator of learning by guiding experiences in a social context.

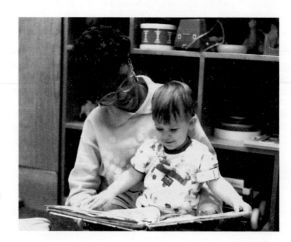

Children need to be exposed to literacy early in life in the form of books and writing. Early attempts at literacy need to be encouraged and rewarded.

Definitions of Whole Language

From a content analysis of sixty-four professional articles related to whole language, Bergeron (1990) composed this definition:

> Whole language is a concept that embodies both a philosophy of language development as well as the instructional approaches embedded within, and supportive of, that philosophy. This concept includes the use of real literature and writing in the context of meaningful, functional, and cooperative experiences in order to develop in students motivation and interest in the process of learning. (p. 319)

Like so many others, after reading the literature, I have come up with my own definition of whole language. The ideas presented here may not be shared by all.

Whole language is a philosophy concerning how children learn, from which educators derive strategies for teaching. Some of its concepts and their implications for instruction follow.

Literacy learning is child-centered because it is designed to be meaningful and functional for children. The function and meaning are drawn from the child's life experiences at home or those created in school. For example, if a beehive is discovered at school and removed by an exterminator, children may be interested in discussing, reading, or writing about bees. Although it is not built into the prescribed curriculum, the teacher allows this spontaneous interest to be pursued.

Literacy activities are purposefully integrated into the learning of content area subjects such as art, music, social studies, science, math, and play. The use of social studies and science themes, such as the study of ecology, links the content areas and literacy experiences. Equal emphasis is placed on the teaching of reading, writing, listening, and oral language, because all help to create a literate individual. In the past, this has been referred to as *an integrated language arts approach*. Varied genres of children's literature are the main source of reading material for instruction. This is called *literature-based instruction*. Classrooms must be rich with literacy materials for reading and writing throughout the room and also housed in special literacy centers. This is often called *the rich literacy environment*.

In a classroom that uses holistic strategies, more emphasis is placed on learning than on teaching. Learning is self-regulated and individualized, with self-selection and choices of literacy activities. Rather than only lessons in literacy, teachers provide models of literacy activities for children to emulate. There is adult and peer interaction as children observe each other and adults engaged in literacy acts. There is the opportunity for peer tutoring and collaboration with each other in active literacy experiences. There is the opportunity to learn through practice by engaging in long periods of independent reading and writing and sharing what is learned—by reading to others and presenting written pieces to an audience. Literacy learning is an active, interactive social process. A major objective for literacy instruction is the development of a desire to read and write.

Skills are taught in classrooms that use holistic approaches when they are relevant and meaningful—for example, when studying a theme such as dinosaurs, the teacher may focus on some of the letters and sounds in the initial consonants found in the names of dinosaurs. Now that teachers have been using whole language strategies, the concept of skill development has become an issue of concern. In early implementation of whole language programs, it was interpreted by some, that skills were not taught in any systematic way, and that children would acquire those that they needed by being immersed in experiences with reading children's literature and writing. Certainly skills would be assimilated through this immersion, but specific skills such as how to use decoding strategies to approach unknown words may require some explicit instruction by the teacher. It is not realistic to assume that in natural settings the skills needed for the development of competent readers and writers would all be acquired by children without some planned objectives. Although whole language strategies suggest authentic approaches for skill development, teachers need to have a planned set of objectives for making sure that students have the opportunity to experience activities that will help develop skills necessary to become competent readers and writers. Occasionally that means, some very traditional explicit instructional techniques.

In a whole language approach, assessment is continuous and takes many forms: teachers collect daily performance samples of work; they observe and record children's behavior; they audio- and videotape them in different situations; and they build a portfolio filled with information about each youngster. The evaluation process is for both teacher and child, and conferences are held to discuss progress.

In a whole language orientation, teachers along with children are the decision makers about instructional strategies, the organization of instruction, and instructional materials used. Commercial materials do not dictate the instructional program although they may be used if desired.

Literacy learning is consciously embedded throughout the curriculum in the whole school day. Large blocks of time are needed for process projects. There will be whole-group, small-group, and individualized instruction, and children will have time to read and write independently for long periods of time.

Whole language can be implemented in many different ways, based on the needs and interests of those involved. There is no one right way because different teachers and children make up the population in schools. One program could not satisfy everyone's needs. Those involved in whole language should feel comfortable with what they are doing and help with the decisions about how to proceed. Change should be slow and include appropriate information for individuals unfamiliar with the techniques. Regardless of what strategies are used, teachers must understand the processes involved in literacy development.

Thematic Instruction

As mentioned earlier, literacy instruction should be meaningful and taught in combination with other content areas. Themes create meaning for children by integrating the language arts. In classrooms that utilize an integrated language arts approach, literacy is not taught as a subject, but as a mechanism for learning in general. Literacy learning becomes meaningful when it is consciously embedded into the study of themes and content area subjects.

Thematic units take several shapes; however, the main goal is to teach literacy skills in an interesting way. Thematic units may revolve around the exposure to certain types of children's literature, such as the study of fables, fairy tales, informational books, and so on. In this type of unit, a child would be exposed to one type of children's literature. The teacher would read several samples of the genre or children would read them to themselves if they were able. There would be discussions about the style of the works. Children would then have the opportunity to engage in writing their own stories that followed the genre being discussed.

Another type of thematic unit involves the selection of a topic that usually has a science or social studies thrust, such as the farm, and the identification of several pieces of children's literature about the topic as the source of reading instruction. All writing activities would revolve around the topic and would be driven by the children's literature. There could be art and music activities as well, but they would evolve from and revolve around the stories being read. For example, if the theme were the farm and one of the stories used in the unit was *The Little Red Hen,* some related activities might be to bake some bread, role-play the story, or write another version of the story in which the animals are all helpful in making the bread. One problem with using literature to drive the unit is that one piece may be overused for general activities and skill development. This practice could ruin the pleasure that can be received from the book. In addition, the literature often restricts the extension of ideas that could be generated.

The third type of thematic unit is one that utilizes a science or social studies topic and consciously integrates literacy into all content area lessons, including music, art, play, math, social studies, and science. Many selections of children's literature are used as a major part of the unit; however, the literature does not drive the unit—the topic of the unit is the main focus. In this type of unit, the classroom centers are filled with materials that relate to the topic, and literacy materials are placed in all of them to encourage reading and writing. In all science and social studies lessons, reading and writing are purposefully incorporated. Skills are taught when they seem appropriate—for example, in the unit on the farm, when the class hatches baby chicks in an incubator, journals may be kept on the progress of the chicks, and the digraph *ch* could be emphasized. Unit topics are incorporated into the entire school day in all content areas. Topics may be predetermined by the teacher, selected by the children and teacher, or decided upon spontaneously based on something of interest that occurs in the school, in someone's home, or in the world. Chapter 10 elaborates on the use of thematic units and provides an entire unit sample. A description of how units are implemented throughout the school day is also included. Appendix A provides a list of popular early childhood unit topics with related selections of children's literature to use when studying those topics.

The Radical Middle: A Balanced Approach to Literacy Instruction

Another perspective for literacy instruction that is being discussed is a balanced literacy program. A balanced approach to literacy instruction includes careful selection of the best theory and learning strategies to match the learning styles of individual children. Balance suggests that we use some constructivist ideas with problem-solving strategies, and more explicit direct instruction as well. When preparing such a program, we want to include different strategies to ensure learning. However, a balanced approach is not simply a little bit of this and a little bit of that. A teacher may select strategies from different learning theories to provide balanced instruction. Common sense tells us that a balanced diet makes us healthy with appropriate amounts of protein, fats, carbohydrates, and so on. So too in reading we need appropriate amounts of literature, skill development, guided reading, and independent reading. If, however, we are allergic to one of these, we must substitute another. One child may be a visual learner and not benefit much from instruction in phonics; another child's strength may be auditory learning and this child learns best from phonics instruction. The balanced approach is a thoughtful approach and a mature approach. Educators can feel comfortable saying that it doesn't matter what the latest fad is, let's think about what's best for kids.

Balanced instruction is grounded in a rich model of literacy learning that encompasses both the elegance and the complexity of the reading and language arts processes. Such a model acknowledges the importance of both form (phonics, mechanics, etc.) and function (comprehension, purpose, meaning) of the literacy processes and that learning occurs most effectively in a whole-part-whole context. This type of instruction is characterized by meaningful literacy activities that provide children with both the skill and desire to become proficient and lifelong literacy learners. A balanced program includes the following components.

Strategies and Structures in a Balanced Literacy Program

Reading and Writing Experiences
1. Shared Reading and Writing Aloud by students and teachers
2. Guided Reading and Writing: An Instructional Setting for oral and silent reading
3. Independent Reading and Writing
4. Collaborative Reading and Writing

5. Performance of Reading and Writing
6. Content Connections for Reading and Writing

Types of Instruction
1. Explicit, direct, and systematic
2. Construction of meaning, problem solving, open ended
3. Spontaneous, authentic

Structural Settings
1. Whole Group
2. Small Group
3. One-to-One Instruction
4. Teacher Directed
5. Center Settings
6. Social Settings with adults and peers

Materials
Hands on, pencil and paper, literature, and textbooks

Professional Associations and Related Journals Dealing with Early Literacy

What we have learned over the years concerning learning theory and early literacy development is due to research by college professors and classroom teachers. Professional associations hold conferences and publish journals to inform and move the field forward. Following is a list of such groups and journals for future study and reference.

American Library Association, 50 E. Huron Street, Chicago, IL 60611.

American Montessori Society, Inc. (AMS), 150 Fifth Avenue, New York, NY 10010.

Association for Childhood Education International (ACEI), 11141 Georgia Avenue, Suite 200, Wheaton, MD 20902.
Journal: *Childhood Education*

Child Welfare League of America, Inc., 67 Irving Place, New York, NY 10010.
Journal: *Child Welfare*

Children's Bureau, Office of Child Development, U.S. Department of Health, Education and Welfare, Washington, DC 20201.
Journal: *Children Today*

College Reading Association (CRA), Department of Curriculum and Instruction, College of Education, Appalachian State University, Boone, NC 28608.
Journal: *Reading Research & Instruction*

Education Today Company, 530 University Avenue, Palo Alto, CA 94301.
Journal: *Learning*

Educational Resource Information Center/Early Childhood Education (ERIC/ECE), University of Illinois, 804 West Pennsylvania Avenue, Urbana, IL 61801.

Gordon and Breach Science Publishers, Inc., One Park Avenue, New York, NY 10016.
Journal: *Early Child Development and Care*

Highlights for Children, P.O. Box 269, Columbus, OH 43216-0269.
Journal: *Teacher K–8*

International Reading Association (IRA), 800 Barksdale Road, P.O. Box 8139, Newark, DE 19711.
Journals: *Reading Teacher; Reading Research Quarterly*
brochures, pamphlets, and monographs

National Association for the Education of Young Children (NAEYC), 1834 Connecticut Avenue NW, Washington, DC 20009.
Journals: *Young Children* and *Early Childhood Research Quarterly*
pamphlets and monographs

National Council of Teachers of English (NCTE), 1111 Kenyon Road, Urbana, IL 61801.

Journal: *Language Arts*
pamphlets and monographs

National Education Association (NEA), 1201 16th Street NW, Washington, DC 20036.
Journal: *Today's Education*

National Reading Conference (NRC), 1070 Sibley Tower, Rochester, NY 14604.
Journal: *Journal of Literacy Research*

Scholastic Inc., 555 Broadway, New York, NY 10012.
Journals: *Early Childhood Today* and *Instructor*

Society for Research in Child Development, 5750 Ellis Avenue, Chicago, IL 60637.
Journal: *Child Development*

Stages of Child Development

The early childhood learning theories described were very concerned about the physical, social, emotional, and cognitive development of the child. The curriculum was to emphasize all four areas equally. This early perspective, which remains with us today, makes it necessary to know what children are like developmentally, what they are capable of doing, and what they already know. This information is needed when preparing instructional environments. This knowledge will also help to determine if children have special needs related to learning disabilities, giftedness, or communication disorders, for example. The following description of developmental characteristics of children from birth through eight years (Seefeldt & Barbour, 1986, pp. 63–69) is provided to be used as a reference throughout this volume and in your teaching. A more complete description of language development is found in Chapter 4.

◆ **BOX 1.1** *Developmental Characteristics of Children*

Infancy (birth through twelve months)

Physical

Develops rapidly.

Changes from waking because of hunger and distress to sleeping through the night with two naps during the day.

Changes eating patterns from every three hours to regular meals three times a day.

Develops control of muscles that hold up the head. By four months enjoys holding up head.

Focuses eyes and begins to explore the environment visually.

Begins to grasp objects at about sixteen weeks. Can grasp and let go by six months.
Rolls over intentionally (four to six months).
Holds own bottle (six to eight months).
Shows first tooth at about six months. Has about twelve teeth by age one.
Sits well alone, can turn and recover balance (six to eight months).
Raises body at nine months. May even pull self up to a standing position.
Starts to crawl at six months and to creep at nine or ten months.
May begin walking by age one.

Social
Begins to smile socially (four or five months).
Enjoys frolicking and being jostled.
Recognizes mother or other significant adult.
Notices hands and feet and plays with them.
By six months likes playing, alone or with company.
Begins to be wary of strangers.
Cooperates in games such as peekaboo and pat-a-cake.
Imitates actions of others.

Emotional
Differentiates crying according to specific discomforts, such as being hungry, cold, or wet.
Shows emotions by overall body movements such as kicking, arm waving, and facial expressions.
Begins to show pleasure when needs are being met.
By six months shows affection by kissing and hugging.
Shows signs of fearfulness.
Pushes away things not liked.

Cognitive
First discriminates mother from others; later, discriminates familiar faces from those of strangers.
Explores world through looking, mouthing, grasping.
Inspects things for long periods.
As a first sign of awareness, protests disappearance of objects.
Discovers how to make things happen and delights in doing so by repeating an action several times.
Between six and twelve months becomes aware of object permanency by recognizing that an object has been taken away and by looking for a hidden object.
Begins intentional actions by pulling at an object or removing an obstacle to get at an object.
Becomes increasingly curious about surroundings.

Toddlers (one and two years)
Physical
Begins to develop many motor skills.

(continued)

BOX 1.1 *Continued*

Continues teething till about eighteen months, develops all twenty teeth by two years.

Develops large muscles. Crawls well, stands alone (at about a year), and pushes chair around.

Starts to walk at about fifteen months; may still be wobbly at eighteen months.

Places ball in and out of box.

Releases ball with thrust.

Creeps down stairs backwards.

Develops fine motor skills. Stacks two blocks, picks up a bean, and puts objects into a container. Starts to use spoon. Puts on simple things—for instance, an apron over the head.

By end of eighteen months, scribbles with a crayon in vertical or horizontal lines.

Turns pages of book.

During second year, walks without assistance.

Runs but often bumps into things.

Jumps up and down.

Walks up and down stairs with one foot forward.

Holds glass with one hand.

Stacks at least six blocks and strings beads.

Opens doors and cupboards.

Scribbles spirals, loops, and rough circles.

Starts to prefer one hand to the other.

Starts day control of elimination.

Social

At age one, differentiates meagerly between self and other.

Approaches mirror image socially.

By eighteen months, distinguishes between terms *you* and *me*.

Plays spontaneously; is self-absorbed but notices newcomers.

Imitates behavior more elaborately.

Identifies body parts.

Responds to music.

Develops socialization by age two. Is less interested in playing with parent and more interested in playing with a peer.

Begins parallel play, playing side by side, but without interaction.

By age two learns to distinguish strongly between self and others.

Is ambivalent about moving out and exploring.

Becomes aware of owning things and may become very possessive.

Emotional

At age one is amiable.

At eighteen months is resistant to change. Often suddenly—won't let mother out of sight.

Tends to rebel, resist, fight, run, hide.

Perceives emotions of others.

At age one, shows no sense of guilt. By age two, begins to experience guilt and
    shows beginnings of conscience.
Says no emphatically. Shows willfulness and negativism.
Laughs and jumps exuberantly.

Cognitive
Shows mental imagery: looks for things that are hidden, recalls and anticipates
    events, moves beyond here and now, begins temporal and spatial orientation.
Develops deductive reasoning: searches for things in more than one place.
Reveals memory: shows deferred imitation by seeing an event and imitating it
    later. Remembers names of objects.
Completes awareness of object permanence.
By age two or three distinguishes between black and white and may use names
    of colors.
Distinguishes one from many.
Says "one, two, three" in rote counting, but not often in rational counting.
Acts out utterances and talks about actions while carrying them out.
Takes things apart and tries to put them back together.
Shows sense of time by remembering events. Knows terms *today* and *tomorrow,*
    but mixes them up.

Preschoolers (three to four years)
Physical
Expands physical skills.
Rides a tricycle.
Pushes a wagon.
Runs smoothly and stops easily.
Climbs jungle gym ladder.
Walks stairs with alternating feet forward.
Jumps with two feet.
Shows high energy level.
By four can do a running broad jump.
Begins to skip, pushing one foot ahead of the other.
Can balance on one foot.
Keeps relatively good time in response to music.
Expands fine motor skills for dressing. Manipulates zippers, maybe
    even buttons.
Controls elimination at night.

Social
Becomes more social.
Moves from parallel play to early associative play. Joins others in activities.
Becomes aware of racial and sexual differences.
Begins independence.
By four shows growing sense of initiative and self-reliance.
Becomes aware of basic sex identity.

(continued)

BOX 1.1 *Continued*

Not uncommonly develops imaginary playmates (a trait that may appear as early as two and a half).

Emotional
Begins enjoying humor. Laughs when adults laugh.
Develops inner control over behavior.
Shows less negativism.
Develops phobias and fears, which may continue until age five.
At four may begin intentional lying but is outraged by parents' white lies.

Cognitive
Begins problem-solving skills. Stacks blocks and may kick them down to see what happens.
Learns to use listening skills as a means of learning about the world.
Still draws in scribbles at age three, but in one direction and less repetitively.
At age four, drawings represent what child knows and thinks is important.
Is perceptually bound to one attribute and characteristic. "Why" questions abound.
Believes everything in the world has a reason, but the reason must accord with the child's own knowledge.
Persists in egocentric thinking.
Begins to sort out fantasy from reality.

Early Primary (five and six years)

Physical
Well controlled and constantly in motion.
Often rides a bicycle as well as a tricycle.
Can skip with alternating feet and hop.
Can control fine motor skills. Begins to use tools such as toothbrush, saw, scissors, pencil, hammer, needle for sewing.)
Has established handedness well. Identifies hand used for writing or drawing.
Can dress self but may still have trouble tying shoelaces.
At age six begins to lose teeth.

Social
Becomes very social. Visits with friends independently.
Becomes very self-sufficient.
Persists longer at a task. Can plan and carry out activities and return to projects next day.
Plays with two or three friends, often for just a short time only, then switches play groups.
Begins to conform. Is very helpful.
By age six becomes very assertive, often bossy, dominating situations and ready with advice.

Needs to be first. Has difficulty listening.
Is possessive and boastful.
Craves affection. Often has a love–hate relationship with parents.
Refines sex roles. Has tendency to type by sex.
Becomes clothes-conscious.

Emotional
Continues to develop sense of humor.
Learns right from wrong.
At age five begins to control emotions and is able to express them in socially
    approved ways.
Quarrels frequently, but quarrels are of short duration.
At age six shifts emotions often and seems to be in emotional ferment.
New tensions appear as a result of attendance at school all day. Temper tan-
    trums appear.
Giggles over bathroom words.
At age five develops a conscience, but sees actions as all good or all bad.
At age six accepts rules and often develops rigid insistence that they
    be obeyed.
May become a tattletale.

Cognitive
Begins to recognize conservation of amount and length.
Becomes interested in letters and numbers. May begin printing or copying let-
    ters and numbers. Counts.
Knows most colors.
Recognizes that one can get meaning from printed words.
Has a sense of time, but mainly personal time. Knows when events take place in
    his or her day or week.
Recognizes own space and can move about independently in familiar territory.

Late Primary (seven and eight years)

Physical
Great variation in height and weight, but rate of growth slows.
Masters physical skills for game playing and enjoys team sports.
Is willing to repeat a skill over and over to mastery.
Increases in fine-motor performance—can draw a diamond correctly and form
    letters well.
Has sudden spurts of energy.
Loss of baby teeth continues and permanent teeth appear.
Physique begins to change. Body more proportionately developed and facial
    structure changes.

Social
Beginning to prefer own sex—has less boy/girl interaction.
Peer groups begin to form.
Security in sex identification.

(continued)

BOX 1.1 *Continued*

Self-absorption.
Begins to work and play independently.
Can be argumentative.
Seven still not a good loser and often a tattle teller.
By eight plays games better and not as intent on winning.
Conscientious—can take responsibility for routine chores.
Less selfish. Able to share. Wants to please.
Still enjoys and engages in fantasy play.

Emotional
Difficulty in starting things but will persist to end.
Worries that school might be too hard.
Beginning of empathy—sees other's viewpoint.
Sense of humor expressed in riddles, practical jokes, and nonsense words.
Discriminates between good and bad, but still immature.
Is sensitive and gets hurt easily.
Has sense of possession and takes care of possessions (makes collections).

Cognitive
Attention span is quite long.
Can plan and stay with a task or project over a long period.
Interested in conclusions and logical ends.
Aware of community and the world.
Expanding knowledge and interest.
Some sevens read well and by eight really enjoy reading.
Can tell time—aware of passage of time in months and years.
Interested in other time periods.
Conscious of other's work and their own. May comment "I'm good at art, but
    Sue is better at reading."
Differences in abilities widening.

Reprinted by permission of Charles E. Merrill Publishing Co. Figure 2–1, pp. 63 to 69 in Seefeldt and Barbour, *Early Childhood Education: An Introduction.*

An Idea for the Classroom from the Classroom

The following experience was created by an early childhood teacher for the children in her classroom. The ideas reflect theories discussed in this chapter. You may find them useful for your teaching.

◆ **Preschoolers Go Restaurant Hopping**

As part of a unit dealing with nutrition, I have individual conferences with my preschoolers to help them create their own restaurant menus to be used during dramatic play. The children can either write their menus themselves (any form of early writing will be accepted—from drawing a picture, scribble writing, to random letters), or if they prefer they can dictate their menus and I will write them down. Their menus contain such savory items as fried chicken on the bone; apple juice; pink ice cream with sprinkles, whipped cream, and chocolate sauce; and cherry tacos. The children decorate covers for their menus and choose a name for their restaurant. The children have the opportunity to discuss and share their menus with the class during our "Morning Message" time.

The next step is to transform our housekeeping area into a restaurant. The play food and utensils are already there. We add items such as a tablecloth, serving trays, and small writing pads and pencils for taking orders. I've made large signs with every child's restaurant name on it. I rotate the names so that each child has a chance for his or her restaurant to be the restaurant of the day. When the children come to school, the first thing they do is rush over to the play area to see whose restaurant sign is posted.

During a typical play time, a great deal of literacy behavior occurs. Children read menus and take orders. They discuss the specials of the day and how the food tastes and pay the check. This science unit on good nutrition is conducive to providing meaningful literacy experiences for young readers and writers.

Meeting with each child on a one-to-one basis in a conference allows me to identify and deal with his or her individual needs. The needs span from finding strategies for early reading and writing that suit his or her learning style to realizing that he or she can share his or her diverse background. For example, in addition to traditional hamburger and pizza places, we had a Japanese restaurant, one that featured Hispanic delicacies, and a Jewish deli.

Marcia Wesalo, Teacher
Play and Grow Nursery School, Somerset, NJ

Activities and Questions

1. Answer the focus questions at the beginning of the chapter.

2. Using one of the literacy skills (reading, writing, speaking, listening), create an experience for an early childhood classroom that reflects the doctrines of Piaget. Repeat for Froebel, Montessori, and Dewey. In other words, teach the same lesson four different ways.

3. In the section of the chapter entitled "Influences for Change in Early Literacy Practices," research and theory are described that have implications for new strategies in early literacy. Most of this book is devoted to describing these strategies. Try and predict one strategy for each of the literacy areas discussed (oral language, reading, and writing) that reflects the theory described. After you have read the entire book, come back to your answer and see how well you did.

4. Observe an early childhood classroom (preschool through second grade). Decide which theoretical influences have determined the type of practices carried out. Document your findings with specific anecdotes illustrating the theory.

Case Study Activities

◆ *Case 1*

An idea for the classroom was presented by a teacher in an early childhood classroom. Refer back to the idea to refresh your memory and identify the theories and research discussed in the chapter that influenced the strategies used.

◆ *Case 2*

Mr. Migel and Mrs. Colon are kindergarten teachers in an inner-city school district teaching in the same building. The children in their classrooms are mostly African-American and Latino. Both teachers are very dedicated to their profession and take it very seriously. They have created classroom settings that demonstrate their philosophy and theory about what they believe early childhood education should be like.

Mr. Migel has his room designed in centers for the different content areas such as science, social studies, art, dramatic play, block play, and music. Each of the centers reflects a theme being studied. For example, now that the children are studying spring, he has added plants to the science corner; tapes about spring in the music center; and books about plants, bugs, and new baby animals in the library corner. A zoo has been designed in the block center where baby gerbils have just been born, and a live setting hen is sitting on her eggs. There are tickets to buy to visit the zoo, signs on the real and play animal cages, and receipts for money spent.

In the morning when they arrive at school, the children get together with Mr. Migel and sing songs about spring, talk about spring, and discuss what they are going to do in school. A good portion of the day is spent at centers with children working with each other, and with the manipulative materials. Often there is a lot of noise, and sometimes children are not productively engaged. Mr. Migel has no formal lessons for reading or writing. When children wish to look at books they are there for them. If children decide to write a story, there are materials for them to use, and Mr. Migel is always happy to help. Children are very happy in his classroom. Mr. Migel is kind, supportive, warm, and caring. He believes that building a positive attitude about school and themselves is the most important part of the children's kindergarten experience. He emphasizes social, emotional, and physical development. He also believes that the children will learn reading and writing as a result of their exposure to books and print in a spontaneous way and that formal lessons in this area are inappropriate and unnecessary.

Mrs. Colon's classroom is very different from Mr. Migel's. She too cares a great deal about the children. She is warm, kind, and supportive. She has her tables organized such that there is a definitive front of the room for her to carry out lessons. She feels that the children need to learn school behavior and be ready for first grade. According to Mrs. Colon, many of these children know almost nothing about reading and writing since their parents rarely work with them. She believes that they need to know the alphabet, and be able to match sounds to their correct symbols as an aid to early literacy. She teaches a letter of the alphabet a week and children use worksheets to reinforce what has been learned. The writing that takes place is mostly for the development of fine motor control to help the children learn to formulate letters, which they practice. Mrs. Colon's classroom is orderly, quiet, organized, with specific objectives to be accomplished. Children do have the opportunity to play in her room. She views this not as a time to learn, but as a time to relax after they have done their work.

The reading specialist in the district is worried about both Mr. Migel and Mrs. Colon. She likes some of the things that both of them do, and feels that each is lacking some important classroom strategies. What theories do Mr. Migel and Mrs. Colon embrace, based on the descriptions given of their classrooms, and why do you feel the reading specialist is concerned about each? What do you suggest could be done in each classroom to improve instruction? If you feel strongly that one teacher or the other provides instruction in kindergarten as it should be, support your premise with the appropriate theory.

Chapter 2

Observing and Assessing the Needs of Children

Multicultural and Special Learning Needs

Classroom strategies should enhance learning in our multicultural society through understanding of cultural differences, and their effect on lifestyle, values, and world view.

Bill of Rights for Children

Let me grow as I be
And try to understand
Why I want to grow like me
Not like my parents hope I will be
Or like my teacher thinks I should be,
Please try to understand and help me grow
Just like me.

—Gladys Andrews, 1954
Creative Rhythmic Movement for Children

Questions To Focus On As You Read

◆ Define authentic assessment.

◆ Describe the nature of standardized tests and standardized testing.

◆ What are the pros and cons of authentic assessment and standardized measurement?

◆ Who are children with special needs? What implications for instruction do special needs children present in the classroom?

◆ What is meant by early intervention programs? What is meant by Inclusion?

◆ How do we plan for early literacy instruction with children from diverse cultural backgrounds in our classrooms?

When the teacher passed out the standardized test booklets, Rosa was confused and frightened. She had limited English skills and had been in her present second grade for just four months. She had been learning English little by little, but her ability was limited. She could read Spanish quite well and was capable of decoding printed English, but with little comprehension. As she looked at the test, she knew that she could not understand the questions or answers. Not wanting to be obvious, she decided the only thing to do was to fill in the answers by marking an *X* in a box for each of the questions. She appeared busy at work filling in all the boxes without reading one question or answer. She felt better about doing this than letting the teacher know that she could not read the test.

In her book *First Grade Takes a Test,* Miriam Cohen describes the experience of a first grade class taking a standardized test, and the consequences of the test results to the dynamics of the interpersonal relationships within the class. In one section of the story she writes:

> George looked at the test. It said: Rabbits eat
>
> ☐ lettuce, ☐ dog food, ☐ sandwiches.
>
> He raised his hand. "Rabbits have to eat carrots or their teeth will get too long and stick into them," he said. The teacher nodded and smiled, but she put her finger to her lips. George carefully drew in a carrot so the test people would know. (pp. 5–6)

In both of these incidents, children answered incorrectly on the standardized tests given to them but for different reasons. Rosa, of course, could not read the test since she was not able to read English. Although she was reading at grade level in Spanish, she was jeopardized due to her cultural background. George, relating his own experience to the question at hand, actually had a more sophisticated answer than those provided. His answer was marked incorrect since his background experience with rabbits was obviously different from the background experience of the person who wrote the test. In addition, George did not understand how to take the test, that is, to fill in the box beside the best answer provided. Students may not supply their own.

In both incidents, children answered incorrectly, but not because they did not know the answer. Rosa failed due to her limited language ability, which was not acknowledged when she was asked to take the test. In George's case, problems with the design of the test caused him to fail.

In this chapter, we deal with two critical issues facing early childhood educators today: Recognizing and addressing special needs of children, and assessing individual performance. The issues are different but have many things in common. Assessment must be sensitive to childrens' different backgrounds and abilities. Only when we recognize individual differences based on our assessment of special needs can appropriate instructional strategies be planned.

I will address both of these topics in this chapter as an introduction to the issues that surround them. The practical applications for addressing the individual needs of children from diverse cultures and having diverse abilities, as well as assessment of all children's performance, will be discussed in all chapters that deal with instructional strategies. Both these issues are tied to instruction and need to be integrated into discussions dealing with instruction. However, both need an introduction.

Authentic Assessment

Early literacy educators, with their concern for children's interests, learning styles, and individual levels of ability, have made us begin to take a closer look at our methods for assessing performance. It has become apparent that the same standardized group paper-and-pencil tests are not sensitive to strategies drawn from early literacy constructs. In addition, it has become quite apparent that one measure cannot be the main source for evaluating a child's progress. Rather than testing children, we need to assess their performance for growth in many areas and under many conditions. Assessment should help the teacher, child, and parent determine a child's strengths and weaknesses and plan appropriate instructional strategies. Assessment should match educational goals and practices. To meet the needs of the different populations in our schools, assessment measures need to be diverse, because there are children who perform better in some situations than in others.

In the International Reading Association's Policy Statement on Early Literacy Development (1985), the following recommendation was made: "Use evaluative procedures that are developmentally and culturally appropriate for the children being assessed. The selection of evaluative measures should be based on the objectives of the instructional program and would consider each child's total development and its effect on reading performance."

The type of assessment referred to is often called *authentic assessment.* There are many definitions for the term, but one that seems to capture its essence is assessment activities that represent and reflect the actual learning and instructional activities of the classroom and out-of-school world.

Several principles emerge from an authentic assessment perspective as outlined by Ruddell and Ruddell (1995).

1. Assessment should be primarily based on observations of children engaged in authentic classroom reading and writing tasks.
2. Assessment should focus on children's learning and the instructional goal of your curriculum.
3. Assessment should be continuous, based on observations over a substantial period.
4. Assessment should take into account the diversity of students' cultural, language, and special needs.
5. Assessment should be collaborative and include the active participation of children, parents, and teachers.

6. Assessment should recognize the importance of using a variety of observations rather than relying on one assessment approach.
7. Assessment must be knowledge-based and reflect our most current understanding of reading and writing processes.

To accomplish these goals, assessment must be frequent and include many types. The main goal is to observe and record actual behavior that provides the broadest possible picture of a particular child. Every chapter in this book that deals with a specific area of literacy development contains a section with suggestions for collecting material related to assessment for that particular skill. A list of generic types of authentic assessment measures that will help to paint a comprehensive picture of a child is provided here.

• *Observation Forms.* Teachers create their own forms for observing and recording children's behavior. Observation forms usually have broad categories with large spaces for notes about children's activities.

• *Checklists.* Inventories including lists of behaviors or skills for students to accomplish are a common form of authentic assessment. The list is prepared based on objectives a teacher may have for instruction. Therefore the inventory is designed to determine if goals set forth have been accomplished.

• *Daily Performance Samples.* These are samples of the child's work in all content areas that are done on a daily basis. Various types of samples should be collected periodically. Samples of writing, artwork, and science and social studies reports can be collected throughout the school year.

• *Anecdotes of Observations.* Anecdotes of observations can be used for many different purposes. Teachers will want to write down interesting, humorous, and general comments about the child's behavior in the classroom. Observations, sometimes called *running records,* could focus on one particular aspect of the child's performance, such as oral reading, silent reading, behavior while listening to stories, or writing.

• *Audiotapes.* Audiotapes are another form of assessment that can be used to determine language development and to analyze progress in oral reading. They can also be used in discussion sessions related to responses to literature to help understand how youngsters function in a group, and the types of responses they offer.

• *Videotapes.* Videotapes relate information similar to that in audiotapes with the additional data that can be gained by seeing the child in action. Because writing is not an auditory activity, videotapes of children in writing situations would be useful for assessment purposes. Audio- and videotapes are methods teachers can also use for assessing their own performance.

• *Surveys.* These can be prepared by teachers to assess children's attitudes about how they think they are learning or what they like or dislike in school. Surveys can be in the form of questionnaires or interviews with written or oral answers.

• *Teacher-Prepared Pencil-and-Paper Tests.* These tests will probably match instruction better than measures designed by commercial companies; therefore, teachers need to provide this type of experience for children.

• *Standardized Tests.* As long as standardized measures are a fact of life, children need to learn how to take them. We must realize, however, that the results of these measures are but one form of assessment among many others. As professionals, we should minimize their importance and improve their content so that they match instructional procedures. As teachers, we need to see that children are familiar enough with their format to take them to the best of their ability.

◆ **FIGURE 2.1** *A Daily Performance Sample of Nicole's Writing at the End of Her Kindergarten Year.*

• *Student Evaluation Forms.* Authentic assessment must involve the child. Forms are prepared for children to evaluate their own performance. Children should regularly evaluate their performance by collecting samples of their work, discussing them with the teacher and other children. Children are an integral part of the assessment process.

• *Parent Assessment Forms.* Authentic assessment also involves parents as evaluators of their children. Parents may be asked to collect work samples from home and to write anecdotes about behavior, for which they may be provided forms for observing and recording behavior. Children should talk about their work with their parents in the home. The parent is an important resource for providing more information about the child from the home perspective.

• *Conferences.* Conferences allow the teacher to meet with a child on a one-to-one basis to assess skills such as reading aloud, to discuss a child's progress, to talk about steps to improve, to instruct, and to prescribe activities. Children should take an active role in evaluating their progress and are equal partners in the assessment process. Parents also are involved in conferencing with teachers about their child's progress. They meet with teachers alone and with their child. They bring materials they have collected at home to add to the packet of information.

Portfolio Assessment

A portfolio provides a way for teachers, children, and parents to collect representative samples of children's work. The portfolio can include work in progress and completed samples. The portfolio provides a story of where children have been, and what they are capable of doing now, to determine where they should go

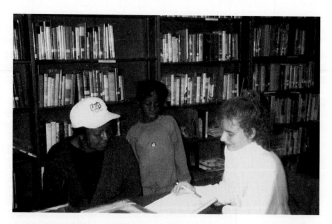

A conference that includes the teacher, parent, and child all taking an active role in assessing the student's progress.

from this point forth. The teacher's portfolio should include work selected by the child, teacher, and parent. It should represent the best work that a child can produce and illustrate difficulties they may be experiencing. It should include many different types of work samples, and represent what the child has been learning about.

The physical portfolio is often an accordion-type folder with several pockets to hold work. The folder can be personalized with a drawing by the child, a picture of the child, and his or her name. Since portfolios often are passed on to the next grade, the pieces collected need to be carefully selected since the size of the folder can be a problem. The portfolio should include different samples representing different areas of literacy and the best work the child has to offer. You will want to include, for example, daily work performance samples, anecdotes about behavior, audiotapes of oral reading, language samples, story retellings, checklists recording skill development over the course of a year, interviews, standardized test results, a child's self-assessment form, journals, expository and narrative writing samples, and artwork. A portfolio should also be prepared by the child with the teacher that he or she can keep and take home at the end of a school year (Valencia, Hiebert, & Afflerbach, 1994).

Throughout the chapters of this book, assessment will be discussed at the end of sections that deal with specific skill development. Multiple measures will be offered to include a portfolio of assessment materials for children. These materials should help teachers create appropriate instructional strategies, help parents understand their child's development, and make the child aware of his or her strengths and weaknesses and how he or she can improve.

Standardized Tests

Standardized tests measure what students have learned. They do not, however, concern themselves with how they learn. The product is more important than the process in standardized tests.

Standardized tests are prepared by publishers and are norm-referenced, that is, they are administered to large numbers of students in order to develop norms. Norms are the average performance of students who are tested at a particular grade and age level. When selecting a standardized test, it is important to check its validity for your students. That is, does the test evaluate what it says it tests for and does it match the goals you have for your students? The reliability of the test is important as well. That is, are scores accurate and dependable?

Other features of standardized tests are as follows:

1. *Grade Equivalent Scores* are raw scores converted into grade level scores. For example if a child is in first grade and receives a grade equivalent score of 2.3, his performance would be considered above grade level.

2. *Percentile Ranks* are raw scores converted into a percentile rank. They tell where the child ranked as compared to all children who took the test at his/

her grade and age level. Therefore, if a youngster received a percentile rank of 80, it would mean that he or she scored better than or equal to 80% of those students taking the test at his/her grade and age level, and that 20% of the children taking the test scored better.

Although many criticisms are associated with standardized measures, they do present another source of information about a child's performance. Parents often like receiving the information from the test since it is concrete information as to where their child ranks among others in the same grade. It must be realized, though, that it is just one type of information that is no more important than all of the other measures discussed earlier. Taking a standardized test does expose children to another type of literacy situation that they are likely to encounter in later years both in and out of school. Many question, however, whether it is necessary to use such a measure in the early childhood grades.

Problems Associated with Standardized Testing

There are a number of problems associated with standardized tests. *First,* we must recognize that they represent only one form of assessment; their use must be coordinated with that of other assessment measures. *Second,* some standardized tests for early literacy test only reading readiness strategies. These tests evaluate children on skills different from those identified in this book as characteristic of emergent literacy. For the most part, they deal with skills abstracted from the reading process and then designated as precursors of reading. Those skills include such things as auditory memory, rhyme, letter recognition, visual matching, school language, and listening. By contrast, practices that nurture emergent literacy emphasize children's prior knowledge, book concepts, attitudes about reading, association of meaning with print, and characteristics of printed materials. One child might pass all portions of a standardized reading readiness test yet not be able to begin to read, whereas a second child might not pass any portion of the test but may already be reading.

Reading readiness training was a major emphasis in my first year of teaching. Imagine my surprise, then, when I saw some of my kindergarteners reading during free-choice time. I had no idea that any of them could read. The results of their reading readiness tests certainly gave no indication of this. I was so busy getting them ready to read that I never stopped to ask them if they could read or if they would read to me.

Some standardized tests may not match the instructional practices suggested by the latest research and theory on early literacy. This leads to a *third* problem. Unfortunately, because school districts are often evaluated on how well children perform on the standardized tests, teachers may feel pressured to teach for the test. Teachers who succumb to this temptation are likely to be using inappropriate strategies for teaching young children. In addition, such teachers spend an enormous amount of time preparing children for standardized tests by drilling them on sample tests similar to the real ones. The sample tests are graded, and instruction geared to remedy student weaknesses indicated by the test. If teachers do not prepare children for the test with practice sessions, and do not teach to the test, their children may not score well. Aside from the content of the test, the knowledge of how to take the test is crucial for success. Thus, teachers may feel they are putting their own jobs on the line if they refuse to teach to standardized tests. It is a frightening dilemma.

A *fourth* problem with standardized tests is that the results of such tests are commonly used in placing children in specific classrooms and reading groups. Once placed, a child may never be moved to a different group. Yet, the standardized tests on which placement decisions are based can yield information that is inaccurate. Figure 2.2 (p. 40) illustrates the subscores and overall percentile ranks of three kindergarten children on a typical standardized reading readiness test.

Child A scored well in auditory and visual discrimination skills, and poorly in language skills. The child's overall score is at the fiftieth percentile. Child B has good auditory skills, poor visual skills, and good language skills and also scored overall at the fiftieth percentile. Child C scored fairly consistently across visual, auditory, and language skills and likewise scored overall at the fiftieth percentile. All three children will go to the first grade and could be placed in the same reading group, even though Child A has a possible language deficit and is missing one of the most important ingredients for reading success—a strong language base. These three children are quite different in ability yet have scored at the same overall percentile on a standardized test. It is very unlikely that the three will achieve similar success in reading, although they might be expected to on the basis of their test scores.

Another problem with standardized tests is bias. For example, standardized test scores are less reliable with younger children than with older children. Furthermore, some standardized tests are still biased in favor of white, middle-class children despite genuine attempts to alleviate the problem. Their use tends to place rural, African-American, and bilingual youngsters at a disadvantage. Prior knowledge plays a large role in how well children will do on the test. Children from white, middle-class homes tend to have experiences that lead to better achievement on the tests. In addition, following test directions such as "Put your finger on the star" or "Circle the goat that is behind the tree" is often a problem for the young child. Children who have never seen a goat may not circle anything, because the animal on the page might look like a dog to them.

The policy statement of the International Reading Association on *Literacy Development and Early Childhood (Preschool through Grade 3)* (IRA, 1985) suggests that evaluative procedures used with young children be developmentally and culturally appropriate and that the selection of evaluative measures be based on the objectives of an instructional program and consider each child's total development and its effect on reading performance. Various steps can be taken to remedy the abuse of standardized testing in early childhood education. Administrators and teachers must understand the shortcomings of standardized tests and the use of multiple assessment tools given frequently throughout the school year would tend to prevent undue emphasis on standardized test results.

◆ **FIGURE 2.2** *Hypothesized Subtest Profiles on Three (3) Kindergarten Children Achieving about the Same Test Performance Rating.*

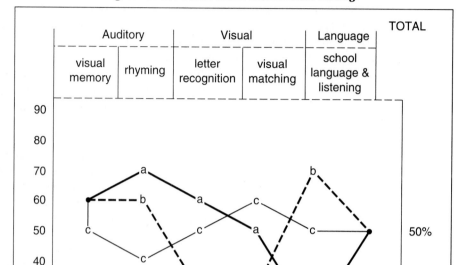

Although standardized tests are problematic with young children, if they are used, teachers need to help youngsters learn about them. Children need to learn how to follow the directions and how to fill in the answers. Children must have the advantage of knowing what the test is like before they are faced with taking it.

Finding suitable tests is a difficult task. However, some test makers are becoming aware of the discrepancies between new instructional strategies and the design of the present tests. There are tools for assessing many aspects of early literacy that acknowledge and reflect the instructional strategies suggested in this book, specifically Marie Clay's (1979) Concept about Print Test and the Early Reading Test (Mason, Stewart, & Dunning, 1986). The Early Reading Test examines such things as children's ability to read environmental print, their attempts to read predictable books, and their awareness of how they are learning to read. In addition to any standardized test, portfolio assessment measures such as interviews, anecdotal records, collection of work samples, and others described throughout the book should be used frequently.

Literacy and Diversity: Understanding and Addressing Children's Individual Needs

Many of the theoretical, philosophical, and psychological perspectives presented in Chapter 1 discuss the necessity for meeting the individual needs of children. Early childhood education has always been child-centered and concerned about the social, emotional, physical, and intellectual needs of children. In early childhood, every youngster is seen as a unique individual with his or her own special needs. There is, however, greater diversity than ever in classrooms today, and there are more and more individual needs to meet.

Frequently texts such as this devote a separate chapter to a discussion about meeting individual needs. In addition, special needs that deal with physical, social, intellectual, and emotional diversity are often separated from special needs associated with cultural and language diversity. Although these are very different concerns, for me they all fit under the heading of *Literacy and Diversity: Understanding and Addressing Children's Individual Needs*. Therefore, I address them together in this chapter, and instead of a separate chapter on each, I bring them to your attention in most of the chapters, because of their importance. We have become aware that appropriate instructional techniques for all children will probably be appropriate with some modifications for those with special needs.

Identifying special needs is the first step in dealing with them. Identification makes us more aware that they exist and then helps us determine the educational implications for instructional programs.

Children with Physical Impairments

Physical impairments refer to visual or hearing impairments, communication disorders, and orthopedic impairments. Children with minimal problems in these areas will be in the regular classroom. Others will be mainstreamed for portions of the day. *Mainstreaming* means that children who are in special classes will be integrated into regular classrooms for part of the school day.

Children with *visual impairments* are legally blind, have no useful vision, or have low vision with very limited sight. For these children, strategies that include auditory and tactile experiences are important. There are learning materials available in large print for the low-vision children. Children with no vision must learn to read through the use of Braille, a system of reading for the blind consisting of characters represented by raised dots on paper. These materials are available in basal readers from the American Printing House for the Blind (Ward & McCormick, 1981). For the most part, only children with minimal visual problems will be present in the regular classroom.

Hearing impaired children are completely deaf or have some useful limited hearing. Some hearing impaired youngsters can be helped through the use of a hearing aid, which amplifies sounds for them. Hearing impaired children who are likely to be mainstreamed into regular classrooms or are in regular classrooms will be those with some hearing ability. Visual and tactile methods for learning are encouraged with these youngsters. Those who are deaf or have very limited hearing may use sign language to communicate. Some knowledge of signing would be helpful for classroom teachers.

Mobility impairment in this context refers to handicaps that are often congenital or acquired during childhood through such diseases as cerebral palsy, muscular dystrophy, spina bifida, and rheumatoid arthritis. Children who suffer from these problems to a severe degree are not usually in regular classrooms; however, those with mild cases may be in the classroom or mainstreamed in. Children with these problems may have normal intelligence but often need help with mobility. Learning strategies will be similar to those used with all children. If the ability to use fine motor control is compromised, alternative methods for writing need to be found, such as using a computer or having a teacher or peer take dictation. Youngsters with diseases that cause mobility problems may need more time to complete assignments, not necessarily because of their intellectual ability, but because of motor coordination problems. Because their disability is more obvious than others, an important goal with these youngsters is helping non-special needs children feel more positively toward them so that all are comfortable in each other's presence. Discussing the problems, how they occurred, and how everyone feels about them will often help.

Children with *communication disorders* are likely to be a part of the regular classroom. These are children who have speech or language difficulties. Speech impairments include problems in articulation, voice disorders (abnormal loudness, pitch, or voice quality), and fluency disorders such as stuttering.

Children with *language disorders* have difficulty acquiring and using language. Delayed language children are significantly behind their peers in both the production and comprehension aspects of language development. These children will go to special classes for help with their problems. For the most part, strategies that are appropriate for all children will be appropriate for these youngsters in the regular classroom. Chapter 3, which deals with language development, discusses instructional contexts appropriate for children with minimal language problems.

The Learning Disabled and the Gifted

Gifted youngsters are those who develop academic or other skills such as playing a musical instrument at an ability level far above that expected of a same-age child. These special talents need to be encouraged, but not at the expense of recognizing the social, emotional, and physical needs of the child. Differentiating assignments to make them more challenging for the ability levels of these children will accommodate their special talents.

Learning disabled youngsters are those who perform at a level below what is expected for their age or grade. Children are learning disabled for a variety of reasons, including mental retardation, emotional problems, and neurological problems. These children are often easily distracted and have short attention spans. Techniques for instruction need to be concrete and include active involvement. Helping these youngsters stay on task is an important goal. Activities that will grasp their attention are those that are most likely to be successful. Working with them on an individual basis is crucial to finding out the best ways for these children to learn. As with the gifted child, differentiating regular classroom activities to meet their ability levels will accommodate their needs.

Following are some instructional guidelines that can prove helpful when dealing with children who have physical impairments or developmental learning differences, whether they are learning disabled or gifted (Ruddell & Ruddell, 1995).

1. Observe students on a regular basis for indications that they may have some physical impairment or developmental learning differences. For example, a child who seems to have difficulty seeing the chalkboard, who copies things incorrectly, and who squints to see things may have a visual problem that needs attention.
2. Seek help from your district's support services with children you find are experiencing problems. Be sure you have suspected problems identified and appropriate assistance given to children in need.
3. When you find out the nature of the problem a child may be experiencing, become informed about it by discussing it with special education teachers and other staff members.
4. Use learning principles that are successful with all youngsters, such as encouragement, praise, and positive feedback.
5. Adapt instruction to meet special needs. Good strategies are often good for all children, with some adaptations to meet their individual differences.
6. Involve parents with children who have special needs. Discuss the help the school is providing, inform them of additional help they might seek outside the school environment, and enlist their help with activities they can do with their youngsters at home.

Multicultural Concerns: Needs to Address in a Multicultural Society

As we approach the 21st century, the demographics of the United States population are becoming more racially and ethnically diverse. Projections are that by the year 2050, a third of the students enrolled in American public schools will be from African-American and Latino backgrounds (Paulu, 1987). In the early 1900s, diversity was disregarded, and children were expected to ignore their cultural backgrounds and language differences and learn the English language and American customs. If we are to live in harmony in a pluralistic society, it seems imperative that educational leaders accept the charge to provide a culturally relevant education for all students. We must be sensitive toward cultural and language differences and recognize that children can and should maintain their cultural heritage, that they can still be considered Americans and learn English without abandoning their native language (Templeton, 1991).

Cultural Diversity

Multiculturalism is a complicated issue. Cultural influences often guide an individual's behavior. Multiculturalism refers not only to race and ethnicity, but also to class, religion, sex, and age (Sue, Arredondo, & McDavis, 1992). The multiracial, multiethnic, multicultural, and multilingual nature of our dynamic society mandates that we teach tolerance and understanding of differences as an ongoing process involving self-reflection, self-awareness, increasing knowledge, and developing relevant skills (Pedersen, 1994). We need to welcome diversity in our schools. It adds a richness to the classroom and to topics of study. By recognizing students' diverse backgrounds, we will enhance their self-image. Differences can become the norm rather than the exception. Differences in cultural backgrounds often provide explanations of why children behave as they do. Behaviors that are acceptable in one culture might be thought of as disrespectful in another. Goals for classrooms in our multicultural society need to be as follows:

1. An improved understanding of cultural differences, and their effect on lifestyle, values, world view, and individual differences;
2. An increased awareness of how to develop strategies to enhance learning in a multicultural environment; and
3. A framework for conceptualizing ways to create a climate conducive to learning and development.

The goals we need to pursue for children in ethnically diverse classrooms and for children whose language is other than English are as follows:

1. Children need to learn to accept and be comfortable with their ethnic identities.
2. Children need to learn to function in other cultures, particularly in the dominant culture.
3. Children need to relate positively with individuals from varied ethnic backgrounds.
4. Children who do not speak English or standard English need to retain and value their first languages but learn English as well.

Teachers need to develop their own understanding of the multiethnic groups they serve. They must first recognize that the children they deal with are multiethnic. Teachers must also be aware of their own ethnic heritages, traditions, and beliefs. They must value and respect the ethnic identities, heritages, and traditions of others (Schickedanz, York, Stewart, & White, 1990).

Language Differences

Language differences vary. There are children who do not speak any English and are often classified as *English-as-a-second-language (ESL)* learners. These children come from homes where English is not spoken at all. There are children with very limited English proficiency who are often referred to as *bilingual*. The English proficiency of these youngsters varies. Many of them are more proficient in the home language than in English. The goal is for them to become truly bilingual—that is, equally proficient in English and the home language.

Children also come to school speaking different dialects. A *dialect* is an alternative form of one particular language used in different cultural, regional, or social groups (Leu & Kinser, 1991). These differences can be so significant that an individual from a region with one English dialect may have difficulty understanding someone from another region since the pronunciation of letter sounds is so different. Dialects are not inherently superior to one another; however, one dialect typically emerges as the standard for a given language and is used by the more advantaged individuals of a society. Teachers must be aware of different dialects and help youngsters with the comprehension of standard dialects. Children are not to be degraded or viewed as less intelligent for speaking different dialects. Although it is important for children to achieve a level of standard English to help them succeed in society, emphasizing the need to become a standard English speaker before learning literacy is inappropriate and likely to create more difficulties for the children by slowing their literacy development. Chapter 3 discusses strategies for dealing with language differences and also provides an outline of language development from birth through eight years of age.

A variety of theoretical, educational, philosophical, and psychological perspectives for instruction have been presented in this chapter. Special needs are accommodated by finding a perspective that best suits a given problem and child. Classroom teachers must deal with children from diverse cultural and language backgrounds, students who have minimal learning disabilities and minimal physical impairments, as well as those who are gifted. Generally, good teaching strategies adapted to specific problems are those that work best. When appropriate, reference to youngsters with special problems with implications for instruction will appear throughout the book. Children's literature can be helpful in dealing with special needs, whether they be physical disabilities or cultural differences. Appendix A presents a list of books that deal with cultural diversity and lists books that discuss physical disabilities, learning disabilities, communication disorders, and the gifted.

Early Intervention

Meeting individual needs is a major concern in our country. There are children with language differences and children who are considered "at risk" or are experiencing difficulty based on performance in kindergarten or first grade or on a test given by their school. There are many programs that have been used throughout the years to help these youngsters, and it has become apparent that meeting individual needs requires time with a teacher and child working together. Early intervention programs are based on the premise that more can be done and needs to be done in school to support young children's literacy learning. Many children, often from "at risk" populations, do not have access to good quality instruction and could be more successful if early intervention were available (Heibert & Taylor, 1994).

The term *early intervention* refers to programs in the primary grades that encourage instruction that is developmentally appropriate and uses authentic reading and writing experiences. The purpose is to improve and enhance the literacy development of children entering school who have not achieved early literacy abilities similar to their peers. In programs that have been implemented, it has been found that children can be prevented from falling behind their peers and from experiencing failure (Slavin & Madden, 1989; Stanovich, 1986).

The difference between the newer early intervention programs and programs from the past, with the same intention, is the instructional focus. Head Start, for example, concentrates on social, physical, and emotional development and views the fostering of early literacy as developmentally inappropriate (Spodek, 1988). The new programs do not promote a reading readiness approach by teaching isolated skills but engage children in activities such as reading stories aloud, writing, sharing big books, and reading silently.

Another issue with early intervention is whether it is more appropriate for intervention to occur in the classroom with the support of special teachers who work with the classroom teacher, or whether **Pull-Out** programs are more successful, in which youngsters go to a special teacher to work on skill improvement.

The ultimate goal of such programs is to provide supplemental instruction to accelerate literacy development with the use of quality instruction in reading and writing. There is a movement toward integrating the intervention into the regular classroom rather than pulling children out of class. The rationale for this trend of **Inclusion** is to limit the movement of children in and out of the classroom during the school day, and for the special instruction to be an integral part of the regular classroom instruction. In this way, children do not miss what is going on in the regular classroom. The instruction is coordinated with their classroom instruction. The stigma of being taken out for special help is eliminated and the classroom teacher and special teacher work together toward helping children.

A well-known early intervention program is *Reading Recovery*, developed in New Zealand (Clay, 1987) and studied extensively at Ohio State University (Pinnell, Freid, & Estice, 1990). Reading Recovery is a program for young readers who are having problems in their first year of reading instruction. Children receive daily thirty-minute one-to-one instructional sessions in addition to their regular classroom reading instruction. Reading Recovery lessons are tailored to the special needs of children and contain authentic literacy experiences that are collaborative and active between teacher and child. A typical Reading Recovery lesson includes (1) the child reads a familiar story, (2) the teacher keeps records of the text reading and analyzes the strengths and weaknesses of the child, (3) work is carried out with letters and features about print that are associated with the book reading, (4) a message or story is written, and (5) a new book is read. Teachers who participate in Reading Recovery receive special training that emphasizes the development of their ability to observe and describe the behavior of children when they are engaged in literacy acts. Reading Recovery teacher training emphasizes how to respond to children with appropriate modeling and scaffolding to help them progress. Another feature of the program is the use of authentic literacy experiences such as using children's literature as the source for reading instruction and writing stories, instead of a skill–drill approach.

Reading Recovery has demonstrated increased performance by "at risk" children. It is, however, expensive to train teachers to become Reading Recovery teachers, and it is a program designed just for first graders with whom teachers work on a one-to-one basis.

Because of the expense of the program, many schools are creating their own versions of Reading Recovery with high quality instructional strategies used to work with children who are not performing well. Of course, it is good common sense that if a teacher works with a student on a one-to-one basis using good strategies, the child is likely to do better due to the extra attention.

A brief description of two intervention programs designed for "at risk" children by school districts themselves follows.

The *Early Intervention in Reading* program was designed for first-grade children in diverse communities. The purpose was to supplement instruction for groups of low-achieving students provided by their teachers. Teachers took 20 minutes a day to provide supplemental reading instruction to a group of five to seven children. Children in the program demonstrated improved literacy skills (Taylor, Strait, & Medo, 1994).

An early intervention program entitled *A Storybook Reading Program* was incorporated into a regular class for kindergarten children identified as "at risk." In addition to traditional instruction in reading readiness types of activities, the following were added to their literacy program: (1) Directed listening and thinking activities when reading to children, (2) Retelling of stories read to the children, (3) Repeated readings of storybooks so that children could engage in attempted readings of these stories from hearing them frequently, (4) Active discussions to construct meaning from stories read to the children, (5) Provision for classroom reading and writing centers containing materials that encourage literacy activity, and (6) Time for children to engage in periods of independent reading and writing to practice skills learned (Morrow & O'Connor, 1995). Work took place in whole class, small group, and one-to-one settings when teachers worked with children to discover their strengths and weaknesses. Basic skills teachers worked along with the classroom teachers in the room during the small group and one-to-one periods to help with instruction. Students in this program made significant improvement over children also identified as "at risk" who did not have the advantage of the intervention described.

When deciding to implement intervention programs, consider the children involved, the resources you have, and how best to use the talent within your own school.

Recognizing that special needs exist and what they are is the most important step for a teacher. Next is to respect and accept differences that exist in the children that you teach.

In a speech given at the National Reading Conference meeting (1995), Lisa Delpit spoke about teaching "Other People's Children." She discussed general characteristics for a successful literacy program in urban school settings with children from diverse backgrounds and disadvantaged backgrounds. Some of the main points in her presentation were as follows:

1. Learn and respect the child's home culture.
2. Do not teach less content to children from disadvantaged backgrounds. They can learn as all other children learn. Teachers, parents, children, and the community should recognize children's ability and teach them accordingly.
3. Whatever instructional program or methodology, critical thinking should be a goal. Children achieve because of teachers who believe in them and have a vision for them. Poor children practice the use of critical skills on a regular basis since they have had to be independent and have many responsibilities at home.
4. All children must gain access to basic skills, the conventions and strategies that are essential to succeed in American education and life. Adults need to help children learn the skills they need to succeed outside of school.
5. Help children view themselves as competent and worthy. Provide them with ego strength.
6. Use familiar metaphors and experiences from children's lives to connect what they already know to school knowledge. If you can't justify what you are teaching, you shouldn't be teaching it.
7. Create a sense of family and caring in your classroom. Make the children your own while you have them. Tell them they are the smartest children in the world and expect them to be. Then they will learn for the teacher, not just from the teacher.
8. Monitor and assess needs and then address them with a wealth of diverse strategies.
9. Recognize and build on strengths that children and families already have.
10. Foster a connection between the child and the community so there is something greater than themselves to use for inspiration. Help them to understand that they go to school for their community and predeces-

sors. If they fail, they fail not only for themselves but their community as well; if they succeed they succeed for everyone including themselves.

Strategies described throughout this book will emphasize accommodations for children with diverse needs. For the most part, quality instruction is appropriate for all.

An Idea for the Classroom from the Classroom

The following experience, which reflects concerns for cultural diversity, were created by an early childhood teacher for the children in her classroom.

◆ *Where In The World Are You From?*

At the beginning of the school year, I sent home a notice with the heading ***"Where In The World Are You From?"*** The parents were asked to fill in a little information on the heritage of their child. The responses were more than I anticipated. Parents were happy to cite the countries of origin and offered information about these lands. This exercise helped me begin my year with a clear view of the cultural diversity within my class.

From the information returned, I found that one of my children was related to Daniel Boone, and another had a grandfather who was one of the first African-American pilots in the Air Force. One child, who was adopted from Peru, had an American father, his mother was German, and his brother, who was also adopted, was from Colombia. I received photographs and artifacts from the various countries as well. With this information, I was able to weave books and activities into my classroom that represented the diversity within my class. I was also able to have parents come to school to share information about their heritage.

We began a class book about the countries represented by the heritage of the children and called it *The Passport.* I met with all children on a one-to-one basis about their page in the book for which they could dictate things about their backgrounds. In addition, I featured one child a week on a small bulletin board where I placed a photograph of the child with information about his or her heritage. We tried to include things that are interesting to children such as food, stories, songs, dances, and clothing pertaining to the featured child's heritage. A map showing the country of origin was also included. Parents were invited to share their backgrounds.

This project gave me an immediate wealth of knowledge about my class and a glimpse into each child's background. It was a wonderful way to celebrate diversity, involve parents, read, write, and be involved with social studies within a meaningful context.

Katherine Heiss, Preschool Teacher
Summit Day Care Center, Summit, New Jersey

Activities and Questions

1. Answer the focus questions at the beginning of the chapter.

2. Begin a portfolio for yourself that will reflect the work you do in this course. Place in the portfolio pieces of work that you and your instructor would like to have there. From time to time, look over the materials and at the end of the semester review them again to help you remember things you have learned and to assess your own accomplishments.

3. Parents in your district are not pleased with the authentic measures for assessment being used. They want to know if their children are doing as well as others. Based on a test, they want to know if their child is above, below, or at grade level. You are convinced that authentic assessment is the right way to evaluate children. What can you do to help parents understand and accept the authentic assessment strategies?

4. The term *special needs* includes children with language differences (those who are non-English speaking or have limited English proficiency); children with learning differences (gifted, learning disabled); children with physical impairments (visual, hearing, mobility, communication disorders); and children from different cultural backgrounds. Select a special need and describe a theory that you feel has implications for instructional strategies appropriate for a child with that special need. Outline the strategies for learning.

5. Throughout the book, strategies will be presented for teaching literacy learning in classrooms. At all times have the interest of children with special needs in mind, and decide the strategies appropriate for these youngsters.

Case Study Activities

◆ *Case 1*

Refer back to **"Ideas for the Classroom from the Classroom"** to refresh your memory. Describe accommodations the teacher has made for meeting the special needs of the children in her classroom, that is, children from culturally diverse backgrounds, children with physical disabilities, etc. What other things might have been done to accommodate special needs in the activity described? What other special needs could be addressed in the situation described?

◆ *Case 2*

Your district uses standardized tests in the early childhood grades, and all teachers keep portfolios on students with daily work samples, checklists of skills accomplished and those that still need improvement, anecdotes about the children, audiotapes of language and story retellings, and videotapes of the children working in social settings. The material on the standardized test does not reflect the teaching that is occurring in the classroom.

Mr. Manson is aware that standardized tests will be coming up soon. Although he uses holistic strategies for literacy instruction most of the time, he also makes sure that his instruction reflects the contents of standardized tests which he knows his students will be taking. About a month before the standardized tests, he stops much of his usual instruction and spends an hour a day preparing his children for the test. He gives them samples of test materials to teach them the content and format of the test. He spends a good deal of practice time on how to fill in the correct box, how to press hard with the pencil, how to be sure to check the appropriate answer box for the particular question, how to make good guesses, what students should do if they cannot answer a question, how much time to spend on each question, etc. He checks the children's work and spends time helping those who are having difficulty.

Mrs. Kimmel uses holistic strategies for teaching similar to Mr. Manson. She knows she must administer the standardized tests, but she does not pay much attention to them, since she feels they are inappropriate for children in the early childhood grades. She also does not want to waste valuable instructional time preparing for them. The only preparation she offers her students for the test is a discussion a week before they are administered when she describes what they are like, tells how long they will take, and generally plays down their importance.

Mr. Manson's students score much better on the tests than Mrs. Kimmel's children, although on informal measures the children do similarly, that is, on story retellings, and rewritings.

There are concerns by parents and administrators about the approaches to testing taken by both teachers. What would your advice be to Mr. Manson and why? What would your advice be to Mrs. Kimmel and why? If you were a teacher in this school district, what would your plan for assessment be?

Chapter 3

Family Literacy Partnerships

Home and School Working Together

Parents, or family members who care for a child, are the first teachers children meet.

You may have tangible wealth untold:
Caskets of jewels and coffers of gold.
Richer than I you can never be—
I had a Mother who read to me.

—Strickland Gillian
"The Reading Mother"
from *Best Loved Poems*
of the American People

Questions To Focus On As You Read

◆ List and discuss three factors described by Leichter that help to promote rich family literacy environments in the home, thus making the home conducive to literacy development.

◆ What reading and writing materials should be present in a home, and where should they be placed to help promote children's literacy development?

◆ What reading and writing activities can families involve their children in to help promote literacy development?

◆ Define the term Family Literacy.

◆ What are the differences between parent involvement and intergenerational family literacy programs?

◆ What are some concerns surrounding family literacy intervention programs with diverse, multicultural populations?

◆ What elements make for a successful family literacy program?

Mrs. Feller spread the newspaper out on the floor as her two grandchildren (Adasha, 6 and Jonnelle, 4), started to put down the paint jars, water can, brushes, and paper to paint. She always spread newspaper out to protect the floor when the girls did something messy. As she spread the paper, she said, "Now let's see what section of the newspaper we have out on the floor today." "Oh look," said Adasha, "It's the sports section. Some team won that baseball game 7 points to 0." "That's right," said Mrs. Feller, "the Mets beat the Dodgers 7 to 0." Mrs. Feller always made a point of having the girls look at the contents of the newspaper they spread on the floor. The children would often continue to investigate the newspaper and almost forget their clay or paint. Sometimes they would paint about what they had just read. Mrs. Feller was taking advantage of the print in her environment that was a familiar part of the children's lives and was making it a pleasurable experience that would enrich their literacy knowledge.

Roxana, a student in one of my graduate courses, said, "When I was young I don't remember being read to. What I do remember is storytelling. I remember listening to personal stories told over and over by my parents, grandparents, and relatives that had to do with funny, sad but all real-life happenings about the family. Everyone took a part in telling the stories, adding parts they felt were missing. This was a special and favorite family tradition that took place every Sunday after church as we sat around the table having lunch in my grand-mother's kitchen. I remember looking forward to it. The stories were often the same, but I wanted to hear them again and again."

What Is Family Literacy?

The term family literacy is a complex concept. It is many things. Here are some descriptions of family literacy as reported in a brochure published by the International Reading Association entitled, *Family Literacy: New Perspectives, New Opportunities* (Morrow, Paratore, & Tracey, 1994).

1. Family literacy encompasses the ways parents, children, and extended family members use literacy at home and in their community.
2. Family literacy occurs naturally during the routines of daily living and helps adults and children "get things done."
3. Examples of family literacy might include using drawings or writing to share ideas; composing notes or letters to communicate messages; keeping records; making lists; following written directions; or sharing stories and ideas through conversation, reading, and writing.
4. Family literacy may be initiated purposefully by a parent, or may occur spontaneously as parents and children go about the business of their daily lives.
5. Family literacy activities may also reflect the ethnic, racial, or cultural heritage of the families involved.

6. Family literacy activities may be initiated by outside institutions or agencies. These activities are often intended to support the acquisition and development of school-like literacy behaviors of parents, children, and families.
7. Family literacy activities by outside agencies may include family storybook reading, completing homework assignments, or writing essays and reports.

Family Literacy: Why Is It Important?

Parents, or the family members who care for a child, are the first teachers children meet. They are also children's teachers for the longest periods. Beginning at birth, children's experiences affect their success in becoming literate. The success of the school literacy program frequently depends on the literacy environment at home. Studies carried out in homes have been a major catalyst for the new look in early literacy strategies. Because many children come to school already reading and writing, apparently without formal instruction, investigators began to study the characteristics of those children and of their homes. Such children were said to have "learned to read naturally," a phrase that suggests that their ability to read developed similarly to their acquisition of language or their learning to walk.

This line of investigation has been extremely helpful from two points of view. First, the findings reveal home practices that could be successful in school settings. Second, they provide information on the crucial role a family plays in the development of children's literacy and on how they can help. The school can disseminate this information to parents.

I can attest to the vital role of the home in the development of early literacy. From the day of our daughter Stephanie's birth, my husband and I read to her. I read to her daily while she sat on my lap, always in the same chair. We looked at books. I talked about the pictures and read the stories. By five months, Stephanie would listen as we read to her. We chose mostly cardboard picture storybooks with only a few words on each page. From time to time, her eyes focused intently on the brightly colored pictures. First she would be serious; next she would break into a broad smile. Sometimes she reached out to touch the book. Occasionally she made pleasant sounds that seemed attempts to imitate my reading voice. Because the experience was daily and positive, she became familiar with story readings and welcomed them.

As Stephanie grew older, her responses to the readings increased. Before she could talk, she pointed to pictures and made sounds as if naming objects or characters. As she acquired oral vocabulary, she labeled things in the book as I read. Quite naturally I responded with pleasure, reinforcing her attention and understanding of the concepts. Often I explained things beyond the words in the book. Both of us looked forward to these times we shared. They were relaxing, warm, and pleasurable. The practice has been referred to as the lap technique in story reading (McCracken & McCracken, 1972).

By the time she was fourteen months old, Stephanie could often be found sitting on the floor reading a book—that is, reading as a fourteen-month-old child can. She knew how to hold the book right side up, she knew which was the beginning of the book and which was the end, and she knew how to turn the pages. She looked at the pictures and chanted in tones similar to the sound of my reading. Except for a word here and there, little of her language was understandable, but from a distance one might think that this baby was reading. Actually she was—not in the conventional manner, but by demonstrating early literacy behavior.

Books were all around the house. Stephanie had an accessible shelf of books in her room. We kept a crate of books with her toys on the floor of a closet, and she was free to use them at all times. There were books in the kitchen, the bathroom, and play areas. My husband and I had many books of our own, and we read a lot, both professional literature and recreational materials such as novels, magazines, and newspapers. Stephanie saw her parents reading frequently. At times she joined us with her own books just to feel like part of the group.

In addition to books, Stephanie had access to pencils, crayons, and markers, along with large supplies of different kinds of paper. Before three years, it was quite natural for her to pick up a pencil and a sheet of paper, sit down and draw a picture, and even write about it. I could not identify what Stephanie had drawn, but she would talk about it. She was well aware of the difference between drawing and writing, and the squiggles of "print" looked different from the scribbles of the drawing. Although not yet capable of either drawing or writing in the conventional sense, she attempted to do both and differentiated between them.

In the house and on trips to the supermarket or post office, environmental print surrounded her as it does other children. Cognizant of its importance in the development of early literacy, I pointed out STOP signs at street corners and asked her to name as many signs as she could as we drove along. At home we read cereal boxes, directions for assembling new toys, and letters that came in the mail. As a result, her awareness of the print around her and of its functions was heightened. She quite naturally learned to ask what labels said and looked to print for information.

When she was three and four, our story readings became more interactive. Stephanie asked questions and commented about pictures and episodes. I responded with answers and comments that expanded the discussion. She began to narrate familiar stories with me as I read. Occasionally she asked what certain words were as her attention focused more and more on print as well as on pictures.

One day, Stephanie was sitting in the back seat of the car on the way home from our weekly trip to the library. She was looking through one of the books she had selected and began reading it out loud. It was a humorous story called *Ten Apples Up on Top* (LeSieg, 1961). The book used a limited number of words, repetitive vocabulary, and rhyme. The attractive illustrations reflected the text. As she read, I first assumed that the book was one we had read together. Suddenly I realized it was not. I pulled to the side of the road and with great excitement confirmed what I thought was true. Stephanie was reading, actually reading on her own! She had made the transition from part-reading, part-narrating stories to reading each word.

Stephanie had reached this point in her literacy development quite gradually and naturally. I had not offered school-like formal reading instruction, nor was there any such instruction in her nursery school. Because of her constant exposure to books and print from birth, she had developed a large sight vocabulary as well as a number of reading skills. Her ability to read, in other words, did not just happen. Rather, it developed in a natural way within a rich literacy environment and through the guidance, modeling, and encouragement of supportive adults.

Factors That Promote Literacy Development in the Home

The information that follows on the next few pages comes from the parent involvement or parents and reading framework, suggesting an American mainstream approach to family literacy. The constructs are appropriate in homes in which mainstream, school-like literacy activities are a comfortable and natural part of the environment. It assumes that the parents have the literacy and language ability to share literacy experiences discussed; however, they would certainly be appropriate if used in the native language of any family. After this initial presentation, which sets the groundwork for some basic ideas and strategies, a broader perspective will be discussed to take into consideration families who have limited literacy ability, speak a different language, and are not comfortable with typical mainstream American school-like literacy activities.

According to Leichter (1984), families influence literacy development in three ways: (1) interpersonal interaction, (2) physical environment, and (3) emotional and motivational climate. *Interpersonal interaction* consists of the literacy experiences shared with a child by parents, siblings, and other individuals in the home. The *physical environment* includes the literacy materials available in the home. The *emotional and motivational climate* comprises the relationships among the individuals in a home, especially as reflected in the parents' attitudes toward literacy and their aspirations for their children's literacy achievement.

Various researchers have studied homes in which children read and write early without direct instruction (Clark, 1976; Durkin, 1966; Morrow, 1983; Teale, 1978). The results have consistently established that certain characteristics are common to these children and their homes. The IQ scores of early readers are not consistently high; they range from low-average to above average. Early readers can accomplish Piagetian concrete operational tasks and are interested in pencil-and-paper activities, letters, and words. Their parents read to them, readily help them with writing and reading, and often read themselves. These parents read a great variety of material, including novels, magazines, newspapers, and work-related information. They own or borrow books, both for themselves and for their children. Reading and writing materials can be found throughout their

The interactive behavior between parent and child during storybook reading involves negotiating, mediating, and constructing meaning related to the print.

homes, in living rooms, bedrooms, family rooms, playrooms, kitchens, and bathrooms. Parents in these homes often take their children to libraries and bookstores (Morrow, 1983). The homes hold ample supplies of books and writing materials, and reading and writing are generally valued as important activities. Books are associated with pleasure, and literary activities are rewarded. The homes are well organized, with scheduled daily activities, rules, and designated responsibilities for family members. They provide a setting where interactions between adults and children are socially, emotionally, and intellectually conducive to literacy interest and growth (Holdaway, 1979).

Children in these homes are also offered many experiences that broaden their background information. They go to the post office, the supermarket, parks, museums, and the bank. Talk surrounds their daily excursions, which enhances language development.

The families of early readers and writers tend to be small. Many of the parents have college educations, but Hansen (1969) argues that it is a literacy-rich environment, not parents' education, occupation, or socioeconomic level, that correlates most highly with children's early literacy ability. Children with an early interest in reading and writing tend to spend playtime at home writing and drawing with paper and crayons or looking at books. They watch television and use video games fewer hours a week than children who do not show an early interest in literacy. Parents in these homes enforce rules for selecting and limiting television viewing. These children are rated by their teachers as higher than average in social and emotional maturity, work habits, and general school achievement. They also perform well on standardized readiness tests (Applebee, Langer, & Mullis, 1988; Morrow, 1983; Sticht & McDonald, 1989).

Durkin (1966), Holdaway (1979), Taylor (1983), and Teale (1984) describe home environments in which the ability and desire to read and write develop quite naturally. These homes provide rich literacy environments that include reading and writing materials from which children are free to select. They offer social contexts in which children are actively involved with others who serve as models of involvement in literacy activity. The adults reinforce the interest of children in reading and writing by cooperating with them in literacy activities.

Parents frequently ask teachers what they can do at home to help their children learn to read and write. In the past teachers suggested that parents drill children on the alphabet or help them with the sounds of letters. Many parents became convinced that formal teaching of skills would help their children get a head start. The newer research on early literacy suggests otherwise. When parents provide a rich literacy environment at home, teaching reading and writing becomes easier for both the teacher and the child at school. Because most children do not enter public school before age five and nursery school before age three, if at all, schools need to take responsibility for disseminating information in the community that parents can implement at home. The information that follows includes mainstream strategies and assumes that parents have the literacy ability and language ability to implement the suggestions offered.

Materials to Read in the Home

Researchers have found that books were readily accessible to children who read early (Applebee, Langer, & Mullis, 1988; Morrow, 1983; Sticht & McDonald, 1989). Parents can provide library corners for their children, preferably in their bedrooms; even a little space is sufficient. Two cinder blocks and a piece of wood make a fine bookshelf, low enough for a child to reach. Books can be placed in a cardboard box or plastic crate with their spines showing, to serve as a bookshelf. In addition, books can be made available all around the house. Kitchens and bathrooms are important, because children spend considerable time in both places. If there is a playroom or a place for toy storage, it should contain books. Virtually every room can hold books that are visible and accessible. Before babies are crawling or walking, books can be brought to them in cribs and playpens; waterproof books are available for bathtubs.

A variety of books should be selected for the home. For babies up to eighteen months, brightly colored concept books with cardboard, plastic, or cloth pages are appropriate. They must be safe, with rounded edges, and sturdy enough to withstand chewing and other rough treatment. As the child becomes a toddler, preschooler, and kindergartener, nursery rhymes, fairy tales, folktales, picture storybooks, realistic literature, informational books, picture books, alphabet books, number books, poetry, books related to favorite television programs, and easy-to-read books (those with limited vocabularies, large print, and pictures closely associated with the text) should be made available. Children's magazines offer attractive print material for children and are a special treat if they come in the mail. In addition to children's literature, print material for adults, including books, magazines, newspapers, and work-related material, should be obvious in the home.

Reading as a Home Activity

Research indicates that children who are read to regularly by parents, siblings, or other individuals in the home, and who have parents who are habitual readers themselves, are the youngsters who become early readers and show a natural interest in books (Teale, 1984). That is not surprising. Through frequent story readings, children become familiar with book language and realize the function of written language. Story readings are almost always pleasurable, which builds a desire and interest in reading (Cullinan, 1992; Huck, 1992). Continued exposure to books develops children's vocabularies and sense of story structure, both of which help them learn to read (Chomsky, 1972; Morrow, 1985).

It is quite clear that verbal interaction between adult and child during story readings has a major influence on literacy development (Cochran-Smith, 1984; Ninio, 1980). Such interaction offers a direct channel of information for the child and thus enhances literacy development (Heath, 1982; Morrow, 1987). It leads children to respond to story readings with questions and comments. These responses become more complex over time and demonstrate more sophisticated thinking about printed material. Research on home storybook readings has identified a number of interactive behaviors that affect the quality of read-aloud activities. Those behaviors include questioning, scaffolding (modeling dialogue and responses), praising, offering information, directing discussion, sharing personal reactions, and relating concepts to life experiences (Applebee & Langer, 1983; Cochran-Smith, 1984; Roser & Martinez, 1985; Taylor & Strickland, 1986). Many parents engage their children in such interactive behavior rather naturally.

Print materials such as books and magazines need to be readily available for children to use at a very young age.

The following transcription from the beginning of a story reading between a mother and her four-year-old son Ian (Morrow, 1986) illustrates how the adult invites and scaffolds responses, answers questions, offers positive reinforcement, and responds supportively to the child's questions and comments. As a result of the prompts, information, and support, Ian pursues his questions and receives additional information.

> *Mother:* Are you ready for our story today, Ian? This is a new book. I've never read it to you before. It's about a mother and her baby bird.
>
> *Ian:* (points to the title on the front cover) Hey, what's this for?
>
> *Mother:* That's called a title. It says "Are You My Mother?" That's the name of the book. See, it's right here, too: "Are You My Mother?"
>
> *Ian:* (long pause, then points to the words) "Are You My Mother?"
>
> *Mother:* Right, you read it. See, you know how to read.
>
> *Ian:* It says "Are You My Mother?" (points again with finger)
>
> *Mother:* You read it again. Wow, you really know how to read!
>
> *Ian:* Um, now read the book and I'll read it, too.

Ian's mother read the story. Each time they came to the words *Are You My Mother?*, she paused and looked at Ian, pointed to the words, and exaggerated her reading of the sentence. After two such episodes, Ian no longer needed prompting and simply read along each time they came to the phrase.

Research findings suggest that teachers should encourage parents to read to their children daily. Reading can begin the day a child is born. It must be recognized, however, that an infant's ability to listen attentively is generally limited and varies from one reading to the next. An infant may prefer to chew on the book or pound it rather than listen to it. However, babies read to from birth begin very early to be attentive in story reading situations.

One of my graduate students shared this story in his class journal about his first literacy experience with his new baby. She was born during the semester he was taking a course with me.

Our First Literacy Experience by John T. Shea

When my wife and I packed for the trip to the hospital on the night before her scheduled caesarean procedure, one of the items that I included in my travel bag was my childhood copy of The Real Mother Goose, *a book my mother had given back to me when she learned that she was going to be a grandmother. I planned on reading some of this much treasured work to my child in a family literacy experience sometime after the birth procedure. My first literacy experience with Casey came much sooner than I had expected, and it happened in a rather unique, spontaneous, and intimate way.*

After she was born, Casey was taken to the nursery and placed under a heat device designed to help her body adjust to the change in temperature she experienced at birth. There were some chairs set up next to the heat devices for new fathers. As I sat beside my daughter and marvelled at her

By six months the baby can be purposefully involved in story readings, pointing to pictures and demonstrating interest and pleasure.

beauty, it suddenly occurred to me that I wanted to read to her at that very moment. I asked the nurse if I could take a book into the nursery to read to my child. The nurse smiled and said, "You're the first father in my 20 years as a maternity nurse to make such a request. I guess it's okay."

I was with Casey for the first hours of her life in the nursery, sitting by her side, listening to her breathe, and reading selections from The Real Mother Goose *to her. Prior to my reading she had been moving and crying, on and off. When I started reading she became very quiet and hardly stirred.*

Reading to Children at Home from Birth to Eight

From ***birth to three months,*** a child's attention to book reading is erratic. The baby who stares at the pictures and seems content and quiet can be considered receptive. If the baby wiggles, shows discomfort, or cries, the adult might just as well stop reading until the next time.

From ***three to six months,*** babies become more obviously involved in book readings. They begin to focus on pictures and to listen. Often, they will grab for a book, pound it, and try to put it in their mouths. So as long as they seem content, they are probably involved with the reading.

Six- to nine-month-olds can be purposefully involved in story readings. They might try to turn pages. They might respond to changes in the reader's intonation or make sounds and movements to demonstrate involvement and pleasure. They sometimes begin to show preferences for books that have been read to them before.

One-year-old babies will show strong involvement in being read to. They might take a leadership role in turning pages, or babble along in tones that sound like reading. They actively look in the book for familiar things that they remember from other readings.

By ***fifteen months,*** babies who have been read to can tell which is the front and which is the back of a book and if the book is right side up or not. They begin to identify and name characters in the book. They take an active part in reading along with the adult, verbalizing a great deal (Schickedanz, 1986).

Fathers, mothers, grandparents, baby-sitters, and older siblings should all read to younger children. Let reading become a ritual, done at the same time and in the same place each day. Bedtime is a favorite time and bedtime stories are a good reading habit to establish. Both child and parent look forward to it as a time to share at the end of the day. Reading before children go to sleep has a calming effect; it establishes a routine for the children, who will eventually read by themselves before going to bed.

Spontaneous readings are encouraged as well, and if a parent finds it easier to read at different times of the day, it is certainly more desirable to do this than not to read at all. Reading to babies requires that the infant be held in the parent's arms. When the youngster is able to sit up alone, parent and child should be close to each other, preferably with the child on the adult's lap. The book with its pictures and print must be visible to the child. Children should be considered active participants in the story reading. Their comments and questions should be encouraged and acknowledged. Parents should relate comments about

Father, mothers, baby-sitters, grandparents, and older siblings should read together.

the story to life experiences whenever possible and question children about familiar things in a relaxed manner to encourage their involvement.

Reading to children does not end when they begin to read themselves. This is a crucial time to continue to support and guide them in this activity. When children are able to read, the bedtime story tradition can change to the child's reading to the parent. Or it can continue with the parent's reading books above the reading level of the child. **Six- to eight-year-olds** are often interested in books with chapters but are not yet ready to read them themselves. Parents can take this opportunity to share more grown-up pieces of literature with these youngsters to encourage their interest. Another important parent motivation is making sure that children have new material to read that is always accessible and of interest to them. Keep track of what your youngster has read and if he or she needs new things. Sometimes we must continually put new books right in their hands even as they grow older and seem to have the reading habit established. As soon as we stop our interest in their reading, their reading interest is apt to wane.

Parents also need to read themselves. Children learn by emulating adult behavior. It has been found that children whose parents read at home become avid readers themselves. The parents become models for reading behavior that the child is likely to emulate.

In addition to reading to their children and reading themselves, parents should make a point of providing time for the family to read together. Sitting together around the kitchen table or in the living room, each member of the family reading his or her own book, makes for a pleasant, rich literacy activity. Talking about what each family member is reading is an important part of the experience.

Materials for Writing in the Home

Some of the researchers who reported characteristics of early readers also found that these children spend a great deal of time and show a great deal of interest in pencil-and-paper activities (Morrow & Tracey, 1996). The parents of many such children reported that the interest in writing began with scribbling in babyhood. Certain scholars have suggested that writing develops naturally before reading. Many children, they point out, invent writing systems of their own that seem to have meaning for them. Whether reading comes before writing or writing before reading is an unsettled issue. What we have come to recognize, however, is that learning to read is enhanced by concurrent experiences with writing and that the development of writing is facilitated by experiences with reading.

One implication of these findings is that writing materials should be made available for children at home. A variety of sizes of unlined white paper is preferable, especially for babies. As children get into their preschool years and kindergarten, smaller sheets can be added to the household supply. A child approaching kindergarten might like lined paper as well. Pencils, crayons, colored pencils, a chalkboard and chalk, and markers are appropriate home writing tools. Manipulatives such as magnetic, felt, or wooden letters are also useful. Children should be exposed to them early and have free access to them. Typewriters and home computers encourage writing and are appropriate for preschoolers. (A list of computer software for young children can be found in Appendix C.)

As with book reading, youngsters need to see their parents involved in writing activities. Parents should communicate with their children through writing as often as possible. When children begin preschool, notes can be placed in lunch boxes that say simply, "Hi! Love, Mommy and Daddy." Notes on pillows can say "Good night" or "Good morning."

As with reading, make writing a family event whenever possible. Ask your child to help you write a thank-you note or a letter to his or her teacher. Fill out school forms with them or make up the family grocery list together. Children will emulate parents who take opportunities to communicate through writing.

Responsive Adults Encourage Literacy

In Chapter 1, we discussed that the parents of early readers answered their children's questions about books and print, offered information, provided experiences that enhanced literacy development, and praised children for participating in literacy behaviors. Such channels of information and support systems in the home naturally encourage the development of reading. Durkin (1966) found that parents who attempted to teach children more formally were not as successful as parents who simply responded to children's requests for information about reading.

Responsiveness between parent and child needs to begin with babies and be cultivated. Responsive adults respond in many ways. Language provides a primary opportunity for developing this behavior. Responsive adults not only answer questions, they initiate activities that promote literacy. While dressing, diapering, or feeding an infant, for instance, a parent can talk, sing, recite nursery rhymes, and tell stories. The baby responds by smiling, cooing, and moving, encouraging the parent to continue, and a cycle of mutual responsiveness develops.

Environmental print surrounds children and holds meaning for them. This natural source of reading material offers a way into literacy through things with whose function children are already familiar (Neuman & Roskos, 1993). Children begin to read and ask about environmental print probably before they are interested in the print found in books. Parents who are aware of the importance of environmental print can point out familiar labels and other information on cereal boxes, vitamin bottles, detergent containers, and food packages. Children are naturally interested in telephone books, cookbooks, television guides, advertisements, and mail. They are particularly interested in personal letters, fliers, greeting cards, bills, catalogs, and magazines. The outside world presents a wealth of environmental print: road signs, street signs, and the names of fast food restaurants, gas stations, and other well-known chains. Parents note the environmental print that is meaningful to children and encourage children to do the same, pointing out specific letters in these familiar words and even sounding the letters. This gamelike involvement in skills has been found to promote early literacy.

In addition to responding to requests about books and print, parents of early readers generally respond to the need to provide varied experiences for their children. They take them to libraries and bookstores. They talk to them a great deal, which builds the children's vocabulary. Trips to zoos, fire stations, airports, and parks all foster literacy growth if they are accompanied by oral language and positive social interactions. It should be emphasized that a trip not only broadens a child's experience but allows verbal interactions between parent and child before, during, and after. Those interactions include providing the child with background about the place to be visited and the things to be seen, answering questions about the experience, offering information, reading stories related to the experience, and discussing the trip afterwards so that new ideas are absorbed. Suggesting that the child record the experience by drawing a picture about it and dictating a story for the parent to write will further expand literacy growth.

Television is part of our lives and definitely here to stay. To make the most of TV viewing, parents should watch some programs with their youngsters, posing questions, raising critical issues, and changing passive viewing into responsive interaction. Choose programs for which parallel books are available, such as "Sesame Street," "Reading Rainbow," and "Mister Rogers." When specific stories are scheduled on television, such as *How the Grinch Stole Christmas* (Seuss, 1957), borrow or purchase the book. (Books associated with TV shows are listed in Appendix B.)

In a series of informal interviews with parents whose children were early readers, it became apparent that literacy was embedded in daily activities that were meaningful, functional, and part of the mainstream of their lives. Various print materials were visible in the homes. Language was used interactively and frequently, in all its forms and in a positive emotional climate. There was praise for literacy activity and pleasure and joy in reading and writing. When asked what they believed helped their children become literate so early, the parents found it difficult to answer because they had not viewed the experiences they offered their children as attempts to promote reading and writing. Most of these activities had other functions, such as keeping the house running smoothly. Many of the experiences had social objectives—to promote positive interpersonal relationships and to teach responsibility and manners, for example. Here are some anecdotes related by some of these parents:

> *"I started a baby book for each of my children from the day they were born, with information about their weight and height, and I included pictures. I made sure to report major events, such as first words, first steps, likes and dislikes concerning food, and events of interest to me. I found myself looking at the book frequently and my toddler snuggling beside me showing great interest. I've continued the books and as the children are getting older they*

add to them and read them over and over. They are without a doubt among their favorite books."

"As a grandfather I don't get to see my grandchildren as frequently as I would like. In order to keep close contact, I often send them things through the mail. I'll enclose games cut from the children's section of the newspaper which I'll ask them to complete. I send them pictures of famous people and ask them to call and tell me who they think they are. Sometimes I include questions and tell them it is a contest for which they can win a prize if all their answers are correct."

"From the time they were very young, my children were required to write thank-you notes for gifts received. At first they dictated them and I wrote down what they said. Later they were able to write simply 'thank you.' One good incentive for the task was to allow them to choose their own stationery for note writing."

"The public library has provided many fine experiences for my children. One in particular is to help prepare them for experiences to come and allow them to relive experiences they have. Before we went to the circus, we took a circus story out of the library in preparation for our trip. After seeing the circus we enjoyed another circus story from the library. No one's home library could ever be as complete as the public library and going to the library for books is such a good habit to get into."

"I started leaving notes for my children in surprise places before they could read. Somehow they managed to find out what the notes said, even at the pre-reading stage. Now I put messages in their lunch boxes. The notes often just say 'hello.' Sometimes I'll write a riddle or a joke, and sometimes the note may require an answer. This has become a family tradition and lately I find surprise notes addressed to me left in the most unusual places."

"The amount of TV viewing by our three- and four-year-old children was a source of aggravation to us. To make the experience a more meaningful one, we read the television program guide to decide on what programs to watch and to limit the number of selections that the children are allowed to make in one day. We try to watch at least some programs with them and ask who, what, when, *and* where *questions to elicit recall of facts. We also ask* why *questions to encourage more interpretive responses."*

"I've always kept a journal recording my daily experiences. My four-year-old found me writing in it one day and asked about what I was doing. She wanted to do the same thing, so we started a joint journal. I'd write things that happened to me during the day and she'd tell me what to write for her. Soon she was able to do her own writing. Sometimes I'd ask her questions

about what she'd written. I did this by writing in the journal, of course, and she would have to answer. The journal had no formal format, except that each of us wrote about an event of the day, and we would share the same journal page."

Researchers have found that home environments possessing the characteristics described here will generally instill an interest in reading and writing, a desire to read and write, and the ability to read and write early. It should be noted that most of the data from the investigations that provided this information were correlational. Therefore, it is difficult to draw conclusions about cause and effect. There are children from homes that display all of the characteristics described who are not early readers and writers and have difficulty learning to read and write. There are early readers and writers from environments lacking the characteristics described. Obviously there are factors other than the environment that affect successful literacy development. But it has been demonstrated that environmental factors do play a strong role in fostering literacy. A rich literacy environment at home gives children a better chance to learn to read and write easily and to enjoy reading and writing as well.

Including a Family Component in Your Literacy Program: What Teachers Can Do

Teachers need to view parents as partners in the development of literacy. Every teacher has the responsibility to inform parents about what is happening in school on a regular basis, how they can help their child, involve the parent in school activities during the day, and provide activities for parents to do at home. Parents should be made to feel that they are welcome in school, they should know what is happening there, and they should know how to help their youngster. Parents should be made to feel that they are partners with the school in the education of their child. Parents should be given the opportunity to offer input on what they would like their child to be learning, to express how they feel about what happens in school, and to offer suggestions for change. Following are some suggestions on ways to make parents an integral part of the school.

1. At the beginning of the school year, send home the goals to be achieved for the grade level you teach for literacy development, in a format that can be understood by all.
2. With each new unit of instruction or concept being taught in literacy, send a newsletter to let parents know what you are studying and what they can do to help.
3. Invite parents to school for informational workshops, for parent meetings about curriculum decisions, for parent conferences, and for school programs.

4. Invite parents to help with literacy activities in the classroom such as reading to children, helping with bookbinding, and taking written dictation of stories.

5. Send home activities for the parents and child to do together regularly. Require some feedback from the parents or child about working together. Include activities such as writing in journals together, reading together, visiting the library, writing down print in the environment that they see, writing notes to each other, cooking together and following recipes, putting toys or household items together that require following directions, and watching and talking about specific programs on television.

6. Invite parents to school to share special skills they may have, about their cultural heritage, etc.

7. Send home notes when a child is doing well. Do not wait to send notes only for bad things.

8. Provide lists of literature for parents to share with their children. Appendix A provides suggested books. They include lists of children's literature about varied social studies and science topics, and multicultural selections, as well as children's literature published in Spanish.

9. Parents should be invited to school to participate with their children in literacy activities. During periods of social-cooperative reading and writing, for example, parents can read and write with their children, see what the literacy environment is like at school, and become an integral part of the child's literacy development at school.

10. Have parent and child meetings in which parents and children come to school to work together on projects.

Parents should be invited to school to work together with their children on literacy projects regularly.

11. Include parents in helping to assess their child's progress. Provide forms for them to fill out about their child's literacy activities, and things they do with their child at home. Have them contribute information about their child's progress at parent conferences. Figure 3.1, *Guidelines for Promoting Early Literacy at Home,* and Figure 3.2, *Observing my Child's Literacy Growth,* are forms that can be used for this process.

The school needs to take on the responsibility of getting information to homes about the need for rich literacy environments even before children enter school. Information can be disseminated at a special meeting for expectant parents; in hospital maternity wards; in obstetricians' and pediatricians' offices; and through churches, synagogues, and community agencies.

A succinct handout such as the one that follows will be a helpful start and should be printed in languages commonly found in the community in which you live. Here it is provided in both Spanish and English. (Books and pamphlets on the development of literacy at home can be found on pages 80–81.)

◆ **FIGURE 3.1** *Guidelines for Promoting Early Literacy at Home*

Your youngster's ability to read and write depends a lot upon the things you do at home from the time he or she is born. You can do many things to help that will not take much of your time. The following list suggests materials, activities, and attitudes that are important in helping your child learn to read and write. Check off the things you already do. Try and do something on the list that you have not done before.

Materials

☐ 1. Have a space at home for books and magazines for your child.
☐ 2. If you can, subscribe to a magazine for your child.
☐ 3. Place some of your child's and some of your books, magazines, and newspapers in different parts of your home.
☐ 4. Provide materials that will encourage children to tell or create their own stories, such as puppets, dolls, and story tapes.
☐ 5. Provide materials for writing, such as crayons, markers, pencils, and paper in different sizes.

Activities

☐ 1. Read or look at books, magazines, or the newspaper with your child. Talk about what you looked at or read.
☐ 2. Visit the library and take out books and magazines to read at home.
☐ 3. Tell stories together about books, about your family, and about things that you do.
☐ 4. Look at and talk about written material you have such as catalogues, advertisements, work-related materials, mail.
☐ 5. Provide a model for your child by reading and writing at a time when they can see you.
☐ 6. Point to print outside, such as road signs, names of stores.
☐ 7. Write with your child and talk about what you write.

☐ 8. Point out print in your home such as words on food boxes or recipes, directions on medicine, or instructions on things that require assembly.

☐ 9. Visit the post office, supermarket, zoo. Talk about what you saw and read. When you get home, draw and write about it.

☐ 10. Use print to talk to your child. Leave notes for each other. Make lists to do things, such as food lists, lists of errands, lists for holiday shopping.

Foster Positive Attitudes toward Reading and Writing

☐ 1. Reward your child's attempts at reading and writing, even if they are not perfect, by offering praise. Say kind words like:
"What nice work you do." "I'm happy to see you are reading." "I'm happy to see you are writing. Can I help you?"

☐ 2. Answer your child's questions about reading and writing.

☐ 3. Be sure that reading and writing are enjoyable experiences.

☐ 4. Display children's work in your home.

☐ 5. Visit school when your child asks. Volunteer to help at school, attend programs in which your child is participating, attend parent conferences, attend parent meetings. This lets your child know you care about him or her and school.

Visit School and Speak to Your Child's Teacher

☐ 1. If you want to volunteer help in any way.

☐ 2. If you want to visit your child's class during school hours.

☐ 3. If you have concerns about your child's reading and writing.

☐ 4. If you feel your child has any special problems with his or her vision, hearing, or other things.

☐ 5. If you need help because the language you speak at home is not English.

☐ 6. If you need help with reading and writing yourself.

☐ 7. If you would like to know more about how you can help your child at home.

☐ 8. If you want to know more about and better understand what your child is learning at school.

◆ **FIGURA 3.1** *Guía para fomentar en el hogar el desarrollo temprano de la capacidad de leer y de escribir*

La capacidad de su jovencito de leer y de escribir depende mucho de las cosas que hacen en casa desde el momento de su nacimiento. Usted puede hacer muchas cosas que no ocuparán mucho de su tiempo. La lista siguiente sugiere materiales, actividades, y actitudes que son importantes en ayudar a su hijo(a) a aprender, a leer y a escribir. Ponga una marca al lado de la sugerencia que usted ya practica en su casa. Procure hacer algo de la lista que no ha hecho antes.

Materiales

☐ 1. Prepare un lugar en su casa para poner libros y revistas para su hijo(a).

☐ 2. Si es posible, subscríbase a una revista para su hijo(a).

☐ 3. Coloque algunos de los libros de su hijo(a) y algunos de los suyos, incluyendo revistas y periódicos, en diferentes lugares en su casa.

(continued)

◆ **FIGURE 3.1** *Continued*

☐ 4. Provea materiales, tales como títeres, muñecos, y cuentos grabados, que animarán a los niños a contar o a crear sus propios cuentos.

☐ 5. Provea materiales para escribir, tales como creyones, marcadores, lápices, y papel de varios tamaños.

Actividades

☐ 1. Junto con su hijo(a), lean u hojeen libros, revistas o el periódico. Hablen sobre lo que hayan hojeado o leído.

☐ 2. Visiten la biblioteca y saquen algunos libros y algunas revistas para leer en casa.

☐ 3. Juntos, cuenten cuentos sobre libros, sobre su familia, y sobre las cosas que hacen.

☐ 4. Hojeen y hablen sobre el material escrito que tengan en su casa, tal como catálogos, anuncios, material relacionado con su trabajo, correo.

☐ 5. Sea un modelo para su hijo(a) leyendo y escribiendo en los momentos cuando él o ella le pueda observar.

☐ 6. Llame a la atención de su hijo(a) cosas impresas afuera, tales como letreros en la carretera y nombres de tiendas.

☐ 7. Escriba con su hijo(a) y hablen sobre lo que hayan escrito.

☐ 8. Indique palabras impresas en su casa, tales como las que están en cajas de comida, en recetas, en las instrucciones para medicinas, o en objetos que hay que armar.

☐ 9. Visiten la oficina de correos, el supermercado, el jardín zoológico. Hablen sobre lo que hayan visto y leído. Cuando regresen a su casa, hagan dibujos y escriban sobre estas experiencias.

☐ 10. Use la escritura para hablar con su hijo(a). Déjense notas el uno para el otro, hagan listas de cosas que hacer, tales como listas de comida para la compra, listas de tareas que hacer, listas de cosas que comprar para los días de fiesta.

Fomente actitudes positivas hacia la lectura y la escritura

☐ 1. Recompense con elogios los intentos de su hijo(a) por leer o escribir, aun cuando sus esfuerzos no sean perfectos. Use palabras bondadosas, tales como:
   "¡Qué trabajo más bueno haces! Estoy muy contento(a) de ver que estás leyendo. Estoy muy contento(a) de ver que estás escribiendo. ¿Te puedo ayudar en algo?"

☐ 2. Responda a las preguntas de su hijo(a) sobre la lectura y la escritura.

☐ 3. Procure que el leer y el escribir sean experiencias agradables.

☐ 4. Exhiban el trabajo de sus hijos en la casa.

☐ 5. Visite la escuela cuando su hijo(a) se lo pida. Ofrezca su ayuda en la escuela, asista a los programas en los cuales su hijo(a) esté participando, asista a las conferencias y reuniones de padres. Esto permite que su hijo(a) se dé cuenta de que usted se interesa por él o por ella y por la escuela.

Visite la escuela y hable con el maestro o la maestra de su hijo(a)

☐ 1. . . . si usted quiere ayudar de alguna manera.

☐ 2. . . . si usted quiere visitar la clase de su hijo(a) durante las horas cuando la escuela está en sesión.

☐ 3. ...si usted tiene dudas acerca del desarrollo de la lectura y la escritura en su hijo(a).

☐ 4. ...si usted cree que su hijo(a) tiene problemas especiales con su visión, con su oído, o con cualquier otra cosa.

☐ 5. ...si usted necesita ayuda porque el idioma que habla en casa no es el inglés.

☐ 6. ...si usted necesita ayuda con sus propias habilidades de lectura y de escritura.

☐ 7. ...si a usted le gustaría saber más sobre cómo puede ayudar a su hijo(a) en el hogar.

☐ 8. ...si a usted le gustaría saber más y comprender mejor lo que su hijo(a) está aprendiendo en la escuela.

Multicultural Perspectives Concerning Family Literacy

In this chapter, family literacy has been approached from the perspective of parents helping children to support their reading and writing development. In our country today we must recognize that many families do not speak English and therefore are not able to help their children in the ways that schools have suggested. In addition, there are many parents who have limited literacy ability and although eager to help cannot do so in the mainstream approach. In some cases the parent is a teenager who has dropped out of school. Therefore, when we speak of family literacy, in many situations we need to recognize that it must be an intergenerational matter in which environments are created to enable adult learners to enhance their own literacies, and at the same time promote the literacies of their children. It has been generally accepted that poverty and illiteracy are linked. However, there is evidence that many low-income, minority, and immigrant families cultivate rich contexts for literacy development. Their efforts are, however, different from the school model we are accustomed to. We must learn from and respect parents and children from cultures in which books are not readily available, yet there is evidence of literacy activity, such as storytelling (Morrow, 1995).

Research shows that the types and forms of literacy practiced in some homes are largely incongruent with those that children encounter in school (Auerbach, 1989; Heath, 1993; Taylor & Dorsey-Gaines, 1988). Although literacy activity is present in one form or another in most homes, the particular kinds of events that some parents or caregivers share with children may have little influence on school success. Conversely, the kinds of literacy practiced in classrooms may have little meaning for some children outside school walls. As mentioned earlier, low-income, minority, and immigrant families cultivate rich contexts for literacy development and support family literacy with exceptional effort and imagination (Auerbach, 1989). Literacy is woven through the fabric of their social lives. Family literacy must be approached to avoid cultural bias, and intervention must be supportive rather than intrusive.

◆ **FIGURE 3.2** *Observing My Child's Literacy Growth*

Child's Name _____   Date _____

	Always	Sometimes	Never	Comments
1. My child asks to be read to.	☐	☐	☐	_____
2. My child will read or look at a book alone.	☐	☐	☐	_____
3. My child understands what is read to him/her, or what he/she reads to himself/herself.	☐	☐	☐	_____
4. My child handles a book properly. Knows how to turn pages, knows that print is read from left to right.	☐	☐	☐	_____
5. My child will pretend to read or read to me.	☐	☐	☐	_____
6. My child participates in the reading of a story, with rhymes and repeated phrases.	☐	☐	☐	_____
7. My child will write with me.	☐	☐	☐	_____
8. My child will write alone.	☐	☐	☐	_____
9. My child will talk about what he/she has written.	☐	☐	☐	_____
10. My child reads print in the environment: signs, labels.	☐	☐	☐	_____
11. My child likes school.	☐	☐	☐	_____

Comments about Your Child

Family Literacy: What Is Being Done?

Based on work done by the Family Literacy Commission of the International Reading Association, three areas in which family literacy initiatives are taking place are as follows (Morrow, Paratore, and Tracey, 1994):

Studying the Ways Literacy Is Used by Families

Researchers working on this aspect of family literacy are interested in advancing understanding of the ways in which literacy is used within families. In these studies, emphasis is placed on the richness of one's heritage and experiences rather than on perceived educational deficits. In some cases, researchers are exploring literacy events that occur naturally within diverse families. In other cases, researchers are describing the effects family literacy has on children's developing concepts about literacy. With the knowledge gained from such studies, educators can better understand the literacies that exist in diverse families and can help to make literacy instruction in school more meaningful for both parents and children.

A study of the ways in which families use literacy was carried out by Delgado-Gaitan (1992). The purpose of the study was to determine the attitudes of Mexican-American families toward the education of their children and the roles played by these families. A major goal was to observe and describe the physical surroundings, emotional and motivational climates, and interpersonal interactions between parent and child.

The subjects in the study were six working-class Mexican-American families with second graders. Three of the children were in advanced reading classes and three were in novice classes. Parents were interviewed and observed in spontaneous parent-child interactions.

Results of the study demonstrated that the Mexican-American parents provided special areas for study for their children, in spite of space limitations. The parents expressed a desire that their children succeed in school. Parents sought the help of friends, relatives, among others to assist them or their children with school-related matters. Parents punished their children for poor grades and rewarded them for doing well. Parents' attempts to help children with homework sometimes were fruitless, because they could not understand the directions and often misled their children. All parents believed that a person cannot be considered well-educated through "book learning" alone but must also learn to be respectful, well mannered, and helpful to others. Family stories about life in Mexico guided the children's moral learning.

From the findings about these families, it seems that schools need to respond to Latinos' concerns that children learn good manners and respect in the curriculum. The schools need to be aware of and help with language problems that parents encounter when they want to help their children. They also need to incorporate oral history and storytelling into the curriculum, since it is an important aspect of the Latino culture familiar to both parents and children.

Parent Involvement Initiatives

Parent involvement initiatives include programs that are designed to involve and inform parents about activities that will promote their children's literacy learning in school. Such programs involve parents as agents in supporting their child's literacy development and may originate from school, the library, or other community agencies. Often they are collaborative efforts among these agencies. A basic premise of parent involvement programs is that parents are both willing and committed to helping their families with literacy activities that will lead to improved school performance.

Running Start (RS) is an example of a parent involvement initiative. This school-based project created by Reading is Fundamental (RIF) is designed to get books into the hands of first grade children and to encourage and support family literacy. The goals of RS are (1) to increase first graders' motivation to read so they eagerly turn to books for both pleasure and information, (2) to involve parents in their children's literacy development, and (3) to support schools and teachers in their efforts to help children become successful readers. Participating classroom teachers are provided with funds to select and purchase high quality fiction and informational books for their classroom libraries. Children are challenged to read (or have someone read to them) 21 books during the 10-week program. A Reading Rally is held to involve the community in supporting literacy development, and parents are encouraged to support their child in meeting the 21-book challenge by sharing books and stories with their children in a variety of ways. When a child meets the 21-book goal, he or she gets to select a book for his or her own personal library. Studies have demonstrated that first graders' reading motivation as well as parents' involvement in literacy activities in the home significantly increased in families that participated in the program (Gambrell, Almasi, Xie, & Heland, 1995).

Intergenerational Literacy Initiatives

Intergenerational literacy initiatives are specifically designed to improve the literacy development of both adults and children. These programs view parents and children as colearners, and are generally characterized by planned and systematic instruction for both adults and children. Instruction may occur when parents and children work in either collaborative or parallel settings. The instruction for adults is intended to improve their literacy skills and at the same time teach them how to work with their children to aid their development.

Parents and Children Together is a nationwide intergenerational family literacy program established by the National Center for Family Literacy (NCFL) in Louisville, Kentucky. Parents who lack a high school diploma and their three- and four-year-old children attend school together between three to five days a week. An early childhood program is provided for the children, while the parents attend an adult education program to learn reading, math, and parenting skills.

In the adult education portion of the program, parents work on improving their reading and math skills, and are taught to set goals and collaborate with other parents in the program. "Parent Time" is a component of the program during which the adults discuss a variety of topics ranging from discipline to self-esteem. The last component of the program is "Parent and Child Together" time. During this hour, families play together. The activities are led by the children. Parents find they can learn both with and from their children. Early childhood teaching strategies are taught to parents (National Center for Family Literacy, 1993).

Some resources you may find useful concerning the establishment, administration, and evaluation of family literacy programs are:

Morrow, L. M. (1995). *Family Literacy Connections at School and Home.* Newark, DE: International Reading Association.

Morrow, L. M., Tracey, D.; Maxwell, C. (1995). *A Survey of Family Literacy in the United States.* Newark, DE: International Reading Association.

What Makes a Family Literacy Program Successful?

Since no two communities are the same, family literacy programs need to be tailored to the needs of the individuals they serve. Here are some tested guidelines to follow that will help programs to be successful.

- Respect and understand the diversity of the families you serve.

- Build on literacy behaviors already present in families. Although they may be different from conventional schoollike literacy, most families use literacy in the routine of their daily lives. These behaviors should be identified, acknowledged, respected, preserved, and used in family literacy programs.

- Be aware of the home languages used within the community so that materials can be translated and understood.

- Family literacy programs should not take a "fix the family" attitude. Rather, they view intervention as a supplement to the interactions that already exist.

- Hold meetings in accessible locations that are friendly and unthreatening. Transportation needs to be provided if no public transportation is available, or if parents do not have a way of getting to meetings.

- Provide childcare and refreshments at meetings.

- Follow sound educational practices appropriate for literacy development of children and adults. Use varied strategies for literacy learning. Include writing together, reading together, and sharing materials that are fun and interesting for all.

- You may work with parents alone, children alone, and with parents and children together. There should be sharing times when both parents and children come to work together.

- Programs should provide support groups for parents to talk about helping their children and to find out what they want to know about. Parent input is crucial.

- Family literacy programs not only seek to help with literacy development but to improve interactions between parents and children.

Successful family literacy programs respect and understand the diversity of the families they serve.

• Programs should provide parents with ideas and materials to use at home.

• Good programs provide functional literacy learning activities that parents consider useful such as talking and reading about child rearing concerns, community life problems, housing, applying for jobs and keeping them, and dealing with migration issues.

• Programs should include the opportunity for parental participation in school activities during school hours.

• Portions of school and home programs should parallel each other. Activities done in school should be the same as those sent home for parents to do with children. When this occurs children can enlist their parents as participants in their learning.

Models for family literacy programs must be developed in which family literacy activities are intended to promote parent/child interaction in a wide range of literacy events, and that view participating families from the perspective of the richness of their experiences and heritage, rather than from the perspective of their deficits and dilemmas.

Home school programs need to be easy to use. Materials sent home should be introduced to children in school first. For example, one program used *Highlights for Children* magazine as the home-school connection material. Teachers featured articles in the magazine at school and each child had a school copy. Another copy was sent home with activities for parents to participate in with their children that were similar to what was being done in school. The program was very successful since children knew what to do with the materials. In addition, the magazine provided the following features which should be present in any home-school connection material: (1) multiple options for families to select activities from, (2) a nonthreatening format that is not schoollike, (3) activities appropriate for many age levels and abilities, (4) culturally diverse content, (5) some activities that do not require the ability to read, and (6) activities that are fun and therefore engage parents and children in literacy together (Morrow, Scoblionko, & Shafer, 1995). The features just outlined should be present in whatever home-school connection materials are selected for use.

Following are comments by children, teachers, and parents concerning their participation in the family literacy program just discussed.

Children Said

• My mom could never work with me even though she wanted to 'cause she don't speak English. Well the magazine has Spanish things in it and you can do things in it that you don't need to read. You just look at the pictures. I teach her to read the English too. She's learning new words.

• When I work with my Mom and Dad at home, it makes you feel like a family and that's what families are supposed to do—sit and do things together.

• Working with my mom at home makes me feel happy, 'cause when your mom works and has lots of kids, you think she don't love you much or care about you, but when she does work with you, you feel special like you're the only one and you know she cares.

Teachers Said

• Parents who never work with their kids are doing so. It makes the children feel good.

• William is doing much better in school. He reads the magazine from cover to cover because he can take it home. There aren't any other reading materials for him there. His mother has worked with him once in a while, which is something she never did before. I notice a big difference in his reading.

Parents Said

• This is a good idea, sending the magazine home from school. I never knew what to do with Geremy, and this helps a lot. I don't like doing homework with him. But I don't mind working in the magazine.

• When we work in the magazine together my child helps me with my English. He can read it and he shows me. I can do some things since it has pictures. It makes me feel good that I can do school work with him.

Educators are recognizing that the family is the key to successful literacy development for both children and their parents. Policymakers from a wide range of agencies need to collaborate and form partnerships in their efforts to create and support effective family literacy programs. Literacy programs in school will be more successful if they have home support; therefore, family literacy programs are crucial.

Appendix A provides a bibliography of children's literature about families for teachers and parents to share with children. There are some general books for all, and books representative of diverse cultural backgrounds. Each book illustrates some very special relationship between family and extended family members. It could be parents, grandparents, an aunt or uncle, sisters or brothers, or a person who becomes like family although he or she is not actually related.

Learning More about Family Literacy

Agencies, associations, and organizations that deal with family literacy can be contacted for further information on ways to establish, administer, and evaluate family literacy programs. A few are listed here as a starting place.

Barbara Bush Foundation
   for Family Literacy
1002 Wisconsin Ave., NW
Washington DC 20007

Even Start Program Compensatory
   Education Programs
U.S. Department of Education
400 Maryland Ave., SW
Room 2043
Washington, DC 20202

International Reading Association
   800 Barksdale Road
   PO Box 8139
   Newark, DE 19714–8139

National Center for Family Literacy
Waterfront Plaza
Suite 200
325 West Main Street
Louisville, KY 40202

Reading Is Fundamental (RIF)
600 Maryland Avenue, NW
Suite 500
Washington, DC 20024

Resources for Parents

Books

Barton, B. (1986). *Tell me another*. Exeter, NH: Heinemann Educational Books.

Butler, D. (1980). *Babies need books*. New York: Altheneum.

Butler, D., and Clay, M. (1982). *Reading begins at home*. Exeter, NH: Heinemann Educational Books.

Hearne, B. (1981). *Choosing books for children: A commonsense guide*. New York: Delacorte.

Kimmel, M. M., and Segel, E. (1983). *For reading out loud*. New York: Delacorte.

Larrick, N. (1985). *A parent's guide to children's reading* (5th ed.). New York: Bantam.

Taylor, D., and Strickland, D. S. (1986). *Family storybook reading*. Exeter, NH: Heinemann Educational Books.

Trealease, J. (1982). *The read aloud handbook*. New York: Penguin.

White, D. (1986). *Books before five*. Exeter, NH: Heinemann Educational Books.

Pamphlets and Booklets

Choosing a children's book. New York: Children's Book Council.

Free with stamped, self-addressed envelope sent to National Association for the Education of Young Children, 1834 Connecticut Avenue, NW, Washington, DC 20009. (800-424-2460)

Janes, D. *Reading in the home*. New York: Scholastic Magazines.

Free from Scholastic Magazines, 50 West 44th Street, New York, NY 10036.

IRA Micromonographs and brochures. Published by the International Reading Association, 800 Barksdale Road, P. O. Box 8139, Newark, DE 19714. This series of pamphlets focuses on answering questions parents ask about the reading education of their children. Some titles include:

You can help your young child with writing. Marcia Baghban.

Creating readers and writers. Susan Mandel Glazer.

How can I prepare my young child for reading? Paula C. Grinnell.

Helping your child become a reader. Nancy L. Roser.

Beginning literacy and your child. Steven B. Silvern, Linda R. Silvern.

Schickedanz, J. (1983). *Helping children learn about reading*. Washington, DC: NAEYC.

Free with stamped, self-addressed envelope sent to National Association for the Education of Young Children, 1834 Connecticut Avenue, NW, Washington, DC 20009. (800-424-2460)

Children and television (free).

Parents and beginning readers (free).

Available from U.S. Government Printing Office, North Capitol and H Streets, NW, Washington, DC 20401.

Good books make reading fun for your child. Glenna Davis Sloan.

Summer reading is important. John Micklos, Jr..

† *You can use television to stimulate your child's reading*. Nicholas P. Criscuolo.

---

*Also available in French.
†Also available in French and Spanish.

An Idea for the Classroom from the Classroom

A newsletter follows that is to be sent to parents describing a unit that their children are involved in entitled Life on the Farm. *A similar newsletter can be sent with every unit taught during the school year. This gives parents information about the unit and asks for their participation in working with their child at home and sending materials to school or coming to school to make presentations. This newsletter will heighten parents' awareness of activities to do at home that corre-*

spond with what their children are doing at school. It also makes parents active participants in school experiences.

◆ Life on the Farm Newsletter
Message to Parents

Dear Parents:

This month your child is participating in an exciting unit about farm life. This unit includes the study of people and the jobs they do on farms, farm animals and their babies, farm machinery, farm buildings, and products that come from farms.

The unit is organized so that all subject areas, social studies, science, math, art, play, reading, and writing, are incorporated within the farm theme. Reading and writing will have a special emphasis in all activities including those in art, music, and so on.

We would like to ask you to participate in the farm unit and feel that each and every one of you can help in some way. If you have any pictures, materials, or personal experiences to talk about related to the topic, please let me know and come to school to share them with us. There are a wide variety of topics dealing with the farm, and I'm sure each of you would have something to share. The following topics would be appropriate:

Jobs on the farm (growing plants, caring for animals, selling products, equipment), farm animals and their babies (cats, dogs, and their care, etc.), farm machinery (tractors, trucks, plows, etc.), farm buildings (barns, animal housing), the products that come from farms (corn, wheat, cotton, wool, fruit, vegetables, meat, milk, etc.), the preparation of food from farm products (apple pie, cheeses, etc.) and the preparation of other items from farm products (goose down pillows, wool sweaters, etc.). We always need help with projects in class so please volunteer to help at school one day regardless of whether you have a farm idea to share or not.

Featured Farm Activities in School

In school, your child will participate in the following experiences:

- In science, the children will learn to keep a journal to record the growth of their very own lima bean plants.
- In social studies, we will discuss cooperation when we read and act out the story of *The Little Red Hen.*
- In the dramatic-play area, we will learn about care of animals and the role of doctors and nurses by setting up a veterinarian's office that has prescription forms, books, and magazines in a waiting room, and stuffed animal patients. Materials in this area encourage reading and writing as children role-play.
- In the Library Corner, we will add books, poems, and songs about the farm to read to your children. Some of the titles are:

1. *Petunia* by Roger Duvoisin
2. *Over in the Meadow* by Ezra Jack Keats
3. *Go Tell Aunt Rhody* by Aliki

4. *Rosie's Walk* by Pat Hutchins

5. *Ask Mr. Bear* by Marjorie Flack

Things to Do at Home with Your Child about the Farm

- Ask your child about the activities he or she is doing in school. Some of them have been mentioned, and you can focus on those. Ask your child to draw a picture about the farm and write about it also.
- Try and get some of the books we are reading in school from your local library and reread the stories to your child. Ask your youngster to retell the story using the pictures if necessary. Talk about the issues discussed in the stories.
- The unit focuses on cooperating with others while doing a job. To reinforce this idea, encourage your child to help you with any household tasks or with the care of a pet or plant.
- When you prepare food at home, point out the products that come from the farm. Notice newspaper or magazine articles that relate to the farm and read and discuss them together.
- If possible, visit a farm, a petting zoo that has farm animals, a pet store, a plant nursery, or the supermarket where you can look at and talk about the products that come from the farm.

* * *

Thank you very much for your interest and enthusiasm which we appreciate and which are greatly appreciated by your child.

I will be happy to answer any questions you may have about this unit and your child's development. I hope to hear from you.

Sincerely,

Susan Burks

Susan Burks, Teacher
North Plainfield, NJ

Activities and Questions

1. Answer the focus questions posed at the beginning of the chapter.

2. Interview members of your family or friends who are parents. Ask them to relate specific activities they have done with their children to promote literacy with natural events that arose from daily living. Collect ideas from all members of the class and put them together in a newsletter or pamphlet format to distribute to parents of early childhood youngsters.

3. Using the memories of your own home when you were a young child or the home of a friend or family member who is a parent of a young child, observe the physical characteristics and record activities done with children that pro-

mote literacy development. Determine elements that could improve the richness of the literacy environment you analyzed.

4. Select a child and his or her family to begin a portfolio of assessment materials to collect throughout the semester. Start a portfolio in a folder for the child that you will keep and provide a folder for the family. Make a copy of the **Guidelines for Promoting Early Literacy at Home** on page 70 for yourself and one for the family you will be working with. Ask a family member to fill out the form for themselves, and a copy for you. Provide the parent with two copies of the form entitled **Observing my Child's Literacy Growth** on page 74. Have them fill it out at the beginning of the semester and at the end. Be sure to get a copy for your folder as well.

5. Create a family literacy program for a community that you are familiar with. If it is a community in which parents have literacy and English skills, you will probably want to develop a parent involvement program; if it is in a community where parents speak other languages, or have limited literacy ability, you may need to engage in an intergenerational program that involves development of literacy skills for parents as well as training them to help their children. Be sure that, whichever program you design, a portion of the home and school activities are similar to each other.

Case Study Activities

◆ **Case 1**

Refer back to the "Idea for the Classroom" section. This newsletter was created by an early childhood teacher for the parents in her classroom. After reading the newsletter, consider the following: David Hernandez will take the newsletter home to his mother who does not speak any English but is literate in Spanish, and Tiffany Jones will take the newsletter home to her mother who has minimal literacy skills. What is likely to be the response to the newsletter in each of these homes?

Review the newsletter as if for a journal that focuses on literacy development. Concentrate on the following: What are the most important items included in the newsletter? What is missing? Present those ideas you feel are missing. This newsletter was written for kindergartners or first graders. What changes would you make for second and third graders?

What accommodations has this teacher made for meeting the needs of all the children and parents in her classroom? What else could she have included to accommodate special needs better? Present those ideas you feel are missing.

◆ **Case 2**

Mrs. Connor graciously accepts and solicits parent volunteers. She thinks it is very important to have parents involved in their children's education. When parents come to help out she has done the following:

Mr. Chan helps with photocopying activity sheets on Mondays. Mrs. De'Angelo works in the teacher's room on Tuesdays and makes materials that are needed for Mrs. Connor to use in the class. Mrs. Jones can't come to school since she has a baby at home so she does some typing for Mrs. Connor, which her daughter brings to school for her. Mrs. Gallagher collates and staples all of the extended reading activities needed for several days of the week.

Has Mrs. Connor selected a productive route for the use of parent volunteers? Would you make any changes to the manner in which she has involved parents? If yes, what would you do differently? In what ways could the parents from different cultural backgrounds contribute to her class?

Chapter 4

Language and Literacy Development

Playing with puppets will encourage language as children tell stories and create their own. Participating in dramatic play will stimulate language from real life.

"The time has come," the Walrus said,
"To talk of many things:
Of shoes and ships and sealing-wax,
Of cabbages and kings...."

—Lewis Carroll
"The Walrus and the Carpenter"

Questions To Focus On As You Read

◆ According to the different theorists described in the chapter, how is language acquired?

◆ What are the general stages of language development that a child progresses through from birth to age eight?

◆ What do we mean when we speak of children with language differences?

◆ What are the objectives for language development in early childhood?

◆ What strategies can teachers and parents carry out to encourage language development from birth to age two?

◆ What strategies can teachers and parents carry out to encourage language development from preschool through second grade?

◆ What techniques can be used for a portfolio of materials that assesses children's language development?

The kind of talking to which Lewis Carroll refers in his poem is very much the language babies need to hear in their first steps toward literacy. From the moment of birth, the infant is surrounded by oral language. The development of language is one of the child's first steps toward becoming a literate individual; it helps to make reading and writing possible. Using newer research methods that involve close observation of children, investigators have been able to describe the strategies by which youngsters learn and use language. Among the many things these researchers have observed is that children are active participants in their learning of language. In order to learn, children involve themselves in problem solving, first creating hypotheses based on background information that they already have and then interacting with those individuals around them who are generating language. These strategies have implications for initial instruction in early literacy.

A parent of a child in one of my kindergarten classes related an anecdote concerning a conversation she had had with her daughter Melody. Mrs. Tracey said they were outside looking at the sky one evening, and she noticed that the moon was full. She said to her daughter, "Look, Melody, the moon is full tonight." Melody looked up at the moon with a slightly confused expression on her face and said, "Why is it full, Mommy, did the moon eat too much for dinner?" Melody used her background language information to help her understand her mother. Until this time the word *full* meant filled up, and Melody made sense of the discussion with what she knew. Her mother went on to explain what she meant by a full moon and that different words can have different meanings depending on the situation in which they are used.

Children do not learn language passively; they actually construct—or reconstruct—language as they learn.

We were talking about what the children in my classroom wanted to be when they grew up. It was Michael's turn. He started by telling us that his dad is a doctor and recently he had taken him to see the operating room where he works. Michael said, "I liked the people and all the machines that my daddy uses and so when I grow up, I want to be an *operator,* just like my daddy." Michael constructed a word for the situation that made wonderful sense under the circumstances. This illustrates the construction of language previously mentioned.

The discoveries of how language is acquired laid the foundation for a new way of looking at how early reading develops. Researchers realized that, because reading is a language process, it must be closely associated with oral language.

Language Development and Reading

Now that language processes are commonly recognized as the basis for learning to read, *language learning* is considered an important part of *learning to read*. Ruddell and Ruddell (1995) define reading as the use of one's language ability to decode and comprehend. Goodman (1967) calls it the interaction between the reader and the written language. He states that reading is the attempt by a reader to reconstruct the author's message, that the graphic sequences and patterns that appear as print represent the oral sequences of language. In the process of reading, we look and listen for recognizable grammatical sequences and patterns that trigger appropriate phrasing. Using what we already know of language structure, we then test how each word fits into the context of what we are reading. Lennenberg and Kaplan (1970) see the reader as continually assigning tentative interpretations to the text and then checking those interpretations. As readers, we use syntactic and semantic cues that enable us to predict what comes next. Our skill in processing semantics (meaning) and syntax (language structure) makes us more adept readers. The reader who encounters unfamiliar language structures and unfamiliar concepts in material to be read has difficulty understanding it. Familiarity with both syntax and semantics enables even the very young reader to anticipate the format and content of sentences in print. Past theory held that it was our accumulation of letters and words that led to competent reading. Now we realize that our ability to understand what we are reading is based on our *reconstruction* of the meaning behind a printed word. Such reconstruction is based on our previous experience with the topic, our familiarity with its main concepts, and our general knowledge of how language works.

The relationship between reading and language is evident in studies of children who are early readers. It has been found, for instance, that early readers score higher on language screening tests than children who were not reading early. Early readers come from homes where rich language and a great deal of oral language are used (Snow & Perlmann, 1985). When interviewed, parents of early readers revealed that their children tended to use very descriptive language and sophisticated language structures. The youngsters invented words, used humor, and talked a lot. The mother of a four-year-old early reader reported that while watching the first snowfall of the year, her youngster said, "The snow is swirling down and looks like fluffy marshmallows on the ground." One spring day a few months later, the same child noted, "Look, Mommy, the butterflies are fluttering around. They look like they are dancing with the flowers."

Halliday (1975) notes that, among other functions, language helps children learn how to ascertain meaning from the world around them. Early readers demonstrate an awareness of story language (Snow, 1983). They can retell stories using such literary conventions as "Once upon a time" and "They lived happily ever after." When telling stories they tend to use delivery and intonation like those of an adult reading aloud. Cazden (1972) suggests that such "book language" takes children beyond their own language patterns and is distinctively characteristic of early readers.

How Children Acquire Language

Although we do not have all the answers about language acquisition, there are many theories that help explain how babies learn to speak. Knowing how language is acquired has strong implications for providing environments that promote language development. It also implies how reading and writing skills develop.

The Behaviorist Theory

The **behaviorists** have influenced our thinking about how language is acquired. Although behaviorism does not present the total picture, it still offers ideas about language acquisition that ought to be considered for instruction. Skinner (1957) defined language as the observed and produced speech that occurs in the interaction of speaker and listener. Thinking, he said, is the internal process of language; both language and thought are initiated through interactions in the environment—interactions such as those between a parent and a child, for instance. According to behaviorists, adults provide a language model that children learn through imitation. The child's acquisition of language is enhanced and encouraged by the positive reinforcement of an adult.

It is evident that children imitate adult models and are motivated to continue using language because of positive reinforcement. Children surrounded by rich language begin to use the language they hear, even though imitation sometimes occurs with erroneous comprehension or no comprehension at all. A child can imitate the sounds of the "words" of a familiar song, for instance, with no concern at all for meaning. A three-year-old girl sang "My country 'tis of thee" as "My country tis a bee." A four-year-old sang "Torn between two lovers" as "Torn between two mothers." Both children were imitating what they heard and were thus acquiring language. But when they came upon unfamiliar words in context, both substituted similar-sounding words that had meaning for them from their own experiences.

Social Interaction and Language Acquisition

Early attempts at language are often rewarded, which leads to additional responses by children, but they are also **interactive,** that is, the language is mediated by adults through interactions designed to elaborate and extend meaning (Neuman & Roskos, 1993). When newborns coo or make other verbal sounds, most parents are delighted and respond with gentle words of encouragement. The infant, in turn, responds to the positive reinforcement by repeating the cooing sounds. As babies get older and are able to formulate consonant and vowel sounds, they try them out. It is not uncommon to hear a six-month-old playing with sounds such as *ba, ba, ba,* or *ma, ma, ma.* The responsive interactive parent perceives such sounds as the child's first words and assumes that the child's *ma-ma* means *mommy.* The delighted adult says more warm and loving things to the baby and adds hugs and kisses. The parent might say, "Come on, now say it again, ma, ma, ma." The baby is pleased with the warm reception and tries to repeat the sounds in order to receive additional interaction and positive reinforcement.

As a child builds an oral vocabulary, he or she tries words more frequently. Children will point to a toy and name it. While playing with a ball, a child may say the word *ball* over and over again. The attentive parent now interacts with the child by expanding and extending the original language (Cazden, 1972). After the child says *ball,* the parent may say, "Yes, that is a nice, big, round, red ball." Through such *expansion* and reinforcement of words by the adult, the child acquires new language. The adult often *extends* upon the baby's words by asking questions, for instance, "Now what can you do with that nice red ball?" Such extension requires the child to think, understand, and act. Positive interactions encourage practice, which helps continue language development.

Unfortunately, the converse is also true. If a baby's babbling is considered annoying, if the parent is aggravated by the sound and responds with negative reinforcement by telling the baby in harsh tones, "Be quiet and stop making so much noise," the child is less likely to continue to explore the use of language.

The Nativist Theory

Chomsky (1965), Lennenberg (1967), and McNeil (1970) have described the **nativist** theory of language acquisition. They contend that language develops innately. Children figure out how language works, say the nativists, by internalizing the rules of grammar, which enable them to produce an infinite number of sentences. They do so even without the practice, reinforcement, and modeling offered by adult language, which are considered necessary by the behaviorists. The ability to learn language must be innate to humans, the nativists believe, because almost all children develop and use language in the first few years of their lives. Language growth depends on maturation: as children mature, their language grows. Children learn new patterns of language and unconsciously generate new rules for new elements of language. The child's rule system increases in complexity as he or she generates more complex language. Lennenberg (1967), an extreme nativist, finds nothing in the child's environment to account for language development. Rather, language acquisition is motivated *inside children;* learning language is a natural ability. Although maturation does play a role in language development, and it is innate to humans, newer theories offered by Piaget and Vygotsky have come to be the more accepted ideas concerning language acquisition.

Piagetian and Vygotskian Theory

Piaget's theory of *cognitive development* is built on the principle that children develop through their activities. Children's realization of the world is tied to their actions or their sensory experiences in the environment. According to this theory, children's first words are egocentric, or centered in their own actions. Children talk about themselves and what they do. Their early language as well as their general development relates to actions, objects, and events they have experienced through touching, hearing, seeing, tasting, and smelling (Piaget & Inhelder, 1969).

Vygotsky's theory of *basic learning* also has implications for language development. According to Vygotsky, children learn higher mental functions by internalizing social relationships. Adults initially provide children with names of things, for instance; they direct youngsters and make suggestions. Then, as children become more competent, the adults around them gradually withdraw the

Children learn language from social interaction with a responsive adult who provides a language model and positive reinforcement for the child's early language attempts.

amount of help they need to give. Vygotsky (1978) describes a *zone of proximal development,* a range of social interaction between an adult and child. Theoretically, the child can perform within that range, but only with adult assistance. Proximal development ends when the child can function independently. The implications for language instruction are clear: to promote language development, adults need to interact with children by encouraging, motivating, and supporting them (Sulzby, 1986).

The Constructivist Theory

The more contemporary perspective of language acquisition is the **constructivist** theory emerging from the work of Piaget and Vygotsky and described and supported by those who have studied language development (Brown, Cazden, & Bellugi-Klima, 1968, and Halliday, 1975). **Constructivists** describe children as the creators of language on the basis of an innate set of rules or underlying concepts. They describe language as an active and social process. The child constructs language, often making errors. But making errors is a necessary part of learning how language works. We need to accept language errors in a child's first years.

The implications are important for early literacy development. Even though language development charts tell us when to expect certain stages of development on average, we do not discipline babies who have not uttered their first words at eight months or their first complete sentences by two-and-a-half years. Sometimes we find their errors cute. We seem to respect their individuality and their right to grow at their own pace. Yet when children enter school, we neglect to recognize developmental differences; we prescribe tasks based on a curriculum, not on the child.

The process of acquiring language is continuous and interactive; it takes place in the social context of the child's interacting with others. Children also learn by playing with language themselves. They try out new words, involve themselves in monologues, and practice what they have learned. The acquisition of language varies from child to child, depending on his or her social and cultural background (Jagger, 1985). Their remarks illustrate that children do not *simply* imitate adult language. It is as if children need to express themselves but do not have sufficient conventional language to draw upon, so they create their own based on their backgrounds and their awareness of semantics and syntax.

A three-year-old girl named Erica saw a freckled youngster for the first time and said, "Look, Mommy, that little girl has *sprinkles* on her nose." A four-year-old boy named Matthew observed an elderly man with deep wrinkles and said, "I wonder why that man has *paths* all over his face." A father and his three-year-old daughter Stacey were toasting marshmallows; the little girl said, "Mmmm, I can smell the taste of them." After a quick summer rain, a three-year-old boy observed the sun returning to the sky and the water evaporating all around him. "The sun came out and ate up all the rain," he observed. Toward the end of the winter as the snow was melting, a four-year-old girl observed, "See how the grass is peeking out from underneath the snow."

Halliday's Theory of Language Development

Halliday (1975, p. 7) describes language development as a process by which children gradually "learn how to mean." According to his theory of developmental language, what a child can do during interactions with others has meaning and meaning can be turned into speech. In other words, children's initial language development is based on **function**: what can be said reflects what can be done. Language is learned when it is relevant and functional. The seven functions evident in the language of young children Halliday (1975, pp. 19–21) identifies are found in the chart below, with examples.

Halliday's Functions of Language
1. *Instrumental:* Children use language to satisfy a personal need and to get things done.
    Example: Cookie Mommy.
2. *Regulatory:* Children use language to control the behavior of others.
    Example: No sleep now.
3. *Interactional:* Children use language to get along with others.
    Example: You want to play?
4. *Personal:* Children use language to tell about themselves.
    Example: I'm running now.
5. *Heuristic:* Children use language to find out about things, to learn things.
    Example: What are cows for?
6. *Imaginative:* Children use language to pretend, to make believe.
    Example: Let's play space.
7. *Informative:* Children use language to communicate something for the information of others.
    Example: I'll tell you how this game works.

The several theories just discussed help us to understand how language is acquired. Each has something to offer but none by itself presents a complete picture. We *do* know, however, that children's language grows according to their need to use it, their interests, and the meaning it has for them. In other words, according to Halliday (1975), what can be said reflects what can be done. Children's language is acquired through exploration and invention and is controlled by their own maturity, the structure of the language, and its conventions. Language acquisition is fostered by positive interactions regarding language between the child and an adult.

Stages in Language Development

Children acquire language by moving through predictable stages. In doing so, they discover the rules that govern the structure of language—specifically, those of phonology (sound), syntax (grammar), and semantics (meaning).

There are forty-four separate sounds, or *phonemes,* in English. With them we produce oral language. Children who grow up in a language-rich environment can learn these sounds quite easily. They learn appropriate articulation, pronunciation, and intonation. *Intonation* involves pitch, stress, and juncture. *Pitch* refers to how high or low a voice is when producing a sound, *stress* to how loud or soft it is, and *juncture* to the pauses or connections between words, phrases, and sentences (Hittleman, 1983).

Syntax refers to the rules that govern how words work together in phrases, clauses, and sentences. Internalizing the syntactic rules of our language helps children understand what they hear and what they read. Syntax includes rules for forming basic sentence patterns, rules for transforming those patterns in order to generate new sentences, and rules for embedding, expanding, and combining sentences in order to make them more complex. Brief examples follow:

1. Some Basic Sentence Patterns
   a. Subject–verb: *The girl ran.*
   b. Subject–verb–object: *The girl ran the team.*
   c. Subject–verb–indirect object–direct object: *Susan gave Lynn a dime.*
   d. Subject–to be–noun or adjective or adverb complement: *Tom was the captain. He was happy. He was there.*
   e. Subject–linking verb–adjective: *Jane is tall.*
2. Some Basic Sentence Transformations
   a. Question
      (1) kernel: *Jim went to the store.*
      (2) transformation: *Did Jim go to the store?*
   b. Negative
      (1) kernel: *Jane is a cheerleader.*
      (2) transformation: *Jane is not a cheerleader.*

      c. Passive
         (1) kernel: *Jennifer gave Lisa some bubble gum.*
         (2) transformation: *Some bubble gum was given to Lisa by Jennifer.*
   3. Some Embeddings (sentence expansion and combination)
      a. Adding modifiers (adjectives, adverbs, adverbial and adjective phrases)
         (1) kernel: *The boy played with friends.*
         (2) transformation: *The boy in the red pants played with three friends.*
      b. Compounding (combining words, phrases, or independent clauses to form compound subjects, verbs, etc.)
         (1) kernel: *Jane ran. Jane played. Jack ran. Jack played.*
         (2) transformation: *Jane and Jack ran and played.* (Morrow, 1978)

Semantics deals with the meaning that language communicates, both through content words and through function words. It largely governs vocabulary development. *Content words* carry meaning in themselves. *Function words* have no easily definable meanings in isolation, but they indicate relationships between other words in a sentence. Function words include prepositions, conjunctions, and determiners (Pflaum, 1986).

Although we have identified stages of language growth, the pace of development may differ from child to child. An individual child's language development also tends to progress and then regress, so that the stages of growth are not always easily recognized. However, language development has been studied to the extent that it can be described generally.

From Birth to One Year

In the first few months of infancy, oral language consists of a child's experimenting or playing with sounds. Infants cry when they are uncomfortable and babble, gurgle, or coo when they are happy. Parents are able to distinguish cries. One cry is for hunger and another is for pain, for instance. Infants learn to communicate specific needs by producing different cries. They communicate nonverbally as well as by moving their arms and legs to express pleasure or pain.

When a baby is about six months old, its babbling becomes more sophisticated. Children at that age are usually capable of combining a variety of consonant sounds with vowel sounds. They tend to repeat these combinations over and over. As mentioned earlier, it is at this stage that parents sometimes think they are hearing their child's first words. The repeated consonant and vowel sounds, such as *da, da, da,* or *ma, ma, ma,* do sound like real words, ones that the parents are delighted to hear. Most parents tend to reinforce the child's behavior positively at this stage. Repetition of specific sounds and continued reinforcement lead the child to associate the physical mechanics of making a particular sound with the meaning of the word the sound represents.

From eight to twelve months, children increase their comprehension of language dramatically; their understanding of language far exceeds their ability to produce it. They do, however, tend to speak their first words, usually those most familiar and meaningful to them in their daily lives: *Mommy, Daddy, bye-bye, baby, cookie, milk, juice,* and *no,* for instance. As they become experienced with their first words, children use holophrastic speech—one-word utterances that express an entire sentence (Smith, 1972). For example, a baby might say "cookie," but mean "I want a cookie," "My cookie is on the floor," or "I'm done with this cookie."

From One to Two

A child's oral language grows a great deal between one and two. Along with one-word utterances, the child utters many sounds with adult intonation as if speaking in sentences. These utterances are not understandable to adults, however. Children begin to use telegraphic speech from twelve months on—the first evidence of their knowledge of syntax. Telegraphic speech uses content words, such as nouns and verbs, but omits function words, such as conjunctions and articles. In spite of the omissions, words are delivered in correct order, or syntax: "Daddy home" for "Daddy is coming home soon," or "Toy fall" for "My toy fell off the table."

Language grows by leaps and bounds once the child begins to combine words. By eighteen months most children can pronounce four-fifths of the English phonemes and use twenty to fifty words (Biehler, 1976).

From Two to Three

This year is probably the most dramatic in terms of language development. Typically, a child's oral vocabulary grows from 300 words to 1000. The child can comprehend, but cannot yet use, 2000 to 3000 additional words. Telegraphic sentences of two or three words continue to be most frequent, but syntactic complexity continues to develop, and the child occasionally uses such functional words as pronouns, conjunctions, prepositions, articles, and possessives. As their language ability grows, children gain confidence. They actively play with language by repeating new words and phrases and making up nonsense words. They enjoy rhyme, patterns of language, and repetition (Brown, 1973). Consider the following transcription of Jennifer's dialogue with her dog. Jennifer was two years ten months at the time. "Nice doggie, my doggie, white doggie, whitey, nicey doggie. Good doggie, my doggie, boggie, poggie. Kiss doggie, kiss me, doggie, good doggie." Jennifer's language is repetitive, playful, silly, and creative, demonstrating some of the characteristics of language production typical for a child her age.

From Three to Four

A child's vocabulary and knowledge of sentence structure continue to develop rapidly during the fourth year. Syntactic structures added to the child's repertoire include plurals and regular verbs. Indeed, children of this age are prone to overgeneralization in using these two structures, mainly because both plural formation and verb inflection are highly irregular in our language (Jewell & Zintz, 1986). Four-year-old Jonathan illustrated both problems when he had an accident in class and came running over very upset. He said, "Mrs. Morrow, hurry over, I knocked over the fishbowl and it broked and all the fishes are swimming on the floor." Jonathan knew how to form the past tense of a verb by adding *ed,* but he didn't know about irregular verbs such as *broke.* He also knew about adding an *s* to form a plural but again was unaware of irregular plural forms such as *fish.*

As they approach age four, children *seem* to have acquired all the elements of adult language. They can generate language and apply the basic rules that govern it. However, although their ability with language has grown enormously and they sound almost as if they are using adult speech, they have really acquired only the basic foundations. Language continues to grow throughout our lives as we gain new experiences, acquire new vocabulary, and find new ways of putting words together to form sentences. At the age of three to four, children talk about what they do as they are doing it. They often talk to themselves or by themselves as they play. It seems as if they are trying to articulate their actions (Seefeldt & Barbour, 1986). While painting at an easel, four-year-old Christopher said to himself, "I'm making a nice picture. I'm making colors all over. I'm painting, pit, pat, pit, pat. I'm going back and forth and up and down. Now I'm jumping as I paint." He carried out this monologue while painting *this* picture. As he talked and painted, he did exactly what he said, words and actions coinciding.

From Five to Six

Five- and six-year-olds sound very much like adults when they speak. However, their vocabularies are always increasing, and so is the syntactic complexity of their language. They have vocabularies of approximately 2500 words, and they are extremely articulate. Many, however, still have difficulty pronouncing some sounds, especially *l, r,* and *sh* at the ends of words. They become aware that a word can have more than one meaning. When they are embarrassed or frustrated at misunderstanding things, they say something silly or try to be humorous. They also tend to be creative in using language. When they do not have a word for a particular situation, they supply their own. Adults often find the language used by children of this age to be amusing as well as delightful and interesting (Seefeldt & Barbour, 1986):

> *Benjamin ran into school very excited one morning. "Mrs. Morrow," he said, "you'll never believe it. My dog grew puppies last night!"*

> *My husband and I were going to a formal dance one evening. My five-year-old daughter had never seen us dressed up like this before. When I walked into the room wearing a long gown and asked Stephanie how I looked, she said, "Mommy, you look soooo pretty. What is Daddy's costume going to be like?"*

> *Escorted by her mother, Allison was on her way to her first day of kindergarten. She seemed a little nervous. When her mother asked her if she was okay, Allison replied, "Oh, I'm fine, Mommy. It's just that my stomach is very worried."*

There are other characteristics of kindergarteners' language. Kindergarteners have discovered bathroom talk and curse words, and they enjoy shocking others by using them. They talk a lot and begin to use language to control situations. Their language reflects their movement from a world of fantasy to that of reality.

From Seven to Eight

By the time children are seven years of age, and continuing on to eight and older, they have developed a grammar that is almost equivalent to that of adults. Of course they do not use the extensive numbers of grammatical transformations found in adult language nor do they have the extent of vocabulary found in adult speech. Seven- and eight-year-olds are good conversationalists who talk a lot about what they do.

Recognizing Language Differences in Young Children

A major instructional concern in early childhood literacy programs is the varied language backgrounds of the children who come to day-care centers, preschools, kindergartens, and first and second grades. Any given group may contain children using words, syntax, and language patterns quite different from those of standard English. Particularly in the United States, there are many different forms of English usage. There are, for example, distinct grammars in rural New England, Appalachia, and in some African-American communities. There are children whose families have immigrated from Latin America, the Middle East, or Asia. Foster (1982, p. 14) compiled the following six categories that represent the diverse language abilities of young children.

Diverse Language Abilities of Children

1. Recent immigrants with little or no English.

2. Children whose home language is something other than English, but who are themselves likely to know at least some English because of their experiences with television and their contacts outside the home.

3. Children who speak both English and another language fluently. Such children are usually easily assimilated into the majority group. Often English becomes the major language with which they communicate. They then risk losing the advantages that fluent bilingualism gives them.

4. Children who speak mainly English but who have poor skills in their parents' or family's language. Often these children speak English at home, but their parents speak to them in another language. Children in this group sometimes deny their heritage and are ashamed of the cultural differences between themselves and their majority classmates at school.

5. Children who speak nonstandard English because the English spoken at home is nonfluent or a dialect. Although they need to learn a more standard English at school, they must not be made to feel that their home language is inferior.

6. The vast majority of children, those who are monolingual in a pluralistic society. Their "understanding and appreciation of the various cultures in America," said Foster, "would be greatly enhanced through study in another language besides English."

All six categories represent major concerns because a firm base in oral language bears a strong relationship to literacy development. A child fluent in any form of nonstandard English may have difficulty reading and writing without some proficiency in standard English. Along with this concern for skill development are affective concerns. Unfortunately, teachers have been known to look down on children with language differences and to classify them as students with potential learning problems. We have come to realize, however, that differences do *not* mean deficits. Linguists have found, for example, that black English is a systematic, rule-governed dialect that can express all levels of thought (Robinson, Strickland, & Cullinan, 1977). Teachers must be sensitive to the differences in language among youngsters in their classrooms. Children must not be embarrassed or made to feel inferior because they do not speak standard English. Teachers need to respect language differences and help children take pride in their backgrounds. Diversity in language and heritage should be shared in classrooms to enrich the classroom experience.

Children's Responses to Language Differences

Children tend to choose playmates who speak the same language, presumably because it is easier to communicate. They usually do not reject those who speak a different language, however, and will use gestures and other means of communication. Bilingual children will often act as interpreters for their parents and friends who are less skilled in the language of the classroom.

While children are curious about differences in speech and will often "correct" each other, they have not developed the biases that adults have toward nonstandard usage.

Pragmatically, children must become somewhat fluent in the language used at school. If they are expected to read standard English, they need a foundation in speaking standard English. According to Pflaum (1986), young children do not have a great deal of difficulty acquiring new language. She suggests that the typical preschool seems to provide a linguistic environment that enables young children to learn standard English if they are encouraged to speak it. An environment that provides varied experiences and opportunities to converse helps the child acquire the ability to speak the language. Children who speak nonstandard dialects, such as black English, need the opportunity to use their own dialects in school during creative dramatics or in storytelling and discussions. Any child given the opportunity to use language frequently and effectively, even if it is not standard English, will be receptive to language learning in general (Robinson, Strickland, & Cullinan, 1977). Frequent opportunity to use language in varied situations will help children become more fluent. As Gonzales-Mena (1976, p. 14) has pointed out:

1. Children are eager to learn English or any other new language when there is an openness and an acceptance of them, their culture, and their native language.

2. Language should not be taught in isolation from any of the other basic school activities, but as a part of the total, integrated program, which includes a focus on language development. Listening, speaking, reading, and writing are all a part of math, social studies, art, and science.

3. Children learn through their senses, including their muscles. Concepts as well as new words and phrases are learned better when children can participate in some action. They need to examine and explore real objects and act out new expressions. Pictures can help, but action imprints the message in a stronger fashion.

The strategies to help develop young children's language discussed on the following pages will also be successful with children who have language differences or special language needs.

Strategies for Language Development

The review of theory and research suggests how we can help children acquire and develop language pleasantly, productively, and appropriately. Children acquire language by emulating adult models, interacting with others when using language, and experiencing positive reinforcement for their efforts. If language is innate, it can develop naturally as individuals pass through common stages of development at certain times in their lives. As children mature, they become capable of generating ever more complex language structures. They learn language by doing, by acting upon and within familiar environments. Their first spoken words are those that are meaningful for them within their own experiences. Their earliest language is an expression of needs. They learn language through social interaction with individuals more literate than they, whether adults or older children. Children also create their own language, play with it, and engage in monologues.

Using what we know of language acquisition and developmental stages as guidelines, we can begin to create and prepare appropriate materials, activities, and experiences in a suitable atmosphere to nurture a youngster's language development. The following objectives are formulated for a program fostering language development in children from birth to age seven.

Objectives for the Development of Receptive Language

1. Provide children with an atmosphere in which they will hear language frequently.
2. Children should be able to associate the language that they hear with pleasure and enjoyment.
3. Children are given the opportunity to discriminate and classify sounds they hear.
4. Children should hear a rich source of new words on a regular basis.
5. Children will be given the opportunity to listen to others and demonstrate that they understand what is said.
6. Provide children with opportunities for following directions.
7. Children are provided with good models of standard English. They also get to hear their home language in school.

Objectives for the Development of Expressive Language

1. Give opportunities for children to use their own language freely at any stage of development. This could be a different dialect or mixtures of English and Spanish. Their desire to communicate will be encouraged, accepted, and respected.
2. Encourage children to pronounce words correctly.
3. Help children to increase their speaking vocabularies.
4. Encourage children to speak in complete sentences at appropriate stages in their development.
5. Give children opportunities to expand their use of various syntactic structures, such as adjectives, adverbs, prepositional phrases, dependent clauses, plurals, past tense, and possessives.
6. Encourage children to communicate with others so that they can be understood.
7. Give children the opportunity to use language socially and psychologically by interpreting feelings, points of view, and motivation and by solving problems through generating hypotheses, summarizing events, and predicting outcomes.
8. Give children opportunities to develop language that involve mathematical and logical relations, such as describing size and amount, making comparisons, defining sets and classes, and reasoning deductively.
9. Give children the opportunity to talk in many different settings: In the whole group with the teacher leading the discussion, in teacher-led small groups, in child-directed groups for learning, or in conversation in social settings.

Providing children with rich sources of new words in storybook reading, for example, will develop receptive language and vocabulary.

Language is best learned when it is integrated with other communication skills and embedded within topics or content areas that have meaning for children. Approaching language development, reading, and writing as skills to be taught in isolation without meaning or function will not promote the development of lifelong literacy. For growth, natural settings are optimal. Children are constructive learners. They are active meaning makers, who are continuously interpreting and making sense of their world based on what they already know, that is, on what they have constructed and reconstructed in their minds.

Language is the major system by which meanings are communicated and expressed in our world. Because language is used for various purposes, our meanings are expressed in various ways. Language cannot be understood or interpreted unless it is related to some meaningful context. Language is learned through use, as part of our daily social activities. In addition to being aware of all of the above, we need to be accepting of language differences and help youngsters with special needs to acquire skills when trying to help children develop, enhance, and practice language. (Pappas, Kiefer, & Levstik, 1995).

Strategies for Language Development from Birth to Two

"Hi, Michael. How's my great big boy today? Let's change your diaper now, upsy-daisy. My goodness, you're getting heavy. Now I'll put you down right

here on your dressing table and get a nice new diaper for you. Here, want this rubber ducky to hold while I change you? That's a good boy. You really like him. Let's clean you up now. This is the way we clean up Michael, clean up Michael, clean up Michael. This is the way we clean up Michael, so he'll feel so much better. You like that singing, don't you. I can tell. You're just smiling away, and cooing. Want to do that again? This is the way we clean up Michael, clean up Michael, clean up Michael. This is the way we clean up Michael, so he'll feel so much better. Wow, you were singing with me that time. That's right, ba-ba-ba-ba, now do it again. Mmmmm, doesn't that smell good? The baby powder is so nice and smooth."

Developing Language in the Child's First Year   Michael was four months old when his mother's conversation with him was taped. Here in print, it reads like a monologue; in reality it was not. Michael was a very active participant in the conversation. He stared intently at his mother's face. He cooed, he waved his arms, he smiled, he became serious. His mother was providing a rich language environment for her baby. She encouraged his participation in the dialogue and acknowledged his responsiveness in a positive way. She provided him with the environmental stimuli necessary for his innate language ability to flourish. She engaged him in this type of conversation during feedings and while changing, bathing, and dressing him. She talked to him even when he was in his crib and she in another room or while in the same room but involved in other things. The baby knew that communication was occurring because he responded to the talk with body movements, coos, babbles, and smiles. When he responded his mother responded in turn; response brought response, back and forth.

Surround Infants with Sounds: Infants need to be surrounded by the sounds of happy language. Whether from mother, father, caregiver at home, or teacher or aide in a day-care center, sounds and interaction should accompany all activities. Adults responsible for babies from birth through the first year need to know nursery rhymes, chants, finger plays, and songs. It is important for children simply to hear the *sounds* of language as well as the meanings. Thus, adults can make up their own chants to suit an occasion, as Michael's mother did when she spontaneously adapted "Here We Go Round the Mulberry Bush" to the situation at hand. Such experiences make the baby conscious of the sounds of language. Children learn that they can have control over language and that oral language can be a powerful tool as well as fun.

In addition to the conversation of nearby adults, infants should experience other sounds and other voices: soft music from a radio, record player, or music box. They need to hear the sounds of "book language," which differs in intonation, pitch, stress, juncture, and even syntax from normal conversation. They need familiarity with language in all its variety so they can learn to differentiate among its various conventions and patterns. Speaking to infants, singing to them, reading to them, and letting them hear the radio and television provide sources of language that help their own language grow. In addition, there are sounds in the immediate environment that need no preparation and are not the sounds of language but that provide practice in auditory discrimination—the ringing of the doorbell, the hissing of the teapot, the chimes on the clock, the hum of the vacuum cleaner, a dog barking, a bird singing, a car screeching, and so on. Bring them to the baby's attention, give them names, and heighten the child's sensitivity to them.

Surround Infants with Sensory Objects: In addition to hearing a variety of sounds, the baby needs objects to see, touch, smell, hear, and taste. They should be placed in the baby's immediate environment—the crib or playpen. They will stimulate the baby's activity and curiosity and become the meaningful things within the environment from which language evolves. Some of the objects should make sounds or music when pushed or touched. They can have different textures and smells. They should be easy to grab, push, kick, or pull. They can be placed so they are visible and within the child's reach, and at least one item should be suspended overhead: stuffed animals, rubber toys, music boxes made of soft material, plastic or wooden mobiles that can be kicked or grasped, mechanical mobiles that hang from the ceiling and rotate by themselves, and books with smooth edges. Books can be propped open against the side of the crib or playpen when the baby is lying on its back, or against the headboard when the baby is on its stomach. Certain familiar objects should always remain, and new objects frequently be made available. In addition to allowing the child to play independently with these objects, the adults in charge need to talk about them, name them, occasionally join the child in playing with them, and discuss their characteristics and what they are capable of doing. Objects should have different textures and scents, make different sounds, and provide different visual effects. Some should be chewable.

From three to six months, the baby gurgles, coos, begins to laugh, and babbles. Recognize an infant's sounds as the beginning of language. Reinforce the infant positively with responses aimed at encouraging the sounds. When the baby begins to put consonants and vowels together, again reinforce the behavior, imitating what the baby has uttered and urging repetition. When the baby becomes aware of the ability to repeat sounds and control language output, he or she will do these things. Babies will also begin to understand adult language, so it is important to name objects, carry on conversations, and give the baby directions. At the end of its first year, assuming he or she has experienced appropriate sounds of language as well as encouragement and pleasant interaction, the baby will be on the verge of extensive language growth during its second year.

Language Development at Ages One and Two   Through the second year of a child's life, the adults in charge need to continue the same kinds of stimulation suggested for developing oral language during the first year. However, because the baby is likely to develop a vocabulary of up to 150 words and to produce two- and possibly three-word sentences during the second year, additional techniques can be used to enhance language growth. As described earlier, one- and two-word utterances by children at this age usually represent sentences. When a twelve-month-old points to a teddy bear and says "bear," the child probably means "I want my bear." Parents and caregivers at home or in day-care centers can begin to expand and extend the child's language at such times by helping to increase the number of words the child is able to use in a sentence or by increasing the syntactic complexity of their own utterances.

Scaffolding to Help Language Develop: One method for helping a child develop ability with language is a kind of modeling called *scaffolding* (Applebee & Langer, 1983). In scaffolding, an adult provides a verbal response for a baby who is not yet capable of making the response itself. In other words, the adult provides a language model. When the baby says "bear," for instance, the adult responds, "Do you want your teddy bear?" or "Here is your nice, soft, brown teddy bear." In addition to expanding on the child's language, the adult can extend it by asking the youngster to do something that demonstrates understanding and extends his or her thinking. For example, "Here is your nice, soft, brown teddy bear. Can you hug the teddy? Let me see you hug him." In addition to questions that require action, the adult can ask questions that require answers. Questions that require answers of more than one word are preferable—for example, "Tell me about the clothes your teddy is wearing." *How, why,* and *tell me* questions encourage the child to give more than a yes/no answer and more than a one-word response. *What, who, when,* and *where* questions, on the other hand, tend to elicit only one-word replies. As the child's language ability develops, the adult provides fewer and fewer such "scaffolds"; the child learns to build utterances along similar models.

New Experiences Help to Develop Language: Select songs, rhymes, and books for one- to two-year-olds that use language they can understand. They are capable of understanding a great deal of language by now, and the selections should help expand and extend their language. Both vocabulary and conceptual understanding are enhanced by experiences. For the one- to two-year-old, frequent outings are desirable. Visits to the post office, supermarket, dry cleaners, and park provide experiences to talk about and new concepts to explore. Household tasks taken for granted by adults are new experiences that enrich children's language. Involve them in activities. For example, an eighteen-month-old can put a piece of laundry into the washing machine or give one stir to the bowl of gelatin or some other food that is being prepared. During such daily routines, surround the activity with language, identifying new objects for the baby and asking for responses related to each activity (Schickedanz, 1990).

Overgeneralizations and Language Development: As the child becomes more verbal, the adult sometimes wants to correct the child's mispronunciations or overgeneralization of grammatical rules. The child who says, "Me feeded fishes," for instance, has simply overgeneralized the rules for:

- Forming most past tenses (*feeded* for *fed*)
- Using pronouns (objective *me* for subjective *I*) and
- Forming most plurals (*fishes* for *fish*)

Children can also overgeneralize concepts. A child who has learned to associate a bird with the word *bird* might see a butterfly for the first time and call it a bird, thinking that anything that flies is a bird. Correcting such an overgeneralization is best done positively rather than negatively. Instead of saying, "No, that's not a bird," simply refer to the butterfly as a *butterfly,* commenting on its beauty, perhaps, and thus expanding the child's verbal repertoire. Eventually, with positive reinforcement and proper role models in language, the child will differentiate between birds and butterflies as well as between regular and irregular grammatical conventions and forms.

Correcting overgeneralizations negatively as absolute error, on the other hand, is not likely to help young children understand the error or use proper tense and plural forms the next time. Rather, it is likely to inhibit the child from trying to use language. In learning, children need to take risks and make mistakes. Hearing good adult models will eventually enable them to internalize the rules of language and to correct their errors themselves. At least until age five, the child should be allowed to experiment and play with language without direct concern for 100 percent correctness in syntax and pronunciation. The English language is extremely complex and irregular in many of its rules; in time, the child will master these rules in all their complexity and nuance, given good adult models and plenty of verbal interaction. At the same time, encouraging "baby talk" simply because it is cute, for instance, is likely to inhibit growth because children will use whatever language they believe will please the adults around them.

Materials for Language Development at One and Two: Materials for the one- to two-year-old should be varied and more sophisticated than those in the first year. Now that the baby is mobile in the home or day-care center, books need to be easily accessible to the child. Toys should still include items of various textures, such as furry, stuffed animals and rubber balls. Other toys should require simple eye–hand coordination. Three-to-five–piece puzzles, trucks that can be pushed and pulled, dolls, a child-size set of table and chairs, crayons and large paper, and puppets are examples. Choose objects that require activity, for activity encourages exploration, use of the imagination, creation, and the need to communicate.

Strategies for Language Development in Early Childhood Classrooms

From three to seven a great deal of language development occurs. Children should continue to hear good models of language. They need continued opportunities to use language in social situations with adults and other children. Their oral language production must be reinforced positively. They must be actively involved in meaningful experiences that will expand their knowledge and interest in the world around them. Language should be purposeful and its development integrated with other subjects rather than taught separately as a content area unto itself.

To accomplish these continuing goals, early childhood teachers provide an environment in which language will flourish. They organize centers of learning, one for each content area, that include materials for encouraging language use. A science center, for instance, can include class pets such as a pair of gerbils. Gerbils are active, loving animals, fun to watch and handle. Children surround the cage often and generate talk just from watching the animals. Gerbils reproduce in twenty-eight–day cycles. When litters arrive, the birth process can be observed. The new babies cause a great deal of excitement and generate questions, comments, and unlimited conversation.

In my own classroom, our parent gerbils reproduced a second litter twenty-eight days after the first and before the first babies had been weaned. The mother looked tired and thin from feeding and caring for ten baby gerbils. One morning one of the children noticed that the mother was not in the cage. We couldn't imagine what had happened to her. A few days later, having almost given up hope, we found her hiding behind the refrigerator in the teachers' room. We never figured out how she got out of the cage, but we hypothesized all kinds of possibilities, and there was a great deal of discussion about why she left. No teacher alone could provide a lesson in which language flourished and grew the way it did during that incident, simply because gerbils were part of the classroom.

Center Materials for Language Development   Here are some examples of centers of learning and appropriate materials in early childhood classrooms that will help to generate language:

>   ***Science:*** aquarium, terrarium, plants, magnifying glass, class pet, magnets, thermometer, compass, prism, shells, rock collections, stethoscope, kaleidoscope, microscope, informational books and children's literature reflecting topics being studied, and blank journals for recording observations of experiments and scientific projects.
>
>   ***Social Studies:*** maps, a globe, flags, community figures, traffic signs, current events, artifacts from other countries, informational books and children's literature reflecting topics being studied, writing materials to make class books or your own books about topics being studied.
>
>   ***Art:*** easels, watercolors, brushes, colored pencils, crayons, felt-tip markers, various kinds of paper, scissors, paste, pipe cleaners, scrap materials (bits of various fabrics, wool, string, and so forth), clay, play dough, food and detergent boxes for sculptures, books about famous artists, books with directions for crafts.
>
>   ***Music:*** piano, record player and records, tape recorder with musical tapes, rhythm instruments, songbooks, books of songs that have been made into books, and photocopies of sheet music for songs sung in class.

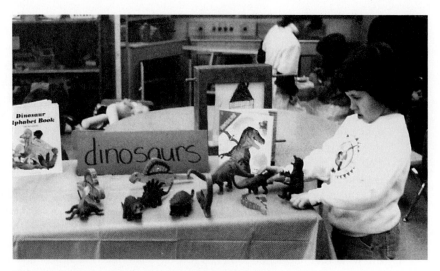

Experiences in science lead to new discoveries, new vocabulary, and reasons to talk and discuss.

Mathematics: scales, rulers, measuring cups, movable clocks, stopwatch, calendar, play money, cash register, calculator, dominoes, abacus, number line, height chart, hourglass, numbers (felt, wood, and magnetic), fraction puzzles, geometric shapes, math workbooks, children's literature about numbers and mathematics, writing materials for creating stories, and books related to mathematics.

Literacy: children's literature, tape recorder, headsets and taped stories, pencils, writing paper, stapler, construction paper, three-by-five cards for recording words, hole punch, letter stencils, typewriter, computer, puppets, storytelling devices such as felt-board and roll movies, stationery with envelopes, letters (felt, wood, and magnetic), sets of pictures for different units (Halloween, seasons, animals, and so on), rhyme games, color games, cards for associating sounds and symbols, alphabet cards, pictures and words representing out-of-school environmental print (*Burger King, Exit, Stop, Exxon*). (The literacy center also includes a library corner, a writing center, oral language materials, and language arts manipulatives, all of which are described in later chapters.)

Dramatic Play: dolls, dress-ups, telephone, stuffed animals, mirror, food cartons, plates, silverware, newspapers, magazines, books, telephone book, class telephone book, cookbook, note pads, cameras and photo album, table and chairs, broom, dustpan, child-size kitchen furniture such as refrigerator, sink, ironing board, and storage shelves. (The dramatic-play area can be changed from a kitchen to a grocery store, beauty shop, gas station, business office, restaurant, etc., with the addition of materials for appropri-

Varied art experiences with different media encourage descriptive language and develop the manual dexterity needed for writing.

ate themes when they are studied.) Include appropriate materials for reading and writing related to the theme of the dramatic-play area.

Block Area: blocks of many different sizes and shapes and figures of people, animals, toy cars, trucks, items related to themes being studied, paper and pencils to prepare signs and notes, and reading materials related to themes.

Workbench: wood, hammer, screwdriver, saw, pliers, nails, worktable.

Outdoor Play: sand, water, pails, shovels, rakes, gardening area and gardening tools, climbing equipment, riding toys, crates, playhouse, balls, tires, ropes.

Children need opportunities to use such areas for interacting with each other and the teacher, and they should be given enough time to touch, smell, taste, listen, and talk about what they are doing. Exploring and experimenting with the materials in the centers are creative, imaginative, problem-solving, decision-making experiences in which children use language and thereby give it the opportunity to grow. The opportunity to *use* language is one of the key elements in language development.

Some materials remain permanently in the centers; others are replaced or supplemented from time to time so that new items of interest become available. Materials added to the centers are often coordinated with thematic units of instruction. For example, if a unit on Indians is introduced, Indian dolls and artifacts are added to the social studies center, and books about Indians to the literacy center. The different content-area centers provide sources for language use and development; the literacy center is devoted *primarily* to language development. Thematic units of instruction that integrate all areas make learning more meaningful and expand concepts. (Interdisciplinary instruction is described more fully in Chapter 10.)

Developing Language with Strategies Used in Thematic Units Each new unit of instruction offers specific language experiences that expand vocabulary, syntax, pronunciation, and the ability to understand others and be understood. Again, these experiences should incorporate all content areas and make use of the senses (Tompkins, 1995). The suggestions that follow can be used each time a new theme is initiated. They reflect or describe activities designed to aid language growth in early childhood classrooms. For purposes of illustration, assume that the topic throughout these suggestions is *winter.* (Virtually any other topic can be substituted.)

1. ***Discussion:*** Hold discussions about the unit topic. What is the weather like in winter? What kind of clothing do the children need to wear in winter? What fun things can they do in winter that they can't do at other times of the year? What problems does winter bring? What is winter like in different parts of the country, for example, New York, Florida, Chicago, and California?

2. ***Word Lists:*** Ask the children to name every word they can think of that makes them think of winter. Your list might eventually include: *snow, ice, cold, white, wet, freezing, sleds, snowman, mittens, scarf, hat, slush, skiing, ice skating, snowballs, fireplace,* and *snowflakes.* Classify the words on the list into how winter feels, looks, smells, sounds, and tastes, or what you can and cannot do in winter. List the words on a chart, and hang the chart in the room. Leave the chart hanging when you go to the next unit. When the wall gets too crowded, compile the charts in a class book.

3. ***Pictures:*** Provide pictures of winter scenes for discussion, each depicting different information about the season.

4. ***Sharing Time (Show and Tell):*** Hold a sharing period during which children bring things from home related to the topic. Give all the children an opportunity to share if they wish, but assign different children for different days, because sharing by more than five or six children in one period can become tedious. Sharing objects from home is an important activity. It gives children confidence because they are talking about something from their own environment. Even the shyest children will speak in front of a group if they have the security of sharing something familiar from home. Encourage children to relate the items to the unit topic, if they can. Model language for children to encourage them to speak in sentences. Coordinate the activity with parents, informing them of their children's scheduled sharing and the general topic under discussion.

5. ***Experiments:*** Carry out a science experiment related to the topic being studied. Involve the children actively. Discuss the purpose and hypothesize what is likely to happen. Encourage children to discuss what they are doing

Experiences related to themes generate oral language that can be written down and then read.

while they are doing it. When the experiment is complete, discuss the results with the class. (Example: Allow water to freeze, then melt. In warm climates use the refrigerator for freezing the water.)

6. **Art:** Carry out an art activity related to the topic; the activity should be process-oriented rather than teacher-directed. Allow children to create their own work rather than making them follow specific directions that yield identical results from child to child. Discuss the project and the available materials before the activity. Provide interesting materials and encourage children to touch, describe, and compare them. While children are creating, it is natural for them to converse about what they are doing. Encourage such conversation. For example, provide blue construction paper, tin foil, white doilies, cotton, wool, tissue paper, and chalk for a winter collage. Discuss why these colors and objects were selected. What is there about them that makes people think of winter? Suggest creating a picture that makes someone think of winter. Discuss the textures of the materials and what can be done with them.

7. **Music:** Sing songs about winter, such as "It's a Marshmallow World in the Winter." Music is enjoyable and lyrics help build vocabulary and sensitivity to the sounds and meanings of words. Listen to music without words, music that creates images concerning the topic. Ask the children for words, sentences, or stories that the music brings to mind.

8. **Food Preparation:** Prepare food related to the unit. Make hot soup, flavored snowballs, or popcorn. Discuss food textures, smells, taste, and appear-

ance. Do they change during preparation? Follow directions and recipes, developing sequence as well as quantitative sense. Allow children to help prepare the food, then enjoy consuming it together, encouraging discussion and conversation throughout about the activity. Food preparation can be a source of new vocabulary, especially because many of its terms take on special meanings—*stir, blend, boil, measure.*

9. **Dramatic Play:** Add items related to the topic to the dramatic-play area—mittens, hats, scarves, boots for dress-up—to encourage role-playing and language about winter. Introduce them by placing each in a separate bag and asking a child to reach in, describe what it feels like, and identify it without peeking. The sense of touch elicits descriptive language.

10. **Outdoor Play:** Encourage spontaneous language and frequent problem-solving situations during outdoor play. For example, provide snow shovels, sleds, pails, and cups during playtime in the snow. Discuss outdoor play before going out, and again after coming in.

11. **Morning Message:** Discuss weather and the calendar in a daily morning message as you begin your day. Encourage children to share news about themselves: a new pair of sneakers, a birthday. Make plans for the school day.

12. **Class Trips:** Take the class on a trip, bring in a guest speaker, or show a film. All three activities can generate language and encourage its use.

13. **Read Stories:** Read stories to the children on the topic under study. Books such as *Katy and the Big Snow* (Burton, 1943) enhance information and expand vocabulary.

14. **Create Stories:** Provide the children with a title, such as "The Big Winter Snowstorm," and let them think of a story about it.

15. **Retell Stories:** Encourage children to retell stories. This activity, of course, encourages them to use book language and incorporate it into their own. Retelling is not always an easy task for young children, so props can be very helpful—puppets, felt-boards and felt characters, roll movies, and pictures in a book. With these same props, children can be encouraged to make up their own stories as well.

16. **Very Own Words:** In any of these activities, children should be encouraged as often as possible to select their favorite Very Own Words about winter. Favorite Very Own Words can be selected from discussions, art lessons, science experiments, songs, books, poems, cooking experiences, or any other activity. Early in the school year, encourage children to collect their favorite Very Own Words. After a particular experience, ask them to name a favorite word. Record children's favorite Very Own Words for them on three-by-five cards and store them in each child's own file box or on a binder ring. When children are capable of recording their own words, assist them with spelling when they ask

for help. Favorite Very Own Words enhance vocabulary and are a source for reading and writing development.

17. **_Summary of the Day:_** Summarize the day's events at the end of the school day, encouraging children to tell what they liked, did not like, and want to do the next day in school.

Children's Literature and Language Development   Among more general suggestions, select and offer children's literature that represents varieties of language and experience. Some children's books feature the sounds of language; they aid auditory discrimination or incorporate additional phonemes into a child's language repertoire—for example, _Too Much Noise_ (McGovern, 1967). Others help develop the syntactic complexity of a child's language through embeddings and transformations and the use of numerous adjectives and adverbs—for example, _Swimmy_ (Lionni, 1963). Craft books require children to follow directions. Wordless books encourage them to create their own stories from the pictures. Concept books feature words such as _up, down, in, out, near,_ and _far,_ or involve children in mathematical reasoning. Realistic literature deals with death, divorce, loneliness, fear, and daily problems. Discussion of such themes leads to sociopsychological language, interpretation of feelings, sensitivity to others, and problem solving. Books of riddles, puns, jokes, and tongue twisters show children how language plays on meaning in certain situations. Poetry introduces children to rhyme, metaphor, simile, and onomatopoeia, and encourages them to recite and create poems. (Children's books are listed by these and other categories in Appendix A.) When children hear and discuss the language of books, they internalize what they have heard; the language soon becomes part of their own language. Research studies have found that children who have had stories read to them frequently develop more sophisticated language structures and increased vocabulary (Chomsky, 1972; Cohen, 1968; Lenz, 1992).

Two anecdotes illustrate how children incorporate into their own language the language of books that have been read to them. My kindergarten class was playing on the playground one early spring day. A few birds circled around several times. Melissa ran up to me and said, "Look, Mrs. Morrow, the birds are fluttering and flapping around the playground." Surprised at first by Melissa's descriptive and unusual choice of words, I thought for a moment, then remembered. The words that Melissa was using came directly from a picture storybook we had read shortly before, _Jenny's Hat_ (Keats, 1966). In the book, birds _flutter_ and _flap_ around Jenny's hat. Melissa had internalized the language of the book and was able to use it in her own vocabulary.

One day after a big snowstorm, my daughter asked, "Mommy, can I go out and play? I want to build a smiling snowman." I was surprised and pleased with this sophisticated language being uttered by my four-year-old. _Smiling snowman,_ after all, represents a participle in the adjective position, a syntactic structure usually not found in the language of children before the age of seven or eight. Then I noticed that Stephanie had a book in her hand, _The Snowy Day_ (Keats, 1962).

In it Peter goes outside and builds a *smiling snowman*. Stephanie had used the book's language and made it her own.

The activities just suggested can be repeated throughout the school year with each new theme that is studied. Such adaptation and repetition make it possible to introduce children to hundreds of new vocabulary words, concepts, and ideas. They will assure children of opportunities to participate in new kinds of spontaneous language as topics and structured experiences change. Word lists and other materials produced during each unit can be maintained and made available for review and reuse.

Most of the suggestions can be followed at home as well as at school. Parents should not be expected to create elaborate centers or carry out units of instruction. But daily living offers holidays, seasons, family events, and other topics and events of special interest. Parents can tap such meaningful occasions for their potential enhancement of language development. They can discuss events, list words, help children collect favorite Very Own Words, involve children in cooking and household chores, take trips, read stories, sing songs, and generally encourage the use of language as a pleasurable activity and a useful skill.

In the learning environment described throughout this chapter, language development is spontaneous and also encouraged. Modeling, scaffolding, and reinforcement make this environment interactive between child and adult, and they guide and nurture language development to an extent that children are not likely to achieve on their own. The strategies discussed are appropriate for children who have language differences and minimal language disorders. These youngsters, however, may need additional attention on a one-to-one basis from the classroom teacher or a resource room teacher.

Formats for Promoting Language in the Classroom

By the time children come to school, they have had varied opportunities for talk in their daily lives. Most of the talk is spontaneous and deals with real life experiences. With their parents, talk has included questions and answers, with the parent directing the discussion. There are conversations in which all involved play a more active role. Conversations can be about information to be shared, or more spontaneous social occurrences. I have discussed strategies that initiate talk. Here I will offer organizational structures in classrooms that will provide different types of talk experiences. These include teacher-directed question and answer discussions, small-group conversations to give and receive information, and spontaneous discussions that are led by the teacher or children in social settings. In addition, conversations that include different types of talk, for example, Aesthetic Talk, Efferent Talk, and Talk that Occurs in Dramatic Activities, will be described.

In **Structured Question and Answer Discussions,** teachers need to provide open-ended questions that will encourage talk such as:

What would happen if?
What would you do if?
Tell us why?

Conversations occur best in small group settings that include three to six children. Any number beyond that can no longer be considered a conversation, but a large group discussion. Guidelines, such as the following, need to be established for conversation to be productive:

Guidelines for Small Group Conversations with the Teacher
1. Listen to others during conversations.
2. Take turns talking; do not do all the talking yourself.
3. Raising hands may be necessary to ensure everyone gets a turn, and individuals do not interrupt each other.
4. Talk should be relevant to the topic of conversation.
5. Teachers can help redirect conversation to its stated purpose, should it stray.
6. Teacher talk should be kept to a minimum as s/he becomes a participant. Teachers should follow the same rules as the children: listen to others when they are talking, take turns, do not do all the talking, etc.

Guidelines for Formal Conversations without the Teacher
A group leader needs to be selected to help direct the conversation when children are in charge of their own discussion. All of the same guidelines for productive conversation when the teacher is present apply when children direct conversations themselves.

1. Listen to others during conversations.
2. Take turns talking.
3. Raising hands may be necessary.
4. Keep the talk relevant to the conversation's purpose.

Informal Conversations without the Teacher

Children need time to talk without leaders or specific outcomes. This type of conversation is likely to occur during free-play periods, center time, or outdoor play. Although classrooms that encourage this type of talk can be noisy, it is important for children to have the opportunity to use language in social settings at school.

In addition to learning the types of organizational structures in which talk should take place, students need to engage in different types of talk. These include Aesthetic Talk, Efferent Talk, and Talk in Dramatic Activities.

Aesthetic Talk This typically revolves around children's literature. In this talk children have the opportunity to interpret what they have read or listened to. Children can participate in aesthetic talk when discussing literature, telling stories, and participating in readers theater. These activities will be discussed further in Chapter 5 which deals with using children's literature in the classroom.

Efferent Talk   This is talk used to inform and persuade. Efferent talk occurs in discussion of themes being studied. Efferent talk will occur in situations such as show-and-tell, oral reports, interviews, and debates. These types of interchange are more formal than previously discussed and often require preparation on the part of the child.

Dramatic Activities   Dramatic activities provide another avenue for different types of talk. When children participate in dramatic activities, they share experiences, explore their understanding of ideas, and interact with peers. Dramatic experiences can include informal role playing in dramatic play areas of the classroom. Use of props and puppets to act out stories provides another avenue for talk.

A teacher who uses these organizational frameworks for language and has children engage in the types of activities that motivate talk will be providing a classroom rich in experiences for talk and topics to talk about. In turn, language development will be enhanced.

Throughout this book—for example, in Chapter 6 concerning children's literature and Chapter 9 concerning writing—the talk that surrounds these activities is a crucial part of language development and the development of literacy skills.

Authentic Assessment of Children's Language Development

It is important to assess children's language to determine if it follows expected stages of development. Assessment also determines how much a child has progressed. The word *assessment* suggests several rather frequent measures by which to judge progress. Assessment should reflect instructional objectives and strategies. It should include evaluation of a wide range of skills used in many contexts. A certain child, for example, may perform better in an interview than on a pencil-and-paper test. Both kinds of evaluation, therefore, should be used. Literacy includes a wide range of skills; it is important to evaluate a child for as many as possible to determine strengths and weaknesses. Unfortunately, many assessment instruments are quite narrow in scope and frequently do not tap a child's total abilities (Heibert, & Chittenden, 1987).

There are several ways to measure children's language development in early childhood. *Checklists* are practical because they provide concise outlines for teachers and appropriate slots for individual children. They are most effective if used periodically over the school year. Three to four evaluations during the year can provide sufficient data to determine progress. Program objectives offer criteria to include on checklists.

Checklist for Assessing Language Development

	Always	Sometimes	Never
Makes phoneme sounds			
Speaks in one-word sentences			
Speaks in two-word sentences			
Identifies familiar sounds			
Differentiates similar sounds			
Understands the language of others when spoken to			
Follows verbal directions			
Speaks to others freely			
Pronounces words correctly			
Has appropriate vocabulary for level of maturity			
Speaks in complete sentences			
Uses varied syntactic structures			
Can be understood by others			

Teacher Comments:

Anecdotal Records

Anecdotal records are another form of language assessment. They tend to be time-consuming but can reveal rich information. Loose-leaf notebooks and file cards offer two means for keeping anecdotal records. These records require no particular format. Rather, the teacher or parent simply writes down incidents or episodes on the days they occur. Samples of a child's language and situations involving language can be recorded. Like checklists, anecdotal samples are necessary periodically to determine growth over a school year.

Tape Recordings

Tape recordings are another means of evaluating language. The process can take the form of an open interview or a hidden recording. (Videotaping equipment can serve the same purpose but may not be readily available in most early childhood classrooms.) Children who are unaware that their conversation is being recorded are likely to be more spontaneous and uninhibited (Genishi & Dyson, 1984). It is often difficult, however, to place a tape recorder where it will record language clearly enough to transcribe and analyze. Interviews with children become more natural when an adult familiar to the child does the interviewing. Allow the tape recorder to become such a familiar tool in the classroom that the child uses it often in the language arts center. Under such circumstances the machine is not threatening when used in an assessment interview. Children become accustomed very quickly to using tape recorders.

To record samples of natural language, discuss the child's experiences. Ask about home, favorite games or toys, TV programs they like to watch, brothers and sisters, trips they have taken, or birthday parties they have recently attended. What you are hoping to collect is a corpus of spontaneous language that provides a typical sample of the child's ability with language.

Tape assessment samples three or four times a year. Let children hear their own recorded voices, enjoy the experience, and learn a bit about themselves. Then, for assessment purposes, transcribe the tapes and analyze them on such items as numbers of words uttered and numbers of words spoken in a single connected utterance (for example, "Tommy's cookie" or "Me want water"). The lengths of such utterances can be averaged to determine mean length. Length of utterance is considered a measure of complexity (Brown, 1973). When children begin to speak in conventional sentences, such as "That is my cookie," measure the length of the t-units. A *t-unit* is an independent clause with all its dependent clauses attached, assuming it has dependent clauses. It can be a simple or a complex sentence. Compound sentences are made up of two t-units. Length of t-units, like length of utterances, is a measure of language complexity. It typically increases with the user's age, and usually the more words per unit, the more complex the unit (Hunt, 1970).

Further analysis of taped utterances and t-units can determine which elements of language a child uses—number of adjectives, adverbs, dependent clauses, negatives, possessives, passives, plurals, and so on. The more complex the transformations, embeddings, and syntactic elements used, the more complex the language overall (Morrow, 1978). Data from several samples over the course of a year can be most revealing.

The following is a verbatim transcription of a taped language sample from a seven-year-old boy who is in the second grade. The child was presented with a picture book and asked to tell a story from the pictures.

Original Verbatim Sample
he's getting up in the morning and he's looking out the window with his cat and after he gets out of bed he brushes his teeth then when he gets done brushing his teeth, he eats he eats breakfast and then when he after he eats breakfast he he gets dressed to play some games then in the afternoon he plays with his toys then in the afternoon he plays doctor and early in the day he plays cowboys and Indians then when it's in the afternoon close to suppertime he plays cops and robbers when he's playing in his castle he likes to dream of a magic carpet he's driving his ship on the waves

he's uh circus uh ringmaster he's lifting up a fat lady I mean a clown is standing on a horse a clown is on a high wire somebody fell and then hurt their head the cowboy is bringing some ice cream to the hurt man that night he goes in the bathroom and gets washed and then he goes to bed then he dreams I don't know what he's dreaming I will think of what he's dreaming he's dreaming of going to play and he's playing the same things over

After the sample is transcribed, the language is segmented into T-units, that is, independent clauses with all dependent clauses attached.

Below is a sample of the segmented sample of T-units:

1. He's getting up in the morning.
2. And he's looking out the window with his cat.
3. And after he gets out of bed, he brushes his teeth.
4. Then when he gets done brushing his teeth, he eats.
5. He eats breakfast.
6. And then (when he) after he eats breakfast he (he) gets dressed to play some games.
7. Then in the afternoon he plays with his toys.
8. Then in the afternoon he plays doctor.
9. And early in the day he plays cowboys and Indians.
10. Then when it's in the afternoon close to suppertime he plays cops and robbers.
11. When he's playing in his castle he likes to dream of a magic carpet.
12. He's driving his ship on the waves.
13. He's (uh) circus (uh) ringmaster.
14. He's lifting up a fat lady.
15. I mean a clown is standing on a horse.
16. A clown is on a high wire.
17. Somebody fell and then hurt their head.
18. The cowboy is bringing some ice cream to the hurt man.
19. That night he goes in the bathroom and gets washed.
20. And then he goes to bed.
21. Then he dreams.
22. I don't know what he's dreaming.
23. I will think of what he's dreaming.
24. He's dreaming of going to play.
25. And he's playing the same things over.

I have discussed oral language separately from the other communication skills in this chapter in order to describe its developmental stages and the theories of how it is acquired. This separation is somewhat artificial, however, because oral language is as important to literacy development as are reading and writing. The whole language approach to early literacy has demonstrated that communication skills develop concurrently, each helping the growth of the others. Coordination and integration of the several communication skills in a single program are described in Chapter 10.

An Idea for the Classroom from the Classroom

The following experience may be useful for your teaching.

◆ The Five Senses and a Fall Theme Generate Language

My first grade class had been studying the five senses. In October, I decided to associate the five senses with the fall season to generate vocabulary and increased language complexity. I asked the children to bring in fall things that one can taste, touch, smell, look at, and listen to. Children were asked to select a sense category, about five children to each, and their groups discuss what each one might bring so as not to overlap. A great deal of excitement occurred within the groups as children collaborated with each other trying to figure out five different things that they could bring related to fall and to the sense they had selected. In addition to bringing in materials, children were to describe what they had brought, with as many interesting words as they could think of. They could also tell how they decided what to bring and where they located their object.

On the day the materials were brought to school, before getting together with the whole class, the children were to have group meetings to show what they had brought and help each other with descriptions.

When we came together as a class, we wrote the names of the five senses, each on a separate piece of experience chart paper. The groups displayed their objects and they were to talk about each item with as many descriptive words as possible. The items were listed on the appropriate sense chart with the descriptive words written under each.

Many rich ideas were generated about the fall materials and the five senses. The children talked about the sound of crunchy dry leaves that were crushed as they walked on them; they described the shape of acorns and how they looked like tiny elves with lumpy hats on their heads. They discussed the slimy texture of seeds inside the pumpkin and the stringy nature of its pulp. They took deep breaths as they discussed the fresh scent of pine cones and their mouths watered as someone described juicy, tart apples that made their lips pucker.

Everyone in the class had an opportunity to describe what he or she had brought. I helped some children who were at a loss for words by scaffolding some descriptions to get them started. This form of the old show-and-tell format attached to themes that we were studying proved to be a rich source for language development.

Jane Roosa, First Grade Teacher
MacAfee School, Franklin Township, NJ

Activities and Questions

1. Answer the focus questions at the beginning of the chapter.

2. Select an objective for language development listed in the chapter. Prepare a lesson that will help a child achieve the goal. Identify the theories of language acquisition used in your lesson.

3. Tape-record children at play or working in a group. Identify which characteristics of their language can be described by various theories of language acquisition. For example, imitation could be explained by the behaviorist theory.

4. Begin a thematic unit that you will continue as you read this book. Select a social studies or science topic. Select three objectives for language development and describe three activities that will satisfy each of the objectives using your theme. An example follows:
   Content Area: Science
   Theme: Creatures That Live in the Sea
   Objective for Language Development: Develop new vocabulary
   Activity: Read *Swimmy* by Leo Lionni. Ask the children to remember two new words they hear in the story. After reading, list words that the children mention on a chart and discuss their meaning.

5. Observe a preschool, kindergarten, first, or second grade class for about three hours. Note the amount of time children are given to talk, the amount of time the teacher talks, and the amount of time during which there is no verbal interaction. Compare the three figures. Then classify talk in the classroom into the following categories:
   a. Questions and answers
   b. Whole-class discussion
   c. Small-group discussion led by the teacher
   d. Interactive discussion among children
   e. Interactive discussion between teacher and children

   Based on the results of this ministudy, determine how often we allow children to use language, and in how many different contexts or situations.

6. Plan an activity that will elicit aesthetic talk and one that will involve efferent talk. How is the language in each setting the same and how is it different?

7. Continue the collection of assessment materials for the child for which you began a portfolio in Chapter 3. Collect one language sample from a child age two through seven. Elicit the language by showing a picture to discuss or asking the child to talk about favorite TV shows, pets, friends, family members, or trips. Tape-record the sample and transcribe it.

a. Check the characteristics of the child's language development according to the descriptions in this chapter and the checklist provided to decide if the child is above, below, or at a level appropriate to his or her age. Have different members in the class study different age groups and compare them.

b. Divide your language sample into t-units and determine the average length per t-unit; then count the number and type of syntactic elements used. Compare your sample to someone else in the class who is working with a child of a different age.

c. Collect three additional language samples for the same child at different times in the year. Evaluate the new samples as you did the first time and check for growth.

Case Study Activities

◆ Case 1

Refer back to the "Idea for the Classroom" section. Read it again and identify the theories of language acquisition that the teacher is incorporating. Has she made any accommodations for children with language differences? If yes, how? If not, how could she do so?

◆ Case 2

All port of entry kindergarten, first, second, and third graders in an urban school district with a large Latino population are separated into an English as a Second Language Classroom. Children who speak both English and Spanish are in classrooms with standard English-speaking children. The rationale for separating the Latino children is to be able to instruct them in Spanish, so their skills continue to improve and grow, while teaching them English.

Mrs. Ruiz, the first grade ESL teacher, works with her children as follows. In the morning when reading and math are taught, Spanish is used. In the afternoon, Mrs. Ruiz is supposed to teach in English. However, Mrs. Ruiz finds that many of the children refuse to speak English and, since she is fluent in Spanish, she often speaks in Spanish in the afternoons out of frustration. Instead of a half English, half Spanish day, the language being used in the classroom is for the most part Spanish.

One child, Joseph Lopez, was placed in a regular first grade by accident. He did not speak English at all. His teacher, Mrs. Mitchell, reported that after only one month in her class Joseph was communicating in English. Since everyone was speaking English, he heard English more, and having a young child's natural ability to assimilate language, he was learning English.

Do you believe that children in the early childhood grades who have no English should be place in separate programs?

What alternative plan would you propose to solve the problem of helping children learn English while continuing to learn literacy skills?

Chapter 5

How Young Children Learn to Read and Write

An Emergent Literacy Perspective

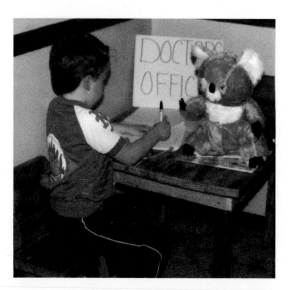

DOCTOR	SERVICE	ROOM	
DATE		Note progress of case, complications, consultations, change in diagnosis, condition or discharge, instructions to patient.	

Pretending to be a veterinarian in the dramatic play center, after examining the stuffed animal, Preston wrote: "This teddy bear's blood pressure is 29 points. He should take 62 pills an hour until he is better and keep warm and go to bed."

Thomas Jefferson articulated three fundamental beliefs about literacy and education that have become part of our national ethos: (1) the ability of every citizen to read is necessary to the practice of democracy, (2) it is therefore the duty of the general public to support the teaching of reading for all youngsters, and (3) reading should be taught during the earliest years of schooling. Among the reasons he cited, "none is more important, none more legitimate, than that of rendering the people safe, as they are the ultimate guardians of their own liberty."

—Thomas Jefferson
The Life and Selected Writings of Thomas Jefferson

Questions To Focus On As You Read

◆ Define the term *emergent literacy*.

◆ How does the emergent literacy approach to literacy instruction differ from reading readiness?

◆ Based on emergent literacy concepts, what are the ways in which reading and writing are acquired?

◆ What are the characteristics of an engaged reader and writer?

◆ Describe Holdaway's theory of developmental learning.

◆ Describe the importance and benefits of small-group collaborative learning.

◆ What developmental trends do children go through as they learn to read and write?

◆ What are the major objectives for emergent literacy development?

◆ How does dramatic play designed for specific themes use theories from the emergent literacy perspective?

Three-year-old Colleen was playing house in the dramatic-play area. She was the mommy and she asked Kevin to be the daddy. They had a doll in the cradle. Colleen got a book and sat in the rocking chair facing the doll and Kevin. She pretended to read *The Three Bears,* although that was not the book she was holding. She rocked and turned the pages while telling the story.

Colleen was engaged in attempted reading behavior that she modeled or emulated after a real-life experience. She was a youngster who was read to regularly by her mother and father. In addition, she was read to daily in her preschool classroom. Because of these experiences, she was familiar with the act of reading; therefore, she found it quite natural to engage in the activity. It was a social activity with another child who took the role of the father.

Mrs. Schenkman created a restaurant in the dramatic-play area of her kindergarten with menus, play money, uniforms, a cash register, and an OPEN and CLOSED sign. Ricky turned the sign to read OPEN and began preparing burgers. Steven joined Ricky and seemed upset. He said, "See that sign, now that says OPEN." He flipped it over. "We're not opened. Now it says CLOSED. We need to clean up the place first before we can open."

In this situation, which is socially interactive, the literacy that takes place is functional. It is something that children had the opportunity to observe and then model. In this play situation, children get to practice and perform literacy skills with each other—all a part of literacy learning.

The examples provided here represent developmentally appropriate practice and an emergent literacy perspective for early literacy development. Teachers provided materials and modeled behavior for children to observe and emulate. In addition, they provided real-life situations to encourage literacy learning in a social and cooperative manner.

Reading Readiness

As noted in Chapter 1, early developmentalists believed in the natural unfolding of the child. At a certain level of maturity, they felt, a child was ready to read, instruction was then appropriate, and the child would learn to read. Some educators became impatient with the notion of simply waiting for maturation, even though they held to the idea that certain levels of maturation were necessary before reading could be taught formally without detriment to the child. This attitude led to instructional programs in reading readiness.

In general, reading readiness programs view getting ready to read as a set of social, emotional, physical, and cognitive competencies. If a child possesses these competencies, adherents say, formal reading instruction can take place. Conversely, a child who has not mastered particular tasks is not considered ready for reading instruction. Strategies for readiness instruction depend on lists of skills in the four areas of development. The skills list provides an outline of activities to be designed to help develop such skills. Typically, these lists include characteristics such as those listed on page 128, on which children are tested.

In programs that follow a ***reading readiness*** perspective, teachers prepare instruction to encourage social, emotional, physical, and intellectual development as outlined on the list.

Social and Emotional Development

For **social and emotional development,** there will be periods of play during which children can select from materials placed in classroom centers. Centers may be for dramatic play, art, science, library, or outdoor play, and may contain blocks and manipulative toys such as Lego, Tinkertoys, or dominoes. The main goal is for children to learn to share, cooperate, develop self-control and a good self-concept, and learn about appropriate school behavior. Discussions will often be focused on the topic of sharing and getting along with others. There will almost always be a unit focused on "All About Me" which emphasizes the building of self-confidence and a positive self-esteem. Food plays an important role in the curriculum; a snack is served daily and is considered a time to socialize and learn to get along with others.

Physical Development

Physical development is a major part of a reading readiness program. Developing large and fine motor control is seen as an important factor in literacy development. Teachers should have indoor and outdoor periods designed specifically to teach children to hop, skip, trot, gallop, jump, throw a ball, and walk a straight line. Often there is music to accompany these activities and specific pieces of equipment such as a balance beam.

To develop fine motor coordination, children can use clay and play with toys that require fitting pegs into holes or snapping things together. These activities supply strength little hands need to develop the coordination necessary to write letters. In developing eye–hand motor control, children are asked to color pictures, stay within the lines, and trace around lines of a particular illustration. Children trace pictures and letters with their fingers and with the use of tracing paper and a pencil. Children practice cutting on lines to enhance fine motor ability, which is needed to write letters. From a reading perspective, there is little concern for children to be engaged in narrative or expository writing. It is assumed they need to learn to read before they can learn to write.

Cognitive Development

Cognitive development is equal in importance to social, physical, and emotional development. It is not considered more important. In a reading readiness program, cognitive development means developing auditory and visual discrimination skills in preparation for reading. To do this, children participate in the following types of activities.

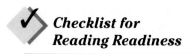

Checklist for Reading Readiness

Social and Emotional Development: The Child	Always	Sometimes	Never
1. Shares			
2. Cooperates with peers and adults			
3. Demonstrates confidence, self-control, and emotional stability			
4. Completes tasks			
5. Fulfills responsibilities			

Physical Development: The Child			
1. Demonstrates large motor control by being able to run, hop, skip, trot, gallop, jump, throw, and walk a straight line			
2. Demonstrates fine motor control by being able to hold a pencil properly, color within lines, and cut with scissors			
3. Demonstrates eye–hand coordination			
4. Can write name, copy letters, draw a human figure			
5. Is generally healthy and vigorous			
6. Shows no visual or auditory defects			
7. Has established dominance (hand, eye, foot)			

Cognitive Development: The Child			
1. Demonstrates auditory discrimination by identifying familiar sounds, differentiating sounds, recognizing rhyming words, identifying initial and ending consonant sounds, and possessing an auditory memory			
2. Demonstrates visual discrimination by understanding left to right eye progression; recognizing likenesses and differences; identifying colors, shapes, letters, and words; possessing visual memory; and showing a sense of figure–ground perception			

Visual Discrimination This reading readiness activity involves children in seeing likenesses and differences in shapes and pictures. Typically a worksheet is used to help children develop this skill. There may be a line of flowers that all look about the same but one will be slightly different from the rest, for example, have one less leaf on the stem or one less petal on the flower. The child is to circle the one that is different from the others. Another visual discrimination activity is color identification. Here children will be asked to fill in pictures using specific colors. They will be asked to classify objects into color groups, or make a collage of pictures cut from a magazine that are all, for example, red, blue, or green. Identifying like and different shapes such as squares, circles, and rectangles is an activity provided on worksheets to develop visual discrimination. Finally, children are taught left to right eye progression, since this is not a natural activity but is necessary for reading. Instead of using print in a book, worksheets have been devised. Children follow a line that goes from left to right and has a return sweep simulating the eye movement used in reading. They do this by following the line with a finger or by tracing the line with a crayon. After working with these visual discrimination skills, teachers move on to identifying letters of the alphabet which are traced and copied. Children memorize the alphabet and learn to identify upper and lower case letters. All of these activities are preparation for reading.

Auditory Discrimination   This is the other cognitive focus in a reading readiness program. It prepares children for learning to use auditory decoding skills. Children are asked to identify sounds that are alike and different. This may be done with sound effects that a teacher prepares for the class or sound effects on a recording. Pictures that represent animals, for example, may also be used, with students asked to circle those that make different or like sounds. Listening to rhymes, identifying rhyming words, and creating rhyme word lists is another auditory discrimination activity. Again, worksheets with pictures of objects are provided, with children asked to circle the ones that rhyme. From rhyme, the teacher progresses to associating letters with their sounds, often with a letter of the week featured. A worksheet is provided to circle pictures that begin with the letter, students collect objects that begin with the sound featured, and may be asked to cut pictures from a magazine to make into a collage for the letter *M* for example. Figure 5.1 shows a typical reading readiness worksheet that asks the child to circle pictures that begin with consonant sounds *d, p,* and hard *c.* These worksheets can be confusing, since the deer could be considered a moose or antelope, and the piano a baby grand or simply a piano. Based on their own experiences, children may identify an illustration as something different from what the artist had in mind and circle the wrong letter.

The list of reading readiness skills can be very long. Previously it was assumed that a child must master all behaviors on the list before being given a book to read, or becoming engaged in what is called formal reading instruction. The activities associated with a reading readiness program do not really teach children very much about the total act of reading. They engage them in a variety of abstract activities that are a part of reading, but not the whole picture. There are many sad stories of kindergarten teachers who have retained children who were unable to master skipping, trotting, or galloping. Parents have become frantic and children have been brought to tears by teachers' insistence on mastery of motor skills. It is still not uncommon to see classes of kindergarten children undergoing skipping lessons to the teacher's cadence of "step-hop, step-hop, step-hop, step-hop."

At least two misguided assumptions lie behind such an approach: (1) children know nothing about literacy before coming to school; and (2) they therefore need an instructional program in readiness. In actuality, some of the listed competencies are irrelevant and inappropriate for early literacy development. Many lists do not include writing and awareness of book and print characteristics that are necessary and important for reading. Instructional practices motivated by the readiness-skills approach abstract activities away from the total act of reading. There have been reports of children who had accomplished few of the tasks on a list of reading readiness skills but were nonetheless already reading. Their ability to read went unrecognized by their teachers because reading readiness tests and activities never do ask children to read. There are also children who can carry out the tasks on a list and still experience difficulty learning to read.

◆ **FIGURE 5.1** *Reading Readiness Worksheet for Sound-Symbol Relationships*

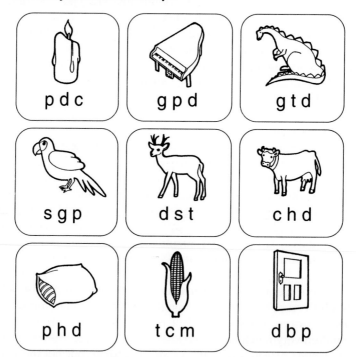

Directions: Circle the letter that each picture begins with, such as c̲ as in candle, p̲ as in piano, and d̲ as in dragon.

Emergent Literacy

Research concerning early readers and what they learn about books, print, and writing before going to school has changed attitudes and ideas about early childhood strategies for literacy development. In the past, reading, writing, listening, and speaking were thought of as separate skills taught independently of one another. Our teacher education programs have tended to separate courses in the teaching of reading from those in language arts. We now realize, however, that literacy involves all of the communication skills and that each skill enhances the other as they are learned concurrently.

Although some of the skills associated with reading readiness are important to literacy learning, new concepts have broadened approaches to early literacy development. The phrase ***emergent literacy,*** first used by Marie Clay (1966), caught the attention of educators interested in early literacy. Emergent literacy assumes that the child acquires some knowledge about language, reading, and writing before coming to school. Literacy development begins early in life and is ongoing. There is a dynamic relationship among the communication skills (reading, writing, oral language, and listening) since each influences the other in the course of development. Development occurs in everyday contexts of the home, community, and school through meaningful and functional experiences that require the use of literacy in natural settings. The settings for the acquisition of literacy are often social, with adults and children interacting through collaboration and tutoring. Literacy activities occur and are embedded purposefully within content areas such as art, music, play, social studies, and science, to ensure there is meaning involved. For example, in art, a recipe is necessary to make play dough, and children should have that recipe to read, in order to be able to make the play dough.

Children at every age possess certain literacy skills, although these skills are not fully developed or conventional, as we recognize mature reading and writing to be (Teale, 1986). Emergent literacy acknowledges as rudimentary writing a child's scribble marks on a page, even if not one letter is discernible. The child who knows the difference between such scribbles and drawings certainly has some sense of the difference between writing and illustration. Similarly, when a child narrates a familiar storybook while looking at the pictures and print and gives the impression of reading, we acknowledge the activity as legitimate literacy behavior, even though it cannot be called reading in the conventional sense.

Emergent literacy constructs are sensitive to children with special needs because they look for strengths youngsters have rather than weaknesses. The emergent literacy perspective is sensitive to cultural diversity, since children learn literacy skills through the study of themes that often focus on their heritage. Literacy development approached in this manner accepts children at whatever level of literacy they are functioning and provides a program for instruction based on individual needs.

A blend between the emergent literacy perspective and some more explicit instruction from reading readiness will provide a balanced approach for early literacy development.

Theories on the Acquisition of Early Reading and Writing

Reading and Writing Are Acquired through Social Collaborative Interaction

Teale (1982) views literacy as the result of children's involvement in reading and writing activities mediated by more literate others. It is the social, collaborative interaction accompanying these activities that makes them so significant to the child's development. Not only do interactive literacy events teach children the societal functions and conventions of reading, but they also link reading and writing with enjoyment and satisfaction and thus increase children's desire to engage in literacy activities. Teale's emphasis on the social aspects of literacy development reflects Vygotsky's (1981) more general theory of intellectual development. Vygotsky suggests that higher order thinking occurs as a result of social relationships that have been internalized. This movement from interpsychological learning to intrapsychological learning is apparent as children become increasingly able to engage independently in literacy activities that previously required interaction with more literate adults or children. This time period has been referred to by Vygotsky as the *zone of proximal development.* It is that moment when the child becomes capable of participating in a particular literacy activity alone and the adult assistance is no longer necessary.

Collaboration plays an important role in the acquisition of writing and reading among small groups of children in different settings. Studies dealing with student cooperation in academic tasks conclude that such cooperation promotes achievement and productivity and yields strong social and attitudinal benefits (Sharon, 1980; Slavin, 1977; Yager, Johnson, & Johnson, 1985). Researchers propose that the positive effects observed are due to the dynamics of cooperative learning, which include a great deal of oral interaction between students and the heterogeneous nature of the groups. Yager, Johnson, and Johnson (1985) found that passive learners particularly benefit from small-group dialogue and interaction. They suggest that cooperative learning succeeds because it allows children to explain material to each other, to listen to each other's explanations, and to arrive at joint understandings of what has been shared. In addition, young children use language and nonverbal signals that other children understand easily.

Dewey (1966) argued that children who engage in task-oriented dialogue with peers can reach a higher level of understanding than that attained by students who listen to a teacher's didactic presentation of information, and Piaget and Inhelder (1969) suggested that childhood peers can serve as resources for one another in their cognitive development.

Teacher-Directed Small-Group Instruction

Learning in small groups can be accomplished with or without adults. The previous discussion referred to the benefits for learning when children worked together without an adult present. A number of researchers have explored the value of small-group instruction when an adult plays an active role in the setting. It has been found that the interactive dialogue between adults and children and between children in small groups improves children's comprehension and oral language (Applebee & Langer, 1983; Palincsar, Brown, & Martin, 1987). Cochran-Smith (1984) and Morrow and Smith (1990) found that transcripts of story readings to groups of three children included more participation by children and more complex discussion in the small groups than transcripts of readings to larger groups.

This review of research suggests the importance of small-group situations for learning in general and for literacy learning in particular. The small-group instruction can be with or without the teacher and should occur both ways. When the teacher is present, he or she needs to allow for interaction to take place between adult and child and between children. There are several formats for learning situations without the teacher. In one, a task is assigned by the teacher; in another, the children decide what they will do when there are several choices involved. The latter situation can take place in independent reading and writing periods when children have the opportunity to make choices. This setting is described in Chapter 6 and is appropriate for children from preschool through the early childhood and elementary grades.

Children Acquire the Ability to Read and Write as a Result of Life Experiences

Some children already have considerable information about reading and writing before they enter school for formal instruction. Some are reading before they come to school; others have had little exposure to literacy. Even though children's strengths in literacy vary with the individual, most children have a general command of their language and a sizable vocabulary and have internalized rules of language. They know the difference between drawing and writing and they associate books with reading. They can read environmental print and they realize the functional purposes of reading and writing. Because their knowledge about literacy to this point is based on meaning and function, they expect that reading and writing will be activities that make sense.

Research since the 1960s has made us aware of early childhood competencies and literacy skills. Studies such as those by Clark (1976), Durkin (1966), and Torrey (1969) have revealed that many children read early—that is, before starting school and without formal instruction. Investigations have also revealed how the environment supports literacy development. Children as young as three are able to read such common words in their environment as *Burger King, McDonald's, Exxon,* and *Sugar Pops* (Goodman & Altwerger, 1981; Hiebert, 1986; Mason, 1980). The results of these investigations indicate that very young children are aware of print, letters, and words, and that their ability to identify familiar printed symbols constitutes the beginning of reading. According to Goodman (1984), the "roots of literacy" are established in early childhood by most children in literate societies. Environmental print helps children discover how print is organized and used as well as what it is used for. Young children also demonstrate such knowledge of books and book handling as (1) where to begin reading, (2) the difference between pictures and print, (3) awareness of the left-to-right progression of print, (4) the difference between the beginning and the end of the book, and (5) how to turn pages. Efforts to expand their reading abilities into reading fluency need to build on their strengths and on what they already know and expect of reading (Harste, Woodward, & Burke, 1984).

The psycholinguistic definition of reading strongly recommends capitalizing on children's prior strengths, knowledge, and past experiences. Goodman (1967) described reading as a psycholinguistic "guessing game" in which the child attempts to reconstruct, in light of his or her own knowledge, what the author has to say. Young children bring to school concepts and understanding from past experiences. Their awareness and use of oral language are particularly helpful. When they read, they anticipate what the written message is likely to say. Reading is an active process. Children search the printed page for cues based on what they already know. They search for *graphic* cues, or cues about print—whether a squiggle is a letter or a word. There are *syntactic* cues such as *The boy ran down the _____*. The child's internalized knowledge of syntax indicates that the word in the blank must be a noun such as *hill, stairs,* or *street.* A verb would make no sense: *The boy ran down the jumped.* From *semantic* clues, children know which words make sense in the slot and which do not. Few if any would guess that the sentence reads *The boy ran down the sky,* for example. Using these graphic, syntactic, and semantic cues, children predict, guess, expect, make associations, and correct themselves to derive meaning from the printed page. The meaning comes from what they know about language and from their own experiences. The most meaningful cues are those in whole pieces of print, rather than in isolated words. All the processes of reading are brought to bear at once within the reader.

Early writing similar to early reading is embedded in real-life experience. Many families do things together that involve meaningful literacy. They write each other notes, lists, holiday greetings, and directions.

Children Acquire Literacy Skills That Have a Purpose

Children are likely to become involved in literacy activities if they view reading and writing as functional, purposeful, and useful. Studies of early reading and writing behaviors clearly illustrate that young children acquire their first information about reading and writing through their functional uses (Goodman, 1980; Heath, 1980; Mason & McCormick, 1981; Taylor, 1983). Grocery lists; directions on toys, packages, household equipment, and medicine containers; recipes; telephone messages; school-related notices; religious materials; menus; environmental print inside and outside the home; mail; magazines; newspapers; storybook readings; TV channels; telephone numbers; conversation among family members; and letters represent but a sample of the functional literacy information with which a child comes in contact daily. Children are familiar with such forms of literacy, they participate in them, they pretend to use them at play, and they understand their purposes. Parents and day-care, preschool, and kindergarten teachers need to provide experiences with reading similar to experiences children have already had. Children expect learning to read to be meaningful and functional.

Being Read to Plays a Role in Literacy Development

Being Read to Develops a Sense of Story Structure   Research indicates that reading to a child benefits the child's acquisition of reading and writing. It provides a model for children to emulate, aids development of literacy skills, and increases interest in books and in learning to read and write. It enhances background information and sense of story structure, and familiarizes children with the language of books (Chomsky, 1972; Cullinan, 1992; Huck, 1976; Morrow, 1985). A well-structured story has a **setting** (a beginning, time, place, and introduction of characters), **theme** (the main characters's problem or goal), **plot episodes** (a series of events in which the main character attempts to solve the problem or achieve the goal), and a **resolution** (the accomplishment of the goal or solving of the problem and an ending). From hearing many well-formed stories, children can predict what will happen next in an unfamiliar story on the basis of their awareness of its structure. Hearing stories with good plot structures helps children to write and tell their own stories (Morrow, 1985). The language of books is different from oral language and provides a model for their writing and speaking. The following passages from two picture storybooks make this quite evident.

> One bad day a tuna fish, fierce, swift and very hungry, came darting through the waves. (Lionni, *Swimmy,* 1963)

> The wild things roared their terrible roars, gnashed their terrible teeth, and rolled their terrible eyes. (Sendak, *Where the Wild Things Are,* 1963)

This next piece is from E. B. White's *Charlotte's Web* (1952) and is appropriate to read to first and second graders.

> At last Wilbur saw the creature that had spoken to him in such a kindly way. Stretched across the upper part of the doorway was a big spiderweb, and hanging from the top of the web, head down, was a large grey spider. She was about the size of a gumdrop. She had eight legs, and she was waving one of them at Wilbur in friendly greeting. "See me now?" she asked.

"Oh, yes indeed," said Wilbur. "Yes indeed! How are you? Good morning! Sal-utations! Very pleased to meet you. What is your name, please? May I have your name."

"My name," said the spider, "is Charlotte."

Being Read to Enhances Comprehension and Knowledge about Books and Print A child's comprehension skills are enhanced from their familiarity with vocabulary and syntactic structures in books that have been read to them. Children who have been read to frequently and early tend to read and write ear-lier than others and to learn to read more easily (Clark 1984; Hiebert, 1981; Mason, 1980). Furthermore, reading to children at school or at home leads them to associate reading with pleasure and provides them with models for reading. In fact, when children begin to read on their own, they often choose books that have been read to them. After I read *The Little Engine That Could* (Piper, 1954) to a four-year-old, she said to me, "Show me where it says 'I think I can, I think I can.' I want to see it in the book." When I showed her the words, she repeated them while pointing to them and then asked to see them again in another part of the book. She proceeded to search through the rest of the book, reading with great enthusiasm each time she found the line "I think I can, I think I can."

Researchers have found that reading to children enhances the development of reading in many ways. Repeated reading of the same story is an important strategy as well (Morrow, 1986; Sulzby, 1985; Yaden, 1985). Smith (1978) sug-gests that reading to children gives them an understanding of the functions of print, a sense of how print is used and of what people are doing when they are reading. Children with storybook experience learn how to handle a book and are sensitive to its front-to-back progression; a story's beginning, middle, and end; and the concept of authorship. Mason (1980) found that reading to children con-tributes to their awareness of the functions, form, and conventions of print. It also develops metacognitive knowledge about how to approach reading tasks. *Metacognition* is one's own awareness of how learning is taking place; it thus nurtures one's own learning.

Being Read to Develops Positive Attitudes Toward Reading and Writing Children who are read to develop positive attitudes toward reading. The warmth that accompanies storybook readings by a caring adult lasts beyond the experi-ence. It involves ritual, sharing, and mutual good feelings. Certain books take on special meanings between an adult and child through repetition or because they are favorites of the one or the other. My daughter and I have had a special rela-tionship with the book *Alexander and the Terrible, Horrible, No Good, Very Bad Day* (Viorst, 1972). I first read it to Stephanie when she was four, and whenever things seemed to go wrong for her I found myself saying, "I guess you're having a terrible, horrible, no good, very bad day." Soon, when things were not going well for me, Stephanie would say, "I guess you're having a terrible, horrible, no good, very bad day."

Being read to and the interaction that occurs during reading play important roles in the acquisition of reading skills.

When Stephanie was in the seventh grade, she came home from school looking terrible one day. She was wearing only one sneaker, and she looked generally distraught.

"What's the problem?" I asked.

"Someone stole one of my sneakers, I got yelled at for talking when my friend asked me a question in class and I answered her, I have tons of home-work, and I lost my assignment notebook."

"I guess you're having a terrible, horrible, no good, very bad day," I said.

She smiled and said, "You're right. I think I'll go to Australia."

"Some days are like that, even in Australia," I replied.

We both laughed. The familiar words of a familiar book created a special ritual between us. Good feelings gained in story readings transfer to the act of reading itself (Hiebert, 1981; Taylor, 1983).

The Importance of Interaction During Storybook Reading Children who have been read to often begin to concern themselves with strategies for independent reading. It is not just the reading itself but the interaction between adult and child that motivates the interest. Studies carried out in school settings illustrate that active participation in literacy experiences enhances comprehension of story and sense of story structure. Role-playing stories they have heard, retelling them, and reconstructing them through pictures enable children to relate parts of a story, integrate information, and interact with teachers and other children (Morrow, 1985b; Pellegrini & Galda, 1982).

Studies of home read-aloud sessions clearly illustrate that active social interaction between parents and children during these sessions is a major factor in literacy development. This interaction offers a direct channel of information for the child. Initially, children are interested in the illustrations and label items pictured or repeat words said by the adult who is reading the story (Yaden, 1985). Such interactive behavior leads children to respond with questions and comments, which become more complex over time and demonstrate more sophisticated thinking about printed material. Eventually, children's remarks about story content reflect interests in interpretation, association, prediction, information, and elaboration. These remarks focus sometimes on title, setting, characters, and story events (Morrow, 1988; Roser & Martinez, 1985), and at other times on print characteristics, including names of letters, words, and sounds.

One of the primary goals of reading aloud is the reconstruction of meaning through the interaction between adult and child. The adult helps the child understand and make sense of the text through their cooperative personal interpretation of the written language based on their experiences and beliefs (Atwerger, Diehl-Faxon, & Dockstader-Anderson, 1985). Particularly helpful behavior includes prompting children to respond, scaffolding responses for children to model when they are unable to respond themselves, relating responses to real-life experiences, answering questions, and offering positive reinforcement for children's responses. We often stop reading to children as they begin to read themselves, usually during first grade. It is crucial to continue reading to youngsters throughout the grades. Reading to children as they grow older continues to enhance skills already learned and to motivate interest in the books featured in the classroom.

Decoding Skills and the Acquisition of Literacy

The emphasis thus far has been on the child's understanding of whole concepts, not isolated reading skills such as letter–sound relationships and decoding. The development of such specific skills has been overemphasized. Their overemphasis has often led to inappropriate home and classroom practices. Yet, we cannot ignore them because research supports their role in literacy development. For instance, children who learn letter–sound relationships have been found to get off to a better start in learning to read and write than other children (Adams, 1990; Baumann, 1984; Chall, Conrad, & Harris-Sharples, 1983). It has been found that early attempts at writing help children with sound–symbol correspondence. On the other hand, there is evidence that teaching many phonic rules does not greatly help most youngsters learn to read, because most of these rules are irregular. Rather, only the most regular letter–sound relationships should be taught. Once those are clear to a child, the best way to refine and extend them is to give the child repeated opportunities to read and write. What needs to be stressed is that the teaching and learning of the alphabet, letter–sound relationships, and decoding skills are only a small part of literacy instruction. The time spent on them should be minimal, and the strategies selected for instruction appropriate for young children.

Reading and Writing Are Acquired through
the Explicit Instruction of Skills

The emphasis in whole language and emergent literacy constructs concerning literacy development is learning through meaning and function and in settings that deal with real life. Skill instruction takes place when the need arises and when spontaneous opportunities occur. If children have an interest in reading and writing because it means something to them, they will want to learn more than if meaningless abstract skills are imposed. However, one must always take into account that, in these natural settings for learning literacy, many children may need additional help, with a focus on one particular skill or another, and opportunities may not occur spontaneously to teach all skills needed. Therefore, there still is the need for explicit instruction of skills for many youngsters. Early in the emergent literacy and whole language movements, direct instruction was looked upon as the skill, drill, teach, test approach and had no place within classrooms using these approaches. As we have spent a few years exploring these ideas, we have come to realize that some of the old can blend and indeed is needed along with the new. Explicit instruction is important for most children. However, this type of instruction needs to be directed at the needs of individuals and to be a small part of the literacy program. Direct instruction can take place on a one-to-one basis and in small groups. The groups form and disband as needed. Chapter 10 deals with organizational strategies for literacy instruction and discusses direct instruction for both groups and individual conference settings. Without this direct instruction component, some children will miss learning many important skills. It is crucial that teachers be aware of the individual needs of their children and accommodate those needs with an appropriate balance of instructional strategies, which might mean some direct explicit instruction.

Holdaway's Theory of Literacy Development

Holdaway's (1979) theory of literacy development provides a summary concerning how reading and writing are acquired:

> The way in which supportive adults are induced by affection and common sense to intervene in the development of their children proves upon close examination to embody the most sound principles of teaching. Rather than provide verbal instructions about how a skill should be carried out, the parent sets up an emulative model of the skill in operation and induces activity in the child which approximates towards use of the skill. The first attempts of the child are to do something that is like the skill he wishes to emulate. This activity is then "shaped" or refined by immediate rewards.... From this point of view, so called "natural" learning is in fact supported by higher quality teaching intervention than is normally the case in the school setting.

Holdaway contends that this form of "developmental" teaching is appropriate for school-based literacy instruction. Characterized by self-regulated, individualized activities, frequent peer interaction, and an environment rich with materials, Holdaway's model is derived from observations of home environments where children have learned to read without direct instruction, homes such as those described in Chapter 3.

Holdaway (1986) explains four processes that enable children to acquire reading and writing ability. The first is *observation* of literacy behaviors—being read to, for example, or seeing adults reading and writing themselves. The second is *collaboration* with an individual who interacts with the child, providing encouragement, motivation, and help when necessary. The third process is *practice.* The learner tries out alone what has been learned, such as reading and writing activities—and experiments without direction or adult observation. Practice gives children opportunities to evaluate their performances, make corrections, and increase skills. In the fourth process, *performance,* the child shares what has been learned and seeks approval from adults who are supportive, interested, and encouraging. The ideas expressed by Holdaway (1986) are also articulated in work on literacy development by Calkins, 1983; Clark, 1976; Read, 1975; and Smith, 1983.

The Engagement Perspective and the Acquisition of Literacy

The engagement perspective defines the goals for literacy instruction. The perspective describes what we believe readers and writers should be like when they reach their fullest potential. According to the National Reading Research Center (1991), engaged readers are **strategic** readers, who have knowledge about print and the meaning of printed materials. They possess multiple skills which enable them to read independently and comprehend what they read. Engaged readers are **knowledgeable** from information they learn through reading. These readers are able to transfer and apply their knowledge into new contexts. Engaged readers are **motivated** to read voluntarily for pleasure and for information, and are **social** in their approach to learning and using literacy.

The engagement perspective is a guide for instructional settings for early literacy development. We need to teach strategies to create strategic readers and writers; we need to expose children to literature to gain information; and we need to provide instruction that will be challenging, offer children choices in literacy learning situations, and provide successful experiences. These are all elements that help to motivate. Finally, we need to do these things in social settings so that children learn the social nature of reading and writing and approach literacy learning by interacting with others.

Developmental Trends in Literacy Acquisition

The concept of emergent literacy suggests that one does not suddenly learn to read and write; rather, becoming literate is a process that begins at birth and continues throughout one's lifetime. Children differ in their rates of literacy achieve-

◆ **FIGURE 5.3** *The Engagement Perspective*

ment; they must not be pressured into the accomplishment of tasks or placed on a predetermined time schedule. Development is not precise. Certain traits of literacy do seem to be acquired by many youngsters before others, but the dividing lines among traits and among youngsters are not always distinct. Acquisition of reading, writing, and language does seem to follow a pattern, however. That is, children seem to be more interested in the **functions** of literacy first, then the **form,** and later the **conventions.**

Researchers have found that children learn how print *functions* as a first step in reading and writing (Mason, 1980; Goodman, 1984; Smith, 1971). The first words a child says, reads, and writes are those with meaning and purpose in their lives, such as family names, food labels, road signs, and names of fast food restaurants.

After function, the child becomes interested in the *forms* of print. Details about names, sound, and configurations of letters and words serve the child's learning more now than simple understanding of how print functions.

Beyond this level, a child becomes interested in the *conventions* of print. This involves recognition that we read and write from left to right, that punctuation serves a purpose in reading and writing, and that spaces demarcate letters and words. Although recognition of the function of print dominates the first stages of reading and writing development in early childhood, the child is at the same time, but to a lesser degree, acquiring an interest in and notions about the form and conventions of print.

Sulzby (1986) describes children's writing behavior which illustrates developmental trends as follows:

1. use of drawings for writing
2. scribble writing
3. use of letterlike forms
4. use of well-learned units or letter strings
5. use of invented spelling
6. writing conventionally

Sulzby warns, however, that children do not systematically go from one developmental stage to the next; for example, they often skip stages or go back to earlier stages.

Sulzby (1985) found developmental trends in two- to five-year-olds in her work on attempted reading of familiar storybooks. Children's first attempts at "reading" familiar stories were governed by pictures, their stories were not well formed, the children sounded as if they were telling a story rather than reading, and they paid no attention to print. In later attempts, the children approached conventional reading behaviors. They attempted to read the print, their stories were well formed, and their language sounded as if they were reading.

In a study of what children know about reading and of their skill in letter and word recognition, McCormick and Mason (1981) established three developmental levels in word recognition. Children first identified words through context, then used letter–sound cues, and finally relied on sounding out words.

Studies of young children's responses to story readings also reveal developmental trends that follow Mason's basic three-strand paradigm. Children's initial questions and comments during story readings are related to the pictures and the meanings of the stories. As they gain experience with story readings, their questions and comments begin to concern the names of letters, the reading of individual words, or attempts to sound out words (Morrow, 1987; Roser & Martinez, 1985; Yaden, 1985). Again, the function of print dominates early responses; the form of print becomes more important in later responses.

Judging from the research, then, there seem to be categories of literacy development in early childhood. Yet reading and writing are obviously complex processes, and individual case studies vary between children. One must never forget that each child is an individual developing at his or her own pace.

Put Yourself in the Place of the Child

It is difficult for us as adults to understand and appreciate the various processes involved in learning to read and write because we have been doing it for many years. To understand better the nature of learning to read or write, put yourself in the place of the learner. With a contrived alphabet called the Confusabet, I have taken college students back to when they were five and six and first taught to read and write. Whole words are introduced in the unfamiliar alphabet, accompanied by picture clues and context clues. They are reinforced with worksheets. After being introduced to about twenty-five words, the students are given a book containing pictures and stories that use these words. They are called upon to read just as they were in a reading group in an early childhood classroom. They are also asked to write one sentence about what they read in the Confusabet alphabet.

After the lesson we discuss how they have just learned to read and write with the Confusabet. Students consistently report similar strategies: they try to relate information they already know about writing and reading to the situation. They realize quickly that Confusabet words have the same number of letters as words written in our regular alphabet, and their knowledge of words in general helps them make sense of Confusabet words. Certain similarities in letter forms help them figure out words. They use context and picture clues as much as possible. Their knowledge of syntax (language structures) and the meanings of words surrounding an unknown word helps them determine words they cannot otherwise identify. They skip around within a sentence looking for words they might know. Some rely on the first letter of a word to identify it. Many try to memorize words by the "look–say" method. Most agree that words with unusual shapes or lengths are easy to identify. They acknowledge that to learn they have to involve themselves actively in the reading process. In short, they guess, make mistakes, and correct themselves.

In addition to the strategies just described, my observations of the students' behavior during this class experience revealed another powerful strategy that they themselves did not seem to recognize—the natural tendency to collaborate and cooperate with each other during their learning. They discussed successes and failures with those around them. They wanted to talk about the words they had figured out and share that excitement with others. They spontaneously expressed frustration when they were experiencing difficulty and they sought help of those nearby. The room was noisy at times because of the social interaction of the literacy-learning experience. At times, two or three of them disagreed about a particular word, finally arriving at consensus. Sometimes problems were solved through peer tutoring, with one student helping another who was having trouble. They demonstrated a natural curiosity as they flipped eagerly through new materials.

All in all, they agreed that working together gave them a sense of security, provided easily accessible sources of information, and made the task more fun. They were almost unaware of their socially cooperative behavior until I pointed it out to them. Most commented that seeking and relying on social interaction when trying to learn to read with the Confusabet seemed to be a natural inclination.

In their descriptions of how they learned to read and write with the Confusabet, the students used emergent literacy and whole language perspectives. In all cases they sought meaning. They approached a printed message as a whole, and they drew on past experience as well as the help of each other. They guessed, predicted, and invented in order to construct meaning. They did use some of the traditional skill strategies such as trying to decode words by focusing on the first letter, using context clues, and the sight word approach. Granted, these college students draw on many more experiences and associations with print and reading than the typical kindergarten or first grade child can, but this only indicates

◆ **FIGURE 5.4**
Illustration of the
Confusabet

look at the red automobile

more emphatically how important it is for initial reading experiences to be based on meaning and function. (The Confusabet lesson can be found in Appendix D.)

Play in the Curriculum: Theories of Emergent Literacy Acquisition Put into Practice

A curriculum area that exemplifies the use of the emergent literacy perspective concerning the acquisition of reading and writing is embedding literacy learning into play. In play settings, children interact and collaborate in small groups. When designed to promote literacy learning, the dramatic play area is coordinated with a social studies or science theme that is being studied to bring meaning to the experience. Materials for reading and writing are provided to support the play theme such that during play children read, write, speak, and listen to each other using literacy in functional ways.

The use of play to promote literacy development is beginning to receive recognition. Although early childhood educators have realized the value of play for social, emotional, and physical development, in the past it has not been viewed as a place or time to develop literacy. From the reading readiness perspective, literacy is taught through a set of discrete skills with pencil and paper assignments.

Recently, play has gained greater importance as a medium for literacy development since it provides meaningful, functional social settings. Literacy development involves a child's active engagement in cooperation and collaboration with peers, builds on what the child already knows, and thrives on the support and guidance of others. Play provides this setting. During observations of children at play, one can see the functional uses of literacy that children incorporate into their play themes. Children have been observed to engage in attempted and conventional reading and writing in collaboration with other youngsters (Morrow, 1990; Neuman & Roskos, 1990).

To demonstrate the importance of the social, collaborative, and interactive nature of literacy development, I take you into a classroom where the teacher, Mrs. Schifflette, has designed a veterinarian's office to go along with their animal theme with a concentration on pets. The dramatic-play area was designed with a waiting room; chairs; a table filled with magazines, books, and pamphlets about pet care; posters about pets; office hour notices; a "No Smoking" sign; and a sign advising visitors to "Check in with the nurse when arriving." A nurse's desk holds patient forms on clipboards, a telephone, an address and telephone book, appointment cards, and a calendar. Offices contain patient folders, prescription pads, white coats, masks, gloves, cotton swabs, a toy doctor's kit, and stuffed animals for patients.

Mrs. Schifflette guides students in the use of the various materials during free-play time in the veterinarian's office, for example, by reminding the children to read to pets in waiting areas, fill out forms with prescriptions or appointment times, or fill out forms with information about a patient's condition and treatment. In addition to giving directions, Mrs. Schifflette also models behaviors by participating in play with the children when the materials are first introduced.

The following anecdotes relate the type of behavior that was witnessed in this setting—a setting that provides a literacy-rich environment with books and writing materials; models of reading and writing by teachers that children can observe and emulate; provides the opportunity to practice literacy in real-life situations that have meaning and function; and has children socially interacting, collaborating, and performing reading and writing with peers.

> *Jessica was waiting to see the doctor. She told her stuffed animal dog Sam not to worry, that the doctor wouldn't hurt him. She asked Jenny, who was waiting with her stuffed animal cat Muffin, what the kitten's problem was. The girls agonized over the ailments of their pets. After a while they stopped talking and Jessica picked up a book from the table and pretended to read* Are You My Mother? *to her pet dog Sam. Jessica showed Sam the pictures as she read.*
>
> *Jennie ran into the doctor's office shouting "My dog got runned over by a car." The doctor bandaged the dog's leg; then the two children decided that the incident must be reported to the police. Before calling the police, they got out the telephone book and turned to a map to find the spot where the dog had been hit. Then they called the police on the toy phone to report the incident.*
>
> *Preston examined Christopher's teddy bear and wrote out a report in the patient's folder. He read his scribble writing out loud and said, "This teddy bear's blood pressure is 29 points. He should take 62 pills an hour until he is better and keep warm and go to bed." At the same time that he read, he showed Christopher what he had written so he would understand what to do.*

Figure 5.6 shows forms that may be used in the Dramatic-Play Center when it is designed as a veterinarian's office during a unit on animals.

Additional play settings that will encourage reading and writing are as follows:

1. *Newspaper Office:* Includes telephones, directories, maps, typewriters, computers, paper, pencils, and areas that focus on sports, travel, general news, and weather.

2. *Supermarket or Local Grocery Store:* Can include labeled shelves and sections, food containers with their labels left on, a cash register, telephone, receipts, checkbooks, coupons, and promotional flyers.

3. *Post Office:* Can be used for mailing the children's letters and would need paper, envelopes, address books, pens, pencils, stamps, cash registers, and mailboxes. A mail carrier hat and bag are important for delivering the mail by reading names and addresses.

4. *Airport:* Can be created with signs posting arrivals and departures, tickets, boarding passes, luggage tags, magazines and books for the waiting area, safety messages on the plane, and name tags for the flight attendants.

◆ **FIGURE 5.6** *Forms to write on for the Veterinarian's Office in the Dramatic-Play Center*

Appointment Card

Name: _____

Has an appointment on _____

❑ Mon. ❑ Tues. ❑ Wed. ❑ Thurs. ❑ Fri. ❑ Sat.

Date _____ at _____ a.m.
p.m.

Prescription

Patient's Name:

Prescription:

Refills: Instructions:

Franklin A. Morrow, D.V.M.

Patient Record Form

Patient's Name: _____   Type of animal: _____

Owner's Name: _____   Date of Visit: _____

Address:_____   Telephone Number: _____

History and Physical Findings:	Treatment:

5. *Gas Station and Car Repair Shop:* Can be designed in the block area. Toy cars and trucks can be used for props. There can be receipts for sales, road maps to help with directions to different destinations, auto repair manuals for fixing cars and trucks, posters that advertise automobile equipment, and empty cans of different products that are sold in stations (Morrow and Rand, 1991).

For materials to be used for literacy to their fullest potential, teachers need to use props that are natural and from the child's environment. The materials in the setting created must serve a real function and be something a child is familiar with. Do not set up several dramatic themes all at once. Have the dramatic-play area match a theme being studied. Change the area when you begin the study of a new theme. Teachers need to guide the use of materials initially. This is not a time for teaching specific skills but a time for literacy to be initiated by the child quite naturally in the setting provided (Neuman & Roskos, 1993).

The materials in dramatic-play areas should be clearly marked and be accessible. All levels of literacy development should be accepted, and reading or writing attempts should be recognized as legitimate literacy behaviors. Teachers might find it useful to record anecdotes of literacy activities as an aid in assessing child development.

In my discussion of play, I have concentrated on cooperative learning to encourage literacy development. Play is typically thought of as a preschool and kindergarten activity; however, this type of setting could and should be used with first, second, and third grades as well. Older children engage in more sophisticated literacy behaviors when participating in play. In Chapter 6, the section "Independent Reading and Writing Periods" discusses opportunities for collaborative, social, and interactive learning that can be provided for kindergarten, first, second, and third grade children.

Strategies for Literacy Development

According to Teale (1987), studies on emergent literacy suggest that to become literate young children must learn about the functions and uses of literacy, conventions of written language, decoding and encoding strategies, and comprehending and composing strategies. They must also develop positive attitudes toward reading and writing. From the theories on reading and writing acquisition and development, we can formulate objectives for emergent and early readers and writers from birth through seven:

1. Develop positive attitudes toward reading and writing.
2. Develop concepts about books.
3. Develop comprehension of story.
4. Develop concepts about print.
5. Develop the functions, forms, and conventions for writing and reading.

These objectives are intended simply as basic guidelines for helping teachers design strategies for instruction.

The instructional strategies described in the next four chapters are designed to serve these objectives. Chapter 6 emphasizes the uses of children's literature and concentrates on the first objective. Chapter 7 deals with the second and third objectives, Chapter 8 concentrates on objective four, and Chapter 9 with objectives one, four, and five. In all of the chapters, the strategies will be guided by the theories of reading and writing acquisition just discussed.

An Idea for the Classroom from the Classroom

The following experience was created by an early childhood teacher. You may find this idea useful for your teaching.

♦ A Bakery in the Dramatic-Play Area

In coordination with a unit on Community Helpers, we set up a bakery in the dramatic-play area. Materials included a baker's hat and apron; cookie cutter; rolling pin; mixing bowls; measuring spoons; and trays and boxes with labels for baked goods, such as donuts, cookies, cakes, pies, and so on. Some classroom recipes that had already been made were hung in the area; a file box with old recipes and blank cards for new recipes was available; and pens and pencils and books with recipes for baking were also placed in the area.

For the purpose of buying and selling baked goods, which were actually made, there were an ordering pad, a cash register, receipts for purchases, number tickets for standing in line, and name tags for the baker and salesperson.

To guide the children in their play, on different days, I modeled the behavior for a salesperson, a customer, and the baker. This was a popular play area in which a great deal of literacy behavior occurred. For example, the salesperson took orders on the phone and in person and wrote them down; the bakers followed recipes in the cookbook and on the wall; and the customers counted out money and read the labels naming the baked goods. Children participated in behaviors that I modeled and generated their own ideas when participating in play in the bakery.

Joyce C. Ng, Kindergarten Teacher
Livingston, NJ

Activities and Questions

1. Answer the focus questions at the beginning of the chapter.

2. Describe how the emergent literacy approach to literacy development is sensitive to children with special needs.

3. Reading and writing are acquired through a child's (a) social and collaborative interaction with adults and other children, (b) association of print materials with real-life experiences, (c) awareness that there is a purpose for literacy, (d) the development of a desire to read and write that comes as a result of being read to, and (e) direct instruction of skills when additional help may be needed. Briefly discuss each of these five areas related to reading and writing acquisition. Then,
   a. Create a learning situation for each of the five categories mentioned.
   b. Observe a preschool, kindergarten, first, second, or third grade and record literacy activities observed. Classify the literacy activities into the categories previously mentioned.

4. Observe a preschool, kindergarten, first, or second grade. List those activities that seem characteristic of an emergent literacy approach to instruction and those that seem characteristic of a reading readiness approach.

5. Observe a child between the ages of three and seven. Identify his or her emergent literacy behaviors.

6. Your principal believes in the emergent literacy and holistic perspective for literacy development. You teach second grade and it has been mandated that

you design an area in your classroom for dramatic play as a source of literacy development. Because your students are studying different countries in Europe, you decide to design a travel agency with books about countries being studied and posters about these lands and their languages, foods, customs, and clothing. During a center time, the children are encouraged to use the area to decide on trips they would like to take and do research about where they are going. They have to write itineraries about the places they will visit and include information about them. They pretend that they have taken the trip and share their experiences with their classmates through a written log that they read to their peers.

Parents are not particularly happy with the dramatic-play period. They do not think it is appropriate for second graders to be spending their time this way in school. Defend your principal's mandate for dramatic play, and how it theoretically and philosophically is good practice for literacy development.

Case Study Activities

◆ Case 1

Review the "Idea for the Classroom" and identify the theories of literacy acquisition that exist in the learning setting described. Would this activity accommodate children with special needs? If yes, explain how; if no, suggest what might be done within this activity to accommodate such children better.

◆ Case 2

Mr. Williams designed a dramatic-play area in his kindergarten classroom for the purpose of stimulating natural literacy occurrences. He chose a pizzeria as the theme, to match a unit the class was studying about nutrition. He was concerned about multicultural issues, and therefore decided that the type of restaurant would change from time to time to represent other cultural backgrounds.

He designed the pizzeria himself after the children had gone home from school. He included a telephone, pads for taking orders and reservations, aprons, pizza pans, a play oven, tables, and chairs. He made an OPEN and CLOSED sign for the restaurant, made menus, and placed a blackboard on the wall for specials of the day. He also included a cash register, receipts, and cookbooks.

The next morning, Mr. Williams introduced the class to their pizzeria and suggested that, when they had free-play time, some of them could choose to play there.

After a week, Mr. Williams was thinking about dismantling the restaurant. Children were using the pizza pans as frisbees, and the order pad near the phone was unused, as were the other literacy materials. The only activity that was going on in the area was wild play.

Help Mr. Williams plan the dramatic-play area better such that it will bring about the literacy activity that he had hoped it would encourage.

Motivating Reading and Writing through the Use of Children's Literature

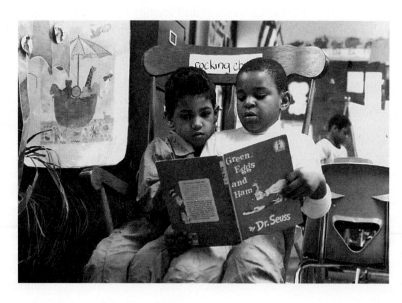

The rocking chair is the Literacy Chair of Honor.

Children who read and write only when they have to are not being taught a love of reading. The best index of the success of literacy instruction is the eagerness with which children approach reading and writing.

Love of reading and writing is not taught, it is created.
Love of reading and writing is not required, it is inspired.
Love of reading and writing is not demanded, it is exemplified.
Love of reading and writing is not exacted, it is quickened.
Love of reading and writing is not solicited, it is activated.

—Russell Stauffer
Adapted from *Wilson Library Bulletin (1970)*

Questions To Focus On As You Read

◆ What does research have to say about the benefits of voluntary independent reading and writing?

◆ What are the physical characteristics of well-designed literacy centers and the benefits of having these centers in classrooms?

◆ Name and define different genres of children's literature.

◆ Describe strategies that can be used by teachers to motivate interest in reading and writing.

◆ Describe the organization of social, cooperative, independent reading and writing periods and the type of activities children participate in during this time.

◆ What characteristics of the literature experiences described in this chapter seem to be appropriate for children with special needs?

◆ What objectives help guide the development of positive attitudes toward literacy activities, thus motivating reading and writing?

During a social cooperative period for independent reading and writing, Tesha and Jamin chose a felt story of the book *Are You My Mother?* The following transpired as they worked together reading the story and manipulating the felt characters:

Jamin: Can I read the story?

Tesha: OK.

Jamin: (Begins reading with enthusiasm and Tesha works the felt pieces on the board.) The baby bird asks the cow, "Are you my mother?"

Tesha: (Puts the cow on the felt-board.) Moooooooo

Jamin: Mooooooooo (Jamin continues to read the book.)

Tesha: Look at this picture. (She points to the baby bird. Both start to giggle. They continue along in the story.)

Jamin: Here I am Mother! (He reads in a high-pitched voice.) Here comes the funny part. (He points to a picture of the mother bird in a red scarf and both children giggle. Jamin again does the bird-pitched voice.) Mother, mother, here I am!

Tesha: I like it when he says to the tractor, You are my mother, Snort, Snort.

Jamin: Snort, Snort!

Tesha: Snort, Snort!

Jamin: I thought I had a mother. (He puts his hand to his head as he says this using a baby bird voice and swaying back and forth pretending he is crying.)

Tesha: (imitates Jamin by putting her hands on her hips) I thought I had a mother!

Jamin: (pointing to the felt-board) Can I do this now and you read? (They trade places and Tesha starts reading. She speaks in a loud dramatic voice and has voices for the two birds. Tesha is reading the story too fast for Jamin to put the characters up on the board.)

Jamin: Wait, wait, will you wait a minute Tesha. (He puts the dog on the felt-board and Tesha continues.) Wait, Wait, Wait! (He puts the mother bird on the felt-board.)

The teacher asks everyone to put all work away because independent reading and writing time is over. Both children are disappointed that they have to put the materials away and suggest they will continue tomorrow.

This dialogue was between two second-grade children engaged in an independent reading and writing period in which they had the opportunity to choose whom they would like to work with and what they would like to do that involves literacy behavior. The children have the opportunity to practice literacy to become proficient, the classroom atmosphere is relaxed, and a desire to read and write has been created through teacher modeling of pleasurable literacy activities. Because children can select what it is they want to do, and whom they do it with, the motivation and desire to read and/or write are high. The atmosphere promotes cooperative and collaborative behavior.

The Extent of Voluntary Readers

Becoming a Nation of Readers (Anderson, Hiebert, Scott, & Wilkinson, 1985) states, among other things, that learning to read requires (1) the motivation and desire to read, (2) practice to the point of proficiency, and (3) continuous and lifelong involvement so that fluency is maintained. One of the first goals in early literacy development is the nurturing of positive attitudes toward reading. Those attitudes usually result in voluntary readers. If children learn to read but have little desire to use their ability, we have not accomplished much (Spiegel, 1981). In a 1984 report to Congress entitled *Books in Our Future,* Daniel Boorstin, then Librarian of Congress, warned that *aliterates*—individuals who can read but choose not to—constitute as much of a threat to our democratic tradition as illiterates. Voluntary reading, or the lack of it, he wrote, "will determine the extent of self-improvement and enlightenment, the ability to share the wisdom and delights of our civilization, and our capacity for intelligent self-government" (p. iv).

Two second graders reading and performing a felt story together.

Unfortunately, substantial numbers of children and adults read neither for pleasure nor for information. Greaney (1980) found that 22 percent of the fifth-grade students he surveyed chose not to read at all, and that those who did read spent only 5 percent of their leisure time at it. Morrow (1982) and Morrow and Weinstein (1982) observed that few primary children chose books during free-choice time in school. A Gallup survey revealed that most of the books read in the United States were read by only 10 percent of the population; half the adults sampled had never read a book all the way through (cited by Spiegel, 1981). An extensive investigation by the Book Industry Study Group (1984) indicated that the number of young people under twenty-one identified as readers dropped from 75 percent to 63 percent in an eight-year period.

One reason for such distressing reports may be that most instructional programs in reading provide little opportunity for students to read for enjoyment (Lamme, 1981; Spiegel, 1981). Children's reading habits develop early in life (Bloom, 1964). If schools do not deliberately and thoughtfully entice children to read during their early years, the desire and motivation to learn to read and to acquire the reading habit may never develop.

Benefits Associated with Voluntary Reading

Apart from the common belief that voluntary reading is desirable, there is considerable empirical evidence that it correlates with success in school. Children identified as voluntary readers in elementary and middle grades demonstrated high levels of reading achievement in comprehension and in vocabulary development (Anderson, Wilson, & Fielding, 1985; Greaney, 1980; Taylor, Frye, & Marugama, 1990). Morrow (1983) found that, in comparison with children whose interest in books was low, kindergarteners who demonstrated a strong interest in books scored significantly higher on standardized reading readiness tests and were rated higher by teachers on work habits, general school performance, and social and emotional development. Children who are introduced to literature at an early age tend to develop sophisticated language structures and vocabulary which correlates with their subsequent success in learning to read. Both vocabulary and language structures can be improved significantly in youngsters by regular listening to stories read aloud. Children who experience literature early accumulate background knowledge, appreciate books, and show increased interest in learning to read. As we saw in previous chapters, they often begin to read early or learn to read more easily (Durkin, 1966). Discussing books provides a foundation for comprehension skills because of the language development, background knowledge, and sense of story structure acquired thereby (Cambourne, 1987; Galda & Cullinan, 1991).

Researchers have repeatedly stressed the importance of providing children with daily opportunities to experience literature pleasurably; to discuss stories through literal, interpretive, and critical questioning; to relate literature activities to content-area learning; and to share the books they read or look at (Cullinan,

1987, 1989; Galda & Cullinan, 1991; Huck, 1976; Stewig & Sebesta, 1978). Research has shown that children's use of literature increases dramatically when teachers incorporate enjoyable literature activities into the daily program and design attractive classroom library corners (Morrow, 1987; Morrow & Weinstein, 1982, 1986).

The information in Chapter 3 for parents of infants and toddlers focuses on techniques and practices to develop positive attitudes toward books that are appropriate as well for aides and professionals in day-care centers. For that reason, the discussion in this chapter focuses on techniques for use with two- to eight-year-olds (much of this information is applicable to younger children, too).

As you read the chapter, think about the characteristics of the strategies presented that would be particularly effective with children from diverse backgrounds.

Strategies for Motivating Reading and Writing

In a survey of classroom teachers concerning priorities for research, motivating children to want to read and write was ranked high on the list of suggestions (O'Flahavan, Gambrell, Guthrie, Stahl, & Alverman, 1992). Teachers recognize the importance of motivation in the development of children's literacy skills, and are most interested in learning new ways to motivate their students.

Motivation is defined as initiating and sustaining a particular activity. It is considered the tendency to return to and continue working on a task with sustained engagement (Maehr, 1976; Wittrock, 1986). A motivated reader chooses to read on a regular basis, and for many different reasons. Researchers have found that experiences which afford students the opportunity for (1) choice, (2) challenge, (3) social collaboration, and (4) success are likely to promote motivation.

Choice

Providing children with the opportunity to make *choices* about which literacy tasks they will participate in gives them responsibility and control over the situation. Choice needs to involve multiple modalities for learning, that is, developing literacy skills may combine traditional avenues that use pencil and paper experiences with modalities that use technology, drama, or the visual arts. Choice instills intrinsic motivation (Lepper, 1988; Morrow, 1992; and Turner, 1992).

Challenge

Students must perceive that there is some *challenge* to an activity, but that it is one that he/she can accomplish. That is, tasks should be perceived as not too hard but not too easy. When tasks are viewed as too easy, children become uninterested, whereas if tasks are too difficult, they become frustrated (Ford, 1992; Spaulding, 1992).

Social Collaboration

Motivation is increased through activities which offer opportunities for *social collaboration*. When children have the opportunity to learn in social situations involving collaboration with the teacher or peers, they are likely to get more done than they could do alone, and are more intrinsically motivated to participate than when they work alone (Brandt, 1990; Oldfather, 1993).

Success

When students complete a task they must consider it a *success*. Often a youngster completes a task that is not completely correct, but if they perceive themselves as being successful, intrinsic motivation is enhanced (Turner, 1992). When a child has met with some but not total success, such as spelling the word *read* as *reed*, he/she should be acknowledged for the part of the spelling that is correct. After all, he/she has gotten three of the four letters right. In other words, the child's success should be noted at the same time he/she is helped with the conventional spelling of the word.

The information presented in this chapter is based on motivation theory, which offers children choice, challenge, social collaboration, and success experiences, and investigations revealing classroom practices that seem to promote children's voluntary reading. Investigators have observed and described such strategies, correlated use of literature to materials in classrooms and activities carried out by teachers, and intervened with programs to see if changes in attitudes toward reading, demonstrated by increased use of books, are possible. The programs or strategies are based on the following objectives to help motivate voluntary use of children's literature.

Objectives for Motivating Voluntary Use of Literature
1. Children should be provided with an environment that is rich, with choices of literacy materials that are challenging but will bring success.
2. The teacher provides models of literacy behavior for children to emulate.
3. Children need to be given the opportunity to participate in social collaborative settings during periods of independent reading and writing.
4. Children must have the opportunity to choose literacy activities in which to participate.
5. Children need to work in cooperative and collaborative settings as well as alone if they choose.
6. Children should have the opportunity to listen to stories read by their teachers and peers in a pleasant, relaxed atmosphere.
7. Teachers should allow for response to literature through discussion, role-playing, the use of puppets to retell stories, and so on.
8. Children need the opportunity to take books home from the classroom literacy center.

9. Children should have the opportunity to experience varied genres of children's literature.

Preparing a Literacy-Rich Environment

Before planning instruction that will entice children to books, the teacher must prepare appropriate materials and a physical setting that sets the stage for pleasurable literacy experiences. As Plato said, "What is honored in a country will be cultivated there." Teachers who honor the development of literacy demonstrate that attitude by providing within their classrooms a rich environment where the use of books can be cultivated. Their students honor literacy development by assimilating the attitudes and atmosphere presented by the teacher.

A classroom literacy center is essential for children's immediate access to literature. Children in classrooms with literature collections read and look at books 50 percent more often than children in classrooms without such collections. The efforts spent in creating an inviting atmosphere for a classroom literacy center are rewarded by increased interest in books (Morrow and Weinstein, 1982, 1986). Morrow (1987) found that well-designed classroom literacy centers significantly increased the number of children who chose to participate in literature activities during free-choice periods. Morrow (1982) observed literacy centers in nursery schools, kindergartens, and first and second grades and identified specific design characteristics that correlated with children's use of the centers during free-choice periods. Conversely, poorly designed literacy centers were among the least popular areas during free-choice periods in early childhood rooms (Morrow, 1982; Rosenthal, 1973). Suffice it to say, the physical features of a classroom literacy center can play an important role in enticing children to use the corner voluntarily.

Features of Well-Designed Literacy Centers

Classrooms need to have literacy centers which include a library corner and writing area. In this chapter, the library corner portion of the literacy center will be described. In Chapter 9 on writing, the writing area is discussed.

A classroom literacy center should be a focal area, immediately visible and inviting to anyone entering the classroom. To provide privacy and physical definition, it should be partitioned on two or three sides with bookshelves, a piano, file cabinets, or freestanding bulletin boards. The dimensions of the literacy center will vary with the size of the classroom. Generally, it should be large enough to accommodate five or six children comfortably (Figure 6.1).

Well-designed library corners in literacy centers have two kinds of bookshelves. The first houses the bulk of the books, which are shelved with the spines facing out. The other type is open-faced, allowing the covers of the books to be seen, which is important for calling attention to special books. Featured books, changed regularly, are placed on the open-faced shelves for easy access.

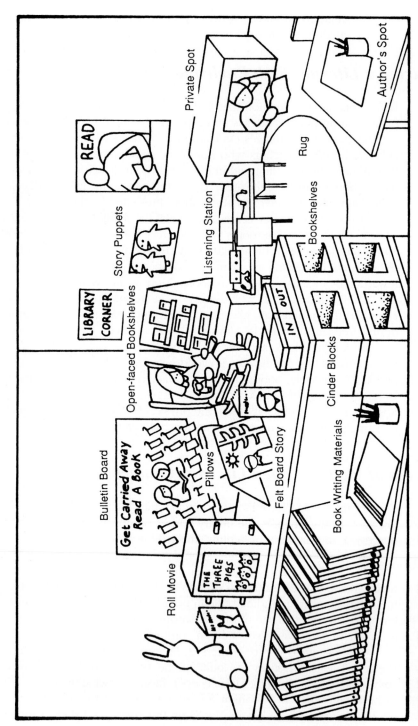

◆ **FIGURE 6.1** *Morrow Literacy Center*

An alternative to open-faced shelving is the circular wire rack, commonly found in bookstores.

Books in the collection should be shelved by category and color-coded according to the type of book. Identify all animal books, for example, by placing blue dots on their spines and clustering them on a shelf marked *Animals,* with a blue dot next to the label. Another color might distinguish books about holidays, a third color poetry, and so on. Color coding introduces children to the idea that books in libraries are organized so as to be readily accessible.

The literacy center should be furnished with an area rug and pillows or beanbag chairs because much of the activity there takes place on the floor. If possible, it should also include a small table and chairs where children can use headsets to listen to taped stories and make their own books. A rocking chair allows comfortable reading: a place for teachers to read to children and children to read to other children. They read their original stories and present literacy projects to the group while sitting in the rocking chair. It is the chair that invited guests use to read to the class or present other information to them. The rocking chair is the Literacy Chair of Honor.

Children are given little privacy in the typical school. It has been found that many children relish privacy. Because it is partially partitioned from the rest of the room, the literacy center provides some privacy. Listening to recorded stories on headsets offers even more privacy, and an oversized carton, painted or covered with contact paper, makes a cozy private reading room. Children have been found reading in coat closets and under shelves.

Attractive posters that encourage reading are available from the Children's Book Council (67 Irving Place, New York, NY 10003) and the American Library Association (50 East Huron Street, Chicago, IL 60611). Stuffed animals also belong in a library, especially if they are related to books available in the corner —a stuffed rabbit next to *Peter Rabbit* (Potter, 1902), for instance. Children enjoy reading to stuffed animals or simply holding them as they look at books. A feltboard, with figures of story characters from favorite books, is one of the more heavily used materials in a literacy center, as are roll movies. A roll movie consists of a box with a picture window cut out that makes it look like a television. A dowel is inserted at the top and bottom of the box. Shelving paper is written on and illustrated and attached to the dowels for presentation (see photograph on page 158). Viewmasters with story wheels are a source of literature for young children, and puppets aid the acting out of stories. The center should also include materials from which children can make their own books, felt stories, and roll movies.

About five to eight books per child is appropriate in a classroom library. Books are not difficult to accumulate. They can be purchased very inexpensively at flea markets. Teachers can borrow as many as twenty books a month from most public libraries, ask for book donations from parents, and hold fund-raisers for book purchases. Children's paperback book clubs offer inexpensive books and free bonus books for bulk purchases.

The library corner is a cozy place where children can relax and read, sitting on a rug, leaning on soft pillows, and hugging stuffed animals.

Children's magazines and newspapers belong in the classroom library even if they are not current. For the cost of mailing and shipping, some publishers and local magazine agencies will donate outdated periodicals to schools.

Children should be involved in the planning and design of a literacy center. They can develop rules for its use, be in charge of keeping it neat and orderly, and select a name for it, such as Book Nook.

To ensure continued interest, the teacher must introduce new books and materials and recirculate others. Approximately twenty-five new books should be introduced every two weeks, replacing twenty-five that have been there for a while. In this way, "old" books will be greeted as new friends a few months later. Recirculation compensates limited budgets.

Books from the library corner should be available for students to check out and take home for a week at a time. The check-out system should be simple. At specified times during the school day, children might bring the books they want to borrow to the teacher, who notes the date, the child's name, and book title. Some kindergarten children have been taught to check out books themselves by copying titles and recording dates on five-by-eight cards filed under their own names. Other youngsters enjoy keeping track of books borrowed by recording titles and dates on three-by-five cards hung on curtain-rod hooks or key rings mounted on a bulletin board, one hook or ring per child. Another method for checking out books is a looseleaf notebook with a page for every child to note books taken out and returned. Figure 6.2 provides a sample check out page.

Books in the Library Corner

Books and other materials selected for the library corner should appeal to a variety of interests and span a range of grade levels. It is advisable to stock multiple

◆ **FIGURE 6.2** *Looseleaf Notebook Page for Checking Out Books*

Name Td(mikd Jones

Name of book	date out	date in
Green Eggs and Hdm	Feb 10	Feb 17
Cdrrot Seed	Feb 20	Feb 26
Curious George	Mdrch 3	Mdrch 9
Where the Wild Thi ngs Are	March 15	Mdrch 21
The Mitteh	Mdrch 27	April 2

copies of popular books. Children sometimes enjoy reading a book because a friend is reading it (Morrow, 1985). Several types of children's literature should be represented:

Picture concept books are appropriate for the very young child. Most picture concept books do not have story lines, though they often have themes, such as animals or toys. Each page usually carries a picture identified by a printed word. Many picture books are made of cardboard, cloth, or vinyl to withstand rigorous handling. Alphabet and number books are also considered picture concept books.

Traditional literature includes nursery rhymes and fairy tales, familiar stories that are part of our heritage and originated in the oral tradition of storytelling. We assume that children are familiar with *Goldilocks and the Three Bears* (Izawa, 1968a) and *The Three Little Pigs* (Brenner, 1972), yet many youngsters have not been exposed to these traditional stories. Children who *do* know the stories welcome them as old friends.

Picture storybooks are most familiar to us as children's literature. Their texts are closely associated with their illustrations. Picture storybooks are available on a wide range of topics, and many are known for their excellence. The Caldecott Medal is awarded annually to the author or illustrator of an outstanding picture storybook. Many of these books have become classics and their authors renowned—Robert McClosky, Dr. Seuss, Ezra Jack Keats, Tomie DePaola, Maurice Sendak, and Charlotte Zolotow, to name just a few. Every child should be given the benefit of hearing some of these books read. However, emergent readers will often find the vocabulary and syntax too sophisticated to read on their own.

Realistic literature is a category within picture storybooks that deals with real-life issues. *Tight Times* (1983) by Barbara Hazen, for example, describes how a family handles the problems that arise when the father loses his job. He tries to explain the situation to his son so he will understand and calls it *Tight Times*. Books in this category deal with issues that many children face, such as fears a child has when it is time to go to sleep or problems that arise with a new baby in the house. Some touch on very sensitive issues, such as divorce, drugs, alcohol, and death. Many of these books can be read to the entire class if they address issues that all share. Some of these books should not be read to the class as a whole. The teacher's use of discretion as to what he or she reads to the class is important with this category of books. Teachers can also recommend specific titles to parents and family members of children who face particular problems.

Easy-to-read books are designed to be read by emergent readers themselves. They have limited and repeated vocabularies, and many of them rhyme, which makes them predictable and aids independent reading. Because of their limited vocabulary, few easy-to-read books rate as quality literature, but many preschool and kindergarten children begin to read independently with them.

Fables and folktales retell many of the myths and traditional stories that are available in picture-book style for the younger child. Many of these stories originate in other countries and cultures and therefore broaden a child's experience and knowledge base.

Informational books or expository texts offer nonfiction for readers. There are books about holidays, plants, animals, foreign countries, communities, dinosaurs, and famous people. They broaden a child's background information, explore new ideas, and often stimulate deep interest in particular topics.

Wordless books carry definite story lines, but use no words. They are often thought appropriate for very young children and are confused with picture books. They are designed not for babies but for children three and older. The child creates the story by reading the pictures, some of which are intricate.

Poetry is too often forgotten in collections of children's literature at home and in school. Many themed anthologies have been compiled for young children, and they are an important part of the literacy center.

Novels are longer books with chapters. We can begin reading novels to young children to expose them to the genre. They are often quite attracted to them and eager to begin to read them. Children often call novels chapter books.

Biography is another genre appropriate for young children. There are simple biographies of historical figures, as well as popular figures in sports and on television.

Big Books are usually large versions of smaller picture storybooks. They can also be original stories. They are oversized books that rest on an easel in order to be read. The purpose of the Big Book is for children to be able to see the print as it is being read, to make the association between oral and written language, and to see how the print is read from left to right across the page.

In addition to these categories of books, young children enjoy joke and riddle books; craft books; cookbooks; participation books, which involve them in touching, smelling, and manipulating; books in a series built around a single character; and books related to television programs appropriate for their age. Magazines and newspapers should be choices for reading in the library corner. They provide a nonthreatening format, diverse topics, and reading matter for diverse ability levels, and include multicultural material. Newspapers and magazines appeal to parents as well.

Children particularly enjoy literature that is predictable, because it helps them to understand the story line more easily and enables them to read along with the individual reading to them. Predictable literature contains rhyme; repetition; catch phrases; conversation; familiar sequences, such as days of the week or numbers; cumulative patterns, in which events are repeated or added on as the story continues; stories about familiar topics; familiar or popular stories; books with uncluttered illustrations that match the text; and stories that have well-developed story structures (setting, theme, plot, episodes, and resolution). (Selected children's books are listed in Appendix A, including books for children with special needs and books that are multicultural. Children's book clubs and publishers of children's literature are listed on page 164, and television programs that feature children's literature are in Appendix B.)

The *Author's Spot* is an integral part of the literacy center. It usually consists of a table and chairs with various writing materials available, such as colored felt-tip pens, crayons, and lined white paper ranging from 8½ × 11 inches to 24 × 36 inches. If possible, include a typewriter or a computer. Materials for making books should also be present, including colored construction paper for covers, plain white paper for inside pages, a stapler, and scissors. (The Author's Spot will be described more thoroughly in Chapter 9).

Teachers and children had the following reactions to literacy centers I designed in their classrooms: teachers said they were concerned that there wasn't enough space in their rooms for literacy centers and were surprised that all the materials could fit. As time went on, teachers themselves provided more space for the literacy centers. Teachers commented that the physical presence of the literacy center made a statement to the children that literacy was so valued that space was taken from the classroom to make room for the area. Teachers agreed that children were attracted to the area by the manipulative materials in the center, such as the felt-board stories and puppets. They found that the elements of comfort, such as the rocking chair, rug, pillows, and stuffed animals made the center relaxing and comfortable for reading:

> *The literacy center became a place where children of all reading and writing abilities mingled. . . . This social context seemed to provide an atmosphere for cooperative learning. The children looked forward to their time there each day.*

A child commented:

> *I liked to cuddle up on the pillows with a book, or crawl into a private spot, or rock in the rocking chair and read. You get to take books home right from the classroom center.*

Children referred to the center as a special place. They felt that the literacy center could be improved by adding more space, more books, and more time to use it. A child commented: "The only thing missing from the literacy center is a snack bar."

Additional Literature Resources

Book Clubs

My Weekly Reader Book Club, 1250 Fairwood Avenue, P.O. Box 2639, Columbus, OH 43216.

Parents' Magazine Read-Aloud Book Club for Little Listeners and Beginning Readers, Division of Parents' Magazine Enterprises, 52 Vanderbilt Avenue, New York, NY 10017.

Rigby, P.O. Box 797, Crystal Lake, IL 60039-0797.

Scholastic Book Services, See Saw Club (K–1), 904 Sylvan Avenue, Englewood Cliffs, NJ 07632.

Troll Book Club, 320 Route 17, Mahway, NJ 07430.

Trumpet Club, P.O. Box 604, Holmes, PA 19043.

Wright Group, 19201 120th Avenue North East, Bothell, WA 98011-9512.

Children's Book Awards

American Book Awards. Association of American Publishers, One Park Avenue, New York, NY 10016.

Caldecott Medal. American Library Association, 50 East Huron Street, Chicago, IL 60611.

Children's Book Showcase. Children's Book Council, 67 Irving Place, New York, NY 10003.

Newberry Award. American Library Association, 50 East Huron Street, Chicago, IL 60611.

The Teacher as a Model to Motivate Interest

The teacher plays a critical role in influencing children's attitudes toward voluntary reading and literature.

> If children live associating reading only with repetition of skill, drill, teach, and test, they will never reach for a book on their own. If, on the other hand, children live in an environment that associates reading with pleasure and enjoyment as well as with skill development, they are likely to become voluntary readers. How children live and learn at home and in the classroom ultimately determines whether they will live their lives as literate or aliterate individuals. (Morrow, 1985, p. 20)

Chapter 3 dealt with literacy activities appropriate for home use and was intended primarily to provide parental models for literacy behavior and to help children associate reading with pleasure. The school must follow a similar agenda.

> One of the clear points to emerge from research into reading failure is that there was no association between reading and pleasure.... The role of teachers in stimulating voluntary reading among children and young people is...potentially the most powerful of all adult influences upon the young. (Irving, 1980, p. 7)

Programs that incorporate pleasurable experiences with literature create interest in and enthusiasm for books that in turn increase children's voluntary use of books (Morrow, 1982, 1983, 1987, 1992; Morrow & Weinstein, 1982, 1986). Among other specific activities in early childhood classrooms, teachers should read or tell stories to children daily. Interest heightens when stories are discussed both before and after being read, especially if they are related to issues that reflect children's real-life experiences or current school topics. Literal, inferential, and critical questions can be introduced even at the preschool level. Skill development can easily be incorporated into storybook reading activities in pleasurable and meaningful ways. The following example describes a discussion about *Goldilocks and the Three Bears* in which inferential and critical comprehension is being developed.

I recently led a discussion with four-year-olds after reading *Goldilocks and the Three Bears*. I asked who were the good and the bad characters. Hands waved in the air and Jennifer answered, "Goldilocks was good and the bears were bad." When I asked Jennifer why she thought that, she said, "Well, the bears scared Goldilocks."

Another hand went up and Tim said, "No, that's not right. The bears are good and Goldilocks is bad. Goldilocks went into the bears' house when they weren't home. She ate their food and didn't even ask."

"That's right," said Megan, "and she broke their chair and went to sleep in their bed and didn't even ask if it was okay."

Chris chimed in, "Yeah, Goldilocks was really bad. She did a lot of bad things because she didn't ask if she could."

"Would you go into a stranger's house and do the things Goldilocks did?" I asked. The whole group called out in unison "Nooooo." I asked why not. Sara answered, "Because that is bad. It's like stealing. She was naughty. If the cops found out, I bet they will arrest her."

Discussion about authors and illustrators also arouses interest. Reading different stories by the same author or a series of books about the same character, such as Madeline (Bemelmans, 1939) or Curious George (Rey, 1941), increases interest as well. Read different kinds of literature to the class and as often as possible coordinate stories with topics being discussed. If the topic is spring, bring a cocoon to class, discuss the life cycle of a butterfly, and follow the discussion with *The Very Hungry Caterpillar* (Carle, 1969), the story of the caterpillar's transformation to a butterfly. Read and recite poetry together regularly. Recruit older children, the principal, the custodian, the nurse, the librarian, parents, and grandparents to read to classes, to small groups, and to individuals. Encourage children to share books with one another. Books from home should be shared with the group and children encouraged to take books home from school.

Many popular folk songs have been made into picture storybooks, such as *Go Tell Aunt Rhody* (Quackenbush, 1973) and *Old MacDonald Had a Farm* (Quackenbush, 1972). These books are particularly good to read to children because the children are familiar with the words and very much want to pretend to read the books themselves and to another person. *Cooking* is another pleasurable activity that can be related to literature. Many picture storybooks feature food—*Blueberries for Sal* (McCloskey, 1948) and *Bread and Jam for Frances* (Hoban, 1964), for instance. After such stories have been read, the class can make blueberry muffins or bread and jam or whatever food is appropriate. *Art* activities can also be motivated by story readings. After reading *The Snowy Day* (Keats, 1962), have the children create a winter collage from blue construction paper, white cotton, wool, doilies, chalk, and silver foil. After reading *Where the Wild Things Are* (Sendak, 1963), ask kindergarteners and first graders to think of a wild thing and draw a picture of it. Gather their pictures into a class book. Class books become favorites and are read frequently by children. Children also enjoy filmstrip and movie stories, which motivate their interest in reading the associated book.

Making Story Reading Pleasurable

To make story reading as enjoyable and pleasurable as possible, select good pieces of literature—well-structured stories with well-delineated characters, clear and uncluttered illustrations, catch phrases, rhyme, and repetition. Read to youngsters in a relaxed atmosphere in a location designated for such readings. Each day let a different child sit close to you while you are reading, with the other children in a single or double semicircle. If you have a rocking chair, use it as the place where you sit when you read. Because children enjoy seeing illustrations in books during story reading, hold the book so it faces the group or turn the book at appropriate pauses so its pictures can be seen. Before reading a story to a group, practice reading it aloud to yourself.

Be expressive in your reading, change your voice when a different character speaks, and highlight special events. Use facial expressions. A story reading is like a dramatic presentation. Read slowly and with a great deal of animation. Record or videotape your readings to improve your technique. Begin a story with an introduction such as, "Today I'm going to read a story about a little girl who wanted to get a present for her mother's birthday. She can't think of anything and asks a rabbit to help her. The title of the story is *Mr. Rabbit and the Lovely Present* [Zolotow, 1962]. The author's name is Charlotte Zolotow and the illustrator is Maurice Sendak. While I read the story, think of which part of the present you like the best." When you have finished reading the story, begin a discussion with a question such as "Who would like to tell me which part of the present you liked best?"

Storytelling: Some Creative Techniques

Storytelling strongly attracts children to books (Morrow, 1982; Morrow & Weinstein, 1982, 1986). It has a power that reading stories does not, for it frees the storyteller to use creative techniques. It also has the advantage of keeping him or her close to the audience. The storyteller establishes direct eye contact with the group. Telling a story produces an immediate response from the audience and is one of the surest ways to establish rapport between the listeners and the storyteller. Long pieces of literature can be trimmed so that even very young children can hear whole stories in one sitting. Considered an art, storytelling can be mastered by most people.

It is not necessary to memorize a story, but be sure you know it well. Use all the catch phrases and quotes that are important to the story. Use expression in your presentation, but don't let your dramatic techniques overshadow the story itself. Look directly at your audience and take their attention into consideration. Storytelling allows you to shorten stories as you go if attention spans seem to be short. It is important to have the original book at hand when you have finished telling a story so that the children can see it and enjoy it again through its pictures and printed text.

Creative techniques help storytelling come alive. They excite the imagination, involve the listeners, and motivate children to try storytelling themselves and create their own techniques. Take clues for creative techniques from the story. Some stories lend themselves to the use of puppets, others are perfect for the felt-board, and still others can be worked up as chalk talks.

Felt-boards are a popular and important tool in a classroom. You can make characters or purchase them commercially. Prepare your own with construction paper covered with clear contact or laminate. Attach strips of felt or sandpaper to the backs of the cutouts so they cling to the felt-board. Stories that lend themselves to felt-board retelling are those with a limited number of characters who appear throughout the story—*Ask Mr. Bear* (Flack, 1932), for example, or *Caps for Sale* (Slobodkina, 1947).

Prop stories are quite easy to develop. Simply collect stuffed animals, toys, and other articles that represent characters and objects in a story. Display the props at appropriate times during the storytelling. Three stuffed bears and a yellow-haired doll aid in telling *Goldilocks and the Three Bears* (Izawa, 1968a), and several toy trains aid in *The Little Engine That Could* (Piper, 1954).

Puppets are used with stories rich in dialogue. There are many kinds of puppets, including finger, hand, stick, and face puppets. Shy children often feel secure telling stories with puppets. Such stories as *The Gingerbread Boy* (Holdsworth, 1968) and *The Little Red Hen* (Izawa, 1968b) are appropriately told with puppets because they are short, have few characters, and repeat dialogue.

Chalk talks are another technique that attracts the listener. The storyteller draws the story while telling it. Chalk talks are most effective when done with a large chalkboard so that the story can keep going in sequence from beginning to end. The same technique can be carried out on mural paper hung across a wall. The storyteller simply uses crayons or felt-tip markers instead of chalk. The chalk talk technique can also be adapted to easel and chart paper or an overhead projector. Choose a story with simple illustrations. Draw only a select few pictures as you tell the story. There are stories that have been written as chalk talks, including an entire series, *Harold and the Purple Crayon* (Johnson, 1955).

Sound-story techniques allow both audience and storyteller to provide sound effects when they are called for in a plot. The sounds can be made with voices, rhythm instruments, or music. When preparing to tell such a story, first select those parts of the story for which sound effects will be used. Then decide on each sound to be made and who will make it. As the story is told, students and storyteller chime in with their assigned sounds. Record the presentation, then leave the recording in the literacy center with the original book. Among books that adapt easily to sound-story techniques are *The Noisy Book* (Brown, 1939), *Too Much Noise* (McGovern, 1967), and *Mr. Brown Can Moo: Can You?* (Seuss, 1970).

Other creative techniques, plus the opportunity to create your own, offer endless possibilities for storytelling (Morrow, 1981). By serving as a model of creative storytelling, you can excite children about literature and motivate them to try their own creative storytelling as well.

I had the opportunity to work with several first- and second-grade teachers concerning sharing literature with children in pleasurable ways. The teachers practiced reading and telling stories and made manipulatives for storytelling to use in their classrooms. These teachers incorporated many of the strategies discussed earlier and one of them commented about their use:

> *The children enjoy being read to and they never grow tired of this activity. I thought that in second grade, reading to youngsters was not that important*

*anymore; however, the benefits of read aloud sessions became quite evident
as I involved my children in them more and more. The stories generated
sophisticated discussion; we'd relate them to the students' own life experiences. We discussed authors, illustrations, and elements of story structure.
Through these story readings and discussions, I found that my students
seemed to appreciate literature more, they became more aware of the different genres of children's literature that exist, and vocabulary and comprehension were enhanced as well. I realized how important it was for me to
model reading to children and in many different ways. I read using felt
characters, roll movies, chalk talks, and so on. I learned how to make reading more appealing for the children. Consequently I saw an increased desire
in my children to read as they modeled my behavior in reading stories I had
read to them and using the storytelling props.*

Second graders who participated in the program were asked what they
learned and liked. They commented:

*I like it when the teacher reads to you. . . . She uses such good expression,
you can learn to read better yourself by listening to her. . . . The teacher
reads and tells stories in many different ways so it is always interesting,
and you can learn to do it the way she does. . . . You learn about authors
and illustrators and that they are people like you and you think that you
could be one.*

One day during a story reading session in a second-grade class with a focus
on making comparisons between styles of illustrators, Ms. Payton told the children that she was going to read two picture storybooks that they had heard
before. She asked the children to concentrate on the pictures or illustrations as
she read the stories, to note their styles so they could describe them. After the
stories were read, she asked if the children thought that the books were illustrated by the same individual. They all said no because they looked very different. Ms. Payton identified the illustrators of the books who were also the authors,
Ezra Jack Keats for *Peter's Chair* and Dr. Seuss for *Green Eggs and Ham.* Then
she asked the children to describe the illustrations for each book.

Tamika said, "Well in *Peter's Chair* the illustrations look like a painting.
They are made like they are real. I think that Ezra Jack Keats is a very good
drawer, I like the colors he uses."

Ms. Payton went on to explain that not only does Mr. Keats paint his pictures but he uses collage as a technique as well. When you look closely at his
illustrations, you see bits of wallpaper, newspaper, doilies and so on blended
into his pictures.

Ms. Payton asked if someone would like to describe the style of the other
book. Marcel raised his hand.

He said, "Dr. Seuss is very different from Keats; he uses lots of lines and
sort of fantasy little shapes. He uses colors on people and things that aren't what

we usually expect. His drawings look like cartoons and the other ones look like real things."

The discussion was followed by the children's illustrating stories they had written. They were told that their illustrations could be their own original styles or that if they wished they could use the style of an illustrator in a storybook that they knew. Ms. Payton walked around to talk about the work the children were doing. Magda decided to make her drawings similar to those of Dr. Seuss and Ms. Payton said to her, "Magda, if Dr. Seuss came through our door he would think that he illustrated your story, your work looks so much like his."

Magda is a child with limited English proficiency. The positive reinforcement in this situation started a conversation about her work with the teacher.

Literature Activities Modeled and Initiated by Teachers

Literature activities need to be modeled and initiated by teachers to motivate children's interest. The following is a list of suggestions to be carried out in classrooms on a regular basis.

Carry Out on a Daily Basis
1. Read or tell stories to children.
2. Discuss stories read in many different ways. Discuss literal, interpretive and critical issues.
3. Have a 30-minute independent reading and writing period (IRWP) three to five times a week which includes the use of books and all the other literature-related materials in the library corner and writing center.
4. During the IRWP, the teacher acts as a model by reading.
5. Allow children to check books out of the classroom library.
6. Encourage children to read during their spare time.
7. Have children keep track of books read.
8. Have children keep the library corner in an order fashion.

Carry Out Once a Week
1. Read poetry to the children.
2. Have the class recite poetry.
3. Allow for literature discussions with the whole class and in small groups.

Do Five of the Following Each Week
1. The principal, custodian, nurse, secretary, or a parent reads to the children.
2. Discuss authors and illustrators.
3. Write to authors.

4. Children read to younger children.
5. Children read to each other.
6. Show filmstrips or movies of stories.
7. Use literature across the curriculum in content area lessons.
8. Do art related to books (e.g., draw a mural of millions of cats related to the book of the same name or create a picture using the technique of a particular illustrator of children's books).
9. Tell stories using a creative storytelling technique such as:

   a. Felt-boards
   b. Roll movies
   c. Puppets
   d. Sound stories
   e. Music stories
   f. Chalk talks
   g. Prop stories
   h. Cut stories

10. Have children tell stories with and without props.
11. Have children act out stories.
12. Prepare recipes related to stories (e.g., make stone soup after reading the story of the same name).
13. Read TV-related stories.
14. Make classbooks and very own books; bind them and store in the library corner.
15. Sing songs that have been made into books and have the book on hand (e.g., *I Know an Old Lady Who Swallowed a Fly*).
16. Make bulletin board related to books.
17. Have children write advertisements for good books they have read.
18. Discuss proper ways to care for and handle books.

Carry Out On a Regular Basis

1. Feature new books in the open-faced bookshelves.
2. Introduce new books on the open-faced shelves.
3. Introduce new books added to the library corner.
4. Circulate 25 new books every two weeks.
5. Provide booklets for children and parents for selecting books to read in and out of school.
6. Have a bookstore in the school where children can buy books regularly.

Carry Out a Few Times a Year If Possible

1. Give bookmarks to children.
2. Give each child a book as a gift.
3. Have a young authors conference (share books children have written, bind books, invite authors).
4. Have a book fair for children to purchase books.
5. Have a book celebration day (e.g., dress up as book characters, tell stories to each other, show movie and filmstrip stories, have stories told creatively).

6. Take a field trip related to books (e.g., book binding factory, town library, publishing company).
7. Have children order books from a book club.

Activities for Parents Related to School Literature Program
1. Provide a newsletter a few times a year about book-related activities in school.
2. Ask parents to participate in some literature-related activity at school (e.g., read to children, helping with book binding, raising money to buy books).
3. Have a workshop for parents that describes the importance, purpose, and activities of the school literature program.
4. Have a workshop for parents describing how they can participate in home recreational reading program.

Literacy Center Time

As discussed earlier in this chapter, elements that help to motivate children include: choice, social interaction, challenge, and success. I have been applying these to instructional settings, that is: (1) the creation of literacy centers in classrooms that provide children choice of activity, and (2) the modeling of literacy activities by teachers that children find challenging to learn to participate in. Now that the environment, materials, and activities are designed and modeled, children need time to look at books and become immersed in literature independently during the school day. Therefore, time is provided for periods of independent reading and writing in social cooperative settings, with activities viewed as ones in which they can succeed. In the past, such periods have been called sustained silent reading (SSR).

Sustained silent reading has generally been defined as quiet time, with little socialization and little student choice beyond selection of the particular book the child chooses to read. If we expect them to become interested in reading, young children (and perhaps older children as well) require more options and greater flexibility than have been characteristic of SSR periods. Setting aside fifteen to thirty minutes three to five times a week for looking at books as well as for engaging in other activities related to literature allows the variety, free choice, social interaction, and flexibility children need if they are to be enticed into voluntary reading. Research has indicated that children of different ability levels worked together during independent reading and writing periods. It was also found that, although many options were available, including felt-boards, roll movies, and taped stories, 70 percent of the free-choice activities selected by children involved reading books. Other materials and options attract children into a free-choice literacy area, but they lead children to choose books (Morrow & Weinstein, 1982, 1986).

Following are descriptions of ways to help teachers and children function effectively during independent reading and writing periods or Literacy Center Time.

Organizing and Managing Periods of Independent Reading and Writing: Literacy Center Time

We know that experience with children's literature helps youngsters to develop vocabulary and enhance background knowledge, thus improving comprehension (Hoffman, Roser, & Farest, 1988). The amount of free reading done by children, both in and out of school, correlates with reading achievement (Anderson, Fielding, & Wilson, 1988; Taylor, Frye, & Maruyama, 1990). Children who read voluntarily develop life-long, positive attitudes toward reading.

Literacy Center Time   In classrooms where teachers incorporate periods of social collaborative literacy activities, time is set aside three to five times a week for about 45-minute periods. During social collaborative Literacy Center Time, children make decisions about what they will do and with whom they will work. Some guidelines for children to follow during this period are shown in Figure 6.3. These are posted in the classroom and reviewed before each session.

In addition to rules pertaining to use of materials, children are taught cooperative skills which are practiced and posted as shown in Figure 6.4. These include helpful things to say and to do for each other during Literacy Center Time.

Independent reading and writing periods can focus around a content area theme or specific literacy skill to practice. If the children are learning about animals, for example, they focus their reading and writing activities on this topic. Likewise, if the teacher features illustrators, children can think about the similarities and differences in style that characterize pictures in the books they read.

When Literacy Center Times are first initiated, some teachers assign children to groups, determine the activity in which they are to participate, and appoint a leader to organize the project. Other teachers have children decide upon activities and groups before the period begins. As a result of participating in the assigned groups with assigned tasks, children eventually can make these decisions about what to do on their own. Children select others to work with, leaders of their groups, and tasks on which to work. To help children select activities, things to do during Literacy Center Time are posted and reviewed, as illustrated in Figure 6.5.

For children who are emergent readers, teachers often include pictures representing activities to help with reading rules and roles on the Activity Cards. But if these lists are reviewed, children learn about what they say and begin to read them.

The purpose of Literacy Center Time is for children to read and write independently of the teacher in a social cooperative manner. Early in the program, some children do not stay on task for long and move from one activity to the next. Within a few weeks, most of the children stay with one or two activities throughout the entire period.

Children spend a great deal of time on projects during Literacy Center Times, some extending over several days or weeks. When the period ends and a

◆ **FIGURE 6.3** *Rules for Using Materials During Literacy Center Time*

1. Decide with whom you will work or if you will work alone.
2. Choose a reading or writing activity from the Literacy Center.
3. Do only one or two activities.
4. Materials can be used in or outside of the Literacy Center.
5. Handle the materials carefully.
6. Speak in soft voices; people are working.
7. Put materials back in their places before taking others.
8. Try activities you haven't done before.
9. Try working with people you haven't worked with before.
10. Be ready to share completed activities with the class.
11. Record completed tasks in your log.
12. Keep the Literacy Center neat.

child has not completed an activity, a place is provided for projects to be stored and worked on in the next period.

It is helpful for teachers to share manipulative materials and books from other classrooms to increase their supply. The children are also involved in making new materials for the literacy center. They can make taped stories, felt stories and roll movies for others to use in the listening center. They can create original

◆ **FIGURE 6.4** *Rules for Cooperating in Groups During Literacy Center Time*

Helpful Things to Do when Working in Groups

- Select a leader to help the group get started.
- Give everyone a job.
- Share the materials and take turns talking.
- Listen to your friends when they talk.
- Stay with your group.

Helpful Things to Say when Working in Groups

- Can I help you?
- I like your work.
- You did a good job.

Check Your Work

- Did you say helpful things?
- Did you help each other?
- Did you share materials and take turns?
- Did you all have jobs?
- How well did your jobs get done?
- What can we do better next time?

◆ **FIGURE 6.5** *Things to Do During Literacy Center Time*

1. Read or look at a book, magazine, or newspaper.
2. Read to or share a book with a friend.
3. Listen to someone read to you.
4. Listen to a taped story and follow the words in the book.
5. Use the felt-board with a storybook and felt characters.
6. Use the roll movie with its storybook.
7. Write a story.
8. Draw a picture about a story you read.
9. Make a book for a story you wrote.
10. Make a felt story for a book you read or a story you wrote.
11. Write a puppet show and perform it for friends.
12. Make a taped story for a book you read or a story you wrote.
13. Check out books to take home and read.
14. Use Activity Cards with directions for the task you select.

stories and make them into books for the classroom library. Participation in these activities increases their feeling of ownership and respect for the area.

The Role of the Teacher During Literacy Center Time   Besides the advance preparation of the environment and the modeling of literacy activities, the teacher also plays an important role during Literacy Center Time. The teacher interacts with the children in the following ways: (1) By facilitating or helping activities get started, (2) by scaffolding literacy behaviors when models are needed, (3) by participating along with the children in their activities, and (4) by modeling reading and writing for pleasure. The goal for this period, however, is for the children to be self-directed in the activities undertaken.

◆ **FIGURE 6.6**
Activity Card

Tell a Story Using the Felt-board

1. Select a leader for your group.
2. Select a book and the matching felt story characters.
3. Decide who will read or tell the story, and who will use the felt characters.
4. Take turns reading and placing the felt figures on the board.
5. Be ready to present the story to the class.
6. Record the activity in your log (see Figure 6.7 for a Log Sample).
7. Check your work:
    How well was the story presented?
    How well did the group work together?

◆ **FIGURE 6.7** *Log Sample*

Log: Circle, Draw, or Write about What You Did During IRWP

Name: _____

Activity:		Date:	
Read by myself	Read to a friend	Told a roll movie	Listened to a taped story
Told a felt story	Wrote a story	Made a felt story, roll movie, or picture	Other

Write or Draw What You Did:

Literacy Skills Developed During Literacy Center Time The data collected in different research studies of students who participated in periods of independent reading and writing revealed that a variety of literacy activities were occurring during this time (Morrow, Sharkey, & Firestorne, 1994). The activities were self-directed and involved the children in making decisions about what work to do and how to carry through with their plans. Children read books and wrote stories and also engaged in active manipulative projects such as creating felt stories and puppet presentations for pieces they had written or read. Most activities were done in groups of two to five and involved peer cooperation and peer tutoring. The groups were composed of single and mixed genders, and were generally friendly. Children took charge of their learning and demonstrated the use of oral reading, silent reading, and writing, while demonstrating their comprehension development in literal and inferential ways.

Literacy Center Time exposes children to reading and writing in many forms and gives them the opportunity to make choices. It is a positive approach toward activating interest in reading and writing, and is a time to practice and learn skills. As mentioned earlier, it can be thought of as a variation of **SSR,** and what some have called **Reading and Writing Workshop.** Because of the element of choice, there is something for everyone: gifted, average, and special needs children. Children from differing backgrounds worked together on similar interests. Children with language differences were welcomed as members of groups doing puppet shows and felt stories, and given roles in which they could participate.

I work with teachers on a regular basis implementing programs with them similar to those that have been described here. I visit the classrooms often. Mrs. Oman had a second-grade class in an inner-city district that I had been working with for an entire school year. I visited her room the last day of school to say good-bye to the children I had grown to know well. Mrs. Oman and I shared a sense of pride while observing the children in their last IRWP for that school year. We saw some children curled up on a rug or leaning on pillows in the literacy center with books they had selected themselves. Louis and Ramon were squeezed tightly into a rocking chair, sharing a book. Marcel, Patrick, and Roseangela snuggled under a shelf—a "private spot" filled with stuffed animals. They took turns reading.

Tesha and Tiffany were on the floor with a felt-board and character cutouts from *The Gingerbread Boy,* alternately reading and manipulating the figures: "Run, run as fast as you can! You can't catch me, I'm the Gingerbread Man!"

Four children listened on headsets to tapes of Maurice Sendak's *Pierre,* each child holding a copy of the book and chanting along with the narrator, "I don't care, I don't care." Yassin and Shawni were writing a story together and bouncing ideas back and forth.

Tyrone had a Big Book and gave several other children copies of the same story in smaller format. Role-playing a teacher, he read to the others, occasionally stopping to ask who would like to read.

Leon asked Tamaika if she would like to hear a story he had written. She agreed and he read it to her. When he finished, she suggested acting out Leon's story with puppets, which they did. Throughout the dramatization, Leon behaved like the director of a play. He knew his story and his characters and wanted them to act in a manner that reflected his intent.

Much of the information discussed here represents the results of studies that involved classroom observation and intervention in kindergarten through second grade. Children in these classrooms participated in literacy programs that included activities that have been described in this chapter. These youngsters scored significantly better on tests of reading comprehension, the ability to retell and rewrite stories, and the ability to create original oral and written stories by including elements of story structure than children in classrooms that did not participate in the program. Children in the treatment rooms also showed significant improvement in use of vocabulary and language complexity (Morrow, 1990, 1992; Morrow, O'Connor, & Smith, 1990).

Teachers and children were interviewed to determine their attitudes toward the Literacy Center Time and the program in general. Teachers commented that the children particularly like the Literacy Center Time because they are able to:

- Choose activities they want to do
- Choose the books they want to read

- Choose to work alone or with others
- Choose manipulatives such as puppets and roll movies

Teachers also said that children enjoyed the Literacy Center Time because everyone participated, and there were few discipline problems.

Teachers said that children learned the following in the program:

- To work together and cooperate with each other
- To be independent and make decisions
- A sense of story structure from the stories they listened to and read, improved comprehension, and vocabulary development
- An appreciation for books and knowledge of different genres of children's literature
- The names of authors and illustrators and an increase in their general knowledge from the amount of reading being done
- That their peers could teach them and were willing to do so
- To like to read and write

By participating in the program teachers said they learned that:

- The social family atmosphere created by the independent reading and writing period is conducive to learning.
- Children are capable of cooperating and collaborating independently in reading and writing activities and learning from each other.
- When there is choice of activity and person to work with, children of all ability levels choose to work together.

Headsets with taped stories and the accompanying storybooks provide a good reading model for children.

During Literacy Center Time, children may choose to tell a roll movie story or a felt-board story. All activities are literature-related and are accompanied by the original book.

- There is something for everyone in this program, advanced and slower children alike.
- The program made me more flexible and spontaneous and a facilitator of learning rather than always a teacher.
- Children who don't readily participate in reading and writing did so during Literacy Center Time. I think it is because they are the ones making the decisions about what they do.

In the student interviews, children were asked what they learned in the literature program, and they answered:

- You learn that reading can be fun.
- You learn to read and write better because you read a lot and you read real books.
- You learn to understand what you are reading and you learn a lot of new words.
- You get to learn how to read better if you don't read real good because kids who know how to read good help you.
- You learn about authors and illustrators and that they are people like you and you think that you could be one.

What do you like about the literature program?

- It makes you want to read and write; it's fun and makes you feel happy.
- You can choose what you want to read, like long books or short books, or hard books or easy books.

- You can write stories.
- You can do felt stories, tape stories, chalk talks, and roll movies, which are all fun, and they have books with them too.
- During Literacy Center Time, the teacher reads to you, and she never does in regular reading.
- During Literacy Center Time, the teacher talks to you one at a time like a friend; in regular reading she talks to you all together. (Morrow, 1992).

It became apparent when speaking with teachers that children's special needs were attended to in this program. Mrs. Bell described an incident about a child who went to the resource room daily, because her reading skills were far below grade level. According to Mrs. Bell, Charlene never read aloud. One day Mrs. Bell noticed her reading aloud to a rag doll as she sat in the rocking chair. Mrs. Bell offered positive reinforcement to Charlene, and the reading aloud continued daily during independent reading and writing.

Mrs. Meechem described another situation with a bilingual youngster who had limited ability in English. This child would not speak in class at all. During an independent reading and writing period, Mrs. Meechem observed Tasha acting as a teacher with a group of children she had organized. She had each one taking turns reading.

Marcel was a gifted child in a classroom with mostly low achievers. He was alone all the time. About two months after independent reading and writing was initiated in his classroom, he found himself able to participate with other children in literacy activities. The first time I observed him with others, he was reading the newspaper and checking out the weather in other parts of the country. Patrick asked Marcel if he could look too. Marcel was pleased and then David joined them. Together they read and discussed how hot and cold it was in Florida, Colorado, and so on.

There were numerous anecdotes from Literacy Center Time describing how children were able to find a way to participate in spite of special problems. One teacher commented, "There seems to be something that every child can find to do during independent reading and writing and do it well."

The recommendations in this chapter for developing positive attitudes toward reading incorporate Holdaway's (1979) developmental approach to literacy. This approach highlights less teaching and more learning, learning that is self-regulated rather than regulated by adults. It has been suggested here that the teacher provide an environment rich with materials and activities from which children are invited to select, plus a social context in which children are actively involved with other children, with the teacher, and with materials. The environment is emulative rather than instructional, providing lively examples of reading skills in action. Teachers present themselves as models involved in literary activities. They serve as sources of support and positive reinforcement for appropriate behavior patterns in the child. Through regularly scheduled literary activities and ready access to attractive and comfortable classroom literacy centers stocked with books and materials that inspire interest and active participation, children associate reading and writing with pleasure and develop an appreciation for books. Given time to use the literacy center and participate in independent reading and writing activities, children reinforce their learning of skills through enjoyable, self-selected practice. The outcome will be children who not only learn to read and write, but who choose to read and write voluntarily.

Assessing Independent Reading and Writing During Literacy Center Time

Assessing the success of a program that incorporates physical and social settings for literacy learning should be carried out on a regular basis.

Teachers discussed Literacy Center Time issues, for example, helping children who were not on task, encouraging different children to work together, helping children try different activities, and seeing that everyone had a leadership role at some time. The opportunity for teachers to meet provided a support system for them. It helped teachers evaluate the program and build their confidence and skill levels as well.

During Literacy Center Time, teachers observed their classes to notice which children were on task, which children needed help getting started, and what activities the children were choosing to participate in. There were changes in the management of Literacy Center Time to help enhance productivity.

Teachers recorded anecdotes of activities and collected writing samples. They made audiotapes and videotapes of the groups at work and of performances of completed tasks. Children were involved in evaluating their Literacy Center Time activities. They discussed how they cooperated and the quality of their completed tasks. When completed activities were presented, peers offered constructive criticism. Children were asked about their suggestions for improving the program and identified materials and books they wanted added to the centers.

Teachers discussed literacy center designs and how they might be improved to increase student productivity. Teachers moved centers from one area of the room to another, because they found a space that was bigger, brighter, or quieter. They added books and manipulatives to provide more choices for children. Figure 6.8 provides a means for assessing available literacy center materials and those that are needed.

Authentic Assessment of Children's Attitudes Toward Books

Direct observation of children's behavior while they are listening to stories, reading, or looking at books independently is probably the most effective method for assessing their attitude toward books. How much attention do they give to the books they are looking at or reading? Do they simply browse? Do they flip through

◆ **FIGURE 6.8** *Library Corner Guidelines and Checklist*

	Yes	*No*
Children participate in some phase of the library corner design (develop rules, select a name for the area, develop materials, etc.)	☐	☐
The area is placed in a quiet section of the room	☐	☐
The area is visually and physically accessible	☐	☐
Part of the area is partitioned off from the rest of the room	☐	☐
Bookshelves are available for storing books with spines facing outward	☐	☐
There is an organizational system for shelving books (e.g., color coding for topic)	☐	☐
Open-faced bookshelves are available for new featured books	☐	☐
Five to eight books are available per child	☐	☐
Many books are available representing three to four grade levels and of the following types: a. picture books, b. picture story books, c. traditional literature, d. poetry, e. realistic literature, f. informational books, g. biographies, h. novels, i. easy to read books, j. riddle and joke books, k. participation books, l. series books, m. textless books, n. TV-related books, o. brochures, p. newspapers, q. magazines	☐	☐
New books are circulated every two weeks	☐	☐
There is a check-out/check-in system for children to check out books daily	☐	☐
There is a rug	☐	☐
There are throw pillows	☐	☐
There is a rocking chair or bean bag chair	☐	☐
There are head sets and taped stories	☐	☐
There are read posters	☐	☐
There are stuffed animals	☐	☐
The area is labeled with a name selected by the class	☐	☐
There is a felt board and story characters and the related books	☐	☐
There is a roll movie and related book	☐	☐
There are materials for writing stories and making them into books	☐	☐
There is a private spot in the corner such as a box to crawl into and read	☐	☐
There is a system for children to keep track of books read	☐	☐
The area occupies about 10% of the classroom space and five to six children can fit comfortably	☐	☐

Checklist for Assessing Attitudes Toward Reading and Writing and Amount of Voluntary Reading and Writing

	Always	Sometimes	Never
Voluntarily looks at or reads books			
Asks to be read to			
Listens attentively while being read to			
Responds with questions and comments to stories read to him or her			
Takes books home to read			
Writes voluntarily at home			
Writes voluntarily at school			

the pages quickly, paying little attention to print or pictures? Do they silently study the text, sustaining attention to pictures and print throughout (Martinez & Teale, 1988)? The teacher should also note how frequently children select looking at books when faced with other options. In occasional interviews with individual children, asking what they like to do best in school and at home might reveal interest in reading. During conferences, ask parents if their children voluntarily look at books or pay close attention when they are read to. At the same time, ask parents how often they read to their children. Gather facts about the home literacy environment that will help you understand the child's attitude toward books.

A Motivation Interview (see Figure 6.9) for a child's portfolio of assessment materials and a checklist for assessing attitudes toward reading and writing is provided. They are useful tools concerning children's interest in reading and writing.

Ideas for the Classroom from the Classroom

I created the following experience when I was teaching children in a mixed-age grouping primary classroom. You may find this idea useful for your teaching.

◆ Felt-Board Story

I wanted to introduce my children to the use of the felt-board as a means for retelling stories and creating their own original stories with characters. I selected a story that was easy to illustrate, had a theme that would generate conversation,

◆ **FIGURE 6.9** *Motivation Interview*

Directions: Tell the child that you would like to find out more about what kids like to do and how they feel about reading and writing. Ask each question in the interview and read the multiple choice responses.

How often would you like your teacher to read to the class?

    (2) every day   (1) almost every day   (0) not often

Do you like to read books by yourself?

    (2) yes   (1) it's ok   (0) no

Which would you most like to have?

    (2) a new book   (1) a new game   (0) new clothes

Do you tell your friends about books and stories you read?

    (2) a lot   (1) sometimes   (0) never

How do you feel when you read out loud to someone?

    (2) good   (1) ok   (0) bad

Do you like to read during your free time?

    (2) yes   (1) it's ok   (0) I don't read in my free time

If someone gave you a book for a present, how would you feel?

    (2) happy   (1) ok   (0) not very happy, disappointed

Do you take storybooks home from school to read

    (2) almost every day   (1) sometimes   (0) not often

Do you read books out loud to someone in your family?

    (2) almost every day   (1) sometimes   (0) not often

What kind of reader are you

    (2) I'm a very good reader   (1) I'm ok   (0) I'm not very good

Learning to read is:

    (2) easy   (1) a little hard   (0) really hard

Do you like to write?

    (2) yes   (1) it's ok   (0) I'd rather do something else

Do you write in your free time?

    (2) a lot   (1) a little   (0) not at all

What do you like to read best?

    (2) books and magazines   (1) schoolwork   (0) nothing

Adapted from L. B. Gambrell, *Me and My Reading Scale,* 1993. In: *The Impact of Running Start on the reading motivation of and behavior of first-grade children* (Research Report). College Park: University of Maryland, National Reading Research Center.

and encouraged the opportunity to write additional episodes for it. The name of the story was *A Bunny Called Nat,* an anonymous tale that I found in a resource book many years ago. The story is about "a bunny named Nat, who was funny and fat, and he could change his color, just like that." This was the repetitive rhyme in the story and at the end of the rhyme, fingers are snapped. The bunny in the story is a gray bunny who doesn't like his color because it is so plain. He is able to change his color and each time he does, he has an unpleasant adventure. For example, Nat changed himself to blue and when he was blue he was blue like the water and blue like the sky. He went down to the pond to admire his reflection in the water. He bent over so far while looking that he fell into the pond and he couldn't swim. He yelled for help, but no one could see him because he was blue like the water. Luckily a turtle came by and pulled him out. Nat said, "Not much fun being blue, but, I'm a bunny named Nat, I'm funny and fat, and I can change my color, just like that." After trying out four different colors, Nat realizes that it's not so bad being just what he was and that's the way he stayed.

When I introduce the story to the children, I ask them to listen for the different colors that Nat becomes and the problems he faces each time. I then tell the story, using the different colored bunny characters on the felt-board to help. When the story is over we discuss Nat and his different colors. We also discuss the ending of the story and its meaning, trying to relate it to the experiences of the children. We discuss if they ever wanted to be anyone other than themselves and why and would it really be better.

After the discussion, I ask the children to think of another color that Nat could become with an adventure attached to it as in the real story. I then ask them to write their story and draw and color a bunny to add to the felt story we already have. The bunnies are made of construction paper and felt strips are glued onto the back to make them stick to the felt-board.

Seven-year-old Lindsey wrote the following:

> "I'm a bunny named Nat, I'm funny and fat, and I can change my color just like that." And suddenly Nat was a red bunny. Red like an apple, red like a cherry, and red like a fire truck. Suddenly a group of bees was coming. They saw Nat in the red color and they were thinking that Nat was an apple. The group of bees was going where Nat was sitting, they wanted to eat him. Then Nat saw the bees. He ran and ran but the bees followed him. So he said as he ran, "Being red is not so good, but I'm a bunny called Nat, I am sassy and fat, and I can change my color, just like that."

In this activity, children were given the opportunity to participate in a pleasurable experience with literature. They were actively involved in the discussion and the creation of a story, using the one below as a model. The underlying theme of this story concerning one's self-image is an important topic for conversation and can help children understand each other's strengths, weaknesses, and special needs.

The story of *A Bunny Named Nat* and a pattern for the bunny follow:

◆ *Sample Felt-Board Story*

A BUNNY CALLED NAT

(adapted version of an anonymous tale)

(As the story is being told, hold up and then place a new colored bunny on the felt-board as each bunny is named.)

Materials—Five bunny characters drawn identically but in the following colors: gray, blue, green, yellow, and orange. The bunny pattern is found at the end of the story.

Once upon a time there was a little gray rabbit and his name was Nat. One day he looked around and saw that all his brothers and sisters, cousins and friends were gray, too. He thought he would like to be different from them. So he said:

> I'm a bunny called Nat,
> I'm funny and fat,
> And I can change my color
> Just like that. (*Snap your fingers.*)

And suddenly Nat was a blue bunny. He was blue like the sky and blue like the sea. He was blue like the twilight and blue like the dawn. It felt nice and cool to be blue. He decided to take a look at himself in the pond. He hurried to the edge and admired his reflection in the water. He leaned over so far that SPLASH! he fell into the pond. Nat fell deep into the blue water and he couldn't swim. He was frightened. He called for help. His friends heard him, but when they came to the pond they couldn't see him because he was blue just like the water. Fortunately a turtle swam by and helped Nat get safely to shore. Nat thanked the turtle. He decided that he didn't like being blue. So he said:

> I'm a bunny called Nat,
> I'm funny and fat,
> And I can change my color
> Just like that. (*Snap your fingers.*)

And this time, what color did he change himself to? Yes, he was yellow— yellow like the sun, yellow like a daffodil, yellow like a canary bird. Yellow seemed like such a happy color to be. He was very proud of his new color, and he decided to take a walk through the jungle. Who do you think he met in the jungle? He met his cousins the lion and the tiger. The lion and the tiger looked at Nat's yellow fur and said, "What are you doing in that yellow coat? We are the only animals in this jungle that are supposed to be yellow." And they growled so fiercely that Nat the bunny was frightened and he ran all the way home. He said:

(Repeat bunny poem above.)

And this time what did he change his color to? Yes, he was green. He was green like the grass and green like the leaves of the trees. He was green like a grass-

◆ **FIGURE 6.10** *Felt Figure for Story* **A Bunny Called Nat**

hopper and green like the meadow. As a green bunny, Nat thought he'd be the envy of all the other bunnies. He wanted to play with his other bunny friends in the meadow. Since he was the color of the grass in the meadow, he could not be seen and his friends just ran and jumped about him not seeing him at all or mistaking him for a grasshopper. So Nat the bunny had no one to play with while he was green. Being green wasn't much fun. So he said:

(Repeat bunny poem above.)

And what color was he then? Right, he was orange. He was orange like a carrot, orange like a sunset, orange like a pumpkin—he was the brightest color of all. He decided he would go out and play with all his brothers and sisters and friends. But what do you suppose happened? When his friends saw him, they all stopped playing and started to laugh, "Ha-ha, whoever heard of an orange bunny?" No one wanted to play with him. He didn't want to be orange anymore. He didn't want to be a blue bunny because if he fell into the pond no one could see him to save him. He didn't want to be a yellow bunny and be frightened by the lion and the tiger. He didn't want to be a green bunny because then he was just like the meadow and none of his friends could see him. And so he said:

(Repeat bunny poem above.)

Do you know what color Nat the bunny changed himself into this time? Yes, you're right. He changed himself back to gray. And now that he was gray all of his friends played with him. No one growled or laughed at him. He was gray like a rain cloud, gray like an elephant, gray like pussy willows. It felt warm and comfortable being gray. From that time on, Nat the bunny was always happy being a gray bunny, and he decided that it's really best being just what you are.

◆ *A Fable Theme for Independent Reading and Writing Period*

Mrs. Martinez assigns themes to periods of independent reading and writing. Following is an account of this when the theme was Fables.

During several independent reading and writing periods over a few days, the theme for my second-grade class was writing fables. This activity inspired reading fable selections. Students selected particular animal characters and settings and wrote responses to the following questions in a prewriting activity:

1. What problem does one character have?
2. What happens?
3. What lesson might one character learn?

The students worked in groups and wrote original fables, accompanied by a moral. The morals were: "Think before you do something" "It's not fun to leave home." "Never run away." After only one mini-lesson on fables followed by the opportunity to create during periods of independent reading and writing, I was amazed at how well the students understood the concept of a fable and incorporated the characters' dialogue and morals into their writing. The students prepared to present their fables in little plays. They worked together in groups during IRWP, planning, writing, drawing, creating, rehearsing, and organizing their presentations.

We have a "Buddy" system with Mr. O'Leary's first-grade class, which gives the classes the opportunity to share literature experiences. My second graders were extremely proud to present their fables, which were well received by the first grade.

Gayle Martinez, Grade 2
Judd School, North Brunswick, NJ

Activities and Questions

1. Answer the focus questions at the beginning of the chapter.

2. Select a piece of children's literature and choose a creative storytelling technique that seems appropriate for the story (e.g., felt characters, chalk talk, sound story). Create materials for the story and tell it to a group of children or to your peers. Evaluate your performance according to the criteria for storytelling discussed in the chapter.

3. Evaluate the literacy center in an early childhood classroom using the form in Figure 6.8. List all the characteristics of the center that reflect criteria described in this chapter. List items that need to be included.

4. Observe in an early childhood classroom on three different occasions. List all the literacy activities carried out by the teacher that you believe contribute to developing positive attitudes toward reading.

5. Continue your portfolio assessment for the child you selected to assess. Observe the child using the assessment checklist provided in this chapter concerning the evaluation of his or her attitudes toward writing and reading. Interview the child using the motivation survey in the checklist on page 184.

6. Continue the thematic unit that you began in Chapter 4. Select three objectives for building positive attitudes toward reading and describe three activities using your theme that will satisfy each of the objectives.

Case Study Activity

Refer back to the "Idea for the Classroom from the Classroom" on p. 183 about *The Bunny Called Nat.* Describe how you think it enhances a child's interest in books. Has the activity made accommodations for children with special needs? If yes, how? If not, how could the teacher do this? Has the teacher made an attempt to use the activity to build awareness of cultural diversity? How could he/she do this? Make a list of books that would help create interest in reading, addressing children with special needs and cultural diversity.

Developing Concepts about Books and Comprehension of Text

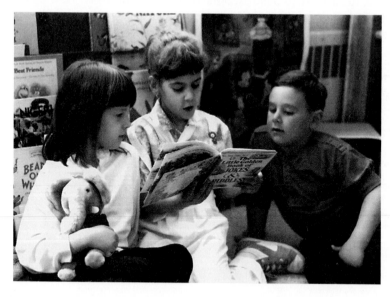

Children learn concepts about books by interacting with other children as they browse through the pictures and by looking at books themselves.

Few children learn to love books themselves. Someone must lure them into the wonderful world of the written word, someone must show them the way.

—Orville Prescott
A Father Reads to His Child

Questions to Focus on As You Read

◆ What are the concepts about books that are important for young children to know?

◆ What experiences enhance a child's concepts about books?

◆ What are the objectives for comprehension development for young children?

◆ Identify and describe strategies that develop comprehension such as: directed reading and thinking activities, mapping, webbing, and story retellings.

◆ List and define the structural elements in a good story.

◆ List and describe strategies that develop aesthetic and efferent stance.

For several months, Mrs. Johnson has been discussing different authors and illustrators with the children in her first-grade class. The class has a chart on which their favorite authors and illustrators are listed. Today she asked them to add names to the list because they had recently read stories by authors and illustrators who were new to them. First she asked for authors and the following names were generated: Ezra Jack Keats, Leo Lionni, Robert McClosky, and Arnold Lobel. Next she asked if they could name some illustrators, and the following names were mentioned and written next to the authors: Maurice Sendak, Dr. Seuss, Eric Carle, and Crockett Johnson. Jamie raised her hand and said, "Hey something weird just happened. I noticed that all of the authors named are also illustrators and all of the illustrators are all authors too." Christopher raised his hand and said, "That's not so weird, I know a bunch of people who are authors and illustrators at the same time. There's me, and Josh, Jennifer, and Patrick." Christopher was looking around the room and naming all the children in the class. When he finished naming his classmates, he continued, "We're all authors and illustrators. We all write books and illustrate them. They are published and they are in our classroom library. How could we forget that?"

Acquiring Concepts about Books and the Ability to Comprehend Text

Investigators have found a number of instructional strategies that nurture children's concepts about books and help them to comprehend text. Those practices include children's role-playing, retelling, and reconstructing with pictures stories that have been read to them. They also include discussions concerning the parts of books, how to handle books, and who authors and illustrators are. The active involvement of children in experiences with literature enhances their comprehension of stories, their sense of story structure, and their language development. Through experiences with literature, young children integrate information and learn the relationships among a story's various parts (Brown, 1975; Morrow, 1985; Pellegrini & Galda, 1982). That interactive behavior plays a leading role in such learning seems to reinforce a model of generative learning: the reader or listener understands prose by actively engaging in construction of and relationships with the textual information he or she hears or reads (Linden & Wittrock, 1981; Wittrock, 1974, 1981).

Teale (1984) has utilized Vygotsky's (1978) definition of higher mental functions as internalized social relationships and applied it to literacy. Literacy develops, according to Teale, from children's interactions with others in specific environments of which reading and writing are a part. Holdaway's (1979) model of developmental teaching, derived from observations of middle-class homes, indicates that a child benefits when early experiences with storybooks are mediated by an interactive adult who provides problem-solving situations. The child is asked to respond and the adult offers information when necessary. In such situations, children and adults interact to integrate, construct, and make relationships with printed text. The strategies to be described in this chapter follow the theory, research, and models just outlined.

Strategies That Develop Concepts about Books and Comprehension of Text

The many benefits of reading to children have been discussed throughout this volume. Strategies for reading to infants and toddlers that are applicable in the home and in day-care centers have been described, as have techniques for reading stories to children that will arouse their interest and entice them to books. The following sections suggest strategies for using children's literature to develop children's concepts about books and the meanings to be found in books.

Objectives for Developing Concepts about Books

A child who has a good concept of books:

1. Knows that a book is for reading.
2. Can identify the front and the back of a book as well as the top and the bottom.
3. Can turn the pages of a book properly.
4. Knows the difference between print and pictures.
5. Knows that pictures on a page are related to what the print says.
6. Knows where one begins reading on a page.
7. Knows what a title is.
8. Knows what an author is.
9. Knows what an illustrator is.

Activities That Develop Concepts about Books

Some adults assume that children know the concepts about books just outlined. To many two- to six-year-olds, however, those concepts are totally unfamiliar. To help children master them, point them out at every opportunity when you read to children. You can introduce a story reading, for instance, by pointing appropriately as you say, "The title of the story that I'm going to read is *Mr. Rabbit and the Lovely Present* [Zolotow, 1962]. This is the title on the front of the book. The author of the book, the person who wrote it, is Charlotte Zolotow. Here is her name. And the illustrator, the person who drew the pictures, is Maurice Sendak. Here is his name. All books have titles and authors, and if they have pictures they also have illustrators. The next time you look at a book, see if you can find the title. It is always on the front cover."

The repetition of such dialogue familiarizes a child with the concepts, which they assimilate easily. Similar dialogues explain other concepts. Point to a picture, then to print. Identify each, then ask, "Which do we read, the picture or the print?" As you get ready to read to them, ask children to point out the top and bottom of the book, the title, and where you should begin reading on a page. Not only will you give the children the opportunity to learn the concepts, you can at the same time determine which children have the concept and which need help. These activities and dialogues can be carried out during story readings to small groups or to individual students. A child's independent exploration of books will reinforce what the teacher has pointed out or explained.

Big Books have become an important part of early literacy instruction. They are oversized picture storybooks that measure from 14 × 20 inches up to 24 × 30 inches. Holdaway (1979) suggested that the enlarged print and pictures in these books help to get children involved with concepts about books, print, and the meaning of text. Big Books are appropriate from preschool through third grade, and because they are used in small to large group situations, active involvement by the group is encouraged. When using a Big Book, a teacher places it on a stand because it is hard to handle otherwise. An easel is usually used for a Big Book stand and makes the print and pictures visible for the children. Class Big Books can be made as well as purchased. When they are made, children become even more aware of book concepts because they are engaged in creating a book. Figure 7.1 provides directions for making a Big Book.

Big Books are quite effective for developing concepts about books mainly because of their size. As the teacher reads the book and tracks the print from left to right across the page, children see that books are for reading and where one begins to read on a page. They also learn to differentiate the print from the pictures. The connection is made that the oral language they hear from their teacher is being read from the print on the page in the book. The correct way to turn pages is easy to see with Big Books because they are so enlarged. The title of the book is prominently displayed on the front of the book and on the title page, as is the name of the author and illustrator.

In addition to using the Big Book to emphasize the concepts of author and illustrator, feature different authors and illustrators on a special bulletin board or in book displays. Carry out discussions about their work. Don't forget to refer to the children in your class as authors and illustrators as they write stories and draw pictures about text.

In Mrs. Johnson's room, children are encouraged always to read the title of a book and the name of the author and illustrator prior to starting to read the text. One day during an independent reading and writing period, Jonathan placed the Big Book *Chicken Soup with Rice* on the Big Book stand. He had gathered three children to sit in front of him to read to. He started by saying, "The title of the book I'm going to read is *Chicken Soup with Rice*." He turned the first page and began reading the text. Patrick popped up and said, "Jonathan, you can't read the book yet; you forgot to read who the author and illustrator are." Jonathan pounded his fist to his forehead, looked somewhat annoyed with himself, and said, "How could I forget that. Let's see, the author of this book is Maurice Sendak and he is the illustrator too."

◆ **FIGURE 7.1** *Instructions for Making a Big Book*

Materials

- 2 pieces of oak tag for the cover (14" × 20" to 20" × 30")
- 10 pieces or more of tagboard or newsprint the same size as the oak tag used for the cover to be used for the pages in the book
- 6 looseleaf rings (¼ ")
- Holepunch

Directions

- Punch three sets of holes in top, middle, and bottom of the cover and paper that is to go inside of the book.
- Insert a looseleaf ring in each hole. The Big Book should have a minimum of 10 pages.
- Print should be 1½ to 2 inches high

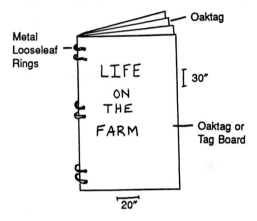

Comprehension of Text

Understanding what is read, or comprehending text, is one of the major goals for reading instruction. The English poet Samuel Taylor Coleridge wrote the following short piece entitled *On Reading Comprehension:*

> There are four kinds of readers. The first is like an hour glass, and their reading being as the sand, it runs out, and leaves not a vestige behind. A second is like the sponge, which imbibes everything and returns it in nearly the same state, only a little dirtier. The third is like a jelly bag, allowing all that is pure to pass away, and retaining only the refuse and drugs. And the fourth is like the workers in the diamond mines of Colconda, who cast aside all that is worthless and retain only pure gems.

How do we get children to cast aside unnecessary information and retain only the pure gems when reading or listening to a passage?

Definitions of comprehension emphasize that it is an active process. In this process, the reader or listener interprets and constructs meaning about what he or she reads or listens to based on what he or she already knows about the topic, thereby making connections between the old and the new (Pearson & Johnson, 1978). This concept arises from research on schema theory that suggests that we have a schemata (background knowledge) for certain information based on prior experience with a given topic. That schemata is never complete because more can always be learned about a subject. For example, if someone told us something about the circus that would give us one bit of information, if we saw pictures of the circus we would have additional information, and if we went to see the circus we would have even more. Then when we read about the circus or listened to a story about it, the new information would expand and refine what we already know. Comprehension of a story or expository piece that is read or listened to involves a child's integration of his or her prior knowledge concerning a topic with the new text to create new knowledge (Johnston & Pearson, 1982). With that background, we can begin to discuss objectives and activities for the development of comprehension.

Objectives for Developing Comprehension of Text

A child is developing comprehension of text when he or she:

1. Attempts to read well-known storybooks that results in the telling of a well-formed story.
2. Participates in story reading by saying words and narrating stories as the teacher reads to him or her.
3. Retells a story without the help of the book.
4. Includes elements of story structure in story retellings: setting (beginning, time, place, characters), theme (main character's problem or goal), plot episodes (events leading toward a solution of the main character's problem or attainment of his or her goal), resolution (problem solution, goal achievement, ending).
5. Responds to text after reading or listening with activities, questions, and comments that are factual, interpretive, and analytical. Responses also include evaluation of text, the author's purpose, and monitoring of one's own understanding of the material presented.
6. Uses reference and study skill materials such as the dictionary, encyclopedia, and magazines to find information; uses study aids in materials such as the table of contents, the index, titles, subtitles, charts, and so on.

In the past the categories most commonly used for classifying comprehension strategy development included literal, interpretive, and critical thought development with subcategories for each. Regardless of the classification system, the types of thought processes we wish children to engage in are the same. The list of cognitive skills usually starts with strategies that require lower level thought processes and progresses to the more sophisticated. The lower level thinking strategies have been considered to be for younger, and the more sophisticated ones for older children. We have come to realize that, whether the child is an emergent or conventional reader, he or she can engage in many levels of thought from those considered lower level to the most sophisticated. They engage in these thought processes, however, at different levels of sophistication. The comprehension experiences we need to provide for young children are as follows:

1. Identify details, sequence events, follow directions, and find the main idea related to the text.
2. Classify ideas, visualize episodes, paraphrase or retell, and focus on structural elements of text.
3. Predict outcomes, make associations, relate story episodes to their life experiences and background knowledge.
4. Put themselves in the place of different characters to determine how they feel and what they would do, to try and determine characters' motives as well as the author's purpose.
5. Compare and contrast, analyze, draw conclusions, apply information in other settings, and problem solve.
6. Evaluate passages and evaluate their own understanding of the text.

Items 1 and 2 would be considered literal skills, 3 and 4 interpretive thought development, and 5 and 6 critical or higher level cognitive processing.

Developing Comprehension through the Use of Children's Literature

Children's literature is especially appropriate for developing a child's sense that print conveys meaning. The stories are attractive; they relate well to a child's real-life experiences; and they are typically well structured, containing clearly delineated settings, themes, plot episodes, and resolutions. Furthermore, the use of children's literature offers ample opportunity for developing comprehension or cognitive instructional strategies.

Children's literature is particularly appropriate for first experiences with books because it is likely that youngsters have had some exposure to this material. Children also need exposure to expository text. This material is usually nonfiction and conveys specific information to readers. We have spent a great deal of time dealing with narrative stories with young children. We must also include experiences with expository text as well.

The following pages will discuss strategies for comprehension development, which also include learning concepts about books and print. In these activities, children play active roles as they respond to literature in many different ways. I begin with an early experience for the emergent reader and continue with experiences that are appropriate for the emergent as well as the conventional reader.

Favorite Storybook Readings

To study emergent reading behaviors, Sulzby (1985) observed children from ages two to six attempt to read favorite storybooks. Although they were not yet readers in the conventional sense, the children were asked, "Read me your book." Sulzby found that, in their "reading," the children produced speech that could indeed be categorized as a first act of reading; that the speech they used as they "read" was clearly different in structure and intonation from their typical conversation; and that different developmental levels could be observed in these "oral readings."

From children's attempts at storybook reading, then, we can determine stages of development. Because the activity is developmental and leads to literacy, teachers should ask children to participate in it, either to evaluate their ability or simply to encourage their emergent literacy.

Sulzby's Simplified Classifications Scheme for Children's Emergent Reading of Favorite Storybooks is found in Figure 7.2.

◆ **FIGURE 7.2** *Emergent Reading Behaviors and Evaluation Form*

1. *Attending to Pictures but Not Forming Stories.* The child "reads" by labeling and commenting on the pictures in the book but does not "weave a story" across the pages.

    yes ☐   no ☐

2. *Attending to Pictures and Forming Oral Stories.* The child "reads" by following the pictures but weaves a story across the pages through wording and intonation like those of someone telling a story. Often, however, the listener too must see the pictures in order to understand the story the child is "reading."

    yes ☐   no ☐

3. *Attending to a Mix of Pictures, Reading, and Storytelling.* The child "reads" by looking at the pictures. The majority of the child's "reading" fluctuates between the oral intonation of a storyteller and that of a reader.

    yes ☐   no ☐

4. *Attending to Pictures but Forming Stories (Written-language-like).* The child "reads" by looking at the pictures. The child's speech sounds like reading, both in wording and intonation. The listener rarely needs to see the pictures in order to understand the story. With his or her eyes closed, the listener would think the child was reading print. The "reading" is similar to the story in print and sometimes follows it verbatim. There is some attention to print.

    yes ☐   no ☐

5. *Attending to Print.* This category has two divisions:
    a. The child reads the story mostly by attending to print but occasionally refers to pictures and reverts to storytelling.
    b. The child reads in a conventional manner.

    a ☐   b ☐

Adapted from Sulzby, 1987.

Directed Listening-Thinking and Reading-Thinking Activities

When children read themselves or are read to, there should always be a purpose that complements content-area learning or develops specific concepts about books or print. The format of the directed listening-thinking activity (DLTA) and the directed reading-thinking activity (DRTA) can be internalized with frequent use by the child and transferred when new material is presented (Anderson, Mason, & Shirley, 1984; Morrow, 1984; Stauffer, 1980). Whatever a DLTA's or DRTA's specific objective, its framework offers the listener or reader a direction and strategy for organizing and retrieving information from the text. In the following outline for *The Little Red Hen* (Izawa, 1968b), there are two main objectives: to emphasize the sequence of events and to involve children in making inferences and judgments from the text. The outline below follows a DLTA or DRTA format. With the DLTA, the child listens to the story; with the DRTA, the child reads the story.

A. *Prepare for Listening or Reading with Prequestions and Discussion*
1. Build a background by introducing the story: "Today I'm going to read a story (or, you will be reading a story) entitled *The Little Red Hen*. Let's look at the pictures to see if you can tell what the story is going to be about." Encourage children to respond as the pages of the book are turned. After they have offered their ideas say, "The story is about a hen who wants to bake some bread and asks her friends for some help."

2. Ask prequestions that build additional background that sets a purpose for listening or reading. Relate the questions to real-life experiences whenever possible: "Have you ever asked people for help? What kind of help? Did they help you? Has anyone ever asked you for help? What kind of help? Were you able to help the person? How? While I'm reading (or, while you are reading), try to decide if you think the little red hen did the right thing with her bread at the end of the story, and why. Try also to remember what happened first, second, third, and at the end of the story."

3. When the children have gained enough experience with your prequestions, you can ask them to think of their own: "Now that I've told you a little about the story, what do you want to find out when I read it to you (or, when you read it)?" When prequestioning, show the pictures in the book to the children as further preparation for their listening or reading.

B. *Reading the Story*
1. Be sure to show the children the pictures as you read the story. Stop a few times for reactions, comments, or questions from the children. If the children are reading the story, remind them to study the pictures. Model or scaffold

responses to guide them in their thinking, keeping in mind the objectives for this particular DLTA or DRTA: "Can you remember what help the little red hen has asked for so far? How have the other animals acted about giving help?" If the children do not respond, scaffold or model responses by changing questions to statements: "These animals aren't very helpful to the little red hen. Each time the hen asks for their help, the animals all answer, 'Not I.'" Also ask for children's predictions of what will happen next. If the children are reading silently, assign stopping points for discussion. If there is oral reading, stop only in a few places.

C. Have a Discussion after Reading

1. The postdiscussion should be guided by the objectives set for listening and reading: "What did the little red hen want help with first? second? and so on." Ask children to retell the story; retelling will demonstrate their knowledge of sequence. Allow children to use the pictures in the book to help them follow sequence. Finally, focus on the second goal, making inferences and judgments: "What would you have done if you were the little red hen? What lesson can we learn from this story?"

A DLTA or DRTA can have many different objectives. The framework, however, is always basically the same: (1) preparation for listening or reading—prequestions and discussion; (2) reading the story; and (3) discussion after the reading. All three steps are focused on the DLTA's or DRTA's specific objectives. A DLTA or DRTA can focus on literal responses (such as recall of facts and sequencing), inferential responses (such as interpreting characters' feelings, predicting outcomes, and relating the story to real-life experiences), and critical responses (such as evaluating, problem solving, and making judgments). It can focus on elements of story structure, such as setting (introduction, time, place, characters); theme (the goal or problem faced by the main character), plot episodes (events leading to solution of the problem or achievement of the goal), resolution (problem solution or goal achievement, story ending). It helps youngsters draw meaning from the print. Research has demonstrated that a DLTA can increase the story comprehension of young listeners (Morrow, 1984), just as a DRTA can increase the story comprehension of young readers (Baumann, 1992; Pearson, Hansen, & Gordon, 1979; Richards, 1979).

K-W-L

K-W-L is a cognitive strategy to enhance comprehension that is mainly used with expository text. It can, however, be adapted for use with stories and shares some similarities to a DRTA and a DLTA. **K-W-L** stands for *What We **Know**, What We **Want** To Know,* and *What We **Learned**.* With this technique students use prior knowledge to create interest about what is to be read. It helps to set a purpose for reading which directs thinking, and it encourages sharing of ideas. The K-W-L chart (Figure 7.3) is particularly useful when reading material for thematic instruction. The following are the steps involved in putting the strategy into practice. Before reading expository text:

1. Children brainstorm what they think they know about a topic. For example, if the book is about spiders a list of *What We **Know*** about spiders is created by the class.
2. Children then list questions about *What They **Want** To Know* as a result of reading the book about spiders.
3. After reading the text, children make a list of *What They **Learned*** about spiders.

Finally children might compare information from the text that they already knew before reading the text, what they learned as a result of reading the text, and what is still on the list of what they would like to learn because it was not included in the book.

Figure 7.3 is a chart for listing items generated in a ***K-W-L*** discussion.

Productive Discussions

Productive Discussions are necessary to help develop comprehension. Discussion includes talking about what is read or listened to with children interacting with each other as well as the teacher. Discussions must include more than a few words by those participating and include questions, clarification, explanations, predictions, and justifications. Discussion questions should reflect a teacher's interest in what children have to say and think rather than the correct answer. Questions should stimulate discussion and elicit responses that reflect what children

FIGURE 7.3 *K-W-L Chart*

Topic: _____

What We **K**now	What We **W**ant to Know	What We **L**earned

think and feel about what has been read. These questions are asking for an aesthetic response since children have to synthesize ideas, sensations, feelings, and images. The following questions will enable the child to give aesthetic responses:

- How did you feel about the story?
- What did this story mean to you?
- What questions do you have about the story?
- What did you learn from what you read?
- How will that information be useful to you?
- Do you agree with what the characters did in the story? Why? Why not? (Gambrell & Almasi, 1994).

The efferent stance is usually taken with expository text that offers content information. Some questions that will elicit efferent responses (Rosenblatt, 1988) include the following:

- How would you describe the central character?
- What idea did you find most interesting?
- What new ideas did you learn?
- How could you find out more about these ideas?
- If you talked to the author, what would you like to ask?

Small-Group and One-to-One Story Readings

The importance and benefits of reading to small groups and to individuals must not be overlooked. Too often considered impractical in school settings, one-to-one and small-group readings yield such tremendous benefits that they must be incorporated into school programs. The most striking benefit of one-to-one story readings at home is the interactive behavior it involves, along with the direct channels of information it gives the child. It also provides the adult with insight into what children already know and want to know. In one study (Morrow, 1988), it was determined that similar readings in a school setting had similar positive results with preschoolers from lower socioeconomic backgrounds, even though the youngsters had little previous experience interacting with adults. Teachers in the study practiced the same interactive behaviors identified by researchers who had studied home storybook readings (Applebee & Langer, 1983; Cochran-Smith, 1984; Heath, 1980; Roser & Martinez, 1985; Teale, 1981). These teacher behaviors included managing storybook reading by introducing the story and providing background information.

Frequent readings by teachers who followed these guidelines (see Figure 7.4) increased the number and complexity of the children's responses. The youngsters offered many questions and comments that focused on meaning. Initially, they labeled illustrations. Later, they gave increased attention to details, their comments and questions became interpretive and predictive, and they drew

◆ **FIGURE 7.4** *Guidelines for Teacher Behavior During Storybook Reading*

1. *Manage*
   a. Introduce story.
   b. Provide background information about the book.
   c. Redirect irrelevant discussion back to the story.

2. *Prompt Responses*
   a. Invite children to ask questions or comment throughout the story when there are natural places to stop.
   b. Scaffold responses for children to model if no responses are forthcoming. ("Those animals aren't very nice. They won't help the little red hen.")
   c. Relate responses to real-life experiences. ("I needed help when I was preparing a party, and my family shared the work. Did you ever ask for help and couldn't find anyone to give it to you? What happened?")
   d. When children do not respond, ask questions that require answers other than yes or no. ("What would you have done if you were the little red hen and no one helped you bake the bread?")

3. *Support and Inform*
   a. Answer questions as they are asked.
   b. React to comments.
   c. Relate your responses to real-life experiences.
   d. Provide positive reinforcement for children's responses.

From Morrow, 1988.

from their own experiences. They also began narrating—that is, "reading" or mouthing the story along with the teacher. As the program continued, some children focused on structural elements, remarking on titles, settings, characters, and story events. Eventually, after many readings, the children began to focus on print, questioning names of words, letters, or sounds. They also began to recognize letters and words and read them as they were able (Morrow, 1987). Compared with one-to-one readings, reading to small groups of children seems to encourage more and earlier responses. Children tend to repeat one another's remarks, and they are motivated to respond to and elaborate on what their peers have said.

The following segments from transcriptions of small-group story readings illustrate the various questions and comments children make when they are involved in the activity, and the wealth of knowledge and information they receive from the responding adult. The transcriptions also illustrate what the children already know and what their interests are, which helps us design instruction.

Story: *The Very Hungry Caterpillar* (Carle, 1970) (questions about a part of the book)

> *Jerry:* (pointing to the picture on the front of the book) Why does it have a picture on it?

Small-group storybook reading with the teacher encourages interesting responses and elaboration of text by children.

Teacher: The cover of the book has a picture on it so you will know what the story is about. Look at the picture. Can you tell me what the book is about?

Jerry: Ummm, I think that's a caterpillar. Is it about a caterpillar?

Teacher: You're right, very good. The book is about a caterpillar, and the name of the story is *The Very Hungry Caterpillar*. When you look at the pictures in a book, they help you find out what the words say.

Story: *Caps for Sale* (Slobodkina, 1947) (asks for a definition)

Teacher: I'm going to read a story today called *Caps for Sale*.

Jamie: What are caps?

Teacher: A cap is a little hat that you put on your head. See, there is a cap in the picture.

Jamie: I never knew that before. I knew about hats, but I never heard about caps.

Story: *Chicken Soup with Rice* (Sendak, 1962) (attends to print)

Chris: Wait, stop reading. Let me see this again. (He turns back to the page that talks about the month of June.) How come they're the same? (He refers to the words of *June* and *July.*)
Teacher: What do you mean?
Chris: Look at the letters, J–U, J–U . . . They look alike.
Teacher: Look more closely at the ends of the words. Are they the same?
Chris: Ohh, nooo, just the front part.

Story: *Caps for Sale* (Slobodkina, 1947) (predicts)

Colleen: I wonder why those monkeys took the caps?
Teacher: I don't know. Can you think why?
Colleen: Well, the peddler was sleeping and those monkeys looked at the caps, and maybe they think they're for them. Or, I know! Maybe they're cold so they want a cap.
Teacher: Those are good ideas, Colleen.

Story: *Madeline's Rescue* (Bemelmans, 1953) (relates to real-life experience)

Jamie: What's the policemen going to do?
Teacher: He's going to help Madeline. Policemen are nice; they always help us.
Jamie: Policemans aren't nice. See, my daddy beat up Dominic and the policeman came and took him away and put him in jail for no reason. And my Daddy cried. I don't like policemans. I don't think they are nice.

Segments such as these reveal children's understandings. Do their comments and questions relate to literal meanings? Do they raise interpretive and critical issues by associating the story with their own lives, make predictions of what will come next in a story, or express judgments about characters' actions? Do comments or questions relate to matters of print, such as names of letters, words, and sounds? The same types of questions and comments occur when small groups of children read together without the presence of a teacher. Recording and then analyzing one-to-one and small-group story readings reveal what children know and want to know (Morrow, 1987). The coding sheet (Figure 7.5, p. 206) aids such analysis.

Although whole-class readings are more practical and have tremendous value in simply exposing children to literature, the interactive behavior between adult and child in one-to-one readings and small-group readings does not occur in the large group setting. If we review transcripts of story readings in all three

◆ **FIGURE 7.5** *Coding Children's Responses During Story Readings*

Child's name _____ Date _____

Story _____

(Read one story to one child or a small group of children. Encourage the children to respond with questions and comments. Tape record the session. Transcribe or listen to the tape, noting each child's responses by placing checks in the appropriate categories. A category may receive more than one check, and a single response may be credited to more than one category. Total the number of checks in each category.)

1. Focus on story structure   _____
   a. setting (time, place)   _____
   b. characters   _____
   c. theme (problem or goal)   _____
   d. plot episodes (events leading toward problem solution
      or goal attainment)
   e. resolution   _____

2. Focus on meaning   _____
   a. labeling   _____
   b. detail   _____
   c. interpreting (associations, elaborations)   _____
   d. predicting   _____
   e. drawing from one's experience   _____
   f. seeking definitions of words   _____
   g. using narrational behavior (reciting parts of the book along
      with the teacher)

3. Focus on print   _____
   a. questions or comments about letters   _____
   b. questions or comments about sounds   _____
   c. questions or comments about words   _____
   d. reads words   _____
   e. reads sentences   _____

4. Focus on illustrations   _____
   a. responses and questions that are related to illustrations   _____

settings, several things become apparent. In whole-group settings, no one child can ask questions or comment repeatedly throughout the story without interfering with the story line for the other children. The teacher might never get through a coherent reading. Dialogue that does occur is managed by the teacher to such an extent that the teacher often says more than the children. A truly interactive situation does not exist due to the size of the group. In small-group and one-to-one readings, by contrast, a teacher may initially do a lot of managing and prompting, but only to encourage and model responses for children. In a short time the roles reverse: most dialogue is initiated by children through questions and comments, and the teacher offers positive reinforcement and answers questions posed by the children (Morrow, 1987).

Children who come from homes that do not offer them one-to-one readings are at a disadvantage in their literacy development. It is necessary to carry out such strategies in school to compensate for what is not provided at home as well as to provide the other benefits. Gains both in literacy skills and in positive attitudes toward books can occur. To learn to associate books with warmth and pleasure, children who have not had the benefit of the lap technique at home can experience it at school. It is difficult to provide one-to-one readings in school because of time limitations and the number of children, but asking aides, volunteers, and older children to do so helps solve the problem. So does reading to small groups of youngsters from time to time, perhaps replacing some of the traditional instruction in reading groups. Many school districts have federal funding for work with young children identified as having potential learning problems. Ratios in such programs may be as low as five children per teacher. Certainly those settings allow one-to-one readings as part of a literacy development program.

Shared Book Experiences

Shared book experiences (Holdaway, 1979) are usually a whole-group approach, although they may be carried out in small groups as well. In one way or another, they enable children to participate in the reading of a book. They also help develop listening skills, for children must listen attentively in order to participate.

Predictable stories are ideal for shared book experiences because they allow children to guess what will come next, thereby encouraging participation. Predictability takes many forms. The use of catch phrases, such as "'Not I,' said the dog," "'Not I,' said the cat," and so on, in *The Little Red Hen* (Izawa, 1968), encourages children to chant along. Predictable rhyme enables children to fill in words, as in *Green Eggs and Ham* (Seuss, 1960). Cumulative patterns contribute to predictability. New events are added with each episode, for example, then repeated at the next, as in *Drummer Hoff* (Emberley, 1967). *Are You My Mother?* (Eastman, 1960) repeats phrases and episode patterns as its central character, a baby bird, searches for his mother by approaching different animals and asking the same question. Conversation can contribute to predictability, as in *The Three Billy Goats Gruff* (Brown, 1957) or *The Three Little Pigs* (Brenner, 1972). All stories become predictable as children become familiar with them, so repeating stories builds up a repertoire for shared book experiences. Fairy tales are already familiar to most children and therefore often predictable to a group. Books that carry familiar sequences, such as days of the week, months of the year, letters, and numbers, are predictable—*The Very Hungry Caterpillar* (Carle, 1970), for instance. Books gain predictability through good plot structures and topics familiar to children. Books in which pictures match text page by page tend to be predictable to children, especially if everyone in the group can see the pictures as the story is being read.

Predictable books are excellent for emergent and conventional readers in shared book experiences as well as in independent reading. They allow the child's first experience with reading to be enjoyable and successful with minimal effort. Such immediate success encourages the child to continue efforts at reading. (A list of predictable books is provided in Appendix A.)

One shared book technique involves reading from a Big Book (Scholastic, 1986) or a similar book made by the class or the teacher. Such a book is designed

Shared book experiences involve the children in some way during the story reading. Often Big Books are used so that they can be seen easily by all and children can see the print as the teacher reads and points to it.

so that everyone in the group can see the pictures and the words of the story clearly while it is being read. If the book is a new one for the class, the children are asked to listen during the first reading. If it is being read for the second time or is otherwise already familiar, immediate participation is encouraged. Often the teacher uses a pointer during the reading to emphasize left-to-right progression and the correspondence of spoken and written words. The teacher encourages participation by stopping at predictable parts and asking children to fill in words and phrases. As the children become more and more familiar with the books, they begin to know them by memory, which enables the children to begin to associate words as they say them with the printed words the teacher points to on the page. Big Books and regular-size copies of the same book should be available for children to use independently after a first Big Book reading.

Shared book experiences can involve children in dramatizations of a story, art activities, or other extended experiences after the story has been read. Shared book experiences can be recorded and made available in the listening station. So can tapes of teachers' readings and commercially recorded tapes. These will provide fluent models with good phrasing and intonation for children to emulate. Shared book experiences can easily be adapted to the DLTA format, as long as it is emphasized that shared book experiences are to be pleasurable, relaxed, participatory, and enjoyable read-aloud events.

Repeated Story Readings

Children enjoy repetition, as we all do. Being familiar with an experience is comfortable, like singing a well-known song. Besides offering the pleasure of familiarity, a repeated story helps develop concepts about words, print, and books. One study (Morrow, 1987a) compared responses of two groups of four-year-olds. One group listened to three readings of each of three stories, the other group a different story at each of nine sessions. The repeated-reading group increased the number and kind of their responses, and their responses differed significantly from those of the different-story group. Their responses became more interpretive, and they began to predict outcomes and make associations, judgments, and elaborative comments.

They also began to narrate stories as the teacher read (their first attempts at reading) and to focus on elements of print, asking names of letters and words. Even children of low ability seem to make more responses with repeated readings than with a single reading (Roser & Martinez, 1985).

We can see that repeated readings are important to youngsters, because they engage in the activity frequently on their own. Children who are able to read themselves or engage in pretend reading behaviors will often select the same book to look at or read over and over again. This is an activity they obviously enjoy, and learn from and from which they experience success. In addition to repeated readings of stories by the teacher to the children, teachers should encourage youngsters to read stories more than once and carry out discussions about books that have been read and discussed previously.

The following dialogue is taken from a transcription of a child's responses to a third reading of *The Little Red Hen*. For the sake of brevity, this excerpt includes primarily the child's comments and questions and the teacher's responses; most of the story text has been omitted.

Teacher: Today I'm going to read the story, *The Little Red Hen*. It is about a hen who wanted some help when she baked some bread. (The teacher begins to read the story.)...Who will help me to cut this wheat?

Melony: "Not I," said the cat. "Not I," said the dog. "Not I," said the mouse.

Teacher: That was good, Melony. You are reading. (The teacher continues reading.)...Who will take this wheat to the mill to be ground into flour?

Melony: "Not I," said the cat. "Not I," said the dog. "Not I," said the mouse with the whiskers.

Teacher: Very nice, Melony. (The teacher continues to read.)

Melony: I want to read that part, but I don't know how.

Teacher: Go ahead and try. I bet you can. I'll help you: The cat smelled it.

Melony: The cat smelled it and she said *umm* that smells good, and the mouse smelled it, and it smelled good.

Teacher: (continuing reading)...Who will eat this cake?

Melony: The mouse, the doggy, the kitty!

Teacher: You're right again, Melony. (The teacher reads to the end of the story.) Did you want to say anything else about the story?

Melony: He was bad so he couldn't have no cake. (Melony searches through the pages.) That's the wrong part.

Teacher: Show me the part you are talking about.

Melony: There it is, almost at the end. She's going to make a cake and she'll say who's going to bake this cake for me. And the cat says, "Not I," the dog says, "Not I," the mouse says, "Not I." And then when she's cooking it they smell a good thing and then they wanted some, too, but they didn't have any, 'cause they didn't plant the wheat.

Teacher: You're so right. They didn't help do the work, so they didn't get to eat the cake.

Melony: Where does it say "Not I"? Show me the words in the book.

Teacher: Here it is. Can you find it again?

Melony: (flipping through the pages) I'm looking for where she bakes the cake. Here it is. Yea. And he smelled it. And he smelled it. And the mouse smelled it. (She turns pages.) They're going in the kitchen. And she said, "All by myself, I cut the wheat. All by myself, I took it to the mill to get it into flour. All by myself I baked the cake. All by myself I'm going to eat it."

Teacher: That's terrific, Melony. That's what the hen said.

Melony: (pointing to the dog) The dog was not happy. Where does it say *dog?*

Teacher: You're right. He doesn't look happy. Here is where it says dog (pointing).

Melony: There's the word, *dog, dog, dog.* How does that dog look?

Teacher: He looks hungry and mad because he can't have any bread.

Melony: You're right. But it's his fault. He didn't help. And that's the end. (Morrow, 1987)

Besides illustrating the value of repeated readings in the responses generated by the child, this exchange demonstrates the encouragement, reinforcement, and rapport that can evolve from one-to-one storybook sessions.

Story Retelling and Rewriting

Letting a listener or reader retell or rewrite a story offers active participation in a literacy experience that helps a child develop language structures, comprehension, and sense of story structure (Morrow, 1985b). Retelling, whether it is oral or written, engages the child in holistic comprehension and organization of thought. It also allows for personalization of thinking as children mesh their own life experiences into their retelling. Retelling contrasts with the more traditional piecemeal approach of teacher-posed questions that require a child to recall bits of information (Gambrell, Pfeiffer, & Wilson, 1985). With practice in retelling, children come to assimilate the concept of story structure. They learn to introduce a story with its beginning and its setting. They recount its theme, plot episodes, and resolution. In retelling stories, children demonstrate their comprehension of story details and sequence, organizing them coherently. They also infer and interpret the sounds and expressions of characters' voices.

Retelling is not an easy task for children, but with practice they improve quickly. To help children develop the practice of retelling, tell them before they read or listen to a text or story that they will be asked to retell or rewrite it (Morrow, 1985b). Further guidance depends on the teacher's specific purpose in the retelling. If the immediate intent is to teach or test sequence, for instance, the children should be instructed to concentrate on what happened first, second, and so on. If the goal is to teach or assess the ability to integrate information and make inferences from text, children should be instructed to think of things that have happened to them like those that happen to characters in the story. Props such as felt-board characters or the pictures in the text itself can be used to help the students retell the story. Pre- and postdiscussion of the story help to improve retelling ability, as does the teacher's modeling a retelling for children (Mitchell, 1984; Morrow, 1985). The procedure in Figure 7.6 is helpful in guiding a child's oral or written retelling. With written retellings, teachers may prefer to have the child write the entire piece first and then conference with him or her afterward.

◆ **FIGURE 7.6** *Guiding Story Retelling*

1. Ask the child to retell the story. "A little while ago, I read the story [name the story]. Would you retell the story as if you were telling it to a friend who has never heard it before?"

2. Use the following prompts only if needed:
   a. If the child has difficulty beginning the retelling, suggest beginning with "Once upon a time," or "Once there was . . ."
   b. If the child stops retelling before the end of the story, encourage continuation by asking, "What comes next?" or "Then what happened?"
   c. If the child stops retelling and cannot continue with general prompts, ask a question that is relevant at the point in the story at which the child has paused. For example, "What was Jenny's problem in the story?"

3. When a child is unable to retell the story, or if the retelling lacks sequence and detail, prompt the retelling step by step. For example:
   a. "Once upon a time," or "Once there was . . ."
   b. "Who was the story about?"
   c. "When did the story happen?" (day, night, summer, winter?)
   d. "Where did the story happen?"
   e. "What was [the main character's] problem in the story?"
   f. "How did [he or she] try to solve the problem? What did [he or she] do first [second, next]?"
   g. "How was the problem solved?"
   h. "How did the story end?" (Morrow, 1985, p. 659)

Retellings can be used to develop many types of comprehension. The prompts should match the goals. In addition to its usefulness as a learning technique, retelling also allows adults to evaluate children's progress. If you plan to evaluate a retelling, let the child know during your introduction of the story you are about to read that he or she will be asked to retell it after the reading. During the evaluative retellings, do *not* offer prompts beyond general ones such as "Then what happened?" or "Can you think of anything else about the story?" Retellings commonly reveal a child's sense of story structure, focusing mostly on literal recall, but they also reflect the child's inferential and critical thinking ability. To assess the child's retelling for sense of story structure, the examiner should first parse (divide) the events of the story into four categories—*setting, theme, plot episodes,* and *resolution.* A guide sheet and the outline of the parsed text are then used to record the number of ideas and details the child includes within each category in the retelling, regardless of their order. *Do* credit a child for partial recall or for recounting the "gist" of a story event (Pellegrini & Galda, 1982; Thorndyke, 1977). Evaluate the child's sequencing ability by comparing the order of events in the child's retelling with the proper order of setting, theme, plot episodes, and resolution. The analysis indicates not only which elements a child includes or omits and how well a child sequences, but also where instruction might be focused. Comparing analyses of several retellings over a year will indicate a child's progress.

The following example uses a parsed outline of *Jenny Learns a Lesson* (Fujikawa, 1980). The story is about a little girl who likes to play "pretend games" with her friends. However, when her friends come to play, Jenny becomes bossy and tells everyone what to do, and her friends leave angry. After several such episodes, her friends leave and do not return. Jenny becomes lonesome and realizes her problem. She apologizes to her friends, invites them back to play, and promises not to boss them. They agree to play, and this time all do as they wish. The following parsed outline is accompanied by transcriptions of two children's retellings of the story. A retelling guidesheet follows with a quantitative analysis of the first transcription told by Beth (Morrow, 1985).

Parsed Story

Setting
a. Once upon a time there was a girl who liked to play pretend.
b. Characters: Jenny (main character), Nicholas, Sam, Mei Su, and Shags, the dog.

Theme
Every time Jenny played with her friends, she bossed them.

Plot Episodes
First episode: Jenny decided to pretend to be a queen. She called her friends. They came to play. Jenny told them all what to do and was bossy. The friends became angry and left.

Second episode: Jenny decided to play dancer. She called her friends and they came to play. Jenny told them all what to do. The friends became angry and left.

Third episode: Jenny decided to play pirate. She called her friends and they came to play. Jenny told them all what to do. The friends became angry and left.

Fourth episode: Jenny decided to play duchess. She called her friends and they came to play. Jenny told them all what to do. The friends became angry and left.

Fifth episode: Jenny's friends refused to play with her because she was so bossy. Jenny became lonely and apologized to them for being bossy.

Resolution
a. The friends all played together and each person did what he or she wanted to do.
b. They all had a wonderful day and were so tired that they fell asleep.

Verbatim Transcriptions

(Beth, age five) Once upon a time there's a girl named Jenny and she called her friends over and they played queen and went to the palace. They had to...they had to do what she said and they didn't like it so then they went home and said that was boring. It's not fun playing queen and doing what she says you have to. So they didn't play with her for seven days and she had...she had an idea that she was being selfish, so she went to find her friends and said, I'm sorry I was so mean. And said, let's play pirate, and they played pirate and they went onto the ropes. Then they played that she was a fancy lady playing house. And they have tea. And they played what they wanted and they were happy. The end.

A retelling by five-year-old Beth when she was in the first part of her kindergarten year was just presented. To demonstrate how retellings can become more sophisticated and improve with practice and time, another retelling by this same child when she was at the end of her kindergarten year follows. The story is called *Under the Lemon Tree*. It is about a donkey who lives under a lemon tree on the farm and watches out for all the other animals. A fox comes in the night to steal a chicken or duck and the donkey hee-haws loudly to protect them. He succeeds in scaring the fox away and in addition wakes the farmer and his wife who never see the fox. This happens frequently until the farmer can no longer take the noise and moves the donkey to a tree far from the farm house where he is very unhappy. The fox comes back and steals the farmer's prize red rooster. The other animals quack and cluck and finally wake up the farmer who chases after the fox. When the fox passes him, the donkey makes his loud noises again, frightening the fox, who drops the red rooster. The farmer realizes that the donkey has been protecting his animals and moves him back to the lemon tree where he is happy again.

Here is six-year-old Beth's retelling of *Under the Lemon Tree:*

Once upon a time there was a donkey, and he was in a farm. He lived under a lemon tree close to the animals on the farm. In the morning all the bees buzzed in the flowers under the lemon tree. He was next to the ducks, the chickens, and the roosters. It was night time. The red fox came into the farm to get something to eat. The donkey went "Hee-Haw, Hee-Haw" and then the chickens went "cluck, cluck" and the ducks went "quack-quack."...Then the farmer and his wife waked up and looked out the window and saw nothing. They didn't know what came into their farm that night. They said, "What a noisy donkey we have. When it gets dark we will bring him far away." So when it get darker and darker they brang the donkey over to a fig tree. And he had to stay there. He couldn't go to sleep alone. That night the red fox came into the farm again to try and get something to eat. All the ducks went quack-quack and the turkeys went gobble-gobble. The farmer and his wife woke up and said, "Is that noisy donkey back again?" They rushed to the window and saw the fox with their red

◆ **FIGURE 7.7** *Story Retelling and Rewriting Evaluation Guide Sheet:*
A Quantitative Analysis

Child's Name _____ Beth _____ Age _____ 5 _____

Title of Story _____ Jenny Learns a Lesson _____ Date _____

General directions: Give 1 point for each element included as well as for "gist." Give 1 point for
each character named as well as for such words as *boy, girl,* or *dog.* Credit plurals (friends, for
instance) with 2 points under characters.

Sense of Story Structure

Setting
a. Begins story with an introduction 1
b. Names main character 1
c. Number of other characters named 2
d. Actual number of other characters 4
e. Score for "other characters" (c/d): 5
f. Includes statement about time or place 1

Theme
Refers to main character's primary goal or problem to be solved 1

Plot Episodes
a. Number of episodes recalled 4
b. Number of episodes in story 5
c. Score for "plot episodes" (a/b) 8

Resolution
a. Names problem solution/goal attainment 1
b. Ends story 1

Sequence
Retells story in structural order: setting, theme, plot episodes, resolution.
(Score 2 for proper, 1 for partial, 0 for no sequence evident.) 1

Highest score possible: _____ 10 _____   Child's score _____ 8.3 _____

From Morrow, 1988.

rooster in his mouth and yelled, "Stop thief, come back." The fox passed
the donkey and shouted "hee-haw, hee-haw." The red fox heard it and
dropped the rooster and ran away. The farmer and his wife said, "Aren't we
lucky to have the noisiest donkey in the whole world." And they picked up
the rooster and put one hand around the donkey and they all went home
together and tied the donkey under the lemon tree.

Retellings can be evaluated for many different comprehension tasks. The
directions to students prior to retelling and the method of analysis should match
the goal. Figure 7.8 provides an analysis form for evaluating oral and written

◆ **FIGURE 7.8** *A Qualitative Analysis of Story Retelling and Rewriting*

Name_____ Date_____

Name of Story_____

	Yes	No
Setting		
a. Begins story with an introduction	☐	☐
b. Names main character	☐	☐
c. List other characters named here: _____		
_____		
d. Includes statement about time and place	☐	☐
Theme		
a. Refers to main character's primary goal or problem to be solved	☐	☐
Plot Episodes		
a. Episodes are recalled	☐	☐
b. List episodes recalled	☐	☐
Resolution		
a. Includes the solution to the problem or the attainment of the goal	☐	☐
b. Puts an ending on the story	☐	☐
Sequence		
a. Story is told in sequential order	☐	☐

Interpretive and Critical Comments: Read through the retelling or rewriting and list comments made or written by students that are of an interpretive or critical nature.

retellings in which checks are used instead of numbers for a general sense of elements children include and to determine progress over time. Also provided in that form is a qualitative evaluation of interpretive and critical responses. Figure 7.9 provides a student evaluation form for oral and written retellings. Self-evaluation with a teacher, with a child, or alone is a crucial part of the learning process.

Webbing and Mapping

Webbing and mapping are graphic presentations for categorizing and structuring information. The strategy builds on a child's prior knowledge and makes children become active in the reading process. It helps the child to retrieve what is known about a topic, expand his or her knowledge, and use the information in reading and listening to text.

◆ **FIGURE 7.9** *Student Oral or Written Retelling Evaluation Form*

Name_____ Date_____

Name of Story _____

	Yes	No
Setting		
a. I began the story with an introduction.	☐	☐
b. I talked about the main character.	☐	☐
c. I talked about other characters.	☐	☐
d. I told when the story happened.	☐	☐
e. I told where the story happened.	☐	☐
Theme		
I told about the problem in the story or the main goal of the characters.	☐	☐
Plot Episodes		
a. I included episodes in the story.	☐	☐
Resolution		
a. I told how the problem was solved or goal achieved.	☐	☐
b. I had an ending on the story.	☐	☐
Sequence		
My story was retold or rewritten in proper order.	☐	☐

Comments for Improvement:
Next time I need to include in my retelling:

Webs and maps are diagrams that help students see how words and ideas are related to one another. They are visual representations of the relationships among ideas underlying a concept. Research has demonstrated that the use of webbing and mapping strategies is successful in the development of vocabulary and comprehension. This research has also demonstrated the effectiveness of the strategy with poor readers and minority and bilingual children (Karbon, 1984; Pittelman, Levin, & Johnson, 1985).

Webs and maps are virtually the same thing. Webs tend to be drawn using a spider-like effect, and maps may have boxes with labels in them that connect in different places.

When used to develop vocabulary concepts and definitions related to a word, the word is written on the board or chart paper. Children are asked to brainstorm ideas related to the word. For example, after reading *The Snowy Day* by Ezra Jack Keats, the teacher asks the children to provide words that describe what snow is like. The word *snow* is written in the center of the chart or chalkboard and the words given by the children are attached to it. A sample of a snow web done by a kindergarten class is shown in Figure 7.10.

Another web about the same story could generate the things that Peter did in the snow in the story and then other things that we can do in the snow. Figure 7.11 is such a web done by a first-grade class.

A map provides a different format for graphically presenting materials before and after listening to or reading a book. Maps deal with more complex representations; therefore, boxes for different categories are needed to present the ideas graphically. Story structures can be mapped to help children learn about the structural elements in the text. Sequence of events can be mapped as well or studies of individual characters. Figure 7.12 is a map of the story *Mr. Rabbit and the Lovely Present* created by a second-grade class. The map illustrates the structural elements in the story.

Collaborative Strategies for Children to Enhance Comprehension

Many strategies for enhancing comprehension have been described. Some are done in whole group, small group, or one-to-one settings with the teacher. The next set of strategies are for children to participate in with other students independent of the teacher. The strategies require teacher modeling before young children are able to participate in them with peers; therefore, they are introduced in teacher-directed settings first. A brief description of each follows.

Literature Circles

Literature circles are formed for children to discuss books they have read with each other. Children can discuss the same book or different stories. Teachers need to model literature circle activities so they can be carried out successfully.

◆ **FIGURE 7.10** *A Web for Expanding Vocabulary*

◆ **FIGURE 7.11** *A Web for Expanding Ideas*

With young children, literature circles will be more successful if topics are raised for discussion, such as telling the parts of your story you liked best, the parts of the story you did not like, and how you might have ended the story if you were the author.

Buddy Reading

Buddy reading is usually a situation in which a child from an upper grade is paired with a child in kindergarten, or first or second grade. The child in the upper grade is given instruction concerning how to read to children. At specified times during the school week, buddies get together for storybook reading.

Partner Reading

Partner reading involves peers reading together. This may simply mean that the children take turns reading to each other, or that they read sitting side by side.

◆ **FIGURE 7.12** *A Story Structure Map*

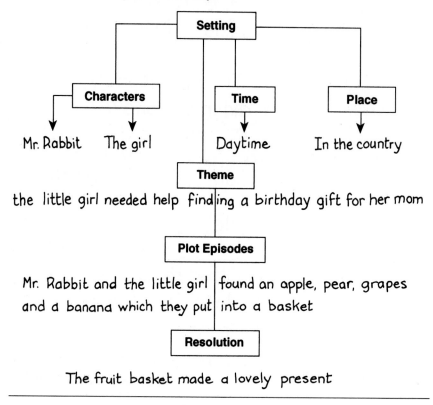

Teachers can structure partner reading similar to literature circles with topics posed for partners to discuss after reading to each other. .

Think, Pair, Share

This strategy involves teacher posed questions, which students are asked to *think* about prior to answering. Students are then *paired* with peers to discuss their answers to the questions. They then come back to a larger group to *share* the answers they have discussed among themselves (Gambrell and Almasi, 1994).

Mental Imagery and Thinkalouds

Mental imagery and thinkalouds involve children in several strategies, alone, together, and with and without the teacher. Mental imagery asks children to visualize what they see after they have been read to or read a passage themselves. We ask children to "Make a picture in your minds to help you to remember and understand what you read or what was read to you." After the mental imagery, we ask children to "thinkaloud" and talk about their images to peers or to the teacher. We also ask children to predict what will happen next in the story. We ask children to ask themselves questions about the story, and to reread when they need to clarify ideas, or remember forgotten details. We often ask them to personalize the text by asking them if they have ever been in a similar situation as the main character and what did they do. Visualizing ideas, and relating those visualizations orally, helps to clarify information and increase understanding (Gambrell & Jawitz, 1993; Brown & Lytle, 1988).

In this chapter, several strategies have been discussed for developing concepts about books and comprehension of text. The strategies are appropriate for both emergent and conventional readers. Most of them can be used with children aged two through eight; however, it is the manner in which they are implemented and the children's literature used that will determine the appropriate age group. With younger children, the teacher will have to do more modeling of strategies with the children. In grades one, two, and three, children are able to participate in some of them in a more independent manner.

Strategies such as the DLTA and DRTA are appropriate with all ages. It is the objectives set for them that will make the difference. Whole-group, small-group, and one-to-one literature sessions are active procedures for preschool through third grade. Shared book experiences, in which the group participates in the story reading as well as repeated readings of books, are appropriate for all early childhood youngsters. Story retellings are one of the most effective procedures for developing comprehension skills and take many forms for children two through eight. There are oral or written retellings, retellings through dramatic role-playing organized by the children, puppet shows, roll movies, chalk talk, and felt-story presentations. When children engage in these types of retellings, they must know the setting, theme, plot episodes, resolution, and story sequence. They infer how characters feel, sound, and act as they take their parts in role-playing stories. They make judgments and decisions about the responsibilities of everyone participating to make the best presentation. With all of these strategies for comprehension development, including mapping, webbing, literature circles, buddy reading, partner reading, think-pair-share, mental imagery, thinkalouds, and discussions, children are active participants in their learning without the teacher's having to ask the typical comprehension questions, such as "How many pigs are in the story?" or "Which house did the wolf go to first, second, and third?" Children demonstrate knowledge as they are actively engaged in the strategies previously discussed. They can engage in them whether in preschool or third grade—the difference is the sophistication of their involvement and the children's literature that is used.

Comprehension Strategies with Special Needs Children

Because many comprehension experiences involve the use of oral language, they are helpful in improving an ESL child's facility with English. The variety of strategies from which children and teachers can choose will accommodate different learning styles of students with learning difficulties. The participation required when involved in the activities discussed also addresses the special needs of children.

Authentic Assessment of Children's Concepts about Books and Comprehension of Text

The techniques described in this chapter are designed to develop concepts about books and comprehension of story through the use of children's literature. These skills listed in the Checklist for Assessing Concepts about Books and Comprehension of Text (p. 223) can be developed and assessed by a broad range of techniques used in various contexts. To determine how much children know about books, such as their front, back, top, and bottom; which part is print and which parts are pictures; how pages are turned; where reading begins; and what titles, authors, and illustrators are, one can observe regularly how youngsters handle books; hold one-to-one interviews with children; question and encourage response in whole-group, small-group, or individual interaction; or use any of the several other techniques described in this chapter. Children's responses can be literal, interpretive, or critical. They can reflect simple recall, detail, sequence, association, prediction, judgment, and evaluation. Children's comprehension of story can be demonstrated and evaluated through their story retelling, story rewriting, attempted reading of favorite storybooks, role-playing, picture sequencing, use of puppets or felt-boards to reenact stories, and their questions and comments during storybook reading. When possible, keep periodic performance samples of activities, such as a story rewriting and audio- or videotapes of retellings.

Throughout this chapter, assessment tools for evaluating strategies have been provided. These materials should be placed in a child's portfolio to evaluate their concepts about books and comprehension of text.

Checklist for Assessing Concepts about Books and Comprehension of Text

◆ **Concepts about Books**

	Always	Sometimes	Never
Knows a book is for reading			
Can identify the front, back, top, and bottom of a book			
Can turn the pages properly			

	Always	Sometimes	Never
Knows the difference between the print and the pictures			
Knows that pictures on a page are related to what the print says			
Knows where to begin reading			
Knows what a title is			
Knows what an author is			
Knows what an illustrator is			

◆ *Comprehension of Text*

	Always	Sometimes	Never
Attempts to read storybooks resulting in well-formed stories			
Participation in story reading by narrating as the teacher reads			
Retells stories			
Includes story structure elements in story retellings:			
Setting			
Theme			
Plot Episodes			
Resolution			
Responds to text after reading or listening with literal comments or questions			
Responds to text after reading or listening with interpretive comments or questions			
Responds to text after reading or listening with critical comments or questions			

◆ *Participates and Responds During:*

	Always	Sometimes	Never
Partner Reading			
Buddy Reading			
Literature Circles			
Mental Imagery			
Thinkalouds			
Discussions			
Think-Pair-Square			

An Idea for the Classroom from the Classroom

The following experience was created by a second-grade teacher in an inner-city school. You may find it useful for your teaching.

◆ Acting Out Stories Demonstrates Comprehension

The experience was motivated by students' interest to create costumes they discovered in a craft book. I was quick to seize the opportunity to attach my youngsters' desire to design costumes and integrate it with a literature selection that I thought would work into a dramatization of a play. I had a collection of T. S. Eliot's poems in a picture storybook format. I decided to read *Growl Tiger's Last Stand* to them and suggested that this might be a poem they could create costumes for and act out because there were several unusual characters. Some of the vocabulary in the poem was difficult for the children, and as I read, I needed to stop occasionally to discuss the meaning of certain words. The children became very engrossed when I read that the tiger was missing an ear and an eye. The children were sprawled on the floor listening, and they drew closer to me to see the pictures more clearly as the story ended.

Immediately following the story, two boys (Yassin and James) took the lead in motivating the rest of the class to act out the poem and make costumes. The children flipped through the pages in order to reread certain lines so that costumes would be accurate. Roseangela decided that Lady Grittlebone must have gloves because this was a ladylike thing to do. There was a long discussion of how to make a costume for Growl Tiger who was missing an eye and an ear. A patch on one eye would be good for depicting the missing eye, but they couldn't figure out what to do about the ear.

During all of this, I was close at hand to facilitate ideas when necessary, or get the children back on track to help them accomplish their goal. Costumes were made and the poem dramatized. In this activity, I drew from the spontaneous interests of my children and created an experience that involved them in demonstrating literal, inferential, and critical comprehension skills. Youngsters had to know the details of the story to act it out and create costumes. They made many inferences about how the characters should act and sound. They engaged in critical thinking as they discussed costumes, roles, and scenery.

Following the project, David and Tamika became involved in a lively debate about whether T. S. Eliot was a boy or a girl. Obviously these youngsters were very much aware of the concept of author and had an interest in it as well.

This classroom experience is an example of one in which I utilized the interests of my children to create a learning experience. This was a comprehension activity in which youngsters were actively engaged, instead of a testing-type question-and-answer session without real child involvement.

Tammye Pelovitz, Second-grade Teacher
McKinley School, New Brunswick, NJ, Public Schools

Activities and Questions

1. Answer the focus questions at the beginning of the chapter.

2. Ask a two-, four-, and six-year-old to read their favorite stories using a story-book. Describe the reading behaviors they attempt. Are developmental differences evident among their performances?

3. Select a child between the ages of three and eight. Meet with the child three-to-five times, each time letting the child practice retelling a story. Tape and transcribe each session. Using the guidesheet provided in this chapter, analyze the tapes for the elements of story structure, details, sequence, and so on that the child includes in retelling. Are there developmental changes in the child's performance from session to session? Have the child evaluate their story retelling and rewriting with the student evaluation form provided in this chapter.

4. Select a piece of children's literature and prepare three literal, three interpretive, and three critical comprehension thinking questions to test a child's knowledge of that story. Now take those questions and change them into activities (such as role-playing stories or creating chalk talks or felt stories) that enable the children to demonstrate their comprehension of the story.

5. Prepare two different directed listening-thinking and directed reading-thinking activities, including pre- and postdiscussions. Select different objectives for each DLTA or DRTA. Use your plans with small groups of children.

6. Use other comprehension strategies discussed in the chapter and create a lesson accompanying the activity with a piece of children's literature you select. Use both expository and narrative texts.

7. Continue your portfolio assessment for the child you selected to assess for language development in Chapter 4. Observe the child using the assessment checklist provided in this chapter concerning the evaluation of concepts about books, comprehension of text, and other measures provided.

8. Continue the thematic unit that you began in Chapter 4. Select three objectives in the area of concepts about books and three in comprehension of text and describe three activities that will satisfy each of the objectives using your theme.

Case Study Activities

◆ *Case 1*

Two first-grade teachers have come to you as the reading specialist in the district for help with students who have limited English proficiency. You are concerned about improving their ability in English and are also aware that they must learn about book concepts and strategies for comprehending text as well. You prepare a workshop to share strategies to help these teachers with these youngsters. You have decided to use children's literature as a resource. Describe the strategies you will be sharing with the teachers.

◆ Case 2

The following passages describe reading lessons taught by three different second-grade teachers. While reading these passages think about the following questions:

1. Do the questions posed by the teachers foster factual or interpretive thought?
2. Is there an emphasis on specifics or understanding of issues raised?
3. Is the plan flexible or predetermined?
4. Is there time for problem solving, looking for the unknown, a disorder period?
5. Is the atmosphere constricted, controlled, supportive, warm, rewarding?
6. Can children raise questions?
7. Are students asked to predict and analyze?
8. Is there an emphasis on higher order thinking or literal levels of thought?

Read Teachers A and B and then answer the questions. If you had to select just one of these teachers, which one would you choose and why. After answering the questions, read Teacher C and then go back and answer all the questions again.

TEACHER A: READING LESSON #1

The teacher begins her lesson by announcing that the class will be reading the story *Goldilocks and the Three Bears.* She introduces new vocabulary from the story such as porridge and middle by writing them on the chalkboard. The story is read orally by the students as the teacher calls on different children. To check their comprehension, the teacher stops after each child reads and asks factual questions about the text such as: Who are the main characters in the story? and What did Goldilocks do first when she got to the bears' house? Similar questions are asked all the way through the passage. Occasionally, the teacher will stop to emphasize the structure or spelling of a word. Throughout the story, the teacher pauses to discuss the pictures. Again, she asks very specific detail questions such as: Who is in the picture?

After reading the story, the children are given a worksheet to complete at their desks. The worksheet is designed to reinforce the details of the story and enhance vocabulary. It includes questions that require the children to circle the correct answer. When the children are finished with the worksheet, the lesson is over.

TEACHER B: READING LESSON #2

Teacher B begins her lesson by asking the students to share things they have done that they knew were wrong. After the children describe their experiences,

Teacher B asks why they did these things. She then tells the children that they are going to read the story *Goldilocks and the Three Bears*. Before reading, she has the children look at the pictures in the book to predict what the story is about. The teacher asks the class to think about who does bad things in the story while they read. The class is then asked to read the story silently from beginning to end. Afterward, the teacher asks questions designed to elicit information about the student's comprehension of the story theme by asking: What are the main events in the story? Who are the good characters and who are the bad ones, and why? Why were they good or bad? Was it okay for Goldilocks to go in the bears' house uninvited? Why yes or why no? Children are asked to discuss favorite parts of the story and read these parts to the class. A discussion follows about the illustrations in the book. Are the pictures important to the story? Do they help tell parts of the story?

The teacher asks the students what types of extended activities they would like to do related to the story, for example, draw a picture or make a felt story. The children decide to act out the story. The teacher helps the children to discuss what the major scenes are and who the main characters are. The children volunteer for roles. They follow the content of the story, but without using the book. The children act out the scenes spontaneously. The class is asked to return to their seats, illustrate their favorite part of the story, and rewrite it in their own words.

Reminder: **Answer the questions posed at the beginning of the case study activity and then read Teacher C.**

TEACHER C: READING LESSON #3

Teacher C begins her lesson by asking the students if they have any special personal things. She asks how they might feel if someone came and took their personal things without asking or used them and ruined them. She introduces the story *Goldilocks and the Three Bears* and asks the class to read the book silently and determine how Goldilocks intruded on the bears' personal things. She asks the class to discuss how they think the bears felt when they got home and found someone had been in their house. All suggestions are accepted as the teacher explains that there are no right or wrong answers here. It is the judgments of the class regarding the situation that are of interest. Students select favorite parts of the story, which are reread and discussed in terms of content and style. Illustrations are discussed in terms of what feelings are being portrayed in the pictures.

Rather than dramatize the story as it is written, the class is asked to create an entirely new story about Goldilocks and the three bears or a new ending for the story. The teacher allows the children to decide with which students they would like to work. In small groups they create their new scenes independent of the teacher, and then act them out for the class. When all groups have made their presentations, the scenes are discussed.

Now answer the questions at the beginning of this case study activity for Teacher C and decide which teacher you would like to be now that you have read Teachers A, B and C. Support your answer.

Chapter 8

Developing Reading through Learning about Print

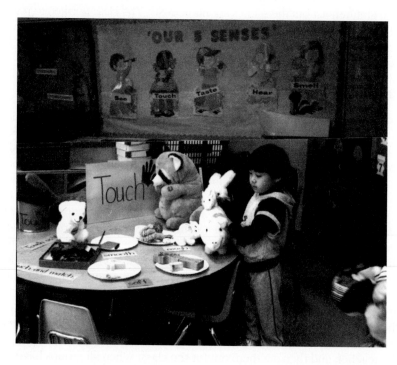

Label the room with words representing topics of study.

First words must have an intense meaning.
First words must be already part of the dynamic life.
First books must be made of the stuff of the child himself,
whatever and wherever the child.

—Sylvia Ashton-Warner
Teacher

Questions To Focus On As You Read

◆ What are the concepts about print that are important for a young child to know?

◆ Define and describe how the use of the following strategies enhances a child's knowledge about print: (1) environmental print, (2) very own words, (3) language experience approach, and (4) context and picture clues.

◆ Define the following terms: (1) alphabetic understanding, (2) phonemic awareness, (3) phoneme–grapheme correspondence, (4) cryptanalytic intent, (5) digraphs, (6) consonant blends, (7) long and short vowel sounds, (8) hard and soft consonant sounds, and (9) phonics.

◆ Describe the characteristics of commercially prepared basal materials designed for literacy instruction.

Mrs. Satterwhite's class was studying nutrition. The dramatic-play area was set up like a supermarket with products displayed separately into food groups. There were the dairy products; breads and cereals; meat, poultry, and fish; and fruits and vegetables. To connect the learning of sound–symbol relationships and letter names with the unit, three letters were featured: *m* for meat, *f* for fish, and *d* for dairy. In addition to creating nonsense stories using the featured letters such as *Fanny the Fish was a Friendly Flounder who liked to Flip her Flippers as she Fluttered through the waves,* the children collected things that began with the featured letters and placed them in boxes labeled with the appropriate symbol. These experiences caused them to talk about letters, sounds, and words in spontaneous play. Kathy and Kelly were pretending that they were shopping in the dramatic-play store. Kathy picked up a can of tuna fish and said, "Kelly, let's see how many foods we can find that begin with the letter *F.*" They looked around and Kathy found a box of Frosted Flakes and some French Fries. Kelly found a can of Fruit Cocktail, Froot Loops cereal, and a container of Frozen Yogurt. The girls were excited when each found some food that began with the letter *f.* They said the word with a strong emphasis on the beginning *f* sound. They each decided to take a piece of paper and copy the names of the food that began with *f.* They decided to do the same thing for the other featured letters in the unit, *m* for meat and *d* for dairy.

Word Analysis Skills and Their Importance

The role that word analysis skill development plays in literacy instruction is being reevaluated. Word analysis skills, or knowledge about print, involve learning strategies that will help children become independent readers. Word analysis skills include the use of context and syntax to figure out an unknown word, the development of a sight vocabulary, the use of configuration or the shape of a word, structural analysis (attending to different parts of words such as prefixes, suffixes, or the root to decode), and the use of phonics that involves the learning of letter and combinations of letter sounds (referred to as *phonemes*) associated with their corresponding letter symbols (referred to as *graphemes*). One of the main problems with phonics is that the English alphabet has at least forty-four different sounds, and sound–symbol correspondence is not consistent—there are many irregularities and exceptions to most rules. Phonics is but one method for decoding and recognizing words. The purpose of phonics is to build independent readers. It is the concurrent use of a combination of several of the word recognition skills mentioned above, however, that will create the most proficient reader.

Research concerning early literacy has made us aware of the importance of meaningful and natural experiences in early literacy instruction (Teale, 1982; Goodman, 1984). When this research was new, word analysis skill development, with an emphasis on decoding, was looked upon as a synthetic approach that lacked meaning for the young child. Now that we have dealt with many of the new ideas in early literacy instruction, skill development is receiving more attention to try and determine the appropriate way to handle this part of literacy development. This area of literacy instruction involves objectives that have existed for many years, including some of the reading readiness objectives that have dominated early literacy programs. Through the years, research has demonstrated that to become a proficient reader, language codes need to be learned. This is not only true in English-speaking countries. There is considerable evidence from both experimental and longitudinal studies from many countries that phonemic awareness and some knowledge of phonics are necessary for success at learning to read and write alphabetic languages (Adams, 1990; Blachman & James, 1985; Juel, 1994; Tunmer & Nesdale, 1985). According to Juel (1989), a child needs to have the following in order to learn to read proficiently: (1) alphabetic understanding (knowing that words are composed of letters); (2) phonemic awareness (knowing that words are composed of a sequence of spoken sounds that have no meaning and being able to hear those sounds); and (3) cryptoanalytic intent (knowing that there is a relationship between the printed letters and spoken sounds). These three elements are in some ways precursors to learning phonics. Therefore, the question no longer is do we deal with these skills in early literacy development; rather, it is exactly what skills are we talking about, when do we introduce them, how do we teach them, and how much time do we spend dealing with them?

Skills and Objectives for Learning about Print

Objectives concerning knowledge about print to enhance literacy development assume that the child:

1. Knows that print is read from left to right.
2. Knows that oral language can be written down and then read.
3. Knows what a letter is and can point to one on a printed page.
4. Knows what a word is, can point to one on a printed page, and knows there are spaces between words.
5. Is aware of print in the environment, knows that it has a message, and is capable of reading some of this print on signs and logos.
6. Recognizes some words by sight.
7. Can identify rhyming words he or she hears and can make up a rhyme.
8. Can identify and name upper- and lowercase letters of the alphabet.
9. Associates letters with their initial and final corresponding consonant sounds including sounds of the same letter (hard and soft) (*c*—cat, city; *g*—goat, George).
10. Associates letters with corresponding long and short vowel sounds (*a*—acorn, apple; *e*—eagle, egg; *i*—ice, igloo; *o*—oats, octopus; *u*—unicorn, umbrella).
11. Knows the consonant blends *bl, cr, dr, fl, gl, pr, st,* and so on (consonant blends are two or three letters that when placed together blend into one sound that represents both letter sounds).

12. Knows the consonant digraph sounds *ch, ph, sh, th,* and *wh* (digraphs are two letters that when placed together make a new sound unlike the sound of either letter).
13. Can blend and segment phonemes in words.
14. Begins to use context, syntax, and semantics to identify words.
15. Knows that words are made up of syllables.
16. Attempts reading by attending to picture clues and to print.
17. Guesses and predicts words based on some knowledge of phoneme–grapheme correspondence.
18. Is aware of different structural elements of words such as prefixes, suffixes, adding *-ing, -ed* and *-s* at the end of a word, and contractions.
19. Knows the following phonic generalizations:
    a. In a consonant-vowel-consonant pattern, the vowel sound is usually short (bat, bet, but, bit).
    b. In a vowel-consonant-*e* pattern, the vowel sound is usually long (cake, cute, bike).
    c. When two vowels come together in a word, the first is usually long and the second is silent (train, receive, bean).
20. Can identify common word families and build words by adding initial consonants to such word families as: *it, an, am, at, ite, ate,* and so on.

In the past, many of these skills were taught exclusively through the use of worksheets that involved mechanical responses on the part of the child. It was also believed that a child could not read until most of the skills were mastered. However, not all skills are necessary for all children. There are many ways for this information to be learned that are more meaningful for the child than methods used in the past. Less time is needed to deal with these skills than was thought in the past.

Instructional activities designed to help youngsters learn about the function, form, structure, and conventions of print should involve the same types of learning experiences as other skill areas dealt with in this book. Children need to be socially interactive when they are learning about print; they need models to emulate; and the learning must be through experiences that are meaningful and connected with real life and incorporate what children already know. If children see a need or usefulness attached to a reading skill, that skill will probably be learned without difficulty.

In the sections that follow, strategies will be described to help children learn about print in meaningful and functional ways. Each strategy is appropriate for youngsters from preschool through second grade—the teacher simply adjusts the activity to the age group he or she is working with. In the past, we selected the behavioristic approach for learning about print. Skills were taught through drill with exercises and worksheets that had little meaning for the child. Learning these skills should be connected to content-area material and functional activities. Activities such as reading to children; pointing out words in the environment; noting their letters and sounds; taking a child's dictation; encouraging children to write in their own way; allowing youngsters to see the print as it is read from a Big Book and tracked from left to right across the page; and using predictable books that rhyme or have patterned language, that allow children to guess and share in the reading all help youngsters to learn about print (Juel, 1989). Through these experiences, children are learning that print is read from left to right, that words in a book are oral language that has been written down and can be read, that letters have sounds, that letters make up words, that words have meaning, that pictures hold clues to what the print says, and that words can be predicted based on the meaning of the text. Some direct instruction of phonemic awareness, phonics, and alphabetic knowledge is needed, which is acceptable so long as it does not dominate instruction. The use of an occasional worksheet will act as reinforcement for skills taught. Children can read several words and simple books through their knowledge of syntax, semantics, and acquired sight vocabulary before there is an emphasis on phonics. When youngsters have experienced success with initial reading, they will seek information about the forms of print, such as the sounds of letters, since they will have a desire to read independently.

Environmental Print

Several researchers have found that children as young as two can read familiar environmental print (Goodman, 1980; Harste, Woodward, & Burke, 1984; Hiebert, 1978). Others, however, have shown that a child is often reading the sign rather than its print; when the print is separated from its familiar environmental context, the young child sometimes can no longer identify it (Mason, 1980). Even so, when very young children associate the McDonald's logo with the word *McDonald's* and try to read it, they are learning that a group of letters make up a word that can be read and thus provides information. Reading environmental print also carries with it a sense of accomplishment and usually elicits positive reinforcement of the child's achievement by caring adults.

As noted earlier, parents can make children aware of environmental print from the first year of life. During daily routines, parents need to point out and read words and labels on food boxes, road signs, stores, and restaurants. The world is filled with environmental print. School, however, is not. With the exception of *Exit, Boys, Girls,* and special names such as *Library* and *Office,* few familiar words appear in the typical school building. Thus, environmental print needs to be brought into school from outside, and classroom teachers need to label items within the walls of their own day-care centers, nursery schools, kindergartens, and first and second grades. Such print, once familiar, becomes part of a child's sight vocabulary.

The environmental print that children tend to know best appears on food containers, especially those for cereal, soup, milk, and cookies, and on detergent boxes and bottles. Among common signs, they recognize fast-food logos, road signs, traffic signals, and names of popular store chains, supermarkets, and service stations. Collect such logos and trade names and make them available in your classroom by posting them on charts, pasting them onto index cards, and making up looseleaf books of environmental print. Most firms distribute various printed materials free, complete with logos. Photograph examples of environmental print yourself to bring to your classroom. Suggest that children read such words and copy them, if they wish.

Fill your room with its own environmental print. Start at the beginning of a school year with only a few signs, such as children's names on their cubbies, and the word *block center* to identify that area of the room. Make labels with five-by-eight index cards and dark felt-tip markers. Begin each word with a capital letter and continue with lowercase manuscript, thus providing youngsters with configuration clues. Hang labels at heights easy for children to see. Point out the labels to the children, and suggest that they read them to friends and, if they wish, copy them. As the school year progresses and things you are learning about are added to the classroom, label these items as well. Refer to the labels as part of your normal routine so that they are used and will then add to the child's sight vocabulary. Label items because they are of interest to the class and serve a function such as identifying important classroom materials and learning centers. Use labels for relating messages such as **Wash Your Hands Before Snack.** Refer to the labels often so the children identify them as useful and functional.

Label items related to content area topics. If you are studying dinosaurs—a very popular topic in early childhood—display model dinosaurs and label each with its name. Even long, difficult words such as *brontosaurus* and *tyrannosaurus* immediately become sight words for many early childhood youngsters. It is not at all uncommon to observe preschool, kindergarten, first-grade and second-grade children reading labels to themselves or to each other. I observed a kindergarten class shortly after the teacher had put up two new labels in the science center, which featured a lesson on the sense of touch and focused on items that were hard and soft. I watched Josh take Jennifer by the hand and heard him say, "See, Jen. See this. This bunny is soft. This word says 'soft.'" Josh continued, "See this, Jen. This is a rock and this word says 'hard.' Touch it. It is hard." The two children stroked the bunny, pointed to the label, and said in unison, "soft"; they then touched the rock, pointed to the label, and said, "hard." They repeated the sequence several times.

Another way to make print part of the classroom environment is to communicate through print, even with children as young as two. Every day have messages and assignments for children. Select a permanent spot on the chalkboard. Use rebus or picture writing along with print to help children make sense of the message. For example:

Happy Birthday, Tyrone!
Happy Valentine's Day!
Read a book to a friend.
We are going on a trip to the town library today.

This routine will have children automatically looking at the chalkboard each day for a special message. They will learn that print carries meaning that is interesting and useful. Some teachers refer to this practice as the ***Morning Message*** and have formalized it into a lesson when the school day begins (Stewart, Benjamin, & Mason, 1987). Continue to communicate in print throughout the day whenever the opportunity occurs. Write at least some of the message with the children watching, so that you provide a writing model for them. Use the message to develop various concepts about print. Emphasize specific words or letters, pursue questions about meaning, or let children add sentences to the original message.

When working with seven- and eight-year-olds, the contents of the morning message and the environmental print displayed in the room will be more sophisticated than when working with younger children. They can be used to point out sound–symbol relationships or phonic generalizations that are appropriate to deal with in first and second grade. For example a morning message such as:

Shelly is wearing *shiny* new *shoes* that *she* just bought yesterday.

is a perfect opportunity to point out the *sh* digraph. In another message such as the following:

Kate's birthday *cake* was *made* in the *shape* of a *kite.*

There are five examples of the phonic generalization that, in a vowel-consonant-*e* pattern, the vowel is usually long. This is a perfect opportunity to observe and discuss this letter–sound pattern.

Computers are a newer part of our print environment. They are now present in many of our homes and schools. Computer literacy is almost a must, and early childhood is the time to expose children to computers. Early exposure makes the computer a part of the child's life rather than a threat. Many adults are intimidated by computers, especially because their introduction came after they were set in their ways. Many avoid using them or approach them with trepidation, but today's children must be made as comfortable with computers as their parents and grandparents have been with typewriters. Children as young as a year can sit on an adult's lap and use a keyboard. The computer places letters of the alphabet before the child and instant left-to-right progression on the screen as keys are pressed. The computer helps with knowledge about print as children compose narrative and expository text.

Many computer programs teach children literacy skills, some better than others. It is important to be selective when choosing software, because some of it is no more creative than the skills-oriented workbooks that have been criticized for years. Other programs, however, encourage active, creative participation rather than simply questions and answers. Selected computer software for children is listed in Appendix C.

Very Own Words for Developing Sight Vocabulary and Knowledge about Print

In *Teacher* (1963), Sylvia Ashton-Warner described Very Own Words as a method for developing sight vocabulary. She encouraged children to write their favorite words from a story or content-area lesson on three-by-five cards, each word on a separate card. Very Own Words are often from a child's home life—*Mommy, Daddy, Grandpa, Grandma, birthday.* They also reflect emotional feelings—*naughty, nice, good, no, punish.* After Very Own Words are recorded on index cards, they are stored in a child's file box, in a coffee can, a zip-lock baggie, or on a loose-leaf ring hung on a bulletin board. Teachers have devised many other methods for storing Very Own Words.

Helping children start their collections of Very Own Words is an exciting experience in school. Before an activity or exercise, let them know that at its completion you will ask them to name their favorite words from the activity. The activity should be a pleasant one that produces interesting language, perhaps popping corn or making play dough. It can also be a favorite word in a story-book or words generated from the study of social studies and science units. Soon children will request their Very Own Words without being asked.

Encourage children to do things with their words—read them to friends or to themselves, copy them, dictate them to the teacher, and use them in sentences or stories. Because they are based on a child's expressed interests in situations at

In our technological world, computers must become a part of literacy development, just as books, pencils, and paper are. Computers should be a part of early childhood equipment and provide a source for literacy development.

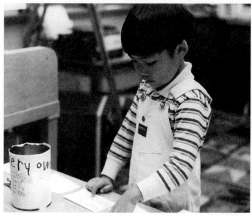

Very Own Words are a source for personal sight vocabulary. Teachers encourage children to copy them, write them, and read them.

home and in school, the collection of Very Own Words is a powerful technique for developing sight vocabulary.

Seven- and eight-year-olds also enjoy and learn from collecting Very Own Words. They should alphabetize them and store them in a file box. Teachers can encourage children to study the letter patterns in their Very Own Words. They can discuss consonant and vowel sounds, blends, and digraphs when applicable, and structural elements such as prefixes and suffixes, as well as phonic generalizations that may be evident. When a child studies letter patterns in words he or she has selected, it will mean more than doing the same task with words selected by the teacher or a textbook.

Very Own Words will be useful with bilingual children. The index card will include a child's Very Own Word in English and can have the word written in his or her native language as well.

The Language Experience Approach

The Language Experience Approach (LEA) has been used for many years in reading instruction. Already tried and true for many teachers, it encompasses in its techniques and suggestions the newer theories of emergent literacy. It can help children associate oral language with written language, teaching them specifically that what is said can be written down and read. It illustrates the left-to-right progression of our written language. In practice, it demonstrates the formation of letters plus their combination into words; it helps build sight vocabulary; it is a source for meaningful teaching of phoneme–grapheme correspondence as well as other knowledge about print; and it is based on the child's interest and experiences.

Many educators have been associated with developing and articulating the Language Experience Approach, among them R. V. Allen (1976), M. A. Hall (1976), and J. Veatch et al. (1973). The LEA is based on the following premises, all from the learner's point of view:

What I think is important.
What I think, I can say.
What I say can be written down by me or by others.
What is written down can be read by me and by others.

The interests and experiences on which the LEA builds come from children's lives both at home and at school. Home experiences, of course, tend to be spontaneous. In school, the teacher needs to plan experiences—for example, class trips, cooking projects, use of puppets, guest speakers, class pets, plants, holiday events—or the study of topics that are exciting to young children, such as dinosaurs, outer space, and other cultures. The language experience lesson is usually carried out with an entire class, but it can also take place with a small group or an individual child.

An LEA lesson begins with oral language. A discussion is usually generated from an interesting or exciting class experience—a recent trip to the zoo, for instance, Halloween costumes, or the pet gerbil's new litter. To begin the discussion, ask open-ended questions that will encourage descriptive responses rather than yes/no answers. For example, if the topic is a trip to the zoo, ask children to name their favorite animal. Why was it their favorite animal? What did the animal look like? What did the animal do while the child was watching it at the zoo? It is important to accept all of the children's responses. Accept nonstandard English without correction, but provide a language model by using standard English to paraphrase what the child has said.

After a discussion has generated several ideas, write them down. With a large group of children, write the ideas on a large sheet of paper (approximately 24 by 36 inches), which becomes an experience chart. It can be taped to the wall or mounted on an easel. Print with a dark felt-tip marker of medium thickness, allowing ample spacing between words and between lines so that the chart is very readable. Use manuscript in upper- and lower-case letters, following the conventions of regular print and thus giving configuration to words that the use of upper-case alone cannot give. Word configuration aids children in word identification.

In recording language on experience charts, teachers should write quickly and legibly, providing good manuscript samples for children to read and copy. Not only is rewriting a chart time-consuming, but a rewritten chart is typically more difficult for children to read because they have not witnessed the writing of the chart firsthand. As you write what children dictate, use their language unless it is difficult for others to understand. When dictation is difficult to understand, ask a child to restate an idea or, if necessary, help the child restate it. It is important to include the comments of as many children as possible. When creating a new chart, try to remember which children have not contributed in the past, and encourage them to contribute to the new chart. It is a good idea to identify who said what. The chart is more interesting to youngsters whose names are included. For example: John said, "I liked the gorilla at the zoo. He jumped around and made funny faces." Jordanna said, "I liked the baby deer. They had big, bright, black eyes, wet black noses, and shiny brown fur." Try to accompany each sentence with an illustration; this will help children to read the charts.

Experience charts should not be very long. Charts dictated by two- and three-year-olds can simply be lists of words, such as names of animals with illustrations next to them. Used occasionally, lists of words make appropriate charts for older children as well. They are a quick way to record and reinforce vocabulary associated with topics being studied. Small-group and individual dictations of experiences can be made into books by the teacher or the child. While writing a chart, take the opportunity to point out concepts about print: "Now I am writing the word 'gorilla'—g-o-r-i-l-l-a. See, it begins here with a 'g' and ends here with an 'a.'" Mentally note which letters or sounds interest children. Ask children to point out on the chart where you should begin to write. Like the Directed Listening (or Reading) Thinking Activity and the Morning Message, the LEA lesson can have a specific skill objective.

The last step in the LEA lesson is to read the chart back to the class. Use a pointer to emphasize left-to-right progression. Let the class read the chart in unison, or ask individual children who contributed different sentences to read them. Leave the chart in a visible spot in the room and encourage the children to read it and copy parts of it, copy words they like, or add to their Very Own Word collection from the chart. Vocabulary charts and experience charts representing the different topics discussed in school can be left hanging in the room so long as space permits, then made into Big Books for children to look at throughout the

The Language Experience Approach provides experiences that interest children, who in turn can write about, develop vocabulary from, and read about them. Experience charts, dictated by the children and written by the teacher, develop language and encourage reading and writing.

school year. If a laminating machine is available, it is wise to preserve charts. They can also be covered with clear contact paper to withstand handling by the children. Children's dictated stories can also be placed in the class library for others to read, as can books made by the entire class. Those made by the class often become the most popular books in the room. Class books can be made by having each child draw and write directly onto a duplicating master. This method allows easy production of multiple copies, one for each child.

The Language Experience Approach, which is appropriate throughout early childhood and beyond, can be used similarly to the Morning Message and Very Own Words for noticing phonic generalizations and sound–symbol correspondences. Learning about print in this situation is done with material that is familiar and meaningful. Occasionally prepare a chart in the language of bilingual children in your class. If necessary solicit help from bilingual parents or colleagues. This strategy will help the bilingual youngsters see that we respect their home or native language and will guide them in making connections between their language and English.

Although the Language Experience Approach has been used for many years, it has often been seen only as a program supplement. Skill drills and standard workbooks on letters and sounds have too often been given instructional priority. Yet, the LEA incorporates all the constructs that are sound principles in nurturing emergent literacy. LEA materials are inexpensive and easy to use. They include chart paper, markers, colored construction paper, white paper, index cards, scissors, staplers, pencils, and crayons. With directions from the teacher, these simple classroom materials record the precious words and pictures created by children from their own meaningful, real-life experiences. The LEA should be central, not supplemental, to literacy instruction in early reading programs.

Using Context and Pictures to Develop Reading

Experiences with literature can lead children to use contextual print and illustrations to recognize that words have meaning and help them decode words written on the printed page. Again, those experiences can take place in whole-class, small-group, or one-to-one settings and through such techniques as directed listening/reading–thinking activities, shared book experiences, and repeated readings of stories. For example, select a story that is predictable, in which the text and illustrations are closely related. Ask children to look at the pictures on a page before reading it to them. Ask them what they think the words will say. Then read the page to demonstrate that print and illustration are closely related and that the pictures provide information that can help the children as they read the story.

The syntax and semantics of a sentence (its grammatical structure and meaning) also help children to identify words. Encourage children to use these elements of written language by stopping your oral reading at predictable points in a story and asking them to fill in words. For example, when reading *The Little Engine That Could* (Piper, 1954), first read the repetitive phrase "I think I can" through, the second time say, "I think I _____," the next time "I think _____," and last "I _____." This technique is most effective with a Big Book because you can point to the words as the children say them. As the children begin to understand the concept of filling in words, choose more difficult passages for your pauses. Prepare charts and sheets with predictable text and leave out words to be filled in as you read. Children unconsciously use their prior knowledge of syntax and context in predicting words. They assimilate and use the strategy when they read themselves.

Identifying Letters of the Alphabet

Many children who cannot yet identify individual letters of the alphabet are able to read. As we have seen, they read sight words from environmental print, from classroom labels, and from Very Own Words lists. They learn other sight words from repeated readings and shared book experiences. It is obviously not necessary to be able to identify and name the letters of the alphabet in order to develop an initial sight-reading vocabulary. It is easier for a young child *initially* to learn whole words already familiar through oral language, rather than learn abstract letters. Familiar words carry meaning for them whereas isolated letters do not.

Children do, however, need to learn the alphabet to eventually become independently fluent readers and writers. There is no evidence that alphabet identification ought to be treated as the first skill in early literacy; it makes more sense for children to learn to identify letters after they have learned a number of sight words. Traditionally, learning the alphabet has often been the first thing parents try to teach their children at home, and it is usually high on any list of reading readiness skills in preschool and kindergarten curricula. Because it is hard to depart from deeply rooted tradition, learning the alphabet will probably always be prominent in emergent literacy programs. The main concern is that it not be overemphasized in experiences provided for learning, in our expectations for the children's performance, and in terms of the time given to it.

Allow children to explore letters by using manipulative materials available in the literacy center. Be sure to have on hand alphabet puzzles, magnetic upper- and lowercase letters with an accompanying magnetic board, a set of wooden upper- and lowercase letters, tactile letters made of sandpaper, alphabet games, felt letters and an accompanying felt-board, letter stencils, alphabet flash cards, and a long alphabet chart posted along the wall of the classroom at the eye level of the children. In addition to these materials, a large supply of alphabet books and taped songs about the alphabet should be in the classroom library. Encourage children to explore these materials, first through play. Later, they will begin to identify the letters they are playing with, and teach letters they know to other children. Provide chalk and a chalkboard so they can make letters themselves. Children also enjoy finger-painting letters, painting them on easels, shaping them out of clay, and eating them in alphabet soup or as cookies or pretzels. Shaping letters with their fingers and whole bodies is an activity often used in early childhood rooms.

Systematic teaching of the alphabet, one letter per week, is not as successful as teaching children letters that are meaningful to them. Many teachers lead children to identify the letters in their own names first. When teaching thematic units, select a few letters to feature that are used in the context of the theme. For example, in a unit on transportation, feature *b* for boat and *t* for train. When children have learned to identify several different letters, ask them to look for the same letters in other contexts, such as magazines, newspapers, and books. Check children individually by using flash cards to determine just which letters they know and which they do not know. Ask children which letters they would like to learn next from their Very Own Words or other sources that allow them to decide for themselves. Give children flash cards of the letters they choose to learn and encourage them to use those letters in all of the activities just mentioned. Letters need to be practiced all year through. Often children forget what they knew yesterday.

A prepared environment rich with alphabet materials to be explored and experienced will help children learn the letters of the alphabet. (Alphabet books are listed in Appendix A.)

Phonemic Awareness and Associating Letters and Sounds

We do have research that supports the importance of learning sound–symbol relationships, and there is no research that suggests we should ignore it in the development of emergent literacy (Adams, 1990). The newer research *does* suggest, however, that traditional early reading instruction ignores many important strategies and practices while abstracting discrete skills from the total act of reading. It suggests that the teaching of letter–sound association has dominated early childhood programs to the point of excluding other practices. As with teaching the alphabet, caution is proposed in the instructional strategies, time allocation, and performance expectations we bring to sound–symbol relationships in the early childhood classroom. Children who have already had substantial experience with books, who are firmly familiar with the structures and uses of language, and who have already acquired large sight vocabularies are perhaps ready to deal with sound–symbol relationships in preschool and kindergarten; children without those backgrounds are not. Like the letters of the alphabet, sound–symbol relationships are abstract and lack intrinsic meaning for children. Only a child who has assimilated concepts about books and print and has acquired a sight vocabulary begins to show an interest in trying to decode unknown words independently. Usually children ask about letters and sounds themselves when they see a need for this knowledge. Studies have demonstrated that children who are taught phonics as part of initial reading instruction do achieve better in the early grades than children who have not (Chall, Conrad, & Harris-Sharples, 1983; Williams, 1985). It must be remembered, however, that the goal of phonics is not to teach a set of rules, but to get across the alphabetic principle that there are systematic relationships between letters and sounds.

Phonemic awareness is a precursor to phonics and necessary for children to benefit from phonic instruction. Phonemic awareness is the knowledge that words are made up of a sequence of spoken sounds. To help children gain this awareness, we expose them to rhymes and jingles and carefully selected children's literature that features language play. Reading books that contain rhyme such as *Green Eggs and Ham* (Seuss, 1960), *Goodnight Moon* (Brown, 1947), and *The Queen of Hearts* (Hennessy and Pearson, 1989) will help develop phonemic awareness. If you do introduce kindergarten children to sound–symbol relationships, deal with initial consonants, initial digraphs, and vowels. Although there does not seem to be a particularly appropriate sequence for teaching specific sounds, it does appear as if the letters used more often should be more familiar to children and therefore easier for them to learn—letters such as initial *s, t, p,* and *m.* After initial consonants, introduce the more familiar beginning digraphs, such as *sh, ch, th,* and *ph.* Then introduce vowels. Teach sounds in meaningful contexts rather than by isolating sounds from words. Using meaningful context tends to avoid the pedagogical distortion of sounds. Rather than asking a child, "Can you think of words that begin with the 'buh' sound?" ask the child to think of words that begin with the letter *b,* such as *baby.* Feature different letters and provide many experiences with the sound–symbol relationship of each letter.

Children need continual practice in order to learn sound–symbol relationships; rarely is a single lesson sufficient. Therefore, provide several experiences with each letter and review frequently, even after proceeding to new letter sounds. Incorporate experiences with sound–symbol association in all content areas whenever possible, and in situations that are meaningful to the child.

Strategies for Developing Sound–Symbol Relationships

How might children be helped to recognize the sound–symbol relationships of consonants and vowels in a meaningful context? Science and social studies themes lend themselves to featuring letters that appear in units. For example, when studying farm, pet, and zoo animals, feature the letter *p,* because it is used frequently within this context.

The following types of activities can follow:

1. Read *The Pigs' Picnic* (Kasza, 1988), *The Pet Show* (Keats, 1972), and *The Tale of Peter Rabbit* (Potter, 1902) during the unit, and point out words that begin with the letter *p* in these books.
2. Make word charts using words from the books that begin with the letter *p.*

3. Make popcorn and bring peanuts to the zoo to feed the animals.
4. Make lists of animals that begin with the letter *p*.
5. Read the book *Animalia* (Base, 1987) and point out the *p* page, which says "Proud Peacocks Preening Perfect Plumage."
6. Collect sensory items about animals that begin with the letter *p*, such as Puppy Chow to smell, peanuts to eat and to feed to elephants when you visit the zoo, peacock plumes to touch, a purring kitten to listen to, and the book *Petunia* (Duvoisin, 1977) to look at and read.
7. List words from the unit that begin with the letter *p*.
8. Write an experience chart of activities carried out during the unit and highlight the letter *p* when it appears in the chart.
9. Ask children to add to their very own word collection with favorite words from the unit that began with the letter *p*.
10. Make a collage of pictures featuring things from the unit and mark those that begin with the letter *p*.
11. Print on a chart the song "Peter Cottontail." Sing the song and highlight the letter *p* when it appears.
12. Have children help you to make up nonsense rhymes for featured letters and chant them, such as:

> *My name is* Penelope Pig
> *I* pick petals off of petunias
> *I* play patty cake
> *and eat* pretzels with pink punch

13. Add a page for the letter *p* to a class Big Book entitled, *Our Own Big Book of Letters, Sounds, and Words*. Have children draw pictures or paste in pictures of words that begin with the letter *p*. (Directions for making a Big Book are in Chapter 7 p. 195.)
14. Complete a worksheet for the letter *p* requiring the student to trace the letter, write the letter, and circle pictures that begin with the letter *p*, such as pig and popcorn.
15. Encourage children to write about their experiences in the units such as their visit to the zoo, the books they read, the songs they sang. In their writing they will be using the letters emphasized and, although their writing may not be conventional, through the use of their invented spellings they are indirectly enhancing their phonemic awareness. When children write, they have to face head-on the problem of mapping spoken language into written language. This can lead to an understanding of the structure of spoken language, and the more children write, the better they become at segmenting sounds in words. This is demonstrated in the following example of Zach's story about *The Pigs' Picnic* when he wrote, Pig wanted the picnic to be perfect, as follows:

Pg wtd tha pcnc to be prfkt

Children's literature is an excellent source for featuring letters attached to themes. Be careful not to abuse the stories by overemphasizing the sounds featured; however, don't pass up the opportunity to feature letters in this natural book setting. For example, in a unit on food, Ms. Fino, a first-grade teacher, featured the letter *b* and read *Blueberries for Sal* (McClosky, 1948), *Bread and Jam for Frances* (Hoban, 1964), and *The Berenstain Bears and Too Much Birthday* (Berenstain, 1987).

These and similar activities can be carried out for any initial consonant. Whenever letters being featured in a thematic unit appear in a language experience chart or a piece of children's literature, take the opportunity to point it out to the children. Alphabet books generally use sound–symbol relationships as they introduce each letter as do picture storybooks that use a particular letter prominently. (See Appendix A for children's literature for building sound–symbol relationships.) For additional practice and individual exploration, include among the language arts manipulatives in the literacy center any materials that help children associate sounds and their symbols—materials in Lotto or Bingo formats, puzzles that require children to match pictures with initial consonants, felt pictures and letters, and boxes of objects representing initial consonant sounds. Letters and sounds introduced need to be reviewed throughout the year.

When we read, we use several skills concurrently to decode and derive meaning from the printed page. We therefore need to encourage children to use multiple rather than isolated skills in their approach to reading. Children should be taught to use context clues and phonic clues simultaneously. One strategy that accomplishes this goal has already been suggested—reading a sentence in which you pause and leave a "blank" to be filled in by the child. For example, say, "The b_____ flew up to the tree and landed on a branch." Supplying the initial consonant for the word, either by sound or by sight, draws on a child's skills with phonics, context, syntax, and semantics.

It must be emphasized that many preschool, kindergarten, and first-grade children are not likely to associate the identification of sound–symbol relationships with reading. Many of them do seem to be able to name words beginning with specific consonants, but they will probably not relate that ability to reading until they approach the end of first grade. Very little time should be spent on such skills before then, and more time spent with the many other strategies already suggested. Although many more phonic rules have been identified, such as those involving final consonants, long and short vowels, and blends, early childhood classrooms should deal mostly with sound–symbol relationships of initial consonants and digraphs and perhaps rudimentarily with the most obvious vowel sounds. There are, however, some children who are capable of dealing with the more complicated skills.

There are several concerns with sound–symbol relationships and phonics generalizations. A major problem is that so many of the rules have exceptions. For example, the sound of *k* in the word *k*ite is its usual sound, but when *k* is followed by *n* it becomes silent as in the word *k*not. It is the opinion of this author that we should teach fewer rather than more rules because the ability to apply them is so limited for young children. Many of the exceptions can wait until the children are older. Exceptions can be dealt with when they come up in print and sometimes treated as sight words when they occur infrequently. In early childhood, our main concern should be with sound–symbol relationships and generalizations that rarely have exceptions.

Another problem when dealing with sound–symbol relationships is dialects. If a teacher from New York taught in the South, he or she would teach long and short vowels with different sounds than those taught by a teacher who was from the South. Children in most parts of the United States are in communities that are made up of youngsters who speak many different dialects and attend the same school. These children may have difficulty dealing with sounds regardless of where their teacher is from.

In addition, there are different types of learners. There are auditory learners and visual learners. A child who is weak in auditory discrimination is not likely to master phonics and is best taught to his or her strength rather than to a weakness. We need to be cautious with sound–symbol relationships. The skills a child acquires as a result of being knowledgeable in this area are important toward becoming a proficient reader; on the other hand, it is just one strategy within the total picture of literacy development, and we need not overemphasize it.

As suggested, a section of the classroom literacy center should be set aside for general language arts manipulatives. This section will include the multipurpose materials preschools, kindergartens, and first and second grades characteristically use to develop eye–hand coordination and sharpen visual and auditory discrimination and memory. Such manipulatives include puzzles; pegboards; sewing cards; beads and string; materials that lace, button, or snap; construction toys such as Legos and Tinker Toys; picture collections for holidays and unit topics; materials for sorting and identification; games such as Concentration, Bingo, Lotto, and Candyland; and card games that involve such skills as use of the alphabet, rhyme, and letter–sound association.

Many of the materials for developing the skills just mentioned can be purchased from school supply companies. Teacher-made items increase the inventory and often suit children's needs better than purchased materials. They also add warmth and help personalize the classroom. Older children, parents, aides, and teachers can all contribute to the classroom inventory by making materials.

Whenever possible take advantage of spontaneous situations that grow out of daily experience to help children learn about print, such as the following example:

> *Christopher, a child in first grade, had just written his name on a picture he drew and exclaimed, "Wow, the word* STOP *is right in the middle of my name. See Chri*stop*her." He pointed to the letters in his name that spelled* STOP. *He continued, "But that doesn't make sense, then I should say my*

name Chri-STOP-her." The teacher immediately seized the opportunity to point out the ph digraph and explain to Christopher that the word STOP was in his name but when the letters p *and* h *come together, they make a new sound as heard in Christopher, like the sound of* F. *She mentioned other words such as* ph*otograph and* ph*antom that illustrated the* ph *sound.*

Transitions

In the last three chapters dealing with reading development, theories and strategies for helping children develop the desire to read, comprehend written text, and learn about the features of print have been discussed. It is my opinion that all the strategies are appropriate for preschool through second grade, with adaptations based on the particular age group. Teachers often want to know how children move from one level of reading ability to another or from attempted reading to conventional reading when children are attending to the print and not depending entirely on pictures and memory. It is a somewhat different process for every child, but trends do emerge. First and foremost we want to be sure that an atmosphere exists in which a child wants to read. Therefore, their attempts at reading at whatever level must be acknowledged and encouraged. Children who are reluctant to read because they think they cannnot, can listen to the attempts of their friends to see that unconventional reading is acceptable. We foster acceptance so that children will attempt reading. As youngsters learn more about phoneme–grapheme correspondence and the predictability of text based on the context and build sight vocabularies, they begin to realize that their attempted reading is not conventional. At this point they begin to ask for help with identifying words as they move into the conventional stage of reading. It may seem as if they are taking a step backward at this time because their reading is suddenly more labored as they try to sound out words rather than fill in words based on their memory or what seems to fit. Their concern for reading correctly has that effect on their performance. This will last for a short time as their skills for independent reading increase and they practice reading more and more. Conventional reading does not just occur one day; it is a gradual process in which a child goes back and forth from conventional to unconventional reading until sufficient proficiency is gained for the reading to be considered completely conventional.

Using Published Materials

Even in the mid-1960s, commercially prepared instructional materials for the development of early literacy were rare. Nursery schools and kindergartens, still very much directed by the doctrines of Pestalozzi and Froebel, used manipulative materials and real-life settings for the child's development. But the burgeoning concept of reading readiness brought with it commercial materials for developing those skills believed to be prerequisite to learning to read. Generally, the reading readiness materials were developed by the same publishers that had produced basal readers for primary grades. What they offered did not look very much like what had been used with children in preschool and kindergarten in the past. Rather, the materials were similar to those used by first, second, and third graders. They consisted mostly of workbooks accompanied by teacher's manuals. Materials prepared by publishers have improved significantly and do include many developmentally appropriate strategies for early literacy development.

Such programs are quite common and will probably continue to be, because they provide a complete package of materials for instruction and are revised to include new findings in early literacy development. Some general rules need to be applied to the selection and use of materials:

- Be sure to study the objectives for the published program and determine if they include those that incorporate the latest findings on strategies for nurturing early literacy.

- Be sure that the materials suit the needs of the children you teach. Urban and rural children may need materials different from those needed by children raised in suburban settings.

- Examine the materials for clarity, appeal to children, and durability.

- Analyze the teacher's editions for clarity of objectives, descriptions of plans, suitability of lesson content, and flexibility given to teachers in using the material.

- You, the teacher, should determine how the materials are to be used; materials should not dictate their use to you.

- Select sequences that seem most appropriate. You need not start at the beginning of a book and follow it page by page to the end.

- Eliminate sections that you feel are inappropriate for your children. On the other hand, material can be repeated if it is particularly good or if children have not grasped its content.

Remember at all times that as the teacher you need to make critical decisions about your instructional program. Published materials are tools to be used by you. Often they are best for providing an organizational framework for instruction and for reinforcing concepts. Published materials can also provide independent work for students when you need to work with individuals or small groups.

It is extremely important to realize that commercially prepared instructional materials are only one part of a program for early literacy development. What has been described thus far in this book is all but devoid of such programs. Many school districts require the use of published readiness and basal materials, and many teachers depend on them as organizational tools. When they are used, select them carefully for quality of content, use them as you see fit, and remember that they are just one part of a literacy program. As the teacher you must be a decision maker about the design of your literacy instruction, the materials you use, and how you use them.

Authentic Assessment and Standardized Measures Concerning Knowledge about Print

Children's knowledge about print and the skills they have mastered in recognizing and using it can be evaluated best through authentic assessment techniques such as running records of their behavior in frequent individual observations, collection of work samples, and personal interviews. Frequent checking and rechecking are required because young children are constantly learning and occasionally they forget. Standardized tests also measure some of the print concepts discussed in this chapter. Because they are used to assess "readiness for reading" in some kindergartens and preschools in the United States, those tests raise issues that need to be addressed. Many of those issues are described in Chapter 2, including:

1. The nature of a standardized test and instructional practice often do not match each other.
2. The results of standardized tests are not particularly reliable with young children.
3. The test results are frequently used for placement into reading groups and special programs. Once placed, a child can be labeled and established in that placement permanently.
4. Standardized tests can be biased in favor of white middle-class children despite genuine attempts to alleviate the problem.

A more authentic assessment measure, a checklist of skills concerning knowledge about print on p. 250, is useful for identifying what children know and need to learn. It should be used at frequent intervals to evaluate a child's progress. It can also be used in several assessment settings such as observation, interview, and daily performance work samples.

Ideas for the Classroom from the Classroom

I created the following experience to try and help teachers incorporate concepts about print into thematic units carried out in early childhood classrooms. The purpose was to connect knowledge about print with content-area learning to make the information about print more meaningful. This was also a way to be sure that all letters in the alphabet were highlighted at some given point in the school year. The order in which the units are studied is not important, and it would be expected that even though a particular letter was featured in a given unit, it would be reinforced in other units when appropriate. You may choose to study unit topics that are not suggested here. If that is the case, try your hand at

Checklist for Assessing Concepts about Print

	Always	*Sometimes*	*Never*
Knows print is read from left to right			
Knows that oral language can be written down and then read			
Knows what a letter is and can point one out on a page			
Knows what a word is and can point one out on a printed page			
Knows that there are spaces between words			
Reads environmental print			
Recognizes some words by sight			
Can name and identify rhyming words			
Can identify and name upper- and lowercase letters of the alphabet			
Associates consonants and their initial and final sounds (including hard and soft *c* and *g*)			
Associates consonant blends with their sounds (*bl, cr, dr, fl, gl, pr, st*)			
Associates vowels with their corresponding long and short sounds (*a*—acorn, apple; *e*—eagle, egg; *i*—ice, igloo; *o*—oats, octopus; *u*—unicorn, umbrella)			
Knows the consonant digraph sounds (*ch, ph, sh, th, wh*)			
Can blend and segment phonemes in words			
Uses context, syntax, and semantics to identify words			
Can count syllables in words			
Attempts reading by attending to picture clues and print			
Guesses and predicts words based on knowledge of sound–symbol correspondence			
Can identify suffixes and prefixes			

	Always	*Sometimes*	*Never*
Demonstrates knowledge of the following phonic generalizations:			
a. In a consonant-vowel-consonant pattern, the vowel sound is usually short			
b. In a vowel-consonant-*e* pattern, the vowel is usually long			
c. When two vowels come together in a word, the first is usually long and the second is silent (train, receive, bean)			
Uses word families such as: *an, at, it,* and *ot,* and initial consonants to build words, eg, man, can, fan, ran.			

---

selecting appropriate letters to feature in other unit topics, making sure to include every letter in the alphabet as a featured letter at least once.

Refer back to this chapter to include as many strategies as possible to use in meaningful ways to feature the letters mentioned.

◆ *Unit Topics with Featured Letters and Words*

All about Me—*h* for home and *m* for mother

Fall—*a* for apples, *l* for leaves, *r* for raking leaves

Learning about Different Cultures—*ph* for photographs illustrating other lands; *f* for food represented in other cultures; *c* for clothing from different cultures

My Five Senses—*s* for sounds, *t* for touch, *q* for quiet

Animals—*p* for pets, *z* for zoo, *j* for jungle

Winter—*sh* for shoveling snow, *i* for ice, *g* for gloves

Jobs in the Community—*x* for X-ray, *n* for newspaper, *o* for office

Nutrition—*d* for dairy, *v* for vegetables, *e* for eggs

Spring—*y* for yellow flowers, *u* for umbrella, *k* for kite

Transportation—*w* for transportation that uses water, *b* for boats, *ch* for choo-choo

◆ *Using the Senses to Learn Letters and Sounds.*

We try to appeal to the different learning styles of our students. With each letter of the alphabet we focus on, we provide sensory experiences of sight, smell, touch, sound and taste. Following is a list of words for the letters and sounds and their associated sensory ideas.

Visual Imagery	Smell	Touch	Auditory	Taste
airplane	apple	acorn	ambulance	apricot
bicycle	bubble gum	blanket	bumble bee	banana
calculator	carnation	cotton	cuckoo clock	carrot
deer	daisy	denim	dog	doughnut
eagle	eggs	earmuff	elephant	eggplant
fork	fish	feather	fiddle	French fries
giraffe	grapefruit	gourd	goose	grapes
horse	hamburger	hair	harp	honey
igloo	incense	ice cube	insect	ice cream
jewelry	jelly	jacket	jingle bells	jello
kite	kiwi	kerchief	kids	ketchup
lion	lemon	lace	lullaby	lollipops
money	mustard	metal	music	milk
nest	nectarine	napkin	nightingale	nuts
octopus	onion	oil	owl	oatmeal
puzzle	peaches	paper	parrot	pears
quail	Quaker Oats	quilt	quiet	quiche
rain	raspberries	rock	rattlesnake	raisin
ship	syrup	satin	siren	soda
turtle	tulips	taffeta	turkey	tomato
unicorn		umbrella	ukulele	
volcano	vanilla	velvet	violin	vegetables
worm	wheat bread	water	weasel	watermelon
Xerox copy	Xmas tree	X-ray	xylophone	extracts
yo-yo	yogurt	yarn	yodel	yarn
zebra	zinnia	zipper	zoo	zucchini

Erica Erlanger and Lisa Lozak
Rutgers University students

◆ *First Grade Phonics Tied to Literature*

In the beginning of first grade, I introduce the concept of word families and try to tie them in with authentic literature. The first family I do is the *at* family and what better piece of literature to use than *The Cat In The Hat* by Dr. Seuss? We read the story, discuss the word family *at*, and brainstorm *at* words. The children draw a picture of themselves, like the cat in the hat, with their face, a hat, and bow tie like the cat in the story. They fill the tall hat with words in the *at* family such as pat, mat, sat, rat, cat. *Green Eggs with Ham* is good for introducing the *am, ould,* and *oat* word families.

Cindy Peters Healy, First Grade Teacher
Harrison School, Livingston, NJ

◆ **FIGURE 8.1** *Story Figures for Learning Phonics*

 ## Activities and Questions

1. Answer the focus questions at the beginning of the chapter.

2. Observe the environmental print in an early childhood classroom. Note what you think could be added to it, both from within the classroom and from the outside world.

3. Select three children from prekindergarten through second grade whose scores on standardized tests are available. Observe the children for oral language ability, competence in comprehension, and print knowledge. Compare what you observe concerning the children's literacy ability with their test results.

4. Write an experience chart dictated to you by children in an early childhood classroom. If you do not have access to children, do this in your college classroom with your peers dictating the contents for the chart. Critique the appearance of your chart and note problems you encountered while writing it. Use your self-evaluation for ideas for improvement.

5. Select five children at random from an early childhood classroom in which they have collected Very Own Words. List all of the words in the children's collections. Compare the list with the words found in basal reading material for the age children you selected. How closely do the basal words and the children's Very Own Words match each other?

6. Select three initial consonants other than *p*. Design classroom experiences that will teach and reinforce the sound–symbol relationships of each. Connect the letters to a thematic topic that is commonly studied in science or social studies in early childhood classrooms. Use traditional and authentic experiences.

7. Continue the portfolio assessment for the child you selected to assess for language development in Chapter 4. Observe the child using the assessment checklist provided in this chapter concerning the evaluation of concepts about print.

8. Continue the thematic unit that you began in Chapter 4. Select three objectives in the area of concepts about print and describe three activities that will satisfy each of the objectives using your theme. (You dealt with sound–symbol associations earlier; select other concepts about print to emphasize.)

Case Study Activities

◆ **Case 1**

Standardized testing and the use of commercially prepared basal reading instructional materials are being questioned in your district. Two committees are formed to deal with issues concerning each. Because you were recently promoted to the position of coordinator of language arts for the district, you are a member of both committees. The committee dealing with standardized tests is trying to decide whether or not to use them in early childhood classrooms. The committee is to write a statement supporting its position. If it decides to use standardized tests, the committee needs to continue that statement and describe how the results of the tests will be utilized.

The second committee is trying to decide whether to continue using commercially prepared basal reading instructional programs for early literacy development, considering the strong emphasis on instruction through the use of children's literature. If you decide to eliminate or maintain basals, provide a statement that supports your decision. If you decide to continue to use basals, continue your statement by describing just how these instructional materials will be used.

◆ **Case 2**

The following describes two first grade teachers' approaches to teaching knowledge about print, specifically the sound–symbol relationship of the letter *s*.

Mrs. G. teaches reading in the morning from 9:00 to 10:30. She works on phonics during that time, and her approach is to teach a letter of the alphabet each week with the associated sound. She uses a commercially prepared program and follows it exactly the way the publisher has it outlined. This means that a letter is introduced through a little story provided by the publisher such as *Sam and the Big Snow Storm*. It is a short story with a lot of words that begin with *s*.

After talking about the featured letter, there are worksheets showing pictures of items that begin with *s* such as *Sam, Snow,* and others in the story. Children are asked to circle the words that begin with *s.* Children are then asked to think of words they know that begin with *s,* and the teacher lists them on a chart. This same lesson is carried out for the next letter presented in the program.

Mrs. H. introduces letters spontaneously as they come up during the entire school day related to something that the children are studying. They are studying the ocean, and Mrs. H reads the story *Swimmy* by Leo Lionni, about a fish who lives in the sea and his adventures there. She points out the letter *s* in the book and other words beginning with *s* that happen to come up, such as sea, sand, swim, surf, sun, sailing, and snails. Children are asked if any of them have the letter *s* in their name, and it is written on a chart. Mrs. H. asks children if they know someone whose name has an *s* in it, or if they know of something in their home that has an *s* in it. After the wall chart is finished, the children sing a song about the sea, and Mrs. H. mentions that the letter *s* is in several words in the song. Mrs. H. does not have a systematic plan for teaching letters of the alphabet. She says, "When they arise in context, I take the opportunity to feature them."

What are the pros and cons of each teacher's approach to teaching the alphabet sounds and symbols? What could each teacher do to improve her presentation? How could they attend to children with special needs?

Chapter 9

Writing and Literacy Development

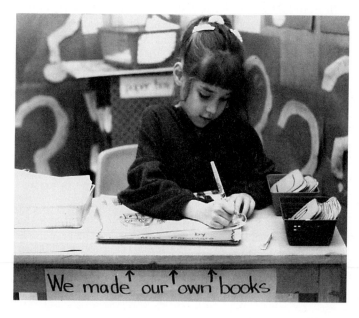

We made our own books

Allison adds her page to the class book while working in the writing center.

Children want to write. They want to write the first day they attend school. This is no accident. Before they went to school they marked up walls, pavements, newspapers with crayons, chalk, pens or pencils . . . anything that makes a mark. The child's marks say, "I am."

—Donald Graves
Writing: Teachers and Children at Work

Questions to Focus on as You Read

◆ How are reading and writing related?

◆ Describe theories concerning how early writing is acquired.

◆ Describe the six categories discussed in this chapter that reflect children's early attempts at writing.

◆ What objectives are appropriate for promoting writing development in early childhood?

◆ What strategies can be used for writing development from birth to two years of age?

◆ What strategies can be used for developing writing in preschool through third grade?

◆ What steps are involved in the process approach to writing?

◆ What are the mechanical aspects of writing with which we need to concern ourselves?

Mrs. Callister read the story *The Old Lady Who Swallowed a Fly*. It is a nonsense tale that is read and also sung. The story is composed of rhymes, and each segment is repeated to make it quite predictable. A portion of the story follows:

> I know an old lady who swallowed a fly,
> I don't know why she swallowed a fly, perhaps she'll die.
> I know an old lady who swallowed a spider
> That wiggled and giggled and tickled inside her,
> She swallowed the spider to catch the fly,
> I don't know why she swallowed the fly, perhaps she'll die.
> I know an old lady who swallowed a bird,
> How absurd to swallow a bird
> (the refrain is repeated)
> I know an old lady who swallowed a cat,
> Now fancy that she swallowed a cat
> (the refrain is repeated)
> I know an old lady who swallowed a dog,
> What a hog to swallow a dog
> (the refrain is repeated and additional verses are chanted).

After the story, Mrs. Callister suggested that the children might think of additional rhymes for the story.

Tasha and Jason decided to work together. Tasha said, "I got one, I know an old lady who swallowed a snake, ummm, ummm, she got a big ache when she swallowed the snake." Jason said, "How about what a mistake to swallow a snake." Tasha agreed she liked that better. They tried another one. Jason said, "I know an old lady who swallowed a frog, what a hog to swallow a frog." Tasha said, "We can't do that, in the real story when she swallows a dog, they say what a hog to swallow a dog." Jason thought and said, "I know—she started to jog when she swallowed a frog." "That's great," said Tasha.

The class came together to see what they had come up with. Many of the rhymes were the same and many were different. There were about ten to add to the story that they wrote out on an experience chart and then chanted together. When they were done, Michael said, "You know, I think what we wrote is better than the original one." Everyone nodded and agreed.

Children love to play. Through play they develop socially and intellectually in fundamental ways. Especially in literate societies, children's play can take the form of making marks on paper. Children enjoy the act of making the marks, the social relationships they develop in the process, the sense of accomplishment mark making brings, and the products of the action. By writing messages, children achieve a sense of identity in their own eyes and in the eyes of others. The movement from playing with drawing and writing to communicating through written messages to writing narrative and expository text is a continuum that reflects the basic theories of emergent literacy (Dyson, 1993; Halliday, 1975; Parker, 1983; Sulzby, 1986a).

Relationships Between Reading and Writing

Readers and writers transform their experiences through verbal symbols. Writers reconstruct meanings by constructing texts; readers reconstruct texts by constructing anticipated meanings (Birnbaum and Emig, 1983).

The parallels between writing and reading are more obvious for young children than for older children and adults. For example, children teach themselves to write in much the same way that they teach themselves to read: experimentally. Through personally motivated and personally directed trial and error—a necessary condition of their literacy development—they try out various aspects of the writing process. They invent and decorate letters, symbols, and words; they mix drawing and writing; they invent messages in various forms and shapes; and they often continue to use invented forms of writing after they have begun to master conventional ones (Figure 9.1).

More specifically, by experimenting with writing, children construct and refine the kind of knowledge about written language that makes reading possible. In Marie Clay's words:

> The child who engages in creative writing is manipulating the units of written language—letters, words, sentence types—and is likely to be gaining some awareness of how these can be combined to convey unspoken messages. The child is having to perform within the directional constraints that we use in written English. The child is probably learning to generate sentences in a deliberate way, word by word. He makes up sentences which fit both his range of ideas and his written language skills. Fluent oral language may permit the young reader to depend almost entirely on meaning and the eye may overlook the need for discriminating details of letters and words. Creative writing demands that the child pay attention to the details of print. To put his message down in print, he is forced to construct words, letter by letter, so he becomes aware of letter features and letter sequences, particularly for the vocabulary which he uses in writing again and again. (1979, p. 2)

In other words, as children write they integrate knowledge of reading with knowledge of writing. They need relatively little direct instruction to do so—just active models, supportive talk about writing and reading, and praise for their efforts.

How Early Writing Is Acquired

Children's early literacy experiences are embedded in the familiar situations and real-life experiences of family and community membership (Gundlach et al., 1985). In fact, ethnographic researchers have discovered that, because these literacy events are so natural, most parents simply do not know about many of their own children's writing and reading experiences until they are pointed out to

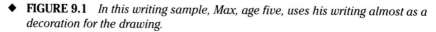

◆ **FIGURE 9.1** *In this writing sample, Max, age five, uses his writing almost as a decoration for the drawing.*

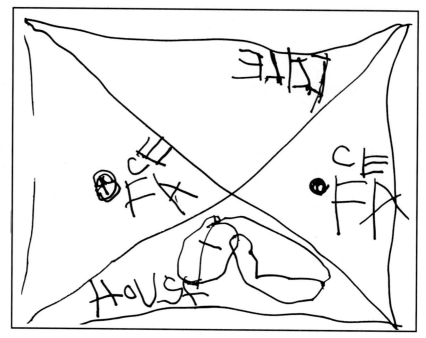

them (Taylor, 1983). Many things that family members do, including the ways they relate to each other, involve literacy. They write each other notes, lists, holiday greetings, complaints, and directions. As Anderson and Stokes (1984) discovered in a study of working-class white, African-American, and Latino families, early literacy experiences and learning are not confined to middle- and upper-class families, even though such experiences may differ greatly from one another. "Literacy," they concluded, "is influenced largely by social institutions and not cultural membership" (p. 35).

As a process, early writing development is characterized by children's moving from playfully making marks on paper, through communicating messages on paper, to creating texts. Children are at first unconcerned about the products of their "writing"; they lose interest in them almost immediately. However, once they begin to understand that the marks made can be meaningful and fun to produce, they are determined to learn how to write (Baghban, 1984).

Children learn the uses of written language before they learn the forms (Gundlach et al., 1985; Taylor, 1983). In observing children scribbling and inventing primitive "texts," researchers have observed that children seem to know what writing is *for* before they know much about how to write in correct forms. The letters to friends or relatives, the greeting cards, and the signs they produce hardly resemble conventional forms. Yet, the children seem impelled by an understanding of the function of written texts. Teale (1986) draws a similar conclusion: "The functions of literacy are as much a part of learning to read and write as are the formal aspects of written language" (p. 9). (See Figure 9.2.)

Children's writing develops through constant invention and reinvention of the forms of written language (Dyson, 1986; Graves, 1994). Children invent ways of making letters, words, and texts, moving from primitive forms through successively closer approximations of conventional forms. As they reconstruct their abilities to produce messages and texts, they simultaneously reconstruct their knowledge about written language (Bissex, 1980; Hansen, 1987). Parents of preschool children who show great interest in writing typically accept and support their youngsters' production of the primitive forms, offering little or no criticism or correction. Just as children's early forms of oral language are sometimes called *proto-language,* their invented writing might be called *proto-writing.* No one teaches them the forms; they invent them from their observations of environmental print and their observing, modeling, and interacting with more literate individuals who write in their presence.

Children's involvement in written language, though typically embedded in social situations and interactions, is essentially self-initiated and self-directed. Most of the time, young children choose when to write, what to write, and how to do it. Parents, teachers, caregivers, other adults, or siblings may encourage them to write, and certain situations (such as playing restaurant or waitress) may require writing. This type of writing works best for young children, that is, voluntarily choosing to participate in writing tasks. Researchers such as Harste, Wood-

◆ **FIGURE 9.2** *Jay, age five, attempts functional writing in a letter to his friend, Peter.*

ward, and Burke (1984) and Newman (1984) emphasize the importance of intent in children's early writing and learning. Children learn to expect written language to be meaningful, and they relate best to those situations in which writing occurs in that manner.

In writing, as in talking, story making is a primary impulse and activity. As humans, we share a deep and fundamental need to turn our experiences into stories (Hardy, 1968). Story making is a fundamental means by which we learn and by which we shape our intellectual development. Making and telling stories play central roles in the development of literacy and the growth of children's minds. Children often surprise us with the things they can do with written language and with what they know about it (Britton, 1982). They seem to grasp important aspects of its functions and forms, using this imaginative awareness to produce primitive but extraordinary manifestations of language because they want to.

Children learn about writing by observing more skilled others and by participating with them in literacy events. People who are more proficient writers play an important modeling role in children's writing development (Temple, Nathan, Burris, & Temple, 1988). Children need to observe adults participating in writing, and they must write having the guidance and support of the adult.

Children need to work independently on the functions and form of writing that they have experienced through interactions with literate others. Teale (1986) calls these activities *explorations* and claims they make it possible for children's literacy to come to "complete fruition." They may involve practicing or rehearsing aspects of writing—letter formation and differentiation, similarities or differences between drawing and writing, spelling, punctuation, and so forth. They are apparently linked to children's evolving knowledge *about* language—their *metalinguistic knowledge*. When children explore their emergent knowledge and their skill in writing independently, they become more conscious of what they know and more explicit. They may even develop language to talk about it (Goodman, 1986). The more they make their knowledge about language explicit, the more children are able to use that explicit knowledge to direct and control their own attempts at writing, and thus the forms and functions of writing.

Two points are important here. First, children practice what they learn about writing, but such practice is most helpful when self-initiated. Second, self-initiated practice contributes to what children learn consciously about writing, an evolving phenomenon that plays a fundamental role in the development of their writing abilities. (See Figure 9.3.)

Theory of Early Writing Development

In the broadest sense, children's language development can be viewed as part of their process of learning to participate in sharing and making social meanings (Halliday, 1975). To achieve this participation, they learn to understand, use, and make various symbols. Though language is just one of the symbol systems used,

◆ **FIGURE 9.3** *Three-year-old Robert separates his writing from his drawing by enclosing each in a circle during self-initiated practice.*

it is the most important and pervasive one. Thus, as part of their broad process of symbol development, children learn to listen, talk, write, and read—that is, they develop language in all four of its uses. Their language learning begins in the prespeech communication that parents and infants construct, and it builds through listening to talking, to gesturing, to playing symbolically, to drawing, and from there to writing and reading (Vygotsky, 1978). Children's main resource for literacy learning is their knowledge of ways to symbolize experience and to communicate through those symbols in pre- and postspeech interactions.

This overall theoretical framework can be summarized as follows:

1. Literacy development is part of language development.
2. Language development is part of symbol development.
3. Symbol development is part of the development of social and cultural meanings.

For most children, the process occurs as a continuum. There are no sharp gaps or transitions from one aspect to another. Under normal circumstances, children's literacy development begins with the continual process of learning to communicate—first nonverbally, then by talking, next with symbolic play, and finally by drawing. Each new phase is rooted in earlier phases and forms a new network of communication resources and potential.

Further, this literacy learning occurs naturally in the interactions of family and community life. In the process, children move from playing with written language to using it to communicate. They invent and reinvent forms. When children first begin making marks on paper, most do so with no knowledge of the alphabetic nature of the written language's symbol system. Initially, they do not conceive of writing as a means of encoding speech (Dyson, 1985; Ferreiro, 1978; Ferreiro and Teberosky, 1982). Shortly thereafter, they view letters as referring to actual people or things, though they still believe that writing, like drawing, only encodes or reflects specific objects, not "filler" words such as articles or adjectives. Only later do they realize that writing represents language (Figure 9.4.)

◆ **FIGURE 9.4** *This scribble writing by Justin (age four) goes from left to right across the page. An illustration accompanies his writing, and the child explained to the teacher what the writing said about the picture. The child understands that writing represents language.*

The Development of Writing Ability

Researchers have arrived at various descriptions of what can be viewed as developmental stages of writing in early childhood (Clay, 1975; Dyson, 1985; Sulzby, 1986b; Teale, 1986). Most agree, though, that if there are indeed stages, they are not well defined or necessarily sequential. Dyson (1986) describes children's writing development as having two broad phases. From birth to about age three, children begin to explore the form of writing by scribbling. Then, as children progress from three to six, their "controlled scribbling gradually develops into recognizable objects which they name, and similarly, the scribbling gradually acquires the characteristics of print, including linearity, horizontal orientation, and the arrangement of letter-like forms..." (p. 118). In fact, as we have noted, children may initially attempt to encode objects directly, as in drawing, and only later attempt to encode language.

Sulzby (1985) identified six broad categories of writing in kindergarten children, cautioning that these should not be considered a reflection of developmental ordering. They do describe, however, children's early attempts at writing.

1. *Writing via Drawing.* The child will use drawing to stand for writing. The child is working out the relationship between drawing and writing, not confusing the two. The child sees drawing/writing as communication of a specific and purposeful message. Children who participate in writing via drawing will read their drawings as if there is writing on them (Figure 9.5).

2. *Writing via Scribbling.* The child scribbles but intends it as writing. Often the child appears to be writing and scribbles from left to right. The child moves the pencil as an adult does, and the pencil makes writing-like sounds. The scribble resembles writing (Figure 9.6).

◆ **FIGURE 9.5** *Writing via drawing: When asked to write something, Brad (age four) drew a picture. The same request over time yielded the same response, a drawing for writing.*

◆ **FIGURE 9.6** *Writing via scribbling: When asked to write, Katie (age three) scribbled randomly. She eventually progressed to a left-to-right scribble and then purposeful marks that could be periods to end the sentence.*

◆ **FIGURE 9.7** *Writing via making letterlike forms. Olivia (age four) wrote letterlike forms from left to right.*

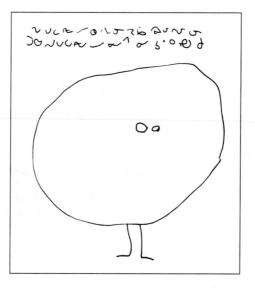

3. *Writing via Making Letterlike Forms.* At a quick glance, shapes in the child's writing resemble letters. However, close observation reveals that they only look like letters. They are not just poorly formed letters, though, they are creations (Figure 9.7).

4. *Writing via Reproducing Well-learned Units or Letter Strings.* The child uses letter sequences learned from such sources as his or her own name. The child sometimes changes the order of the letters, writing the same ones many different ways, or reproduces letters in long strings or in random order (Figure 9.8).

5. *Writing via Invented Spelling.* Many varieties and levels of invented spelling are demonstrated by children. Basically, children create their own spelling for words when they do not know the conventional spellings. In invented spelling, one letter may represent an entire syllable and words sometimes overlap and are not properly spaced. As the child's writing matures, the words look more like conventional writing, with perhaps only one letter invented or left out (Figure 9.9).

6. *Writing via Conventional Spelling.* The child's writing resembles adult writing (Figure 9.10).

◆ **FIGURE 9.8** *Writing via reproducing well-learned units or letter strings written by Brian (age four) go from left to right across the page.*

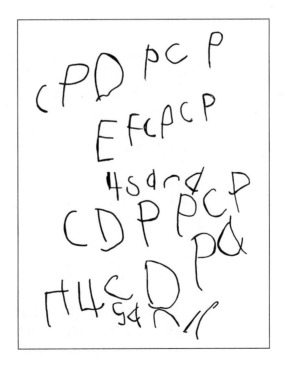

◆ **FIGURE 9.9** *Writing via invented spelling: "I love cats because they are so pretty and I like other animals too. I love my family and they love me back." This was written by Jenny C. Wilkinson in the spring of her kindergarten year.*

◆ **FIGURE 9.10** *Conventional spelling. This story was written by Kevin, who was in second grade.*

Sulzby's general description of early writing is most helpful for parents and teachers when they are observing and describing children's writing. As we have noted, however, Sulzby emphasizes that these categories are not necessarily developmental or sequentially invariant.

Strategies and Objectives for Promoting Writing Development

Parents and teachers can use various strategies to encourage and respond to children's self-initiated writing efforts. They can create situations that will engage children in producing and learning about written language. These situations reflect our growing understanding that children's literacy develops within the context of family and community events that involve writing and reading, but for which literacy instruction is only infrequently an immediate goal.

Of all the ideas, theories, and strategies concerning emergent literacy, the way in which we think about writing represents the most obvious break with tradition. We have allowed children to use crayons and paper to encourage development of motor coordination in preparation for writing, but we never thought of writing to convey meaning as being an integral part of an early literacy program for children as young as two. We now integrate strategies for writing into the daily routines of babies, toddlers, preschoolers, kindergartners, and first graders. We consider even the youngest child's marks on paper as early attempts at writing, rather than as random marks. This perception is necessary in programs for early literacy development.

Generally, the best way to assist children in language and literacy development is to create situations for meaningful use in addition to offering some direct instruction. This principle applies equally in the home, day-care center, nursery, kindergarten, first, second, or third grade. The following objectives are posed from the perspective that children learn language, including writing and reading, by using it purposefully in many situations (for example, in playing or communicating).

1. Children will be provided with an environment in which they are regularly exposed to many kinds of print.
2. Children will experience print as a source of pleasure and enjoyment.
3. Children will regularly observe adults writing, both for work and for leisure.
4. Children will be given opportunities and materials for writing themselves.
5. Children will be assisted in deciding what to write about, but left alone to make such decisions.
6. Children's attempts at writing, whatever the form, will be responded to as meaningful communication (e.g., scribble writing, letterlike forms, random letters, invented spelling).

7. Children will be encouraged to use writing for a wide range of individual and social purposes, such as making lists, cards, letters, signs, announcements, stories, expository pieces, and books.
8. Children will be read stories in a variety of styles, which may serve as eventual models for their writing.
9. The use of writing will be integrated throughout the curriculum.
10. Teachers will take the opportunity through children's writing to point out sound-symbol correspondences as the spoken word is transformed into the written.
11. Children will be exposed to the appropriate way to write letters in manuscript.
12. Children will be exposed to the use of some aspects of punctuation: periods, commas, and quotation marks.
13. Children's invented spelling will be accepted and, as they make the transition to more conventional writing, there will be instruction for spelling.
14. Students will participate in evaluating their own work.
15. Experiences in writing from a constructivist perspective will be balanced with some explicit instruction of skills.

Strategies for Writing Development from Birth to Two

Earlier chapters have described strategies that parents can use in helping children with oral language development and early reading. Some of those strategies can be applied directly to children's early writing development; others can be adapted. Some strategies are helpful specifically with writing development. It is crucial to remember, though, that speaking, reading, and writing are dynamically linked in children's development. When we help children with oral language, we also contribute indirectly to their literacy development by increasing their language experience. Similarly, reading development contributes to speaking and writing, and writing to speaking and reading. This understanding forms the basis for the integrated language arts approach.

In a detailed case study, Baghban (1984) describes observations of her daughter Giti's writing development from eighteen months, when Giti first began marking on paper, to twenty-four months. When Giti began scribbling, her productions sprawled all over the page. By nineteen months she had begun to make dots and her sprawl was noticeably less extreme. By twenty months she had added circles and wavy lines to her repertoire. When she wrote after watching one of her parents write, her productions "more closely resembled English script" (p. 48). At twenty-three months she averaged ten minutes per writing session, and at twenty-four months she began babbling over her own writing. She also attempted to write her first letter, *M* for *McDonald's* and for *Marcia,* her mother's first name. Throughout the period, and later as well, Giti's parents followed her literacy experiences and efforts attentively. Such attentiveness is something we urge all parents and primary caregivers to adopt.

As suggested in earlier chapters, another important way that we can support children's writing development is to become more aware of their experiences with environmental print, including print they see on television, in religious environments, on food cans and boxes, on signs, and in stores. Not only can we become more aware of the variety and frequency of children's experiences with environmental print, we can talk with them about these experiences, commenting, asking questions, and encouraging them to identify and remember signs, letters, and bits of print out of their normal contexts (for instance, an *M* used somewhere other than in a *McDonald's* sign). If we so interact with children, especially from their second year on, we are ready to support them when, as a part of their scribble writing, they try to write one or more of these environmentally learned letters. In fact, some children may make their first attempts to do this between eighteen and twenty-four months, though most children will not begin until twenty-four to thirty-six months.

We can also assist children in their first attempts to make marks on paper. Often, when children begin scribbling (some at eighteen months), they bang on the paper with their writing implements. Only a bit later do they begin using smoother, more deliberate, more coordinated movements to make their marks. When children are in their first, primitive stages of scribbling, we can show them how to hold markers or crayons. We can guide their hands to paper, not making marks for them but helping them understand that the paper is the place for writing.

Our responses to children's early scribbling are important. It is better not to urge children to write particular things. They should make marks spontaneously and decide for themselves when these marks are intended to represent something. It is important not to press them to tell us what their marks mean or represent. It is better to say, "I like that," than to ask, "What is it?" "Can you write some more?" is also a helpful response, but do not insist if the child says no. Expressing genuine pleasure in children's early markings, whether they resemble writing or not, and seeing them as an important step in a long developmental process are positive responses that will encourage children to continue. By continuing their "writing," they will incorporate in it what they are learning about print from the literacy events that fill their lives.

Beyond responding supportively to children, we can model writing for them by writing in their presence. As we have seen, we can let them see us writing letters, lists, and notes and filling out forms and bills, and we can interact with them about what we are doing. For example: "I'm writing a letter to Grandma and Grandpa. I'm telling them that we miss them. Do you want to tell them something? Do you want to write something on the paper to them?" When writing, invite the youngsters to sit with you, watch you, ask questions, and try their own hand at writing. This gives children opportunities to see how we go about writing and to begin to understand that the marks we make convey meaning.

Junk mail is a form of environmental print that can arouse interest in writing. Children enjoy writing or making marks on flyers, brochures, ads, announcements, and forms. They will write over the print and in the blank spaces. Apparently, the look and arrangement of the print gives them the model and inspiration to make their own marks.

Repeating rhymes and singing songs can also contribute to children's early writing. So can using hand puppets and playing with toys and games, such as puzzles that can be taken apart and put back together. Manipulative toys that require dexterity help with the motor development needed to shape letters. Playing with clay or play dough, finger painting, using chalkboards, and painting on easels help build motor coordination as well. Of course, reading to children not only develops oral language and promotes early reading attempts, as discussed earlier, it can also motivate children to emulate the writing or to make their own books, no matter how crude the first attempts. Parents and caregivers in day-care centers can display children's early writings on walls, doors, and appliances, to be enjoyed and not judged or corrected.

Homes as well as day-care centers should provide environments for writing—comfortable spots with rugs and child-size tables and chairs—and storage for writing materials. The latter should include felt-tip markers, pencils, crayons, and chalk. There should be ample supplies and varied sizes of large unlined paper (newsprint works well) and a chalkboard. Materials should be stored consistently in the place provided for writing so that the child can learn how to select materials and put them away independently.

Strategies for Writing Development in Early Childhood Classrooms

Parents and teachers can expect to see rapid development in writing in children from two to eight years of age. As we have seen, it is during this period that most children move from scribbling to producing random letters, to writing letters, to writing words with invented spellings, to beginning to use conventional writing. They will begin to space properly between words and use some marks of punctuation. They tend to write longer pieces, and their productions often represent wider ranges of functions and forms. In short, this is a time when children show intense bursts of writing activity, perhaps alternating these with intense bursts of reading activity (Bissex, 1980). It is important, therefore, that teachers have a sense of children's writing needs and interests at this time and know how to interact with them in order to support their efforts, learning, and growth.

Like younger children, preschoolers and kindergarteners for the most part take more pleasure in the *process* of writing than in its *products*. The act of writing is their center of interest. Gradually they do develop concern for the products. When they play waiter or waitress, for example, and take an "order," they may be concerned that others can "read" it. The same thing might happen with notes or greeting cards sent to relatives or friends. Children begin to evidence concern that recipients are able to read their messages—perhaps so they can write back. Children who have had little experience pretending to write might be reluctant to make marks on paper even by kindergarten age, possibly because they have become aware that their marks are not conventional writing and thus might not be accepted. It is important to let them know that writing that is not conventional will be accepted. Some children may request conventional spellings and will not write unless they know it is correct. They should be given the help they request.

Children in societies such as ours have experienced literacy through pre-school and kindergarten, and they have constructed useful though usually asystematic knowledge about writing and reading. Some may also have begun to write and read on their own, though in unconventional and invented forms. Therefore, it is inappropriate to think of these youngsters as preliterate. The challenge for schools is to provide experiences that complement children's prior experiences and to recognize individual differences in development among youngsters (Calkins, 1986). It is important that adults observe the signs and pace of the growth of children's understanding of writing, of their use of writing for a widening range of purposes, and of their ability to control various writing conventions in less primitive, more adultlike ways. Observing children's early writing development creates a context for the planned learning events and spontaneous interactions through which adults can contribute so fundamentally to children's emerging literacy.

Adults should take children's early writing seriously as interesting evidence of the kinds of experiments with writing that contribute centrally to their literacy development. Children's early writings are to be enjoyed, valued, and understood. At the same time, they should usually not be made the occasion for the hunting and correction of errors or for excessive direct instruction. The latter should follow from children's questions and needs, identified by the teacher and child, and should thus be individualized. Explicit instruction should also be given in proportion to the magnitude of the request. Often, adults respond to children's requests with information and explanations that are appropriate and helpful but too long or detailed.

We must realize that what young children write about and how they approach writing is more important than their mechanics of writing (spelling, handwriting, punctuation, and spacing). Mechanical skills *are* related to writing, but not writing as we are concerned with it in early childhood literacy development. Learning to write involves learning to compose texts that convey meaning. As children gain experience with writing, they will learn the peripheral skills and mechanics of writing through practice and instruction when the need arises and by asking for the information.

When children are free to write in unconventional ways, such as using invented spellings as illustrated in Figure 9.9, p. 268, they are enhancing phonemic awareness and eventually knowledge of phonics. When children write, they have to transform the spoken word into written language. This fosters understanding of the structure of spoken language and how it is related to written language. The more children write, the better they become at segmenting sounds into words, which not only develops their ability to write, but their ability to read independently as well.

No distinctions should be made among the kinds of writing young children undertake. A list of words is as important as a creative story. For young children, the functions of writing are more important than the form or content. They choose to write if a situation has meaning for them. If we impose upon them our selection of what they should write about, we are not likely to see positive results. With these basic ideas in mind, we can create strategies and appropriate environments for helping children write naturally.

The Writing Center

The literacy area in the classroom should include a place designated for writing. It should be easily accessible, attractive, and inviting. This area can be a part of the library corner. It should be furnished with a table and chairs, plus a rug for youngsters who want to stretch out and write on the floor. Writing implements should include plenty of colored felt-tip marking pens, large and small crayons, large and small pencils (both regular and colored), and chalk and a chalkboard. Various types of paper should be available, lined and unlined, plain white or newsprint, ranging from 8½ × 11 inches to 24 × 36 inches. Do not, however, use manuscript practice paper that is lined with different colored and dotted lines specifically to encourage proper size of letters and spacing between lines. Most preschoolers and kindergartners are not ready for such restraints.

Index cards for recording Very Own Words should be stored in the writing area, as should the children's collections of Very Own Words. Very Own Words can be stored in file boxes, coffee cans, or paper bags. Each child should have a

The computer allows young children to communicate thoughts. Early introduction to the computer will make it part of the child's life.

writing folder to collect written samples of his or her work over the course of the school year. If available, a typewriter is useful, as is a computer for word processing. Materials for making books should also be available, including colored construction paper for covers, plain white paper for inside pages, a stapler, and scissors. Teachers can prepare blank books, keyed to special occasions, for children to use. For example, a blank Valentine's Day book shaped like a heart and made of red construction paper with five or six sheets of plain white paper stapled inside provides inviting space that children can fill with their written greetings. (See Figures 9.11, 9.12, and 9.13 on preparing blank books.) Stock *bare books* (books with hard covers but no print inside) for special projects, and blue books used for examinations are perfect for young children's writing. They can be purchased from school supply companies and are very inexpensive. They come with twelve or sixteen pages, which is usually just right for an original story by a young child. Keep a supply of interesting pictures, posters, magazines, and newspapers; these can stimulate, decorate, or illustrate children's writing.

An alphabet chart in easy view helps children identify and shape letters they may need while writing. Tactile plastic, magnetic, wooden, and felt letters should be among the language arts manipulatives. These help develop motor dexterity for the act of writing and aid in letter recognition and formation. A bulletin board should be available for children to display their own writing with a space for posting notices or sending and receiving private messages. "Mailboxes" for youngsters' incoming and outgoing "mail" can be placed in the writing center. The mailboxes for a pen pal program are discussed later in the functional writing section. The writing center should be labeled with a sign that could say "Author's Spot" or whatever name is selected by the children.

◆ **FIGURE 9.11** *Stapled book. Cut colored construction paper and white writing paper into a desired shape. Staple at the side.*

◆ **FIGURE 9.12** *Sewn book. Punch holes into oaktag and white writing paper. Sew together with yarn.*

Basic implements and supplies for writing should be stocked in every other learning center in the room as well. The accessibility of these materials will encourage writing (Morrow, 1990). A child might want to record the outside temperature on a chart in the science center, protect a construction of blocks with a "Do Not Touch" sign, or copy a Very Own Word in the social studies or science area. A group might decide to turn the dramatic-play corner into a dentist's office, including in it an appointment book for recording dates, times, and patients' names; appointment cards; patients' records; and a prescription pad for medication.

In all such situations, children should write independently according to function and interest. The teacher has prepared the environment in which such writing can occur and has introduced the materials and made suggestions to the children. With this preparation, children look naturally to writing as a means of communication.

Allison adds her page to the class book at the writing table in the writing center.

FIGURE 9.13 *Folded, Stitched, and Glued Book*

a. Sew a running stitch down the center of eight to ten sheets of eight-and-a-half-by-eleven plain white writing paper backed with a piece of nine-by-twelve colored construction paper.

b. Place an eleven-by-fourteen piece of contact paper or wallpaper face down. Paste two pieces of six-by-nine oaktag or cardboard on the peeled contact paper a quarter inch apart, leaving about a one-inch border. Fold each corner of the contact paper onto the oaktag to form a triangle (glue if using wallpaper).

c. Fold the edges of the contact paper onto the oaktag (paste down if using wallpaper). Place a twelve-inch piece of Mystic Tape down the center of the contact paper and over its edges. Put glue on the two exposed pieces of oaktag and on the quarter-inch space between them.

d. Place the folded and stitched edge of the construction paper and plain white paper in the quarter-inch glued space. Paste the construction paper onto the oaktag and over the contact-paper border to make the inside covers.

Independent Writing

In Chapter 6, the independent reading and writing period, which gives children the opportunity to participate in literacy activities, was discussed. Children choose what to do based on several options, and they choose to work alone or collaboratively with others. Chapter 6 emphasized pleasurable experiences with reading, and collecting anecdotes concerning reading behaviors during this time. It is difficult to separate reading and writing, especially during this independent time when children direct their own behavior. It is interesting to note when observing children during independent reading and writing periods that equal time is spent at reading and writing. When children decided to engage in writing, it often was a cooperative effort. During this period, children had the opportunity to select from a list of literacy activities, such as:

Read a book, magazine, or newspaper alone or with a friend.

Listen to a story on the headsets at the listening station.

Read or tell a story using a felt-board and story characters.

Read or tell a story using a roll movie.

Read or tell a story using the chalk talk technique.

Read or tell a story using puppets.

Prepare a tape story by recording your reading of a book.

Write a story alone or with a friend.

Write a story and make it into a felt story.

Write a story and record it for the listening station.

Write a story and perform it as a puppet show.

Write a story and make it into a roll movie.

Write a story and present it as a chalk talk.

Present a play based on a story you wrote or read.

Bind a story you've written into a book and place it in the library corner for others to read.

Participate in content-area activities that involve reading and writing.

The following anecdotes relate to the writing that took place during observations of independent reading and writing periods. It is evident how closely reading and writing are linked. So many of the things children chose to do were motivated by what they had read or what was read to them. When writing, they often looked for additional information by going to sources to read more.

After listening to the teacher read *The Magic School Bus Inside the Earth,* Stephanie, Jason, Kevin, and Nicky decided to make a poster about the book that showed key pictures with captions for each picture. The children delegated responsibilities. They made up a title for the poster and called it, *Scenes from the*

Magic School Bus Inside the Earth. They drew episodes from the story and wrote their own captions for the pictures. The poster took several days to complete. (One of the characteristics of independent reading and writing is that projects can be worked on over a long period.) When the poster was complete, the children presented their work to the class. Stephanie and Jason held the poster and Kevin and Nicky were the spokespersons. Kevin explained how the group wanted to illustrate the story in an unusual way and decided on a poster. Kevin and Nicky took turns pointing to the pictures they had all drawn and reading the captions they had written for each.

Heather, Kim, and Tina read a biography about *Willie Mays, the Baseball Star.* They decided to make a roll movie about the book. They wrote dialogue for the pictures they drew. Their information came from the book they had read. Heather was concerned that they might need more information about Willie Mays and suggested they look in the dictionary. Kim told Heather that dictionaries are for finding out how to spell words and getting their definitions and encyclopedias were for finding out information. The girls did find additional information about Willie Mays in the encyclopedia. They copied it down and continued with their work.

Motivated by the story *Aladdin,* Zarah and Shakiera decided to write their own story about a magical fish called Alexander. Shakiera asked Zarah to write the story, and Shakiera suggested that she would do the pictures. Shakiera also offered her help in thinking of the words to write. Zarah began to write the first line: "A fish called Alexander was a talking fish." Shakiera told Zarah to add to the sentence, "and he had magic."

Zarah said, "Magic, I don't know if that's the right word. I think he had powers." Shakiera said, "I think that magic and power are the same thing." The girls agreed and went on to write the rest of the story.

Television shows, rock stars, and current events motivated writing during independent reading and writing. Three girls created a roll movie that included biographies of each member of a rock singing group. Another group made a felt story for an original episode they created for a popular television program.

Current events along with books children read motivated writing. Joey was reading a book about the Civil War. He asked the teacher to read it to the class, which she did. Joey decided to write his own book about the Civil War, and Christopher joined him. Christopher called the book "U.S. Saratoga." As they were drawing pictures, they made bombing sounds. Suddenly Joey said, "Wait a minute, this is weird. We're making airplane carriers fighting in the Civil War." The two boys changed their minds and decided to do a book about a war that could be happening now. It was an intense piece.

On the lighter side, Julia and Katie wrote a script for a play they were going to have some children act out. It was a wedding ceremony, and their text is reproduced in Figure 9.14.

These episodes during independent reading and writing reveal a wide variety of topics that were focused upon. Many of them we would never think to ask children to write about. If we did, they probably would never have the enthusi-

◆ **FIGURE 9.14** *A Play Written by Julia and Katie During an Independent Writing Period*

> *We are gathd her today to jon thes two wondrfal pepel in holey matramony. Silvea*
> *Do you tak Gim to be yor offl weded hasbind, I do. Gim do you tak Silvea to be yr*
> *offel weded wife. I do. Ma we have the rins. Silvea pot this ring on Gims Finger.*
> *Gim pot this ring on Silveas finger. I now prnawns you man and wife. Yo may now*
> *kis the brid*

asm they demonstrated because they had not selected them themselves. We also don't know what all of their interests are. Some of the topics are much more sophisticated than one might have thought would interest children in grades one and two. Children have original ideas that they can draw from their varied and rich life experiences. The topics they select have meaning and function for them, and therefore they write freely and enthusiastically about them.

In Chapter 6, I described Independent Reading and Writing Periods and suggested that these are often called *Reading and Writing Workshops.* The independent writing just discussed has the same characteristics. Some classrooms separate Reading Workshops and Writing Workshops, but it is difficult to differentiate the two. Children's writing draws on their reading, and their reading encourages writing. The characteristics of reading and writing workshops or periods of independent reading and writing include:

1. A mini-lesson by the teacher to set a purpose or theme for the independent reading and writing period.
2. Choices for children to decide what they will do and whether they will work together or alone.
3. Engaged activity with reading and writing that can include functional writing, story writing, writing plays, or using art and other modalities for utilizing writing, such as a roll story, flannel story, and so on.
4. Evaluation among students of how their projects have progressed.
5. Some type of performance of tasks completed.

Many different terms have been used for some of the strategies associated with the integrated language arts related to developing reading and writing. Many of them overlap and have similar and different components. The important thing is that teachers offer varied experiences for their students, such as reading and writing alone, together, with guidance, and without guidance; sharing reading and writing; evaluating reading and writing; and just enjoying reading and writing. As in Chapter 6, these activities can be adapted for children with special needs. Children can write to other youngsters who may share their problems. As

Second-grade girls engage in a cooperative writing experience.

teachers have said, "There is something for everyone during independent reading and writing, the gifted, the child who attended basic skills classes, and youngsters from bilingual backgrounds."

Functional Writing

Children need to see purpose before they write. Class writing projects that are particularly purposeful include **greeting cards** for all occasions to parents, grandparents, sisters, brothers, friends, and relatives. Don't forget birthdays and holidays. Write **thank-you notes** to guest speakers who come to class, to mothers or other adults who help on class trips, to the director of the zoo you visited, or to the librarian who spent time with the class at the public library. Prepare **lists** of things to remember to do in preparing a party, a special program, or a class trip. Make **address and telephone books** with entries from class members. Write notes to parents about activities in school. Encourage individual children to write to their parents about specific things they are doing in school.

Collecting and using Very Own Words offer opportunities for writing and copying and so does using classroom environmental print in one's own writing. Some preschools and kindergartens, as well as elementary classrooms, have established **mail service** and **pen pal** programs (Green, 1985; Martinez & Teale, 1987; Mason, 1986). Children are offered pen pals to write to regularly (once a week is reasonable). Teachers or aides may have to help children write their letters or take dictation. Encourage children to use what writing capabilities they have, even if they cannot produce conventional writing. Teachers may have to read the incoming letters to students who cannot yet read conventionally.

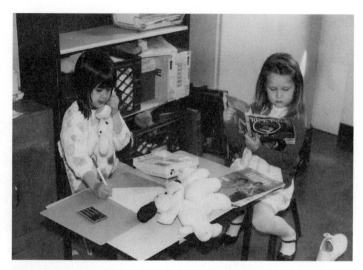

Melissa pretends to be a nurse and writes down an appointment in the dramatic-play center designed to be a doctor's office.

A **notice board** for exchanging messages also motivates functional writing (Newman, 1984). Children can tack up pictures for each other as beginning messages. The teacher needs to provide a model by leaving messages for individuals and for the entire class. Notices about school or class events are appropriate. It is important to draw attention to the board when posting a class message or when leaving messages for individuals, so that children get into the habit of looking for messages and leaving them themselves. There also needs to be a place for private messages. These can be posted on the notice board in an envelope or in student mailboxes. Some teachers have taped brown bags to each child's desk for them to receive private messages. From time to time the teacher will check the messages to see that children are writing. One teacher found the note in Figure 9.15, written by Asia a first-grade girl, to Andra who is a boy in first grade.

Journal writing can be carried out successfully in early childhood rooms, with entries made daily or at least several times a week. Children are encouraged to write anything they want in their journals and to write at their own developmental levels. Thus, some children's journals might include only pictures, scribble writing, random letters, or invented spelling. The teacher models journal writing, perhaps with a personal message such as, "I'm very excited today. My daughter is going to be in a play tonight, and I'm going to watch her." By example the child is given an idea about the kinds of entries that are appropriate. Some children draw or write stories in their journals as well as personal experiences. From time to time the journal can also take on dialogue form, the teacher responding to a child's journal entry with a comment. If the child writes, "I had a

◆ **FIGURE 9.15** *A Private Message Sent by a First-Grade Girl to a First-Grade Boy*

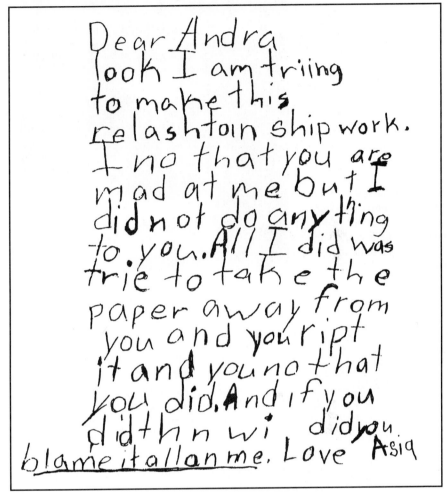

picnic," the teacher might respond, "That sounds like fun. What did you eat?" The length and fluency of children's journal entries show great gains when the activity is continued regularly throughout a school year (Routman, 1991). Journals can be written about a child's personal life. They can be related to topics studied such as recording the growth of a seed that was planted, charting daily temperature, or reacting to a story that was read. Journals can be written in notebooks or pages stapled together to create a book.

Because there are different names for journals, it often becomes confusing as to which one should be used. Once again, it is the concept of journal writing that is important, that is, putting one's thoughts and early writing attempts down

Teachers may need to take dictation for journal writing and for writing to pen pals. Eventually children should be encouraged to do their own writing.

on paper without concern for the mechanics of writing. To help differentiate the different uses of journals, several will be mentioned here.

Personal journals are private journals in which children write about their lives or topics of special interest to them. These are shared only if a child chooses to do so. These are never subject to correction for spelling, punctuation, and so on.

Dialogue journals are similar to the personal journal, but they are shared with teachers or peers who respond to what they have read. They are similar to a conversation only the conversation is done with the written word instead of the spoken word. This provides students with feedback about their thoughts.

Reading response journals are those in which children respond to narrative or informational text read. They write their feelings concerning responses to the story or information. In these response logs they may even record vocabulary learned. Teachers do read response to literature journals.

Learning logs usually involve other content areas, such as social studies or science. This is when children record information being learned, such as charting the growth of a plant or the progress of a setting hen's eggs.

There are many other titles for journals. As with terminology in the integrated language arts, different titles are associated with different and similar tasks. Journal writing has been found to be productive for students in helping them to become more fluent writers, choose topics to develop, learn the mechanics of writing, reflect on ideas, and articulate them. Whatever they are called, some journal experiences should include private reflections about the life of the child, others should include responses to a child's journal writing by the teacher or peers, some should be written in response to literature, and some should be written in relation to information learned.

Children's Literature and Writing

Children's literature and writing is as natural a medium for encouraging writing as it is for encouraging oral language and reading (Routman, 1991). Reading several books by the same author or illustrator can prompt a class letter asking the author how he or she gets ideas to write or asking the illustrator what kind of art materials he or she uses. It is best to identify authors or illustrators who are likely to respond, for it is important to receive a response, even if it comes from a publisher's representative. Series books—those that use the same character in several different books, such as *Madeline* (Bemelmans, 1939), *Curious George* (Rey, 1941), and *Harold and the Purple Crayon* (Johnson, 1955)—can motivate children to write their own books or a class book about the character. Books such as *Swimmy* (Lionni, 1963) and *Alexander and the Terrible, Horrible, No Good, Very Bad Day* (Viorst, 1972) involve the main character in a series of adventures or incidents as the story proceeds. Children can be asked to write still another episode or adventure for the character. Some stories, such as *Alexander and the Terrible, Horrible, No Good, Very Bad Day,* lend themselves to writing about personal experiences. (Figure 9.16 illustrates one child's response to this task.) Shared book experiences, directed listening/reading–thinking activities, and one-to-one and small-group story readings (described in Chapter 7) can all lead to writing

◆ **FIGURE 9.16** *Writing Motivated by Children's Literature*

experiences. Predictable books provide patterns that children can imitate in their own writing through: cumulative patterns, as in *I Know an Old Lady* (Westcott, 1980); repetitive language, as in *Are You My Mother?* (Eastman, 1960); familiar sequences, as in *The Very Hungry Caterpillar* (Carle, 1970); or catch-phrases, as in *Horton Hatches the Egg* (Seuss, 1940). (See Appendix A for a list of such books.)

Children need to share their writing with some audience. When they know they will be sharing their work, they will write for that audience and have a greater purpose for writing. At a designated time during the day, usually at the end when the class gets together to review the day's happenings, a child can be selected as Author of the Day to share something that he or she has written (Graves & Hansen, 1983). More than one piece can be read and more than one child can be Author of the Day. Those authors who read their writings in a particular week should display them on a bulletin board in the writing center along with photographs of themselves. When sharing work, the child can sit in a chair marked "Author's Chair." This is a permanent fixture in the room for all to use at some particular time. Children in the audience should be encouraged to comment about their friends' work with such statements as "I like what you wrote" or "I fell and cut my knee once, too." Because at first the children may not comment readily, the teacher needs to model comments for the audience, whose young members will soon emulate the behavior.

It was Steven's turn in the Author's Chair. He sat down, and organized his materials, and said,

> I've been working on a series of stories. They are all about the same character and in each one he had another adventure. It is sort of like the books about *Clifford the Big Red Dog*. My stories are about a cat and the first one is called *The Cat Named Buster*. I call that Part I; I already have Part II and Part III. Part II is called *Buster Meets Pretzel*. Pretzel is a dog. Part III is called *Buster Gets Lost*. I'll read Part I to you.

After reading Part I of his stories, Philip said, "Can I read one?" Steven replied, "Sure but you should read all of them. They go together." Philip continued, "I just want to read the first one now." Steven said, "O.K., but you don't know what you're missing."

Children's work should be published. "Why publish?" almost answers the question "Why write?" "Writing is a public act, meant to be shared with many audiences" (Graves, 1983, p. 54). When children know their work will be published, they write for a defined purpose. When work is to be published, it becomes special; it needs to be done carefully and refined. Children can publish their work in many ways. The most popular is to bind writings into books, which are placed in the literacy center and featured on open bookshelves for others to read. Other means of publishing include creating felt-board stories or roll movies, telling stories to classmates, role-playing what has been written, or presenting the story in a puppet show. A computer can be used to type, save, and print original material.

The Process Approach to Writing in Early Childhood

For rather experienced early writers, publishing can be the motivation for beginning the **process approach** to writing. The process approach makes children realize that writing involves thinking, organizing, and rewriting before a piece is complete. They become aware that a first writing rarely constitutes a finished product. Typical steps in this approach include prewriting, drafting, conferencing, revising, and editing (Calkins, 1986). **Prewriting** involves some brainstorming related to the topic. Brainstorming can take place with the entire class, a friend, the teacher, or alone. If the topic is the writer's favorite food, brainstorming might include listing the characteristics of the food, the different ways the writer likes it prepared, and what in particular he or she likes about it. The prewriting activity helps generate ideas and organizes thoughts prior to writing. The prewriting ideas made into an outline help determine what to write about first, second, and so on. **Drafting** is the second part in the process. The author makes his or her first attempt at writing the piece by getting the words down on paper. The lists prepared in the prewriting phase are used as a guide. The **conference,** which is next, can be done with a teacher or a friend. This is a time to reflect upon what has been written to see if changes need to be made and, if so, just what they ought to be. It is preferable to reflect with someone else but a child can also do it alone. The fourth part is **revising.** During the conference, suggestions arise that may demonstrate the need for change, and this is the time to make those changes. When the revision is made, the author goes on to the fifth step, which is called **editing.** Editing requires minor changes to the piece, mostly attending to such things as punctuation, grammatical corrections, and spelling.

The process approach should be used cautiously with children in the early childhood years. The prewriting phase may be accomplished through discussion and word lists. The drafting or initial writing can be carried out, but the teacher must be sensitive to the child's attempted writing behavior. The teacher then asks the child if he or she can think of any changes to be made or other ideas to be added. This is the revision stage. The final task is editing, and with young children this means copying the work over. If the child is publishing a book, it might mean copying it into a bound book. (Three ways of making a book are illustrated earlier in this chapter in Figures 9.11 to 9.13).

Some children may be frustrated by revisions and editing, particularly by having to copy their work over. Be selective in choosing the youngster with whom to use the process approach. Involve only those who seem capable of handling it. Try only one or two of the steps in the process in writing experiences.

Writing conferences between a teacher and a child are times to discuss what the child has written, to encourage the child in writing, and to assess progress by observing and reviewing the writing products gathered in the child's folder. During the conference the teacher can take dictation or help the child with a word, a caption, a picture, or a publishing activity. This is an especially

Stephanie created her story into a roll movie.

Stephanie puts the finishing touches on the cover of a book she has written.

good time to work with those students capable of dealing with any of the steps in process writing and to encourage reluctant writers. The process approach is used only occasionally with young children. As they increase their skills, more of the steps can be utilized. Only use the approach with children who seem ready to deal with it.

Writing programs in early childhood should be initiated at the beginning of the school year. Teachers should refer to children as authors and writers so that they perceive themselves as such. Teachers need to model writing through messages on the message board, notes to parents, thank-you notes to children, and experience charts dictated by the class. They must be supportive when working with young writers. Reluctant writers need to be encouraged to write in "their very own way" (Martinez & Teale, 1987; Sulzby, 1986b). Youngsters need to know that their work does not have to look like adult writing. Showing them samples of other children's writing, including drawings, scribble writing, and random letters, helps them see that they can do the same thing. Adults need to facilitate young writers' attempts by taking dictation if children cannot or will not write themselves, spelling words, showing children how to form letters when asked, and answering questions that arise during writing. Like other areas of literacy, writing requires social interaction if it is to promote development. Therefore, teachers need to offer young writers feedback, encouragement, and positive reinforcement.

The Mechanics of Writing

Thus far this chapter has emphasized the importance of promoting children's interest in writing and giving them opportunities to write that will prove to be enjoyable. The mechanics of writing have not been dealt with.

Writing requires dexterity. Although it is unnecessary and often unwise to bog down preschoolers and kindergarteners with the particulars of proper letter formation, they can be encouraged to use manipulatives such as puzzles and sewing cards that strengthen their fine motor coordination. In our earlier discussion of the literacy center, other materials that will help with writing and identifying letters were mentioned, including magnetic letters and letter forms to trace and copy. The letters of the alphabet should be displayed at eye level for children, and the teacher can model the correct formation of upper- and lowercase manuscript (Figure 9.17). We are all individuals; therefore, we need not all write in the same style. Legibility needs to be the main goal for handwriting. Learning about spaces between words is important so that words will not run into each other.

Punctuation and capitalization are best taught when the need arises. Opportunities for dealing with commas, question marks, periods, and capital letters occur when reading a Morning Message, for example, and the mechanics of writing are discussed in a natural setting. There will need to be some direct instruction when dealing with these skills, but whenever possible, they should be handled when opportunities arise to discuss them in the print used in your classroom such as that appearing in experience charts.

Spelling has become an area of concern with the acceptance of invented spelling in the early stages of writing. Many teachers are not sure when to begin formal teaching of spelling or if they should even correct invented forms. Children should be encouraged to write in any way that they can in the early first attempts. However, they need to know that it is "a child's way of writing and not grown up writing." When children are comfortable writing, and do so freely in their own style of early attempts, it then becomes time to point out elements of spelling that will help them make the transition from invented spelling to conventional spelling. The following are some suggestions.

◆ **FIGURE 9.17** *Forming the Letters of the Alphabet*

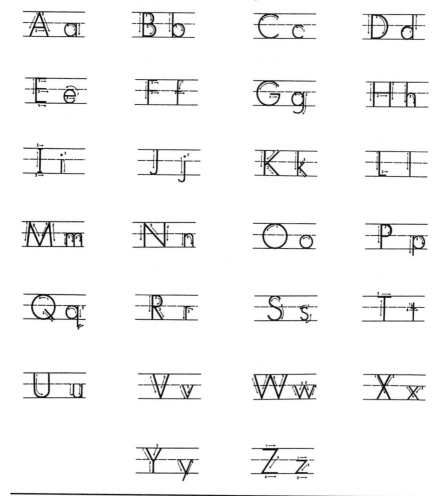

- When you take dictation from a child you can comment on the spelling of some unusual words.
- When children use certain consistent invented forms of spelling in their writing, put the correct spelling on a 3 × 5 Very Own Word card for them to copy the next time they use that word. Get children in the habit of asking for words they do not know how to spell on index cards to help them develop their own spelling word list.
- If when using Big Books, and tracking print, there is a word that you think is worth emphasizing for spelling aspects, this is a perfect time to take advantage of the opportunity.
- A lot of free writing will actually result in improved spelling.

- Phonic lessons which teach about word families and sound–symbol relationships will help with spelling. Make children aware that they should be using their knowledge of sound–symbol relationships when they spell words.
- In writing conferences with children, take the opportunity to make them aware of editing, which includes correct spelling.
- Make children aware of spelling resources, such as the dictionary, and help them learn how to use them.
- Make word lists on wall charts to help with spelling.
- Use word lists of common but difficult words to spell, such as *the,* for children to memorize.
- Encourage children to help each other with spelling words.

It is important to free children to write their thoughts down on paper without concern for the mechanics of writing. Also, when they are ready, it is important to make them aware of writing that is mechanically correct. There are times for free writing, and there are times for edited pieces. Children should know that each type of writing is acceptable, but they occur in different settings. Children should be encouraged to do both.

Transitions

Throughout this chapter theories and strategies for helping children develop the desire to write have been discussed. It is my opinion that all are appropriate for preschool through third grade, with adaptations based on the particular age group. Teachers often want to know how children move from one level of writing ability to another or from unconventional writing to conventional. It is somewhat individual for every child, but trends do emerge. First and foremost we want to provide an atmosphere in which children will write. Therefore, acceptance of what they can do at a given time is acknowledged. Children who are reluctant to write because they think they can't can be shown work done by others of their own age so that they see that unconventional writing is acceptable. We foster acceptance so that children will attempt writing. As youngsters learn more about phoneme–grapheme correspondence, they begin to realize that their invented spelling is not conventional spelling. At this point they begin to ask for correct spelling as they move into the conventional stage of writing. It may seem as if they are taking a step backward because suddenly they will not be writing as much or spontaneously as they did in the past. Their concern for writing correctly has that effect on their performance. This will last for a short time as their spelling vocabulary increases, they learn to use the dictionary, and they seek help from friends and the teacher. Conventional writing does not just occur one day. It is a gradual process in which a child often goes back and forth from conventional to unconventional writing until sufficient proficiency is gained for the writing to be considered completely conventional.

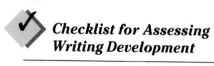
Checklist for Assessing Writing Development

	Always	Sometimes	Never
Explores with writing materials			
Dictates stories, sentences, or words he or she wants written down			
Copies letters and words			
Independently attempts writing to convey meaning, regardless of writing level			
Can write his or her name			
Collaborates with others in writing experience			
Writes in varied genres: narrative (stories), expository (personal and informational reports)			
Writes for functional purposes			
Check (✓) the level or levels at which the child is writing			
____ uses drawing for writing and drawing			
____ differentiates between writing and drawing			
____ uses scribble writing for writing			
____ uses letterlike forms for writing			
____ uses learned letters in random fashion for writing			
____ uses invented spelling for writing			
____ writes conventionally with conventional spelling			

◆ Mechanics for Writing

	Always	Sometimes	Never
Forms uppercase letters legibly			
Forms lowercase letters legibly (see Figure 8.16)			
Writes from left to right			
Leaves spaces between words			
Uses capital letters when necessary			
Uses periods in appropriate places			
Uses commas in appropriate places			

◆ Assessing Your Classroom Writing Environment

	Yes	No
Space provided for a writing center		
Tables and chairs include in center		
Writing posters and bulletin boards for children to display their writing themselves		

✔ Checklist for Assessing Writing Development

	Yes	No
Writing utensils (pens, pencils, crayons, magic markers, colored pencils, etc.)		
Typewriter and/or a computer		
Writing materials (many varieties of paper in all sizes, booklets, pads)		
A message board or private message area for children to leave messages for the teacher and other members of the class		
A place to store Very Own Words		
Folders for children to place samples of their writing		
Materials to make books		

Authentic Assessment of Children's Writing Development and the Writing Environment

As in other areas of literacy, assessment of a child's writing should take place throughout the school year. That way the teacher can determine a child's level of development, monitor progress, and plan programs accordingly. Teachers also need to assess the classroom writing environment. The checklist on pages 292 to 293 provides a resource for the teacher to evaluate characteristics of a child's writing development and the classroom writing environment.

The assessment checklist is used to analyze individual writing samples collected through the school year for the specific characteristics outlined in the measure. Figure 9.18 provides another means of evaluating children's written original stories and oral dictations of stories for sense of story structure as well as the inclusion of interpretive and critical thoughts.

Teachers should maintain a portfolio of materials related to a child's writing development, such as notes of observations as the child writes, samples of the child's writing over a period of time, notes from conferences with the child, notes from conferences with the child's parents, and completed checklists. The portfolio should include the best of the child's work and samples showing need for improvement as well. The portfolio can be used during parent conferences and can accompany a child to his or her next teacher. Children should have their own writing folders in which they keep samples of their writing throughout the year. They should also be involved in the assessment process by participating in parent and teacher conferences, and in conferences with the teacher alone. Assessment should be kept as informal as possible based on children's self-initiated activities and on teachers' observations of and interactions with them. Figure 9.19 provides a means for children to assess their own writing interest and ability. All of these suggestions support the purpose of assessment as a means to (1) enhance the teacher's understanding of children's writing ability, (2) aid in program planning, and (3) help children and parents understand a child's progress and the processes involved to help gain more competence in writing.

♦ **FIGURE 9.18**
Evaluating Oral and Written Original Stories

Name_____ Date_____

Name of Story _____

	Yes	No
Setting		
a. The story begins with an introduction.	☐	☐
b. One or more main characters emerge.	☐	☐
c. Other characters are talked about.	☐	☐
d. The time of the story is mentioned.	☐	☐
e. Where the story takes place is mentioned.	☐	☐
Theme		
a. A beginning event occurs that causes a problem for the main character or goal to be achieved.	☐	☐
b. The main character reacts to the problem.	☐	☐
Plot Episodes		
An event or series of events is mentioned that relates to the main character solving the problem or attaining the goal.	☐	☐
Resolution		
a. The main character solves the problem or achieves the goal.	☐	☐
b. The story ends with a closing statement.	☐	☐
Sequence		
The four categories of story structure are presented in typical sequential order (setting, theme, plot episodes, resolution).	☐	☐

Interpretive and Critical Comments
Read through the oral taped story and the written original story and record comments and responses that demonstrate interpretive and critical thought.

♦ **FIGURE 9.19**
Self-Assessment about Writing for Children

Name_____

The good things about what I wrote are:

The things I don't like about what I wrote are:

I could make this writing better if I:

I used correct spelling:

I used my best handwriting:

Is writing hard or easy for me?

For me writing is (a) fun, (b) not so much fun.

Writing could be better if:

Next time I write something, I will try to do the following things to make it better:

An Idea for the Classroom from the Classroom

♦ *Preschool and First-Grade Pen Pals*

Children from a nearby preschool wrote to my first graders to find out what the elementary school was like. We wrote a class letter back answering their questions; we also included our pictures. One week later, we received a response. Now we had established a letter writing routine. The children in my class took turns writing parts of each letter on chart paper. We went through the writing process steps of brainstorming, revising, editing, and rewriting for our new audience. Three children acted as scribes, while the rest of the class developed the letter. Later, three new children were chosen to revise and edit. Finally, three more children rewrote the letter. Being pen pals became a part of our writing curriculum. We invited the preschoolers for a snack and a paired-reading session, as well as to our end-of-the-year play. In turn, the preschoolers invited our class over for a picnic at the preschool. We developed quite a friendship with the younger students, and our first-grade class learned the purposeful and very rewarding skill of letter writing. In addition, the preschoolers became familiar with our school, which most of them would be entering soon.

Donna M. Ngai, First-Grade Teacher
Basking Ridge, NJ

Activities and Questions

1. Answer the focus questions at the beginning of the chapter.

2. Ask three children of different ages, for example, three, five, and seven, to write about their favorite food, television show, storybook, or game. Take notes on their behavior during writing and analyze the sample of their writing to determine each child's writing developmental level.

3. Many functional and meaningful writing experiences are related in this chapter. Try and think of writing experiences not dealt with in the chapter that you could suggest for children to participate in.

4. Think of several dramatic-play themes that you could create in an early childhood classroom, such as a restaurant. For each theme, think of the writing materials you could provide for that play area for children to use.

5. Continue the portfolio assessment for the child you selected to assess for language development in Chapter 4. Observe the child using the assessment checklist provided in this chapter concerning the evaluation of writing development. Collect writing samples from the child over the course of several months. Evaluate them to determine the child's development in writing over time.

6. Continue the thematic unit that you began in Chapter 4. Select three objectives in the area of writing development and describe three activities that will satisfy each of the objectives using your theme. Be sure that your activities reflect functional and meaningful writing tasks.

Case Study Activities

◆ **Case 1**

Janice Bradley is a first-grade teacher. This year, unlike other years, she has children with many and different special needs. There are several children who have limited facility with English because it is their second language. There is a large group identified as "at risk" due to poor scores on tests that are used in the district, and finally she has a group of youngsters classified as gifted. She is very aware of the importance of writing experiences for children and the need for guided writing, shared writing, independent writing, and collaborative writing. With such a diverse group of children, she feels that she cannot allow independent writing or collaborative writing this year and confines the experiences to guided writing in whole-group lessons, and some sharing of finished products for the entire group. She is concerned that children will not get the skills needed in collaborative groups and independent periods of writing.

Do you feel Janice has made the correct decisions? If not why? If so, why? If you answered no, describe how she might better support the special needs of the children in her class.

◆ *Case 2*

You have been assigned the responsibility to do a workshop for a group of irate parents who do not understand the concept of invented spelling. They feel that the school is teaching the children how to spell incorrectly and that undoing what is incorrect is much harder than learning the right way first. Describe what you will do in the workshop to convince the parents that allowing children to use invented spelling in preschool, kindergarten, and first and second grades is an important aspect of developing fluent writers.

Organizing and Managing the Learning Environment for Literacy Development at School

Children need to experience literacy learning in many contexts. The teacher should arrange for whole-class experiences, small-group learning (pictured here), one-to-one conferences, and activities in which children learn from other children.

"What is honored in a country will be cultivated there." In classrooms in which teachers honor literacy development, it will be cultivated as an integral part of the school curriculum.

—Plato

Questions to Focus On As You Read

◆ Describe environments for classrooms that are rich in literacy materials and support optimal literacy instruction.

◆ What is meant by integrating literacy learning into content areas through the use of themed units?

◆ How can literacy development be integrated into the following content areas: art, music, math, science, social studies, and play?

◆ Identify different grouping methods, or organizational arrangements, for working with children to meet their individual needs.

◆ How can literacy learning be integrated into activities throughout an entire school day?

Mrs. Youseff wanted to integrate literacy activities in content-area subjects. The children often found science boring with only the textbook, because it did not feature real-life situations. She decided to use selections of children's literature that related to different topics in science to make them more relevant.

The children were learning about "The Changes in our Earth," a unit that focused on topics such as hurricanes, glaciers, and the composition of the earth. Mrs. Schenkman found several excellent selections of children's literature for this unit. Two of them were *How to Dig a Hole to the Other Side of the World* and *The Magic School Bus Inside the Earth*. Both books combined good children's literature with factual information about the topic. These books motivated a great deal of enthusiasm and discussion in class. Mrs. Youseff asked the children to write a science story—one that told a story, but included many science facts they had learned. This proved to be a difficult task for the children. Most of them wrote informational pieces that gave facts about the composition of the inside of the earth and what a volcano is and does. Those who wrote stories did not include very many science facts. Mrs. Youseff decided to have the children write a whole-class science story by having the students generate science vocabulary and concepts they learned and use those ideas to write the story together. The story they wrote follows.

Our Class Adventure

One sunny day in Sacramento, California, our class went on a camping trip to a mountain. We put down all our bags and set up the tents. Kevin, Alex, Jason, and Keri went to the stream to catch fish for lunch. Antoinette and Emily went to get wood for a fire since it was cold on the top of the mountain. While the other kids were setting up their tents, a bear came out. The bear saw the fish, ate them and went away. Two hours later, our class decided to go for a hike. Along the way we saw a river and rocks that were weathered. We also saw two glaciers which were blocking a river. Suddenly, everything started to rumble and shake and everyone fell to the ground. Little and big rocks tumbled down the mountain. Smoke started coming out of the mountain and everyone started to yell. Amber started running around in circles. Then what we thought was just a mountain blew its top. Lava started coming down out of the volcano and an earthquake started. It was a good thing we brought our earthquake survival kits. We all ran to our camp for cover, but the camp was destroyed. The survival kits were fireproof and lava proof, so they were okay. Inside there were tools which we used to fix up the camp. We fixed it up so well that it looked like new.

This anecdote describes the integration of literacy into a content area, specifically science. The concept of integration is one topic discussed in this chapter. The success of any program depends to a large extent on how it is organized, designed, and managed. Even creative and knowledgeable teachers have difficulty without careful planning, preparation of the environment, organization of lessons, and management of daily routines. This chapter ties together the prerequisites for successful implementation of the ideas described earlier in this book. Specifically, it focuses on (1) preparation of the physical environment, including selection of materials and their placement in the classroom; (2) integration of literacy activities throughout the school day in all content areas; (3) grouping practices to meet individual needs; and (4) a suggested outline for a school day that provides literacy experiences throughout.

This chapter is concerned with the teaching of youngsters from two-and-a-half to eight—preschoolers, kindergarteners, first, second, and third graders. (Chapter 3 addressed home literacy environments and daily routines appropriate for infants and toddlers. Day-care centers for children of that age need to organize rich literacy environments, routines, programs, and activities similar to those described for homes.)

Preparation of the Physical Environment

The physical design of a classroom has been found to affect the choices children make among activities (Bumsted, 1981; Morrow & Tracey, 1996; Morrow & Weinstein, 1982, 1986). The design of the room should accommodate the organization and strategies of the teaching that goes on there. Programs that nourish early literacy require a literacy-rich environment, an interdisciplinary approach to the development of literacy, and recognition of individual differences and levels of development.

Instructional Environments for Language and Learning

Mrs. Shafer's kindergarten is learning about workers in the community. While discussing news reporters, the children decided they would like to have a news office in the dramatic-play area where they could publish their own newspaper. Their teacher helped create the center where they placed writing paper, telephones, phone directories, a typewriter, and a computer. There were pamphlets, maps, and other appropriate reading materials for the different sections of the newspaper, such as sports, travel, weather, and general daily news. The class completed their first newspaper, and Yassin was in charge of delivering the paper the first month. He had a newspaper delivery bag, and each paper had the name of a child on it. As the delivery person, Yassin had to match the names on the papers to the names on the children's cubbies. Later, when the kindergartners read their newspapers, they shared them with great enthusiasm. Each child had contributed something to the paper, for example, a drawing, a story, or a group poem.

In this example, children are participating in functional literacy activities in a classroom environment that was prepared with materials and space that stimulated reading and writing.

Research Concerning Literacy-Rich Physical Environments That Motivate Reading and Writing

Historically, theorists and philosophers who studied early childhood development emphasized the importance of the physical environment in learning and literacy development. Pestalozzi (Rusk & Scotland, 1979) and Froebel (1974) described real-life environments in which young children's learning could flourish. Both described the preparation of manipulative materials that would foster literacy development. Montessori (1965) described a carefully prepared classroom environment intended to promote independent learning and recommended that every material in the environment have its specific learning objective.

Piaget (Piaget & Inhelder, 1969) found that children acquire knowledge by interacting with the world or the environment. Ideal settings are oriented to real-life situations, and materials are chosen to provide opportunities for children to explore and experiment. Dewey (1966) believed in an interdisciplinary approach. In other words, learning takes place through the integration of content areas. He believed that storing materials in subject-area centers encouraged interest and learning.

Based on these discussions, any classroom designed to provide a literacy-rich environment and optimum literacy development will offer an abundant supply of materials for reading, writing, and oral language. These materials will be housed in a literacy center. Literacy development will be integrated with content-area teaching reflected in materials provided in content-area learning centers. Materials and settings throughout the classroom will be designed to emulate real-life experiences and make literacy meaningful to children. They will be based on information children already possess, and will be functional so that children can see a need and purpose for using literacy. Careful attention to a classroom's visual and physical design contributes to the success of an instructional program. Preparing a classroom's physical environment is often overlooked in planning instruction. Teachers and curriculum developers tend to concentrate on pedagogical and interpersonal factors, but give little consideration to the visual and spatial context in which teaching and learning occur. They direct their energies toward varying teaching strategies while the classroom setting remains relatively unchanged. When program and environment are not coordinated, "setting deprivation" often results, a situation in which the physical environment fails to support the activities and needs of students (Spivak, 1973).

While the learning environment is often viewed as background or scenery for teaching and learning, there is another way to view the physical environment and the teacher's role in creating it. This view recognizes that by purposefully arranging the environment, teachers acknowledge the physical setting as an active and pervasive influence on their own activities and attitudes, as well as those of the children in their classrooms. Appropriate physical arrangement of furniture, selection of materials, and the visual aesthetic quality of a room contribute to teaching and learning (Loughlin & Martin, 1987; Rivlin & Weinstein,

1984; Morrow, 1990; Morrow & Weinstein, 1982, 1986; Morrow & Tracey, 1996; Sutfin, 1980). For example, design of spatial arrangements alone affects children's behavior in the classroom. Field (1980) observed that rooms partitioned into smaller spaces facilitated such behaviors amongst peers as verbal interaction, fantasy, and cooperative play more than did rooms with large open spaces. Nash (1981) and Moore (1986) found that children in carefully arranged rooms showed more creative productivity and greater use of language-related activities than did children in randomly arranged rooms.

Pellegrini and Galda (1983) found that dramatic props in the block center elicited more imaginative language than playing with blocks alone. Studies that investigated the role of literacy-enriched dramatic-play areas based on themes being used in the classroom found they stimulated increased literacy activity and the enhancement of literacy skills (Morrow, 1990; Neuman & Roskos, 1990, 1992). Other researchers have found that dramatic play with story props has improved story production and comprehension, including recall of details and ability to sequence and interpret (Mandler & Johnson, 1977; Saltz & Johnson, 1974).

Preparing Literacy-Rich Physical Environments That Motivate Reading and Writing

Research that investigates the physical design of classrooms strongly suggests that, by purposefully arranging the space and materials, teachers can create physical environments that exert an active, positive, and pervasive influence on instruction. Educators must think of their classrooms as places to project a visual atmosphere that communicates a definitive message. The following sections describe the visual presentation of a literacy-rich physical environment to motivate reading and writing based on the research discussed in the previous section.

Environmental Print in Your Classroom   Literacy-rich classrooms are filled with visually prominent functional print—labels on classroom items and areas; signs communicating functional information and directions, such as *Quiet Please* and *Please Put Materials Away After Using Them*; and charts labeled *Helpers, Daily Routines, Attendances,* and *Calendar* to name a few (Schickedanz, 1993). A notice board in a prominent place in the room can be used to communicate with the children in writing. Experience charts are used to display new words generated from themes, recipes used in the classroom, and science experiments conducted. Labels identify learning centers and each child's cubby. Teachers discuss and use the environmental print with the children to ensure it is noticed. Children are encouraged to read, copy, and use words from the labels in their writing.

The outdoor environment should also accommodate literacy development. In addition to the usual playground equipment, new materials that reflect unit instruction add to the interest of outdoor play. Where climates are seasonal, for example, flowers should be planted in the spring; rakes provided in the fall for leaf gathering; and pails, shovels, and other digging and building equipment provided in winter for snow play. Creative materials such as crates, boxes, plastic containers, boards, ropes, and balls give children incentives to play creatively. The materials generate language during play, and in class discussions, and provide information for writing experience charts and class books.

The Classroom Literacy Center   The literacy center, which includes the library corner and a writing area, should be the focal point in a classroom. Children's immediate access to literature and writing materials increases the number of children who participate in literacy activities in the course of the school day. Both areas need to be obvious and inviting but should also afford privacy and be clearly defined. The areas should accommodate four to five children comfortably. The center says to children that as teachers we value literacy by making it an important part of our classroom. The materials range in difficulty to meet individual needs and the different developmental levels of the children. Each set of materials has its own place and is to be respected. The literacy center includes materials for reading, writing, oral language development, and developing concepts about print. The different parts of the center have already been discussed in other chapters (the library corner in Chapter 6, the writing center in Chapter 9, oral language center materials in Chapter 4, and materials to develop concepts about print in Chapter 8). The library corner and writing center will be described again here to pull the entire area together.

The Library Corner: The library corner should house books on traditional shelves with only their spines showing. Shelve books by category and use some sort of coding system. Coding introduces the idea that books in regular libraries are organized systematically for easy access. Other shelves should be open faced to display full covers, thus calling attention to them. Use the open-faced shelving to feature books about themes being studied and rotate new books in every few weeks. To ensure there is something for everyone in the center, include five to eight books per child at three or four grade levels representing different genres of children's literature. Stock multiple copies of popular stories. Children enjoy reading the same book together.

Furnish the area with elements of softness such as a rug and pillows. Include a rocking chair representing **"The Literacy Chair of Honor,"** where the teacher reads to the children as well as other individuals such as parents, the principal, or town mayor. This area is where children read for pleasure, read to other children, or present stories to the class that they have written. Provide a cozy private spot for reading. Teachers have used large cartons from household appliances, painted or covered with contact paper, where children can crawl inside and read.

Posters and bulletin boards that celebrate reading should be used to decorate the area. Devise a method for checking books out of the classroom library to take home and read. Provide materials for active involvement in storybook reading and storytelling, with storytelling manipulatives such as a felt-board with story characters, roll movies, puppets, and headsets for listening to taped stories.

The Writing Area: The writing area requires a table and chairs, plus colored felt-tipped markers, large and small crayons, pencils (both regular and colored), chalk, a chalkboard, and paper in a variety of sizes, kinds, and colors. Include unlined plain paper or newsprint of many different sizes. Have index cards available to record children's Very Own Words. A writing folder for each child can be kept in a large box. A word processor or computer, if available, is important to have in a writing area. Book-making materials include paper, a hole punch, a stapler, and construction paper. Blank books prepared by the teacher and children can be keyed to special occasions and completed by youngsters. Display children's writing on a bulletin board. Equally valuable are *notice boards* on which messages can be exchanged among classmates or between teacher and students.

Involve children in designing and managing the literacy center. They can help develop rules for its use and keep it neat and orderly.

Designing Content-Area Centers to Accommodate Individual Needs

Programs that motivate early literacy development require literacy-rich environments that recognize the need for an integrated approach to literacy learning and recognition of individual differences and levels of development. These classrooms are arranged in centers designed for particular content areas. Centers contain materials specific to topics currently under study and general supplies, materials, and resources. The materials are usually manipulative and activity oriented. They are also designed such that children use them independently or in small groups. Centers are partially separated from each other by furniture that houses their materials. Centers should be labeled and their materials stored on tables, on shelves, in boxes, or on a bulletin board. Each piece of equipment in a center should have its own designated spot so that teachers can direct children to it and children can find and return it easily. Early in a school year, a center need hold only a small number of items; new materials are gradually added as the year progresses. The teacher should introduce the purpose, use, and placement of each item added.

The centers in such classrooms are dedicated to content areas, such as social studies, science, art, music, math, literacy, dramatic play, and block play. Centers contain materials pertinent to the content area, and materials are added that are specific to themes being studied such as nutrition or animals. Each subject-specific center includes literacy materials as well: Things to read, materials with which to write, things to listen to, and things to talk about. These materials create interest, new vocabulary and concepts, and a reason for participating in literacy activities. With each new theme studied, additional books, posters, artifacts, music, art projects, dramatic-play materials, and scientific objects can be added to create new interest. Chapter 4 (pp. 107–113) describes general materials for each content-area center, and then discusses additions made for the study of a particular theme. The classroom floorplans in Figures 10.1 and 10.2, illustrate this type of learning environment from preschool through fifth grade.

Notice in Figure 10.1, in the preschool through first grade floorplan, that the art center is placed by the sink for easy access to water. In this same area are children's cubbies for storage of individual work. Because the working needs of early childhood classrooms are better met by table surfaces than by desks, children need to be provided with these storage areas. The contents of the various centers diagramed in the figure have been described in Chapter 4. In addition to all the materials available in them, it is important that each has books and writing materials. The music center, for example, can include picture storybooks adapted from songs, such as Ezra Jack Keats's *Over in the Meadow* (1971). In addition to looking at the book, children may choose to copy words from the story. Certainly social studies and science centers should hold informational books and children's literature that relate to the topic at hand. The art center might have books with craft ideas, including directions and diagrams. Books are appropriate as well in the dramatic-play area. If the class is discussing space, the area should have books about space and space stories for pretend mothers and fathers to read to their "children." The block center can contain books that help develop ideas for

◆ **FIGURE 10.1** *Classroom Floorplan for Prekindergarten through First Grade*

◆ **FIGURE 10.2** *Classroom Floorplan for Second through Fifth Grade*

building. Books that contain maps or plans of communities might motivate children to create such communities in their block play.

In addition to generating a rich literacy atmosphere and an interdisciplinary approach, the room is designed to cater to different teaching methods, organizational strategies, and grouping procedures so that the differences among the children can be accommodated. The centers provide space for independent or social learning, exploration, and self-direction. The tables illustrated in the classroom floorplan (Figure 10.1) provide a place for whole-class instruction, as does the open area in the music center with the rug on which children can sit. The teacher's conference table is a place for individual learning or small-group lessons. All furniture is, of course, movable so that any other needed teaching arrangement can be accommodated. The centers are located so as to create both quiet, relatively academic areas and places for more active play. The literacy center, for example, which houses the library corner, writing, and oral language areas, is next to the math center. Because these areas generally house activities that require relative quiet, they are in close proximity. On the other hand, dramatic play, woodworking, and block play tend to be noisier activities and so are placed at the opposite end of the room from the quiet areas. The art center can also be a noisy area and is set aside from the quieter sections of the room. The teacher's conference table is situated in a quiet area yet allows the teacher a view of the rest of the classroom. While the teacher is involved, as he or she usually is, in small-group or individualized instruction at the conference table, the rest of the class is working independently. The table's location allows the teacher to see all the children even while working with just a few.

The plan for the physical environment is utilized in many nursery schools and kindergartens, and some first and second grades. The assumption is that it is for younger children. Teachers in first and second grade should consider these designs because they encourage literacy learning. Figures 10.3 is a map to help you decide on general materials for your centers and materials to add that are specific to a particular theme. Evaluate the richness of your literacy environment, using the checklist on pages 310–311.

Thematic Units: The Integration of Literacy Learning into Content Areas

Dewey (1966) was largely responsible for bringing the concept of an interdisciplinary approach to teaching to the attention of educators. This interdisciplinary approach, or the integrated school day, teaches skills from all content areas, within the context of a topic or theme being studied. The themes that are studied at school are derived from children's real-life experiences and topics that they demonstrate an interest in. Learning experiences are socially interactive and process oriented, giving children time to explore and experiment with varied materials. If, for example, a class is studying dinosaurs, the students talk about them, read about them, write about them, do art projects related to dinosaurs, and sing songs related to the theme. In doing so, they learn about dinosaurs and also develop skills in other content areas.

Literacy activities can be integrated into the study of themes and in all content areas throughout the school day. Several are described here to demonstrate how some of the strategies to develop literacy that are discussed in previous chapters can be used in other areas of the curriculum (Pappas, Kiefer, & Levstik, 1995).

Objectives for Art Experiences

In early childhood, art experience should offer children the opportunity to:

1. Be exposed to varied art materials.
2. Explore and experiment with these materials.

◆ **FIGURE 10.3** *General Center Materials and Center Theme Materials*

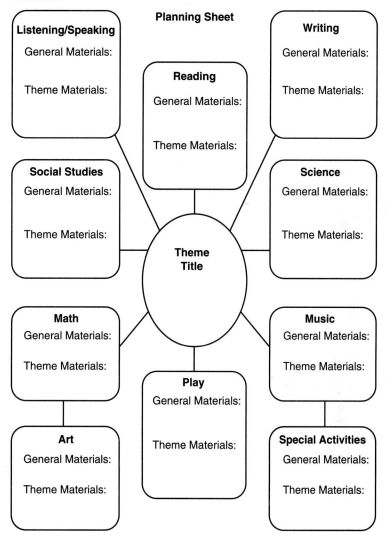

3. Express feelings through art.
4. Represent experience through visual art forms.
5. Gain an appreciation for varied art forms.
6. Name and discuss content of art: line, color, texture, form, and shape.
7. Experience literacy learning in art activities.

Art experiences allow children to explore and experiment with such interesting materials as finger paints, watercolors, printing, string painting, sponge

Checklist for Evaluating and Improving the Literacy Environment

	Yes	No

◆ **The Literacy Center**

1. Children participate in designing the center (e.g., develop rules, select a name for center, develop materials).
2. Area is placed in a quiet section of the room.
3. Area is visually and physically accessible, yet partitioned off from the rest of the room.
4. Rug, throw pillows, rocking chair, bean bag chair, stuffed animals
5. Private spot in the corner such as a box to crawl into and read
6. The Center uses about 10% of the classroom space and fits five to six children.

◆ **The Library Corner**

1. Bookshelves for storing books with spines facing outward
2. Organizational system for shelving books
3. Open-faced bookshelves for featured books
4. Five to eight books per child
5. Books represent three to four grade levels of the following types: (a) picture books, (b) picture story books, (c) traditional literature, (d) poetry, (e) realistic literature, (f) informational books, (g) biographies, (h) chapter books, (i) easy to read books, (j) riddle and joke books, (k) participation books, (l) series books, (m) textless books, (n) TV-related books, (o) brochures, (p) magazines, (q) newspapers.
6. Twenty new books circulated every two weeks
7. Check-out/check-in system for children to take books out daily
8. Head sets and taped stories
9. Felt board and story characters with related books
10. Materials for constructing felt stories
11. Other story manipulatives (e.g., roll-movie, puppets, with related books.)
12. System for recording books read
13. Multiple copies of the same book

| | *Yes* | *No* |

♦ *The Writing Center (The Author's Spot)*

1. Tables and chairs
2. Writing posters and bulletin board for children to display their writing themselves
3. Writing utensils (e.g., pens, pencils, crayons, magic markers, colored pencils)
4. Writing materials (many varieties of paper in all sizes, booklets, pads)
5. Computer or word processor
6. Materials for writing stories and making them into books
7. A message board for children to post messages for the teacher and students
8. A place to store Very Own Words
9. Folders for children to place samples of their writing
10. A place for children to send private messages to each other

♦ *Literacy-Rich Environment for the Rest of the Classroom*

The classroom should include literacy materials in all centers. Materials should be changed often to reflect the unit being studied— for example, in the science center there should be books on the unit topic, and in the music area posters of songs related to themes. Play areas should reflect units with themed play and literacy materials. All centers should contain the following:

1. Environmental print, such as signs related to themes studied, directions, rules, functional messages
2. A calendar
3. A current events board
4. Appropriate books, magazines, and newspapers in all centers
5. Writing utensils in all centers
6. Varied types of paper in all centers
7. A place for children to display their literacy work
8. A place for teachers and children to leave messages for each other
9. Print representative of multicultural groups present in the classroom
10. Content area centers present are:

    Circle centers

    music   art   science   social studies   math   dramatic play painting, colored pencils, felt-tip markers, crayons, colored construction paper, tissue paper, foil, transparent wrap, paste, scissors, yarn, fabric scraps, pipe cleaners, clay, and play dough. If children are encouraged to discuss such materials as they use them, language development flourishes. Children immersed in finger painting, for instance, use such words as *mushy, smushy, gushy,* and *squiggle.* Playing with dough or clay elicits *pound, squeeze, roll, press,* and *fold.* Watercolors stimulate such comments as "Oooh, it's drippy," "The paint is running down the page like a stream of water," "Look how the colors all run together. The red is making the blue turn purple," and "My picture looks like a rainbow of colors across the sky." The teacher can take the opportunity to make word lists from the language generated in art activities and to encourage the children to share and talk about what they are doing. The words that individual children generate are a source of Very Own Words.

Children are often eager to exhibit their creations. This practice is likely to result in children's asking each other how they made their projects. The resulting description provides an excellent opportunity for literacy development. Children sometimes ask to dictate or write sentences and stories about their artwork, or write about it themselves. Individual works of art on similar subjects can be bound together in books that include captions, titles, or stories. Art activities can appropriately highlight concepts such as the letter *p,* for example, through the use of purple and pink paint, paper, and play dough.

Objectives for Music Experiences

In early childhood music experiences should include:

1. Having intense involvement in and responding to music.
2. Exposure to different forms of music (instruments, singing, types of music) to be able to discriminate between them and develop an appreciation for varied forms.
3. Music experiences that involve listening, singing, moving, playing, and creating.
4. Expressing feelings through music experiences.
5. Experiencing literacy learning in music activities.

Music provides ample means for literacy development. Children find new words in songs, thus increasing vocabulary. Songs emphasize syllabic patterns in words, which should be brought to the attention of the children. Songs can be written on charts and sung, the teacher pointing to the individual words. Picture storybooks adapted from songs, such as *Old MacDonald Had a Farm* (Quackenbush, 1972), provide predictable reading material for young children. Listening to classical music often creates images and is a rich source for descriptive language. Children can create stories about the music, describe their feelings, or describe the sounds of various instruments.

Objectives for Play Experiences

In early childhood play experiences include providing opportunities for children to:

1. Problem solve.
2. Acquire new understandings.
3. Role-play real-life experiences.
4. Cope with situations that require sharing and cooperating.
5. Develop language and literacy through play.

Dramatic play provides endless possibilities for development of literacy through the use of oral and written language and reading. The materials and activities typical of dramatic-play areas stimulate considerable language, and the addition of new props and materials provides the opportunity for continued growth. Dramatic play provides realistic settings and functional reasons for using print. New units in social studies and science trigger opportunities to add print materials that stimulate reading, writing, and oral language. A unit on community helpers—a topic familiar to early childhood teachers—invariably leads to a discussion of fire fighters, police officers, supermarket clerks, doctors, nurses, mail carriers, and office workers. The mention of any of these community helpers is an opportunity to add literacy materials to the dramatic-play area.

Role-playing supermarket, for instance, is aided by the addition of food and detergent containers, a toy cash register, play money, note pads, a telephone and directory, store signs, a schedule of hours, advertisements, and posters for food and other products. Teachers or aides might visit a nearby supermarket to note for the classroom the print that is there, and to pick up outdated signs and posters. Store managers readily give away such materials when they no longer need them. Definitely include, among materials for dramatic play about supermarkets, a bookshelf full of magazines and books "for sale." All these materials help children engage in conversation as they role-play a store manager, clerk, or shopper. They read posters, books, signs, and magazines and write shopping lists, orders, and new signs when they are needed.

Many topics lend themselves to dramatic play and incorporating literacy materials. A study of health-care personnel can lead to the creation of a doctor's office. A waiting room can be set up with magazines for the patients to read and pamphlets about good health. There can be a **No Smoking** sign, a notice containing the doctor's hours, and posters on the wall concerning good health habits. There should be an appointment book for the nurse and a pad for writing down appointment reminders for patients to take with them, a pad for writing prescriptions, patient folders containing forms to be filled out, and a patient address and phone book.

When studying transportation, the class can create a travel agency. Here there would be maps, travel posters, pamphlets about places to visit, and tickets to be issued for planes and trains.

Creative play in the dramatic-play center encourages social interaction, vibrant discussion, and language development.

The possibilities are numerous. The materials are easy to obtain, and they encourage functional reading and writing. Dramatic play involves children in literacy that relates to real life. The children enjoy role-playing in these situations because the activity includes meaningful experiences. In dramatic play, children are voluntarily participating in reading and writing.

Dramatic play has been considered appropriate in preschools and kindergartens; however, we seldom leave time for it in first and second grades or think of it as an area in which learning can take place. In classrooms that integrate content themes into dramatic play with six- to eight-year-olds, extremely sophisticated productions of reading, writing, and oral language result. It is suggested that first- and second-grade teachers incorporate play into their curriculum.

Social studies and science themes for the most part provide the meaning and function for learning, particularly for literacy learning. Themes provide a reason to read and write about topics of interest. Skills are learned within a context rather than in isolated lessons for skill development.

Objectives for Social Studies Experiences

In early childhood social studies experiences should include:

1. Fostering self-esteem.
2. Learning social skills for functioning, such as sharing, cooperating, and communicating with others.
3. Recognizing and respecting similarities and differences in others.
4. Increasing knowledge of other cultures and ethnic and racial groups.

5. Increasing understanding of the nature of our social world through the study of history, geography, and economics.
6. Using the content of social studies to promote literacy development.

Objectives for Science Experiences

In early childhood science experiences should include activities that involve:

1. Observing, hypothesizing, recording data, summarizing, analyzing, and drawing conclusions.
2. Increasing understanding in
   a. Biological science, the study of living things
   b. Physical science, including the study of
      (1) astronomy—heavenly bodies and their movements
      (2) chemistry—materials found on the earth and the changes that occur in them
      (3) meteorology—weather and air
      (4) physics—the nature of matter and energy
3. Using the content of science to promote literacy development.

Science and social studies are probably the two content areas that provide the greatest opportunities for literacy development. Their contents typically generate enthusiasm, meaning, and a purpose for using literacy strategies. A unit on the farm can lead to oral language development through discussions about farm work, different types of farms, and farm animals. Word lists of farm animals, crops, and jobs on the farm can be made. Pictures of farm scenes, a trip to a farm, or a visit by a farmer generates discussion, reading, and writing. To encourage positive attitudes toward books, the teacher can carefully select good pieces of children's literature about farms to read to the class. The *Petunia* series (Duvoisin, 1950) deals with a delightful goose who lives on a farm. *The Little Red Hen* (Galdone, 1973), *The Tale of Peter Rabbit* (Potter, 1902), *The Little Farm* (Lenski, 1965), and *Charlie Needs a Clock* (DePaola, 1973) are just a few examples of good children's literature that relate to the farm. These stories will motivate youngsters to pick up the books on their own, retell them, role-play them, and share them with each other. A farm visit can be retold in stories or drawings bound into class books, recaptured in a language experience chart, or reflected in Very Own Words. The teacher can associate letters and sounds in farm words with those in children's names or in environmental print.

Science experiments and food preparation offer opportunities for more discussion, generation of interesting word lists, and reading and writing of recipes. The block center, too, can stimulate literacy activities. For instance, when introducing a unit on transportation, the teacher can add toy trucks, trains, cars, boats, and airplanes to the block corner, along with travel tickets, luggage and freight tags, maps, travel guides, tour brochures, travel posters, and signs common to airports, train stations, and bus depots, such as gate numbers, names of carriers, and arrival and departure signs.

The integrated language arts curriculum includes mathematics within the themed units and literacy learning in math as well.

Objectives for Mathematics Experiences

In early childhood mathematics experiences should include activities that involve:

1. Many opportunities to handle and deal with mathematical materials and ideas.
2. Movement from dependence on the concrete to abstract ideas.
3. Opportunities to classify, compare, seriate, measure, graph, count, identify, and write numbers and perform operations on numbers.
4. Using mathematical vocabulary.
5. Using mathematics to promote literacy development.

In all of the other content areas, a teacher can feel quite confident that he or she is providing a fairly adequate program of study through the themed units used in social studies and science that incorporate music, art, play, and literacy development. Math, however, is a specialized area that needs more attention than can be dealt with in a content-area unit. There are many activities, however, that bring meaning to mathematics through unit topics and include literacy as well. Stories related to numbers can be read; children can count out cookies for snack to make sure there are enough for the class; and children can be in charge of collecting and counting milk money. When studying weather, a chart of daily temperatures can be graphed to observe the variability from day to day.

When literacy skills are developed in an integrated fashion, as in practices and approaches described here, children see purposes and reasons for becoming literate. When we teach literacy skills that do not reflect real-life experience and lack content, children are not likely to perceive the usefulness in those skills. When taught in an integrated, interdisciplinary fashion, children ask for the skills they find they need in order to participate fully in experiences that interest them during their work and play at school and at home (Manning, Manning, & Long, 1994; Walmsley, 1994). During a unit on transportation in a kindergarten class of my own, children asked for even more materials than I had already made available in the several centers. Books on transportation led to requests for books on space travel and various maps of places not already represented in the center. Many children added to their Very Own Words. Children asked for help in preparing signs representing places they wanted to visit and highway signs indicating mileage to various destinations. Some dictated travel directions. The need for literacy information was created by the preparation of an environment that reflected interesting, real-life experiences. In such an environment, learning is to a great extent self-generated.

◆ **FIGURE 10.4** *Curriculum Web for a Thematic Unit on Nutrition*

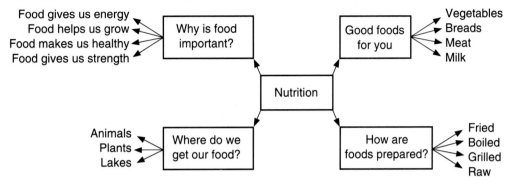

Unit themes can be selected by the teacher and the children. Giving students choices concerning what they will learn is important. When a topic is selected, allow the children to brainstorm what they would like to know about. You might begin by suggesting categories to focus on and letting them fill in subheadings (Rand, 1994). In preparation for a unit on *nutrition,* we asked a class of kindergarten children to help decide what they might like to learn. We used a web to chart their ideas and started it for them with *nutrition* as the theme and four categories to focus on: Why is food important? What foods are good for you? Where do we get food from? and How are different foods prepared to eat? The web in Figure 10.4 illustrates the children's responses and the content to be studied for the unit.

In planning for the unit, the teacher needs to be sure to include activities in all content-areas. The *map* in Figure 10.5 will help to generate activities related to the unit topic and include each of the content areas. From this map the teacher can select activities to schedule throughout the school day. In the section entitled "An Idea for the Classroom from the Classroom," I have included a science unit that integrates literacy learning throughout all the content areas in the early childhood curriculum. Following is a mini unit written by Donna Ngai, a first-grade teacher. As you will see, she integrates activities throughout the content areas as she focuses on her theme.

Thematic Instruction: Fun With Popcorn

Themes can connect our content areas. An interesting theme can make things come alive for children. With food as our theme, and popcorn as our week-long focus, things were really "popping" in our first-grade classroom! Here are some exciting ways to make learning about popcorn fun, while tying in content-area instruction.

The Friday Before: We planted popcorn kernels in wet paper towels. We used baking pans and lined them with paper towels. We spread popcorn in them, watered the seeds, and covered the pans with plastic wrap. In a few days, the roots began to sprout (*science*).

◆ **FIGURE 10.5** *Daily Schedule Planning Sheet to Integrate a Theme Throughout the Curriculum*

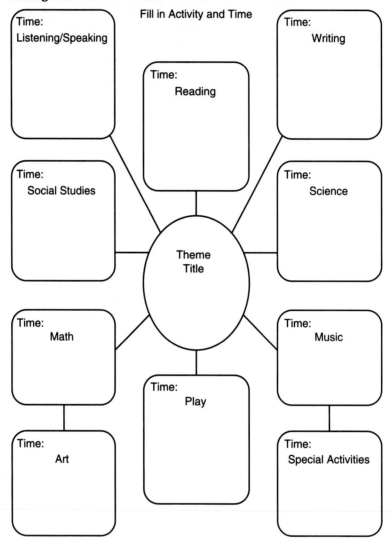

Fill in Activity and Time

Monday: Using a log, we recorded the growth of the seedlings over the weekend. We read *The Popcorn Book* by Tomie DePaola. We discussed that the Native Americans were the first to introduce popcorn to the colonists. We used the compound word "popcorn" to trigger a list of other food compound words, such as cupcake and milkshake. This led to a chart that was left up all week. Anytime a student thought of or came across a compound word, he/she would write it down on the chart. By the end of the week, the chart paper was full (*science, language arts, social studies*).

Tuesday: We set up an experiment chart for making popcorn. We asked ourselves, "What do I want to find out?" (How does a corn kernel change to popcorn?) "What do I think will happen?" "How will I find out?" "What actually happened?" and "What did I learn?" We answered the first two questions. We used an air popper to pop the corn and then completed the experiment chart, answering the remainder of the questions. We also enjoyed the popcorn for *snack*. We planted our seedlings in paper cups filled with soil (*science*).

Wednesday: We made more popcorn to create an estimation lesson for math. Each child grabbed a handful of popcorn from a large bowl, and guessed how many kernels were in his/her hand. Afterwards, we used a simple record sheet to log estimations. We then counted to find the actual number. We tried it a second time to see if we arrived at a more accurate estimation (*mathematics*).

Thursday: One of the ways the Native Americans popped corn was to put an ear of corn on a stick and hold it over a fire until the kernels popped. Another way was to throw kernels into the fire until they popped out all over the place. Still another way was to use clay pots filled with hot sand, in which the kernels were mixed until they eventually popped to the top of the pot. We illustrated the method we thought was the best, and wrote a few sentences as to why we felt that way. We discussed how the Native Americans made necklaces out of popcorn. Using the popcorn from Wednesday, we gave it a try. We used large, blunt needles and heavy thread, and created fun and easy necklaces to wear around our necks (*writing, art, social studies*).

Friday: As a culminating lesson, we had parent volunteers come into our classroom to make popcorn balls. We checked for any growth of our corn plants, and recorded the information in our science logs (*science and cooking*).

We had a *bowlful* of fun incorporating popcorn into our weekly lessons.

Strategies for Meeting Individual Special Needs

There are, of course, a variety of strategies for organizing instruction. Children can be taught as a whole class, in small groups, and individually. Children can be grouped homogeneously or heterogeneously by ability, interests, or skills, or they can be divided into peer groups for cooperative learning. The use of a variety of organizational strategies is important, because some children benefit more in one setting than in another. The use of several different grouping schemes within the same classroom also tends to eliminate the stigmas attached to a single grouping system. Variable grouping makes it likely that children will interact with all others in one group or another. Finally, using varied organizational strategies provides children with a more interesting and broader educational experience.

Whole-Group Instruction

Whole-group lessons are inappropriate until the children are almost three. Children younger than three lack the ability to concentrate or to sit and listen. Whole-group lessons, sometimes referred to as shared experiences, are appropriate when the subject needs to be introduced to all the children and the presentation can be understood by all the children. In early childhood literacy development, story readings by an adult, group singing, class discussions, and brainstorming sessions are appropriate whole-group activities.

Small-Group Instruction

Small groups are effective for guided instruction in specific skills and other more intricate lessons that require careful supervision or close interaction with children. Appropriate literacy activities in small groups include directed listening/reading–thinking activities that involve interpretive or critical thinking, cooperative projects such as creating pictures for a class book on a particular topic, storybook reading, and assignments in a specific center or area (because whole groups cannot fit into these areas at the same time). Teachers often prefer a small, homogeneous group for skill development, because this organizational arrangement allows the teacher the opportunity to work closely with a few children who seem to be at a similar literacy level and have similar needs at the same time. Grouping should be flexible; for example, when members of a small group have mastered a particular skill, the group can be disbanded and new groups formed when necessary.

This flexible arrangement for grouping allows children to work with many others and eliminates the stigmas often attached to fixed homogeneous grouping that assigns general ability labels to groups. When children as young as four are organized for instruction into fixed high, middle, and low groupings, they become as aware of their group placement as children in third or fourth grade.

In addition to teacher-organized groups, children should be given opportunities to select groups they might like to be in because of interest and friendships. Chapter 6 describes periods of independent reading and writing called Literacy Center Time during which choice of activities and the person with whom children work with are based on their decisions.

One-to-one Instruction

Working with children on a one-to-one basis and allowing them to work independently are both forms of individualized instruction. Although children need to work cooperatively with peers and interact socially with both peers and adults, one-to-one instruction offers personal attention and an opportunity for the teacher to learn a great deal about the child. Literacy activities particularly appropriate for one-to-one instruction include (1) story retellings; (2) attempted readings of favorite storybooks; (3) helping children with specific skill needs, such as letters of the alphabet or color identification; (4) assessing a child's ability or knowledge in a particular literacy area; (5) reading stories, with prompts for questions and comments; and (6) taking dictation of original stories or helping children to write themselves.

Regular one-to-one sessions can be extremely productive. A teacher can establish twenty minutes or more of conference time each day, thus allowing a one-to-one session with each child for at least a few minutes each week. During conferences, teachers can assess the child's special needs, record accomplishments, offer instruction, and assign tasks or suggest goals. Conference time lets the teacher accommodate both the child who is already reading and the child who cannot yet differentiate print from pictures. Conference time with one child might best be used for reading a story and encouraging responses, with another child helping record Very Own Words.

At the end of each conference period, the teacher announces which children will be seen the next day, writing their names on the board. The agenda for each conference with each child is determined by the needs, interests, and abilities of that child at that time. Although children can participate in conferences from age three, their maturity determines exactly how a conference is carried out. The typical conference lasts about five minutes, but it can be as short as two minutes or as long as fifteen. The atmosphere is informal, and the session is usually a very special time for both teacher and child.

The value of meeting children one-to-one was made quite apparent to me early in my teaching career. A mother told me that her child liked to be absent from school. I was quite upset by this comment, assuming immediately that he liked being absent because he was unhappy in my class. The mother went on to say that her son liked being absent because when he returned to school he was given "private time with the teacher." I had made a practice of meeting "privately" with absentees on their return to school to share work we had accomplished during their absences.

On another occasion, I noticed several children reading on their own during free-choice time—an ability I was unable to recognize in them during my whole-class instruction in reading readiness skills. I began to work with children one-to-one, discovering what they knew, wanted to know, and needed to know. One-to-one instruction can be more easily and accurately designed to meet children's individual interests and needs. Assignments or suggestions can involve specific materials at a particular center or area of the room. Such targeted instruction not only gives children practice they specifically need, but instills in them a sense of responsibility in accomplishing assigned tasks. Conferencing not only meets the usual needs of children in a given classroom but is also particularly suited to meeting the needs of children with special problems.

To make an assignment "official" and to help the child remember it, the teacher can draw up a contract or assignment sheet. For preschoolers and kindergartners who cannot read conventional print, their contracts are composed of both pictures and words. The teacher and child check off the areas in which the child is to work. At the next conference they read over the contract together to check what the child has done. A typical assignment might be to read a book in the library corner, to read over one's Very Own Words, to copy words from a new word list, or to make a book of pictures about a particular topic. Assignments are based on the needs, interests, and ability levels of individual learners. A sample contract is illustrated in Figure 10.6.

During a one-to-one conference, the teacher takes notes and records anecdotes of the child's behavior. These notes, collected in one folder for each child, become part of the records on the child's progress and prescriptions for future work. The folder also holds periodic samples of the child's drawings, writing, and dictated stories. It is helpful for the teacher to include in each folder copies of the various checklists and sets of objectives described throughout this book as an aid in observing and nurturing a child's development. The checklist on pages 324–327 is a guide to the assessment of early literacy development. The list is a compilation of the objectives and assessment information that appear in chapters throughout the book. Assessment during conferences adds to the child's total assessment portfolio, which contains material collected throughout the school year.

◆ **FIGURE 10.6** *Contract Activities*

Name _____	Contract _____ Date	Done
Things To Do	**Specific Activity**	**Done**
	Reading	
	Writing	
	Oral Language	
	Language Arts Manipulatives	
	Listening Station	
	Math Manipulatives 1 + 2 = 3	
	Other Activities:	

Teachers should keep anecdotal records about children's learning. A loose-leaf notebook with dividers (one per child) provides a place to write quick notes when the opportunity arises. Social interactions, attitudes, progress, strengths, and weaknesses should be noted. Also, a child's self-evaluation form, shown in Figure 10.7, is an important part of a total assessment profile.

Working Independent of the Teacher

Working individually or with a friend can also mean working independently. When teachers are working with small groups of children or in conference settings, the rest of the class must function independently. Children sometimes read alone during independent reading and writing periods. They enjoy working alone or in small groups with their Very Own Words. They listen to books on headsets and create books. They need practice in working independently, especially while the

◆ **FIGURE 10.7** *Children's Self-Evaluation Form*

Name_____ Date_____

1. I know all the letters of the alphabet.   Yes ☐   No ☐

2. I can write the letters.   Yes ☐   No ☐
   Here is a sample of some letters I can write

3. I know letter sounds.   Yes ☐   No ☐
   Here are some letter sounds I know

4. Things I need help with letters are:

---

1. I like to read: Yes ☐   No ☐   Why?

2. Things I like to read are:

3. The things I do well in reading are:

4. The things I need to learn how to do better in reading are:

---

1. I like to write: Yes ☐   No ☐   Why?

2. Things I like to write are:

3. The things I do well in writing are:

4. The things I need to learn how to do better in writing are:

Checklist for Assessing Early Literacy Development

Child's Name: _____

Date: _____

◆ *Language Development*

	Always	Sometimes	Never
Makes phoneme sounds			
Speaks in one-word sentences			
Speaks in two-word sentences			
Identifies familiar sounds			
Differentiates similar sounds			
Understands the language of others when spoken to			
Follows verbal directions			
Speaks to others freely			
Pronounces words correctly			
Has appropriate vocabulary for level of maturity			
Speaks in complete sentences			
Uses varied syntactic structures			
Can be understood by others			

◆ *Attitudes toward Reading and Voluntary Reading Behavior*

	Always	Sometimes	Never
Voluntarily looks at or reads books			
Asks to be read to			
Listens attentively while being read to			
Responds with questions and comments to stories read to him or her			
Takes books home to read			
Reads voluntarily at home			

◆ *Concepts about Books*

	Always	Sometimes	Never
Knows that a book is for reading			
Can identify the front, back, top, and bottom of a book			
Can turn the pages properly			
Knows the difference between the print and the pictures			
Knows that pictures on a page are related to what the print says			
Knows where to begin reading			

	Always	Sometimes	Never
Knows what a title is			
Knows what an author is			
Knows what an illustrator is			

◆ *Comprehension of Text*

Attempts to read storybooks resulting in well-formed stories			
Participates in story reading by narrating as the teacher reads			
Retells stories			
Includes story structure elements in story retellings:			
Setting			
Theme			
Plot Episodes			
Resolution			
Responds to text after reading or listening with literal comments or questions			
Responds to text after reading or listening with interpretive comments or questions			
Responds to text after reading or listening with critical comments or questions			

◆ *Concepts about Print*

Knows print is read from left to right			
Knows that oral language can be written down and then read			
Knows what a letter is and can point one out on a page			
Knows what a word is and can point one out on a printed page			
Knows that there are spaces between words			
Reads environmental print			
Recognizes some words by sight			
Can name and identify rhyming words			
Can identify and name upper- and lowercase letters of the alphabet			
Associates consonants and their initial and final sounds (including hard and soft *c* and *g*)			
Associates consonant blends with the sounds (*bl, cr, dr, fl, gl, pr, st*)			

(continued)

326

Checklist for Assessing Early Literacy Development (Continued)

	Always	Sometimes	Never
Associates vowels with their corresponding long and short sounds (*a*—acorn, apple; *e*—eagle, egg; *i*—ice, igloo; *o*—oats, octopus; *u*—unicorn, umbrella)			
Knows the consonant digraph sounds (*ch, ph, sh, th, wh*)			
Can blend and segment phonemes in words			
Uses context, syntax, and semantics to identify words			
Can count syllables in words			
Attempts reading by attending to picture clues and print			
Guesses and predicts words based on knowledge of sound–symbol correspondence			
Can identify suffixes and prefixes			
Demonstrates knowledge of the following phonic generalizations:			
a. In a consonant-vowel-consonant pattern, the vowel sound is usually short			
b. In a vowel-consonant-*e* pattern, the vowel is usually long			
c. When two vowels come together in a word, the first is usually long and the second is silent (train, receive, bean)			
Uses word families such as: *an, at, it,* and *ot,* and initial consonants to build words (e.g., man, fan, ran)			

◆ *Writing Development*

	Always	Sometimes	Never
Explores with writing materials			
Dictates stories, sentences, or words he or she wants written down			
Copies letters and words			
Independently attempts writing to convey meaning, regardless of writing level			
Can write his or her name			
Collaborates with others in writing experience			
Writes in varied genres: narrative, (stories), expository (personal and informational reports)			
Writes for functional purposes			
Check (✓) the level or levels at which the child is writing			
_____ uses drawing for writing and drawing			
_____ differentiates between writing and drawing			

___ uses scribble writing for writing

___ uses letterlike forms for writing

___ uses learned letters in random fashion for writing

___ uses invented spelling for writing

___ writes conventionally with conventional spelling

◆ *Mechanics for Writing*

Forms uppercase letters legibly

Forms lowercase letters legibly (See Figure 9.18)

Writes from left to right

Leaves spaces between words

Uses capital letters when necessary

Uses periods in appropriate places

Uses commas in appropriate places

---

teacher is holding individual conferences. Montessori schools tend to be very effective in helping young children to be independent, self-directive, and capable of working individually or in small groups without the need for teacher supervision.

Children working individually or in small groups use manipulative learning materials placed in centers on accessible shelves. Teachers illustrate the use of all such materials before placing them on the shelves, each item in its own place. Children select new items only after they replace those they have been using. During conference periods, only relatively quiet materials may be used independently. Teachers need to give children time to practice working independently. This was discussed in Chapter 6, which featured the preparation of the environment, the modeling of materials, and time to work alone.

When children work at centers, teachers can organize and manage this time by having students select what they want to do. Teachers can also assign specific centers to children according to needs and interests. Figure 10.8 provides an example of a form for selecting or assigning centers. This form is for an individual child to use for a week. When selecting a center, the child checks where they intend to go before a conference or center time begins. If a teacher assigns centers, he or she will fill in the form for the children. The form can be used for one school week.

It is important that the teacher use a variety of organizational strategies to meet the individual learning styles and to make the schoolday interesting. Teaching children in groups and on a one-to-one basis may not seem as if one is creating an environment in which literacy can emerge naturally; it may seem structured. Yet, it is not realistic to rely totally on a child's initiative and expect learning to take place. The teacher must create the conditions and plan the learning opportunities within which the reading process can be nurtured and developed.

◆ **FIGURE 10.8** *A form to help teachers organize and manage individual student activities during centers on a weekly basis.*

Center Form

Name_____ Week of _____

Centers	Mon.	Tues.	Wed.	Thur.	Fri.
Reading					
Writing					
Science					
Social Studies					
Math					
Art					
Dramatic Play					
Other:					

The Daily Schedule

Scheduling the daily routine in nursery school, kindergarten, and first and second grade must take into account the social, emotional, physical, and intellectual level of the children. It must also reflect the best from theorists' models of early childhood education, including those of Piaget, Froebel, Dewey, Montessori, the behaviorists, and Vygotsky. The environment should be prepared so that learning can take place naturally, but with the guidance and instruction that will help children achieve their fullest potential.

Young children cannot sit for long periods; their schedule must vary. Whole-class lessons that require sitting and listening must be few and short. Chil-

◆ **FIGURE 10.9** *Evaluation Strategies and Organization of Instruction*

Planning Your School Day: Theme Topic _____

(TD-Teacher Directed, IN-Independent Activity, WG-Whole Group, SG-Small Group, 1 to 1)

CHANGE TIME SLOTS WHEN USING LONGER OR SHORTER PERIODS OF TIME

9:00 to 9:30: <u>Activity and Content Area:</u> <u>Materials Used:</u> <u>Where Activity Takes Place</u> <u>TD or IN:</u> <u>WG, SG, 1-to-1:</u>	**9:30 to 10:30 <u>Activity and Content Area:</u>** <u>Materials:</u> <u>Where:</u> <u>TD or IN:</u> <u>WG, SG, 1-to-1:</u>
10:30 to 11:30 <u>Activity and Content Area:</u> <u>Materials:</u> <u>Where:</u> <u>TD or IN:</u> <u>WG, SG, 1-to-1:</u>	**11:30 to 12:30 <u>Activity and Content Area:</u>** <u>Materials:</u> <u>Where:</u> <u>TD or IN:</u> <u>WG, SG, 1-to-1:</u>
Lunch 12:30 to 1:30	
1:30 to 2:30 <u>Activity and Content Area:</u> <u>Materials:</u> <u>Where:</u> <u>TD or IN:</u> <u>WG, SG, 1-to-1:</u>	**2:30 to 3:00 <u>Activity and Content Area:</u>** <u>Materials:</u> <u>Where:</u> <u>TD or IN:</u> <u>WG, SG, 1-to-1:</u>

dren need large blocks of time for exploring environments. They need play situations, manipulative materials, learning centers, and outdoor areas. Children need small-group and one-to-one instruction. Activities that require sitting and listening need to be followed by ones that allow movement. Quiet times must be followed by noisier times. To nurture literacy, the teacher must allow for rich literacy experiences throughout the day, experiences in using and enjoying language in all its forms and functions.

In scheduling the school day, be sure to include *whole-class, small-group,* and *one-to-one* settings for learning. There need to be *teacher-directed* experiences and activities that children participate in *independently.* Children should have opportunities for *oral reading* and *silent reading* from books and from their own writing. They need to have time for whole-group *shared reading* experiences and *shared writing* experiences. Time should be set aside for periods of *guided reading* and *guided writing,* as well as *reading and writing independently.* Children should have the opportunity to *read and write collaboratively* with peers, and *perform* in formal and informal settings the products of their reading and writing. Figure 10.9 provides an example of a self-analysis form concerning the organization of instruction. The form provides space for recording lessons taught. It also asks that lessons be identified as whole-group, small-group, or one-to-one settings, and as teacher-directed or independent. There is a place to record the materials used in the lesson, and where the activity occurred in the classroom. If you record this information for a few days it will help you to analyze the teaching strategies you are using and identify those that you may need to incorporate.

The sample schedules that follow illustrate where and when specific opportunities to promote literacy can occur. The schedule provides a routine or structure for the day that seems to make children comfortable.

Several examples of early childhood programs are provided. They include:

1. Day-care centers for infants and toddlers
2. Half-day preschool and kindergarten
3. Full-day preschool and kindergarten
4. A program appropriate for kindergarten, first, or second grade

Day-Care Centers

Full-Day Program for Infants and Toddlers

8:00–9:45: Arrival, caring for infants' needs (diapering, feeding). When involved in these routine activities, caregivers talk to babies, sing nursery rhymes, recite poems, reinforce babies' responses.

Activity period consisting of play (in small groups or one-to-one) with blocks, manipulative toys, books, or paper and crayons. Teacher and aides provide language models by identifying materials and talking about their use and provide positive reinforcement for such literacy activities as attempting oral language, looking at books, and using crayons on sheets of paper.

9:45–10:00: Snack for toddlers, accompanied by song or poetry. (Infants are fed whenever necessary.)

10:00–10:45: Rest or nap. Adults sing a napping song before children lie down.

10:45–11:15: Washing, diapering, caring for babies' needs in preparation for lunch. Adults interact with children verbally through conversation, song, or rhymes.

Activity time focuses on reading stories, looking at pictures, and using taped stories, paper, and crayons.

11:15–12:00: Lunch. Conversation involves the taste, smell, and texture of the food. After lunch, babies are readied for nap time with washing, diapering, and caring for infant needs.

12:00–1:45: Naps, begun with a song and carried through with quiet background music.

1:45–2:00: As children wake, their needs are taken care of again and a small snack is provided.

2:00–3:30: Indoor and outdoor play. In either setting, adults work with small groups, reading stories, encouraging responses from children, pointing out print.

3:30–4:00: Teacher attempts a group session involving singing a song or reading a book aloud. The last ten minutes of the day are spent in preparing the children to leave—toileting, diapering, and general care.

As noted in the introduction to this chapter, the day-care center needs to emulate as much as possible homes with rich literacy environments if they are to ensure the natural development of literacy in infants and toddlers.

Preschools and Kindergartens

There is no one daily routine that has been established as the model for all preschool and kindergarten programs. There are, however, basic categories of activities that ought to be included. The daily routines for preschool and kindergarten do not vary much in the blocks of time allocated to specific activities. The tone, content, and means of what actually occurs in those time periods are far more important. Time allotments for activities should be flexible to accommodate spontaneous educational experiences. When activities are particularly productive, they should be continued beyond allotted time schedules.

Two sample schedules follow, one for a half-day and one for a full-day program.

Half-Day Program for Preschool and Kindergarten

8:30–8:50: Arrival at school, storage of outdoor clothing. Quiet activities.

8:50–9:20: Whole-group morning get-together, opening exercises, morning message, discussion of unit topic, songs or musical movement activities related to unit topic, daily news, planning for the school day.

9:20–9:40: Whole-class lesson in language arts, mathematics, social studies, or science, varying from day to day, with an assignment to complete that flows into the next period.

9:40–10:00: One-to-one conference period or small-group work. The rest of the class completes work from the whole-class lesson; children work on individual contracts in small groups or at designated centers (literacy, social studies, science, or mathematics).

10:00–10:35: Center time. All centers open, including art, music, blocks, dramatic play, literacy, science, and social studies. Special projects may be set up at different centers, such as art or science. Children work alone or in small groups independent of the teacher.

10:35–10:50: Clean-up and snack.

10:50–11:10: Literacy Center Time. Children use materials from the literacy center (library corner, oral language area, writing area).

11:10–11:30: Outdoor play, if weather permits, or large-motor games in the gymnasium.

11:30–12:00: Whole-group storybook reading with varied strategies, including shared book experiences, role-playing, creative storytelling. Summary of the school day. Dismissal.

Full-Day Program for Nursery School or Kindergarten
(It should be noted that full-day schedules allow for larger blocks of time and more time for learning through exploration and manipulation of materials.)

8:30–9:00: Arrival at school, storage of outdoor clothing. Quiet activities.

9:00–9:30: Whole-group morning get-together, opening exercises, morning message, discussion of unit topic, songs and musical movement activity related to the unit topic, daily news, planning for the school day.

9:30–9:50: Whole-class lesson, either in language arts or mathematics, varying from day to day, with an assignment to complete that flows into the next period.

9:50–10:15: One-to-one conference period or small-group work with emphasis on literacy development and math skills. The rest of the class completes work from the whole-class lesson or works on individual contracts from small groups or at centers designated for use during this quiet period (literacy center, math, social studies, science).

10:15–10:45: Free play. All centers open, including dramatic play, blocks, and woodworking. Special art or food-preparation projects are set up in the art center once each week for small groups independent of the teacher.

10:45–11:00: Clean-up and snack.

11:00–11:30: Shared storybook reading, creative storytelling, repeated story readings, role-playing, shared book readings, use of Big Books.

11:30–12:15: Literacy Center Time. Children use materials in the literacy center (library corner, writing area, oral language area, language arts manipulatives), including Very Own Words.

12:15–1:15: Lunch and outdoor play, if time and weather permit. Otherwise, large-motor activities in the gymnasium.

Afternoon Schedule for Preschool

The morning schedule would be the same for preschool and kindergarten. In preschool, however, the afternoon would differ somewhat and look more like this:

1:00–1:45: Rest period.

1:45–2:10: Center time. All centers open and a special project is in one of the areas. Work in small groups or alone independent of the teacher.

2:10–2:35: Outdoor play, large-motor play in gymnasium, or large-motor musical movement activities.

2:35–2:50: Work-group circle time. Summary of the day's activities, planning for the next day, sharing items brought from home that are related to the unit, sharing work created by children, songs, story reading.

2:50–3:00: Preparation for dismissal. Dismissal.

Afternoon Schedule for Kindergarten

1:15–1:45: Whole-group lesson in science or social studies incorporating language arts, music, or art.

1:45–2:15: Center time (literacy, mathematics, science, social studies). Special projects can be set up in any of these for small groups to rotate through in a given week. The teacher meets with small groups for instruction in math or literacy skills.

2:15–2:50: Whole-group circle time. Summary of the day's activities, planning for the next day, sharing of items brought from home that are related to study units, performance of work created by children, songs, and adult story reading.

2:50–3:00: Preparation for dismissal. Dismissal.

A Program for Kindergarten, First, Second, and Third Grade

The detailed outline that follows illustrates how literacy development and content-area instruction can be integrated throughout a school day. Let us assume that the topic under study is animals.

8:30–9:00: Arrival and Quiet Activities: Books about animals are featured on the open-faced bookshelves in the library corner. The science and social studies table holds collections of pictures and figures of four different types of animals: farm, zoo, pet, woodland. Farm and woodland animals are particularly featured here; zoo and pet animals are featured in the block and dramatic-play areas. Also in the classroom are one or more live animals, such as fish in an aquarium, gerbils, hamsters, guinea pigs, newts, hermit crabs, or rabbits. They are located near the dramatic-play area, which is designed as a veterinarian's office. Children are encouraged to look at the books, work on written stories or reports that are in progress, explore with the model animals, or play with the pet animals during this quiet activity period. Background pictures of barns, a silo, farm equipment, mountains, trees, and zoo scenes encourage interesting play and language use. Index cards are readily available for labeling animals or making signs such as Deer Crossing, No Hunting, or Endangered Species. A morning message on the chalkboard says, "We will be going on a trip to a farm."

9:00–9:30: Morning Get-together: A child leads the opening exercises. Children are encouraged to tell news for the day, including things that have happened outside of school that they would like to share. The teacher writes on an experience chart what the children have to say—for example, "I got new red sneakers after school yesterday," or "My dad got a flat tire while we were driving home. We had to use the little tire from the trunk until we got to the gas station to buy a new one."

The teacher asks if anyone can read the morning message: "We will be going on a trip to a farm." After children attempt to do so, she reads it with them, asking them to join in unison. To generate discussion and build anticipation she asks, "What do we need to think about before going to the farm?" She generates further discussion about the unit topic, asking the children to name all the farm animals they can think of and listing them as they are named. She then asks the function or purpose of each animal—for example, "Cows give milk for the farmer to sell." The group sings "Old MacDonald Had a Farm" and "The Farmer in the Dell."

The teacher and children discuss plans for the rest of the day and the work children will choose during their independent work period. The teacher reminds the children to look for messages on the notice board and to leave messages there for friends.

9:30–9:50: Whole-Group Language Arts Lesson: The class makes its fourth book about animals. Thus far they have completed one each for pet, zoo, and woodland animals; this one deals with farm animals. The teacher asks each child which animal he or she will draw and tries to include as many animals as possible from the list just completed. The teacher asks the children to write sentences, stories, or simply names connected with their animals. Children who finish early can choose to write to pen pals, write messages for the notice board, copy from charts, or ask the teacher for help with their writing. Children who are hesitant to write are encouraged to dictate to the teacher, who provides a writing model for them.

9:50–10:45: Conference Period or Small-Group Work: The teacher reminds the children that most of them will work independently, alone or with friends, during conference time. Each child's individual folder holds a contract suggesting individual activities to complete. Children use the literacy, math, and science centers. They complete their page for the farm animal class book if they have not already done so.

The teacher meets with three or four children individually, tailoring work to their individual needs, interests, and abilities. For example:

Christopher is functioning below grade level. The teacher tries to provide him with experiences that many of the children have already mastered. She continues a discussion begun at his last conference, encouraging him to differentiate print and pictures. She uses a book that is familiar to him, one she has read to him before. They talk about the book, pointing out its front and back. The teacher reads the story to Christopher, occasionally asking him to point out the print or the picture on a page, or where she should start to read on a new page. For his contract assignment, she asks Christopher to look at books and find their beginning and end, their print and pictures. Before Christopher leaves, she asks him if he would like a new word for his Very Own Word collection. If he does, she writes it for him on an index card.

Jim is beginning to merge narrational reading and conventional reading. Jim has shown an interest in words and asks to have them identified. He likes to associate letters and sounds because it helps him become more independent in his reading. The teacher selects a familiar story, *Are You My Mother?* (Eastman, 1960) and asks Jim to read it. He uses the intonation of conventional reading and looks at the print as he narrates the story. In particularly predictable parts, he attends to the print, a behavior the teacher encourages. She asks him to point out the words *Are you my mother?* wherever the main characters say them in the story. When Jim is finished reading the story, the teacher asks, "If you were the baby bird, would you have looked for your mother or just waited for her?" and follows his response with "Why?" For his contract assignment, she asks Jim to read three familiar storybooks and write down all the words he recognizes in print. Before he leaves, she asks if he would like a new word for his Very Own Word collection. He selects two words from the story he just read.

Jennifer is reluctant to try to write. The teacher initiates a discussion of the child's family. She knows a new baby has just arrived. The baby's name is Joseph. The teacher asks Jennifer if she would like to write something about her new brother. Jennifer responds that she can't write. The teacher explains that she doesn't have to write like a grownup but that children can write in their own ways. The teacher shows Jennifer samples of other children's writing, which include invented spelling, random letters, scribble writing, and conventional writing. Jennifer responds that she would like to write Joseph's name but she can't do it. Because of Jennifer's reluctance, the teacher writes the name *Joseph* on an index card and asks Jennifer if she can copy some of it. Jennifer copies the *J* and comments that it is the first letter of her name, too. As a contract activity, the teacher asks Jennifer to draw a picture of her new brother and to think of things she would like to say about him and try to write them in her own way. The word *Joseph* becomes Jennifer's new Very Own Word.

(These conferences were samples of work with kindergarten or early first-grade children. They would be different in content with children at the end of first grade or second grade.)

10:15–10:45: Themed Play: Children may select activities in any area in the room. This is the only time during the day that blocks, art, workbench, and dramatic-play areas are open. Items that incorporate the animal theme have been added to the areas. The dramatic-play area is set up as a veterinarian's office, with typical signs such as *No Smoking* and *Doctor Is In [or Out]*. There are pictures of pets with their names, waiting room magazines, pamphlets on animal health, appointment pads, a telephone and directory, prescription pads, and health charts. The classroom pets and stuffed animals serve as patients; students role-play the doctor, nurse, secretary, and pet owner.

The block corner is set up as a zoo. It includes tickets for admission, posters of zoo animals with their names, pamphlets and brochures about a real zoo, and pamphlets on zoo animals. Children use figures of zoo animals as they construct a zoo from the blocks. Typical signs include the name of the zoo, *Don't Feed the Animals, I Bite, Petting Zoo, Pony Rides,* and signs identifying various animals.

The art center offers on a large chart a simple recipe for play dough, to be used for making animals. The ingredients and equipment are laid out. The teacher is there to offer assistance.

How to Make Play Dough

Put 2 cups of flour into a bowl. Add 1 cup of water. Add 1 tablespoon of salt. Add 1 teaspoon of food coloring of your choice. Mix together with your hands till it feels like play dough. If it is too sticky, add more salt. If it is too dry, add 1 tablespoon of water. If it is too wet, add 1 tablespoon of flour.

Each child in the art center takes a piece of play dough then shapes it into an animal of his or her choice. Conversation is encouraged as the children follow the recipe, discuss textures, and create their animals. It is advisable that an adult be available for supervision.

The social studies center is set up with materials that focus on farm and woodland animals. It includes a store for selling farm products such as eggs, milk, vegetables, and wool. Also included are signs (*Fresh Farm Products, Open, Closed*), a cash register, order pads, shopping lists, name and price tags for various products, food posters, bags for groceries, play money, and markers for pricing food.

10:45–11:00: Clean-up and Snack: Children receive animal crackers with juice, and conversation is encouraged.

11:00–11:30: Storybook Reading: The teacher has selected *The Little Red Hen* for a shared book reading. She tells the story, using felt figures on a felt-board, and asks the children to participate every time the animal characters say, "Not I." After telling the story, she uses a Big Book to review the pages and points out the words *Not I.* She asks the children if they think the little red hen is right in not sharing her bread with the other animals, and why. She asks if there are other ideas for ending the story. She then leads the children into an independent reading and writing period and says that the Big Book and the felt figures for the story will be in the library corner for those who want to use them.

11:30–12:15: Literacy Center Time: Featured on the open-faced bookshelves are books dealing with farm, zoo, pet, and woodland animals. Animal puppets are available, as are taped stories about animals. The writing area includes animal pictures and word lists, plus all the usual materials needed for drawing and writing. The language arts manipulatives include animal puzzles, labeled pictures of animals that can be alphabetized, animal lotto, animal dominoes, a concentration card game on animals, and animal sewing cards. Although children may participate in any activities in the literacy center during this period, they are encouraged to use books during the period and to write a few times a week. The special writing project this week is making a book about animals, either a book about one of the four types under study or a book about all four. Children are encouraged to use their Very Own Words during this period and to ask for new ones.

12:15–1:15: Lunch and Outdoor Play: Part of the outside play area has been turned into a farm where seeds can be planted and vegetables grown. Markers identify plantings, and other signs say *Careful* and *Don't Step on the Plants.*

1:15–1:45: Whole-Group Lesson in Science or Social Studies: The class discusses its upcoming trip to a farm. With the teacher using an experience chart, the class lists things to remember for the trip: behavior reminders, safety rules, spending money, lunch, animals of particular interest, things they would like to see or do at the farm, questions to ask the farmer. Each child is encouraged to think of a question accompanied by a picture that will be sent to the farmer in advance so he or she will know what to discuss when the class visits.

1:45–2:15: Center Time: The literacy, science, social studies, and math centers are open. At the science center a special project has been set up for churning butter. If possible, have cream and a churn available. If not, five or six children with an adult supervisor can make butter by following a simple recipe posted on a large chart; materials and ingredients should be at hand. Each day, five or six other children can be assigned to the center for this activity.

Recipe for Making Butter
Two children work together. Take one baby food jar. Fill it halfway with whipping cream. Place the lid on the jar tightly. Take turns shaking the jar briskly for a total of five minutes. Let it stand for a few minutes and pour off the liquid. Run cold water over the butter and pour off the water. Add a little salt, spread on a cracker, and eat.

The teacher may meet with small groups or individuals to help with particular needs or projects, or read to small groups during this time.

2:15–2:50: Circle Time and Review of the Day: Several children share items from home that are related to farm, pet, zoo, or woodland animals. They are encouraged to speak in sentences. Other children share on other days. The teacher displays work that students have prepared earlier in the day for the class book on animals. With an alphabet chart visible, she suggests that the book be assembled in alphabetical order and leads the children as they do so in a whole-group activity. Student Authors of the Day are asked to share their part of the letter that will go to the farmer before the class visit to the farm. With a few children sharing each day, over the course of a week each child will have shared some writing. Children also take turns telling about good books they have read. The day's activities are reviewed, with children commenting on things they liked or did not like and things they accomplished or still have to do. As a large-motor musical activity, children listen to music, decide which animals the music brings to mind, then act out how those animals might move, walking like elephants, jumping like kangaroos, waddling like ducks, and so forth. The class sings "Go Tell Aunt Rhody." The words to the song have been posted on a chart, and the teacher points to each word as it is sung. She then reads and displays a book version of the song to end the day.

2:50–3:00: Preparation for Dismissal: Dismissal.

An Idea for the Classroom from the Classroom

On the following pages, you will find a thematic unit dealing with "Healthy Bodies, Healthy Minds," written for children in preschool through third grade. This unit includes all content areas and weaves literacy instruction throughout. When using the unit, adapt and select the ideas for the children you teach, making sure to repeat activities to reinforce the concepts being taught. When carrying out the unit, samples from each student's work should be gathered through formal and informal assessment measures. This is an excellent way to track the student's progress, and can be used in portfolio assessment. Using this unit as a guide, try your hand at creating another thematic unit for the youngsters in your classroom.

◆ *Integrated Language Arts Thematic Unit: Healthy Bodies, Healthy Minds*

FACTUAL INFORMATION

What Does It Mean To Be Healthy in Body and Mind?

Eating nutritious food, exercising regularly, getting enough sleep, keeping ourselves clean, and feeling good about ourselves, are all very important to keeping fit and healthy in body and mind.

Why Should We Eat Healthy Foods?

Good foods are needed to supply your body and mind with the energy it needs to function and grow everyday. All people need food to eat and water to drink to live. Food and water are also necessary for animals and most plants to live. Nutrients are the substances in food that give us the energy and strength we need to grow, work, and play.

What Are the Four Food Groups?

Eating properly, along with plenty of sleep and exercise, will keep a person's body healthy and strong. There are many types of food. Foods are separated into four major groups, and eating a proper amount of each daily will help ensure good health. Foods are categorized in the following manner:

1. *Vegetable-Fruit Group:* Most vitamins and roughage are obtained from fruits and vegetables. A good diet should contain dark green and yellow vegetables and citrus fruits. Some examples include apples, oranges, pears, broccoli, lettuce, carrots, spinach, and squash. It is recommended that four servings be eaten daily from this group.

2. *Bread-Cereal Group:* This group includes breads; rolls; bagels; crackers; cereals, such as oats and rice; and pastas. Carbohydrates, necessary for the energy to work and play, and fiber are the primary benefits of this group. Four daily servings are suggested.

3. *Meat-Poultry Group:* Also included in this group are fish, beans, nuts, and eggs. This group provides minerals and much of the protein in one's diet. Protein is essential for building and maintaining muscles. It is also important for overall growth. Two servings are suggested daily.

4. *Milk-Cheese Group:* This group includes all dairy products, such as milk, cheese, yogurt, and cottage cheese. These products are also high in protein and contain nutrients that build strong bones and teeth. Many products in this group tend to have a high fat content. Three servings are the recommended daily intake.

A proper diet, including ample portions from the four food groups, is essential for a healthy, growing child. However, there are also foods known as "empty calorie foods" or "junk foods." These items provide no vitamins, minerals, or protein and are not necessary for good heath. Foods in this group include soda, candies, potato chips, and some seasonings and spices. On occasion these foods are fine in moderate amounts; however, a well-rounded diet containing items from the four major food groups is best.

People from different cultures eat different food. Because the United States is home to people from many cultures, numerous American dishes have been influenced by Mexican, Asian, French, Italian, and Jamaican cooking, among others. It is fun to try ethnic foods and learn about different multicultural backgrounds.

Why Are Exercise, Rest, and Cleanliness Important?

Exercising by ourselves or with others can be fun. It gives us stronger muscles, healthier hearts, and makes our bodies and minds feel good. It helps circulate our blood and makes us feel refreshed and relaxed.

People around the world exercise regularly to keep healthy. Many of the sports or exercises here in the United States have been influenced by other cultures. For example, baseball was influenced by a British game called cricket, and American football was developed from rugby, a similar contact sport. Regular exercise helps to relieve stress and in getting a good night's sleep.

We spend a third of our lives sleeping. When we sleep, we give our bodies and minds time to rest, during which our heart rate and blood pressure decrease and breathing slows down. This is so our bodies and minds can work hard when we are awake. Getting too little sleep can affect your body and mind's ability to function and grow.

People with clean bodies, hands, faces, teeth, and hair are nice to be around. Clean people are less likely to attract germs and get sick. We can stay clean by washing ourselves and our clothes often.

How Does Self-esteem Affect Your Body and Mind?

People who feel good about themselves have self-esteem. They take care of their bodies and minds, and stay away from junk food, drugs, and alcohol. They look healthy and share their energy and good feelings with others around them.

Good mental health is important for coping with the demands of everyday life. Sometimes when you do not feel very good about yourself, it might help to make a list of all the things you can do, for example, ride a bike, read a book, draw a picture, or cook a dish. People can also help us solve our problems and make us feel better. These people include parents, siblings, friends, and teachers. However, it is important to realize that we all have strengths and weaknesses. This kind of self-knowledge helps in our ability to accept ourselves and to relate well with others.

It is healthy to express our feelings in appropriate ways. When someone does not take the time to think about his or her feelings and speak calmly in words, feelings may come out in other ways. People might show anger, feel sick and tired, or might want to be alone. Getting plenty of sleep, eating nutritious meals, exercising outdoors, and keeping up personal hygiene will help you feel better about yourself.

NEWSLETTER TO PARENTS ABOUT HEALTHY BODIES, HEALTHY MINDS

Dear Parents:

Your child will be participating in a unit that explores what it means to be healthy in body and mind. This unit will include study of why we should eat healthy foods, the four food groups, exercise, rest, cleanliness, and the importance of self-esteem.

The good health unit will cover all subject areas—play, art, music, social studies, science, math, and literacy (reading, writing, listening, and oral language) which will be incorporated in the theme. Some of the exciting activities we do here at school may also be carried out at home with your child.

At School and at Home

Art: Art can be a wonderful learning experience for your child. Your child will refine eye-hand coordination and visual discrimination skills and explore and experiment with different art materials as he or she engages in various art activities. At school we will be creating food collages and abstract bean mosaics. At home you can encourage your child to use his or her imagination by providing these and other food-related materials for art activities. Remember that art is for exploring what can be done with different materials, rather than copying an adult model.

Science: Science explorations will be related to meaningful aspects of your child's life. We will be making homemade applesauce, which will give the children an opportunity to listen, follow directions, and learn where apples come from and how they are grown, as well as how food changes as it is cooked. Making healthy snacks at home, such as a fruit or lettuce salad, and involving your child in the preparation by using simple recipes will help to extend listening skills.

Literacy: The letters *H, F,* and *B* associated with *Health, Food,* and *Body* are being highlighted. Please assist at home by labeling healthy food items with these letters or pointing out words that have these and other beginning sounds. Read signs and point out these letters when you are outside the home as well.

Please read stories, poems, informational books, cookbooks, exercise magazines, and other literature related to our theme of good health to your child. Reading to your child, having her or him read to you using illustrations, and retelling a story are all literacy activities that are valuable and enjoyable. Some books that will be featured in the unit include:

> *Gregory, the Terrible Eater* by M. Sharmat, 1984
> *No More Baths* by B. Cole, 1989
> *Mooncake* by F. Asch, 1983
> *There's a Nightmare in my Closet* by M. Mayer, 1968

We Need Your Help

We would like your assistance with our multicultural food of the week or your favorite food at home. If you are able to prepare a snack one day and discuss it, please sign your name and tell what type of snack you would like to prepare on the attached sheet.

If you can come in and read your child's favorite bedtime story to the class, please sign your name and tell what date you are available on the attached sheet.

If you have any other materials at home related to our theme, such as empty food containers, seeds, nuts, beans, or exercise or yoga magazines that we may use in our dramatic-play area, please send them in with your child.

Other Activities to Do with Your Child

Go to the supermarket with your child. Prepare a list beforehand of the food you need to purchase. Have your child check the things off as you put them in the cart. Try to purchase food from each food group.

Plant watermelon, avocado, carrot seeds at home. Keep a diary or record of their growth, making comparisons between them.

Make simple, nutritious recipes at home, such as fruit salad, mixed green salad, butter, or peanut butter, to help our lessons carry over from class to home.

Take the time to engage in some exercise with your child each day. A brisk walk or bike ride will help your child learn that exercise is fun and should be done often. It is an activity your family will enjoy together.

Remind your child at bedtime that rest is important for our bodies. Share a special bedtime story each night with your child.

Child's Corner

Ask your child to write or draw something he or she did in school related to our theme.

Help your child keep a journal of what foods he or she eats each day. Keep track of any exercises your child does. Keep track of how many hours of sleep your child gets, writing the number in the journal. Graph the numbers. The journal can be written in a notebook, on a pad, or on pieces of paper stapled together like a book.

If you have any questions about the unit or have any additional ideas, please contact me. If you are in a profession that is related to our theme, such as a nutritionist or any fitness-related career, please consider coming into class and talking to us.

Sincerely,

Lisa Lozak

- -

I would like to prepare the following snack for your healthy bodies, healthy minds unit:

Snack: _____ Parent's Name: _____

I am able to come in on the following date for a storyreading: Date: _____

Book: _____ Parent's Name: _____

Preparing Classroom Environment for the Healthy Bodies, Healthy Minds Unit

To begin the unit on healthy bodies, healthy minds, prepare the room so that the theme is evident to those who enter. Begin with some of the following suggestions and continue to add others as the unit progresses. Display environmental signs and labels about nutrition, personal hygiene, exercise, rest, and self-esteem wherever possible. Feature colors that represent the unit, such as white for dairy products, green for vegetables, and yellow and red for fruit.

1. *Dramatic Play:* This center can be turned into either a restaurant or a fitness center. As a restaurant, the center should include menus, receipts, order-taking slips, recipe cards, cookbooks, baking utensils, prop foods, signs commonly seen in restaurants, a cash register, play money, food posters, and waiter and waitress clothing. As a health club, the center could include light weights or dumbbells, jump ropes, balls, a balance beam, mats, gym membership cards, stop watches, heart-rate posters, sign-up sheets for aerobic classes, and towels.

2. *Block Area:* To create places that food comes from such as farms and supermarkets, the following items can be added: farm props (animals and plants), supermarket props (play foods, receipts, money, and bags), environmental print signs and posters displaying food information, and cards for making signs.

3. *Outdoor Play:* A health club/fitness center can be created outside by providing the following items: tables for stands or desks; exercise equipment

including jump ropes, balls and a balance beam; play money; cash register; receipts; signs displaying the hours of business; and paper and pencils, so children learn that this is a place to go to keep our bodies healthy.

4. *Music:* Various songs on nutrition, exercise, personal hygiene, and good self-esteem can be added to this center. All tapes should be accompanied by the written lyrics posted on the wall. Props to act out the songs may also be motivating. Students should also be encouraged to write and sing their own songs about good health.

5. *Art:* Include play dough and a poster with play dough recipes to make play foods. Include cooking and health magazines, dry foods to make collages, fruits, vegetables, shaped sponges for printing with paint, and scraps that represent the nutrition colors—white, green, red and yellow.

6. *Science:* Materials for various health and nutrition projects may be added: a stethoscope, a heart-rate chart, blood pressure device, foods to be classified into the four food groups, seed packages, and planting equipment. All of these items should be accompanied with charts and journals to record ongoing progress. Posters of the human body showing the muscles and skeleton and informational books should also be added.

7. *Social Studies:* Pictures of foods and the four food groups, and maps that depict where certain food comes from, as well as where the children's families are from should be included. In addition, posters displaying various athletic events from around the world may appear in the center. Recipe books representing different cultures may also be added.

8. *Math:* Various foods can be used as counters, such as macaroni or dried beans. Charts and graphs to record various activities, such as favorite fruit, laps around the school yard, or number of hours slept per night, should be included. Blank books for children to create their own number books are also needed.

9. *Literacy Center*

    a. *Writing Center:* Materials needed include a recipe box to share favorite recipes, food-shaped blank books, and a message board on which to share the morning message.

    b. *Library Corner:* Include health and fitness magazines, cooking magazines, pamphlets about good nutrition and general health, and a collection of books pertaining to the unit from all genres. (See the following list and the bibliography at the end of the unit.)

LIBRARY CORNER BOOKLIST WITH SUGGESTED ACTIVITIES

Asch, F. (1983). *Mooncake.* Englewood Cliffs, NJ: Prentice Hall.

Brandenberg, F. (1976). *I wish I was sick, too.* NY: Greenwillow.

Carle, E. (1969). *The very hungry caterpillar.* New York: Philomel.

Chambers, W. (1974). *The lip-smackin', joke-crackin' cookbook for kids.* New York: Golden Press.

Cole, J. (1988). *The magic school bus inside the human body.* New York: Scholastic.

DePaola,T. (1975). *Strega Nona: An old tale.* Englewood Cliffs, NJ: Prentice Hall.

DePaola, T. (1978). *The popcorn book.* New York: Holiday House.

Eberts, M. (1984). *Pancakes, crackers, and pizza.* Chicago: Children's Press.

Faulkner, M. (1986). *Jack and the beanstalk.* New York: Scholastic.

Hoban, R. (1976). *Bread and jam for Frances.* New York: Harper & Row.

Hopkins, L. B. (1985). *Munching: Poems about eating.* Boston: Little, Brown.

Irving, W. (1987). *Rip Van Winkle.* New York: Puffin Books.

Izawa, T. (1968). *The little red hen.* New York: Grosset & Dunlap.

Kellogg, S. (1988). *Johnny Appleseed: A tall tale.* New York: Morrow Jr. Books.

Krauss, R. (1945). *The carrot seed.* New York: Scholastic.

Mayer, M. (1968). *There's a nightmare in my closet.* New York: Penguin.

McCloskey, R. (1948). *Blueberries for Sal.* New York: Penguin.

Numeroff-Joffe, L. (1985). *If you give a mouse a cookie.* New York: Scholastic.

Raffi. (1987). *Shake my sillies out.* New York: Random House.

Sharmat, M. (1984). *Gregory, the terrible eater.* New York: Macmillan.

Shaw, C. (1947). *It looked like spilled milk.* New York: HarperCollins.

Suess, Dr. (1960). *Green eggs and ham.* New York: Random House.

Westcott, N. B. (1980). *I know an old lady who swallowed a fly.* Boston: Little, Brown.

Zolotow, C. (1962). *Mr. Rabbit and the lovely present.* New York: Harper and Row.

INTRODUCTORY LESSON

Objective

A written message will provide for vocabulary development and sound–symbol associations. Print will be recongnized as functional because it relays a message.

Activity: Morning Message—Introduce the students to the good health unit by writing a message on the board. Tell them about some of the interesting facts they will be learning during the unit. The message could look something like this: *"Today, we are going to begin learning about how to keep our bodies and our minds healthy. To take care of ourselves we need to eat good food, sleep, exercise, keep our bodies clean, and feel good about ourselves."* Read the message to the class using a pointer to track the print. Afterwards discuss the content of the message as well as the special words, letters, and sounds. Identify the letters *H, F,* and *B* as letters that will be focused on throughout the unit and associate them with the words *Health, Food* and *Body.* Allow the children to add to the message. Do a morning message daily to inform students of new health facts, as well as any special events or questions that are related to the unit.

CONCEPTS ABOUT PRINT

Objective 1

Increase oral and sight vocabulary through a discussion involving the seeing and writing of Very Own Words. Knowledge of nutrition will be gained.

Activity: *Very Own Words*—Before reading the story *I Know an Old Lady Who Swallowed a Fly,* discuss with the children why it is dangerous to eat inappropriate food. After reading the story, the children will discuss food they should not eat. Then ask them to name foods they like that are also good for them and *The Old Lady.* Write each child's favorite food on a 3 × 5 index card to be stored in their Very Own Word container.

Objective 2

Increase sight vocabulary and the ability to follow directions by using a chart with functional environmental print.

Activity: *Environmental Print*—A helper chart will be made that lists jobs for students to perform. The chart should be located in a visible area and relate directly to the unit. Jobs may include cafeteria monitor, reading the lunch menu, and helping with the daily snack.

Objective 3

The featured letter in a word, story, or song will be identified. The letter's sound–symbol relationship will be made and then copied from a story chart.

Activity: *Featured Letters*—Display pictures of types of exercises that keep a body healthy, using the featured letters: *R—Running, D—Dancing, B—Baseball, W—Walking.* Simple stories and songs with the letters may also be used, e.g., *Barbara plays baseball with Bob in Billy's backyard.* Emphasize the sound the letter makes in each word and have the children write the letter. Students may be encouraged to bring in items from home that begin with the featured letter. Pictures of items that begin with the featured letter may also be made and added to a class book. Do one letter at a time and repeat the activities suggested.

Objective 4

An alphabet book that reviews many nutrition words learned in the unit will be created. Knowledge of letters, both vowels and consonants, and words that are identified with specific letters and sounds will be demonstrated.

Activity: *Nutrition Alphabet Book*—An alphabet book will be made and photocopied for each child in the class. Each letter will relate to nutrition (i.e., *A—apple, B—bread, C—carrot, D—dairy, E—eggs, F—fish.*) and a complete sentence will be written with each letter (i.e., I like ___). The students will read the letters, words, and sentences with the teacher and with each other.

ORAL LANGUAGE

Objective 1

Listening skills will be improved by speaking in complete sentences.

Activity: *Show and Tell*—Have students bring in their favorite foods from home representing different cultural backgrounds. Display and discuss with the class.

◆ **FIGURE 10.10** *A Web of Characteristics of Milk*

Our Poem about Milk

Milk tastes cold and delicious,
Milk is healthy and refreshing,
Milk is a white liquid that is good for you.

Another activity would be to have children share a healthy habit they practice at home or at school.

Objective 2

Appropriate vocabulary for the level of maturity will be used when retelling a story.

Activity: *Story Retelling*—Read a story related to nutrition, such as *The Very Hungry Caterpillar,* and allow the class to retell the story using food props that are in the book.

Objective 3

Oral communication skills will be increased, through participation in a literature circle.

Activity: *Literature Circle*—Children will sit in a small group with the teacher and discuss a book that they read related to the healthy bodies, healthy minds theme. Model appropriate book talk and pose questions to facilitate the group discussion. Encourage the children to continue posing questions to each other, without the teacher as a guide.

Objective 4

Language complexity will be increased through the use of adjectives.

Activity: *Webbing and Creating Poetry*—Brainstorm characteristics of nutritious food, such as milk, and provide a graphic presentation with a web (Fig. 10.10). List the characteristics of the food by writing adjectives to describe it. Create a web on the chalkboard. Encourage children to assist in putting together a poem by using the information on the web. Write the poem on the chalkboard. Encourage children to read it with you, tracking print from left to right as you read. Rewrite the poem on chart paper to display.

DEVELOPING POSITIVE ATTITUDES

Objective 1

Develop positive attitudes toward reading through interaction in a well-designed literacy center.

Activity: The Library Corner—Include different genres of literature related to the theme of healthy bodies, healthy minds (realistic literature, fairy tales, poetry, informational books, magazines, and newspapers). Provide hand/face/stick puppets, taped stories, felt stories, roll movies, and so on.

Objective 2

A story is read by a class parent to increase family literacy. Using the context of the story, outcomes will be predicted.

Activity: If You Give a Mouse a Cookie *Prop Story.* A child's family member will read *If You Give a Mouse a Cookie* to the class. Use props such as a mouse doll, a plastic cup, an empty box of cookies, and so on to tell the story again to the class. Encourage participation by having the children use their knowledge of rhyme and context. Place the props in the library corner for the children to use.

Objective 3

A story will be told through the use of a storytelling technique (chalk talk).

Activity: Mr. Rabbit and the Lovely Present. *Chalk Talk*—Read *Mr. Rabbit and the Lovely Present* and discuss the food in the story. Now retell the story and draw the fruit in the story as you come to each part. Use colored chalk for the chalk board. After repeated story readings, encourage children to retell the story themselves.

Objective 4

Enjoy literature while working with a friend.

Activity: Partner Reading—Have children work in pairs in the literacy center. They may retell a story using props, felt-board, hand or face puppets, or a roll movie. They should also be encouraged to take turns reading and discussing a story with their partner.

CONCEPTS ABOUT BOOKS

Objective 1

Learn to differentiate print from pictures and know what books are for.

Activity: Big Book—Create a class Big Book that contains pictures and sentences of each child's favorite exercise or sport. When it is completed, read the book together. Place the Big Book in the library corner for repeated readings.

Objective 2

See and understand that print is read from left to right.

Activity: *Poetry Reading*—Display a poem (such as "Shake My Sillies Out") about movement or exercise on a large chart and read with the class. Use a pointer to show that print is read from left to right. Act out the poem and then create a class poem. Display and read it in the same manner.

Objective 3

Learn that an illustrator draws pictures in a book.

Activity: *Illustrators*—Read *It Looked Like Spilled Milk* to the class. Discuss the illustrations in the story and allow the students to become illustrators by drawing their own pictures of what they see when they look at a cloud. Create a Big Book of all the pictures.

Objective 4

Learn the function and importance of the title and cover of a book.

Activity: *Title Pages*—Present several books about health and hygiene (refer to book list if needed) to the class. Read the titles and discuss the picture on the cover. Ask students if they can guess what the book is about just by reading the title and looking at the cover. Explain that the title and picture help the reader know what the story or book is about. Have the students create their own title and cover for a book they would like to someday read or write. Create a class Big Book of title pages.

COMPREHENSION

Objective 1

Learn about story structure by identifying story elements (setting, theme, characters, plot episodes, resolution).

Activity: *Story Structure:* The story *There's a Nightmare In My Closet,* has been read to the children in the past. Before reading the story a second time, ask the children to try and remember the time that the story takes place, where the story takes place, and who the characters are. After reading the story the second time, have the children identify the three setting elements: *time, place,* and *characters*. Do the same thing with other story elements such as the *theme, plot episodes,* and *resolution*. Have the children prepare a roll movie with five headings: Setting, Theme, Characters, Plot Episodes, and Resolution. Do one section of the roll movie at a time. Encourage them to draw pictures and include narrative for each of the sections. Repeat with other stories.

Objective 2

Demonstrate literal knowledge by acting out a story using stick puppets, as well as identify details of a story by answering literal questions.

◆ **FIGURE 10.11** *K-W-L Chart*

Topic **Exercise**

What We **K**now	What We **W**ant to Know	What We **L**earned
fun To get in shape Run Walk	Different ways to exercise Exercise properly Eating healthy	Rollerblade Ride Bike How to take pulse Four food groups

Activity: *Literal Activity:* Before reading *The Little Red Hen,* tell the children to remember the things the hen wanted help with when baking bread. After reading the story, have the children dramatize the episodes with stick puppets of the animals and the hen.

Objective 3

Express feelings, predict, generalize and problem solve.

Activity: *Critical Activity:* The story of *The Little Red Hen* is repeated. Role play the "Donahue Show" and have a child take the part of Donahue interviewing the animals in *The Little Red Hen* story, asking why they didn't help the hen and what they think about the fact that she didn't share the bread with them. Then interview the hen as well. Video- or audiotape interviews and place copies in an assessment portfolio. With another story such as *Gregory the Terrible Eater,* interview his parents to try and find out why his eating problem exists. Try and extend this activity to other books as well.

Objective 4

Create a **KWL** chart (what they **K**now, what they **W**ant to know, and what they have **L**earned).

Activity: *K-W-L Activity*—Begin a discussion about exercise and how it affects the body. Ask what the children know about the importance of exercise. List their responses on chart paper under the heading "What We Know." Ask the students what they might want to learn about the subject and list those responses on chart paper as well under the heading "What We Want To Know." Introduce and read several informational books, posters, pamphlets, and magazines about exercise and a healthy body, such as *Shape* and *Muscle and Fitness.* After several days of discussion and activities in conjunction with these books, refer back to the lists you made at the beginning of the lesson. Create a new heading titled, "What We Learned" and ask the students to share things they learned about exercise over the past several days. Compare this list to the list of what they wanted to know about exercise. Ask questions like: How are they different? What could you do if you didn't learn something you wanted to know? Have the students complete similar charts before and after other lessons.

WRITING

Objective 1

Emerging authors and illustrators: Learn that books are written by authors, and that pictures are drawn by illustrators. Children will participate in brainstorming, drafting, conferencing, editing, and revising and engage in an experience chart as a prewriting activity.

Activity: Bed-shaped book—Read the book *Mooncake.* Create a story web on experience chart paper as students talk about characteristics of sleep (why it is important, what happens when you sleep). Each child will be writing a story about sleep while teacher conferences take place. Finished products will be written in books shaped like a bed. This activity can be extended to other topics related to the theme. For example, books may also be shaped like a bathtub or bar of soap if the story is about personal hygiene.

Objective 2

Communicate through writing about exercise and nutrition. See and use functional writing.

Activity: Notice Bulletin Board: A notice bulletin board with student and teacher sections will be prepared in the classroom. Children may display their work on the board, as well as leave and receive messages in their spaces. Students can share messages, such as what they had for lunch and what food group each item belonged to or what exercise or sport they played in gym or at home. They may also decorate their personal space by drawing pictures related to these topics.

Objective 3

Letter writing as a meaningful form of communication.

Activity: Healthy Mail Service: The students will write letters to each other about healthy habits through an in-class mail service. The class as a whole will write to the American Heart Association and other health organizations to request information and pamphlets about good health.

Objective 4

Journal writing as a form of written expression.

Activity: Journal Writing: Read *Green Eggs and Ham* to the class. Explain to the children that journal writing will allow them to use writing to convey meaning about things they have learned in the unit. Emphasize that by doing so, they will become authors and illustrators. As in the story, children should be encouraged to write about a food they do or do not like. Throughout the healthy bodies, healthy minds unit, students will periodically write about their experiences. Conventional or invented spelling, scribbling, and pictures are acceptable entries.

PLAY

Objective 1

Engage in problem solving through dramatic play and environmental print related to the theme of being healthy in body and mind.

Activity: *Dramatic Play. Healthy Food Restaurant*—Turn the dramatic-play area into a health food restaurant by adding menus, cookbooks, recipe charts, receipts, and other signs that would appear in a restaurant. Encourage children to write while taking orders and posting signs.

Objective 2

Block play will be enhanced with theme-related play to acquire new concepts and encourage participation in reading and writing activities.

Activity: *Block Play. Where We Get Food*—Have children create block constructions of the places that our food comes from, such as farms and supermarkets. Provide labels and appropriate props for their construction, as well as paper for children to draw or write about their constructions.

Objective 3

Follow written directions and use print in a functional manner in an outdoor play activity.

Activity: *Outdoor Play. Health Club*—Set up a health club outside with different exercise stations. Have a sign-in sheet at each numbered station. Have children choose roles such as directing an exercise class, pouring water, filling in membership cards, or writing receipts. Encourage the children to name their club and hang posters as advertisements.

Objective 4

Engage in dramatic play while building self-esteem and respect for each other.

Activity: *Dramatic Play. "I'm Glad I'm Me" Kingdom*—Watch Sesame Street's "I'm Glad I'm Me" with Prince Charming Bird. Create an "I'm Glad I'm Me" Kingdom in the dramatic-play area. Hang flags the children have made to represent the things each child is proud of and likes about him- or herself. Supply crowns, robes, scepters, and so on. Place a basket of fairytale books in the center.

ART

Objective 1

Develop perceptual skills and use visual discrimination while copying patterns and colors. Develop concepts about the importance of rest.

Activity: *Body Murals*—Have the children wear their pajamas to school (if possible). Have them listen for rhymes as you read *Rip Van Winkle*. Afterwards, draw the children's body shapes on large paper in a sleeping position. Have children color in the patterns of their pajamas and try to draw their sleeping faces.

Objective 2

Self-esteem and self-assessment will be fostered over the course of the unit.

Activity: *I'm "Thumb" Body Books*—Children will be given blank books to illustrate. On the cover, they will put their thumb print and write the words "I'm (thumb print) Body." Each week, they will draw a picture of something they have accomplished or are proud of. Encourage them to write beginning sounds or engage in invented spelling to accompany their pictures or take dictations in the books. After each entry, collect books and make motivational comments to the children. At the end of the unit, ask children to make a final comment on what they think their biggest accomplishment was.

Objective 3

Learn that parts of most vegetables can be used for print painting as they explore and experiment with these materials.

Activity: *Vegetable Print Painting*—Vegetable printing with ink or tempera paint will be carried out. The ends of discarded vegetables and fruits will be used for print painting. Children will discuss their pictures and describe how they made them. A discussion of conservation and recycling may be conducted.

Objective 4

Gain an appreciation for creativity and ingenuity by designing pictures and jewelry based on different cultures. Increase visual discrimination and enrich vocabulary through observation and discussion.

Activity: *Macaroni Art*—Pictures using macaroni, beans, dried fruits, seeds, and so on can be made. Jewelry can also be made by using macaroni and string. Macaroni can be dyed by placing it in food coloring and water for three minutes. Provide students with pictures, books, or authentic examples of multicultural jewelry, such as Mexican or Native American necklaces, bracelets, or rings. Encourage children to design such types of jewelry. Students will observe and model each other's work and describe their own to the class.

MUSIC

Objective 1

Recall skills will be enhanced, as children relate their own bedtime experiences to the group.

Activity: *Bedtime Round*—Listen to "Bedtime Round" by Tom Chapin. Post the lyrics and track from left to right as they listen. Talk about bedtime and list other things children say in order to delay going to sleep. After practicing, try to sing the song in rounds as in the recording.

Objective 2

Discuss good health habits. Recognize and create rhymes while acting out a song.

Activity: *Brush Your Teeth*—Write the lyrics to Raffi's "Brush Your Teeth" and highlight the rhymes. Listen to the song and track the lyrics as you sing. Try to think of lyrics that would rhyme with the numbers 6 through 10.

Objective 3

Increase sight word vocabulary. Talk about feelings and emotions in a supportive environment.

Activity: *If You're Happy and You Know It*—Sing the song "If You're Happy and You Know It." For each emotion, draw the corresponding face on a paper plate with the emotion written on it. Make a variety of plates, for example, if you're sad and you know it, if you're angry and you know it. Practice the song with the picture cards until the children can recognize the words without the drawings. Talk about each feeling. Make a list of things that make you feel each type of emotion.

Objective 4

Introduce music representative of the Indian culture. Develop an understanding of Yoga as a type of exercise first practiced in India to relax the body and mind.

Activity: *Yoga*—Children will be asked to sit comfortably on the floor. Lights can be dimmed and Indian music played softly. Children can be asked to close their eyes and concentrate on breathing evenly and deeply. They may engage in simple stretches and poses like the lotus (sitting straight and centered with feet pulled in) or the dead man's pose (lying flat on the back). Later you may want to make Indian food such as hummus and pita bread for snack time. Ask children to describe their feelings and experiences with the activity, or write about it in their journals.

SOCIAL STUDIES

Objective 1

Increase writing and oral language abilities and discuss how following directions is important.

Activity: *Strega Nona*—Read the story, *Strega Nona,* to the class. Discuss how the story takes place in Italy and note the use of its native food in the story. Discuss how the character in the story should have followed directions. Students may write a similar story, using new characters and food, perhaps from another country they have studied in the unit.

Objective 2

Gain appreciation for other countries' influences on popular sports. Increase knowledge of geography and other cultures.

Activity: *Sports Study*—Students will work in small groups to research the popular sports of various countries. Each group's contributions can be added to a class Big Book. As an extension activity, students may enjoy playing these sports during outdoor play.

Objective 3

Children are exposed to conflict and resolution, and shown how cooperation and communication are important to developing and maintaining relationships. Cooperation and friendship skills will be increased through role-playing.

Activity: *No More Baths*—Read *No More Baths.* After reading, discuss the story and note children's feelings about bathing on an experience chart. The students can then take turns role-playing the story.

Objective 4

By introducing foods and customs of different countries, an appreciation for the differences and contributions of other people and cultures will be developed. Oral and written communication skills will be increased.

Activity: *Country of the Week*—A "Country of the Week" will be focused on. Customs, foods, and major contributions of each will be highlighted. Children will discuss the differences and similarities among the countries, with an emphasis on foods and the healthfulness of each. The students may also write about their favorite food from each country. Different foods will be featured at snack time.

SCIENCE

Objective 1

Hypothesize what will happen to a heartbeat during exercise. Record observations of any changes as they occur.

Activity: *Heartbeat in Exercise*—Demonstrate how to listen to a heartbeat using a stethoscope or by feeling a pulse. Have children listen to a partner's heart before and after doing jumping jacks. Students can then record observations in their journals. Discuss and write a conclusion of the experiment. Older children may record beats per minute and graph their results.

Objective 2

The connection between oral and written language will be made through a discussion about how you catch a cold.

Activity: *I Wish I Was Sick, Too*—Read *I Wish I Was Sick, Too.* Use an experience chart to record what the children know about catching a cold. Discuss the importance of cleanliness and the prevalence of germs in our lives. Allow each child to collect a sample of germs from objects and place on an agar petri dish. Students can then predict which samples will grow faster than others. Children can then record their observations of any significant growth. Provide microscopes and/or magnifying glasses for more detailed observations.

Objective 3

Hypothesize what will happen during the growth of a planted seed. Record observations of the growth as it occurs.

Activity: *Planting*—Allow each student to plant a lima bean seed and keep the plants in the classroom. Have the students write entries in journals each day to record the progress of their plant's growth.

Objective 4

Observe changes that occur in the form of food while following directions in preparing a recipe.

Activity: *Making Applesauce*—Read *Johnny Appleseed* to the class. Discuss the nutritional value of apple products. Make applesauce with the class. Post the recipe and use it as a reference to point out all the steps involved in making applesauce.

MATH

Objective 1

The connection between oral and written communication will be made by observing and recording the sleep patterns of animals.

Activity: *Sleep Patterns*—Students will observe and record the sleep patterns of the class pet and graph daily results. Compare any differences on the graphs and discuss how animals need different amounts of sleep at different times of the day.

Objective 2

Compose a nutrition counting book by following oral directions for counting and writing numbers to ten.

Activity: *My Nutrition Counting Book*—Explain to the children that they will be authors and illustrators of their own nutrition counting book. Pass out copies of premade number books and review directions. Children will need to color illustrations and trace or write the number on each page. Each page will feature a number and a food. For example, 3 with 3 carrots.

Objective 3

Relate pictures to text and see that pictures and print go together. Classify objects according to shape (triangles, circles, squares).

Activity: *Sort a Food*—Read *Pancakes, Crackers, and Pizza* to the class. Emphasize the different shapes of food as you read: round pancakes, square crackers, and triangular shaped pieces of pizza. Create a chart with three columns (triangles, circles, squares). Encourage children to classify cut out pictures of food from magazines or newspapers in the appropriate columns on the chart. Provide three shoe boxes labeled with each shape so that children can continue to classify different foods on their own.

Objective 4

Practice counting to twelve and matching the correct number of items to number of words.

Activity: *Counting "Eggsactly"*—Display an egg carton with number words printed on the bottom of each hole. Provide a variety of seeds, nuts, and beans for children to match to the correct number by placing them in the egg holes of the carton.

CULMINATING ACTIVITY

Objective 1

Share the products of the unit with children's family, friends, or other classes in the school.

Activities: Prepare a nutritious food, such as fruit salad and applesauce, for a snack to share with guests.

Sing a song related to the importance of rest from the unit, such as "Bedtime Round," or related to the importance of personal hygiene, such as "Brush Your Teeth."

Display art projects related to the unit and describe how they were made.

Show plants from the science portion of the unit and discuss how they grew.

Lesley Morrow with Rutgers Graduate Students: Kathleen Cunningham, Patty DeWitt, Erica Erlanger, Donna Ngai, Katherine Heiss, Pam Kelliher, Lisa Lozak, Melody Olsen

Activities and Questions

1. Answer the focus questions at the beginning of the chapter.

2. During the course of reading and working on the activities in this book, you have been preparing an integrated language arts thematic unit based on a topic in social studies or science. To complete this unit, do the following:

   a. Prepare a classroom environment with materials based on your topic that promote literacy in different content-area centers. Be sure to add materials to the following centers: art; music; math; science; social studies; the literacy center (reading and writing); and block, dramatic, and outdoor play areas. (Refer to the environment portion of the Healthy Bodies, Healthy Minds Unit provided in the "An Idea for the Classroom from the Classroom" section.)

   b. Prepare a newsletter to send home to parents concerning the activities you have designed for this unit and the things they can do at home with their child to enhance learning. (Refer to the newsletter in the unit provided in the "An Idea for the Classroom from the Classroom" Section).

c. Provide a few pages of factual information for the teacher about your unit. Refer to the factual information portion of the unit provided in this chapter.

d. Add activity sections to your unit in these content areas: science; social studies; art; music; and block, dramatic, and outdoor play. Be sure to include activities that reflect the objectives for the content area and literacy development as well. Refer to the content area sections in the unit provided in this chapter.

e. Plan an entire school day for an early childhood classroom of your choice (preschool, kindergarten, first or second grade) and incorporate some of the themed activities and literacy activities prepared in your unit.

f. In your plan for the day, include three conferences to meet individual needs. One of the children you will be working with is gifted, one is a child who attends a basic skills class, and one is from a bilingual background.

3. Observe in an early childhood classroom to evaluate how rich the literacy environment is. Use the "Checklist to Evaluate the Rich Literacy Environment" provided in this chapter.

4. Review the sample materials you have collected in the assessment portfolio you began for a child at the beginning of the book. Write a summary concerning the child's literacy development at this time and the progress he or she has made in the months you've been collecting the materials; include suggestions you have for his or her program of instruction.

Case Study Activity

As a recognized professor in the field of early literacy, you have been asked by the editors of *The Reading Teacher* journal to write a review for this book, *Literacy Development in the Early Years: Helping Children Read and Write*. In your review you are to discuss the content of the text, the organization and writing style, and the special features (such as photographs, illustrations, checklists, activities, ideas for the classroom, case studies, bibliographies, and so on). You are reviewing the book for college professors who might adopt it as a text for a course in early literacy development or for practicing teachers who wish to broaden their knowledge of early literacy development. Let these individuals know why they should or should not adopt or read this text. Is the book appropriate for undergraduates, graduate students, or both? Is this book appropriate for teachers new to the field or those who have been teaching for some time? Because the book is going into a new edition soon, provide suggestions in your review about how the book might be improved. Please send your review and comments to Lesley M. Morrow, Rutgers University, Graduate School of Education, 10 Seminary Place, New Brunswick, NJ 08903. I look forward to hearing from you.

LMM

Afterword

We must reignite our romance with the written word.
—Steven Spielberg, 1987

This volume has presented a theory- and research-based program for developing literacy in early childhood. It has emphasized the importance of literacy-rich environments; social interaction; peer collaboration; and whole-class, small-group, and individual learning with adult guidance. The activities suggested underscore the concurrent, integrated nature of learning how to use oral language, reading, and writing. The volume has outlined education that is functional and related to real-life experiences and is thus meaningful and interesting to the child. It has provided for the integration of literacy activities into content areas through units of study that are based on themes that add enthusiasm, motivation, and meaning. It has suggested careful monitoring of individual growth through direct instruction and frequent assessment using multiple measures and allowing ample space for children to learn through play, manipulation, and exploration. Attending to children with special needs has been a concern throughout the volume.

New information about learning is constantly being generated and subsequently changes the strategies we use to help children learn. Teachers must stay abreast of the constant stream of literature that is available after they complete their formal education. Teachers need to be researchers and reflect upon their own teaching to discover their strengths and weaknesses. When teachers are researchers, they will increase their knowledge and skill. To be a teacher–researcher means to formulate questions about teaching strategies, child development, classroom environment, curriculum development, or other relevant topics that will clarify issues or help generate new information. Questions should generate from your daily experiences in the classroom and be of interest to you personally.

When an area of inquiry is decided upon, the teacher should focus on collecting data that will help to answer questions posed or clarify issues. Data can be collected in the following ways: observe and record anecdotes of classroom experiences that are relevant to the question being asked; videotape classroom segments; collect samples of children's daily work over a period of time; interview children, teachers, and parents; administer formal and informal tests; and try new techniques.

As a teacher–researcher, you will always be on the cutting edge of what is current and appropriate. You will always find your teaching interesting because you will be learning about new things on a daily basis. You will enjoy your work more because you have extended your role to include additional professional activity. As a teacher–researcher, you are practicing both the art and science of teaching. The science involves inquiry, reading, observing, and collecting data. The art involves reflecting on findings and making appropriate changes. Teacher–researchers empower themselves to be decision makers and catalysts for making change in their schools. As they study questions for which they have tangible data, they are more likely to be heard when they propose new ideas and change. Rather than having change mandated based on the research by individuals outside your school district or by administrative personnel, take the responsibility for what change will occur by researching issues yourself. Each year that you teach, select another area of inquiry to study. When appropriate, collaborate with colleagues on research projects. Collaboration with adults, as with children, results in projects that you might not have been able to do alone.

The program described in this volume is meant to be enjoyable for both teachers and children. Enjoyment allows the teacher to work with vigor and enthusiasm. Enjoyment allows the child to associate literacy with a school environment that is pleasurable, positive, and designed to help children succeed. The single most important element in learning to read and write is having a desire to read and write. This desire motivates an interest in learning the skills necessary to become proficient in literary activities. Such an environment ensures a lifelong interest to refine and use literacy skills. The program is designed to help us "reignite our romance with the written word" (Spielberg, 1987).

Appendix A

Children's Literature

Books for Babies

Cardboard Concept Books

Allen, J. (1992). *Up the steps, down the slide*. New York: William Morrow and Co., Inc.

Boone, E. (1986). *It's spring, Peterkin*. New York: Random House.

Day, A. (1992). *Carl's masquerade*. New York: Farrar, Straus, & Giroux.

Dyer, J. (1986). *Moo, moo, peek-a-boo*. New York: Random House.

Hands, H. (1985). *First-look nature books*. New York: Grosset & Dunlap.

Hayes, G. (1986). *Patrick and his grandpa*. New York: Random House.

Hoban, T. (1993). *Black on white*. New York: Greenwillow Books.

Lilly, K. (1982). *Baby animal board books*. New York: Simon & Schuster.

Pandell, K., and DePaolo, T. (1994). *I love you, Sun. I love you, Moon*. New York: G. P. Putnam's Sons.

Cloth Books

Anglund, J. W. (1985). *Baby's first book*. New York: Random House.

Attinello, L. (illus.). (1986). *Baby piggy's purse*. New York: Random House.

Beasley, R. (illus.). (1986). *Baby's cradle songs*. New York: Random House.

Bracken, C. (illus.). (1984). *Baby Strawberry Shortcake's playtime words*. New York: Random House.

Cook, T. (illus.). (1986). *In a popple's pocket*. New York: Random House.

Gleeson, K. (1994). *Yum! Yum!*. New York: Western Publishing Company, Inc.

Marksbury, T. (1986). *Nighty-night teddy beddy bear*. New York: Random House.

Parr, J. (1979). *Baby's animal book*. New York: Random House.

Tucker, S. (1994). *Quack Quack*. New York: Simon & Schuster.

Plastic Books

Anglund, J. (1986). *Tubtime for Thaddeus*. New York: Random House.

Berenstain, S. and J. (1985). *The Berenstain bears bath book*. New York: Random House.

Chauhan, M. (1986). *Muppet babies take a bath*. New York: Random House.

Davis, J. (illus.). (1985). *Garfield's water fun*. New York: Random House.

Hill, E. (1984). *Spot goes splash*. New York: Putnam's.

Miller, J. (1984). *The duck says quack book*. New York: Random House.

Scarry, R. (1984). *Richard Scarry's lowly worm bath book*. New York: Random House.

Sesame Street. (illus.). (1982). *Ernie's bath book*. New York: Random House.

Sustendal, P. (illus.). (1986). *The care bear bath book*. New York: Random House.

Touch-and-Feel Books

Carle, E. (1972). *The secret birthday message*. New York: Thomas Y. Crowell.

George, G. (1986). *If you rub a wrinkle*. New York: Random House.

Hanna, J. (1992). *Let's go to the petting zoo with Jungle Jack*. New York: Doubleday.

Kunhardt, D. (1984). *Pat the bunny*. Racine, WI: Western Publishing Co.

McQueen, L. (1994). *Pet the baby farm animals*. New York: Scholastic.

Penick, E. and I. (1983). *The good morning book*. New York: Western Publishing Co., Inc.

Perryman, J. (1984). *Where are all the kittens?* New York: Random House.

White, E. and P. (1984). *The touch me book*. New York: Western Publishing Co., Inc.

White, E. and P. (1976). *Who lives here?* New York: Greenwillow.

Concept Books

Baker, A. (1994). *White rabbits color book*. New York: Kingfisher Books.

Berenstain, S. and J. (1968). *Inside, outside, upside down*. New York: Random House.

Bond, M. (1990). *Paddington's opposites*. New York: Viking.

Byron, B. (1981). *Wheels*. New York: Thomas Y. Crowell.

Dodds, D. A. (1994). *The shape of things*. Cambridge: Candlewyck Press.

Hoban, T. (1972). *Push, pull, empty, full*. New York: Macmillan.

Robbins, K. (1983). *Tools*. New York: Four Winds Press.

Round, G. (illus.). (1976). *Top and bottom*. New York: Grosset & Dunlap.

Alphabet Books

Agard, J. (1989). *The Calypso alphabet*. New York: Henry Holt & Company.

Base, G. (1986). *Animalia*. New York: Harry N. Abrams, Inc.

Boynton, S. (1983). *A is for angry: An animal and adjective alphabet*. New York: Workman Publishers.

Brown, R. (1991). *Alphabet times four*. New York: Dutton Children's Books.

Feelings, M. (1974). *Jambo means hello: A Swahili alphabet book*. New York: Dial Press.

Gag, W. (1971). *The ABC bunny*. New York: Coward, McCann & Geoghegan.

Hague, K. (1983). *Alphabears*. New York: Holt, Rinehart & Winston.

Seuss, Dr. (1963). *Dr. Seuss's ABC*. New York: Random House.

Van Allsburg, C. (1987). *The Z was zapped*. Boston: Houghton Mifflin Company. Each alphabet letter suffers mishaps.

Number Books

Anno, M. (1977). *Anno's counting book*. New York: Thomas Y. Crowell.

Baum, A. and J. (1962). *One bright Monday morning*. New York: Random House.

Brisson, P. (1993). *Benny's pennies*. New York: Doubleday.

Carle, E. (1968). *1, 2, 3 to the zoo*. New York: William Collins.

Clements, A. and Johnson, L. S. (1992). *Mother Earth's counting book*. Boston: Picture Book Studio.

Feelings, M. (1971). *Moja means one: A Swahili counting book*. New York: Dial Press.

Fujikawa, G. (1977). *Can you count?* New York: Grosset & Dunlap.

Hoban, T. (1972). *Count and see*. New York: Macmillan.

Keats, E. J. (1972). *Over in the meadow*. New York: Four Winds Press.

Oxenbury, H. (1968). *Numbers of things*. New York: Franklin Watts, Inc.

Sheppard, J. (1994). *The right number of elephants*. New York: Harper & Row, Publishers.

Wolff, F. (1993). *Seven loaves of bread*. New York: Tambourine Books.

Nursery Rhymes

Battaglia, A. (1973). *Mother Goose*. New York: Random House.

DeAngeli, M. (1954). *The book of nursery and Mother Goose rhymes*. New York: Doubleday.

DePaola, T. (1985). *Tomie dePaola's Mother Goose*. New York: Putnam's.

Galdone, P. (1966). *The history of Simple Simon*. New York: McGraw-Hill.

Jeffers, S. (1973). *Three jovial huntsmen: A Mother Goose rhyme*. New York: Bradbury Press.

Lobel, A. (1986). *The Random House book of Mother Goose*. New York: Random House.

Piper, W. (1972). *Mother Goose: A treasury of best loved rhymes*. New York: Platt & Munk.

Tudor, T. (1944). *Mother Goose*. New York: D. McKay.

Watson, C. (1971). *Father Fox's penny rhymes*. New York: Thomas Y. Crowell.

Wildsmith, B. (1964). *Brian Wildsmith's Mother Goose*. New York: Franklin Watts, Inc.

Favorite Well-Known Picture Storybooks

The following books represent a careful selection of some distinguished authors and excellent children's literature not to be missed.

Barrett, J. (1970). *Animals should definitely not wear clothing*. New York: Atheneum.

Bemelmans, L. (1939). *Madeline*. New York: Viking.

Berenstain, S. and J. (1966). *The bear's picnic*. New York: Random House.

Brown, M. W. (1957). *Goodnight moon*. New York: Harper & Row.

Carle, E. (1969). *The very hungry caterpillar*. New York: Philomel.

DePaola, T. (1975). *Stregna Nona: An old tale*. Englewood Cliffs, NJ: Prentice Hall.

Eastman, P. D. (1960). *Are you my mother?* New York: Random House.

Flack, M. (1932). *Ask Mr. Bear*. New York: Macmillan.

Galdone, P. (1975). *The little red hen*. New York: Scholastic.

Hoban, R. (1969). *Best friends for Frances*. New York: Harper & Row, Publishers.

Hughes, S. (1979). *Up and up*. New York: Lothrop, Lee & Shepard Books.

Hutchins, P. (1978). *Don't forget the bacon*. New York: Puffin Books.

Johnson, C. (1955). *Harold and the purple crayon*. New York: Harper Books.

Keats, E. J. (1962). *The snowy day*. New York: Viking.

Kellogg, S. (1971). *Can I keep him?* New York: Dial Press.

Kraus, R. (1971). *Leo the late bloomer*. New York: Windmill.

Lionni, L. (1973). *Swimmy*. New York: Random House.

Lobel, A. (1972). *Frog and toad together*. New York: Harper & Row.

Mayer, M. (1974). *One monster after another*. Racine, WI: Western Publishing Co., Inc.

McCloskey, R. (1948). *Blueberries for Sal*. New York: Penguin.

Piper, W. (1954). *The little engine that could*. New York: Platt & Munk.

Potter, B. (1902). *The tale of Peter Rabbit*. New York: Scholastic.

Rey, H. A. (1952). *Curious George rides a bike*. Boston: Houghton Mifflin.

Sendak, M. (1963). *Where the wild things are*. New York: Harper & Row.

Seuss, Dr. (1940). *Horton hatches the egg*. New York: Random House.

Shaw, C. (1947). *It looked like spilled milk*. New York: HarperCollins.

Slobodkina, E. (1947). *Caps for sale*. Reading, MA: Addison-Wesley.

Steig, W. (1969). *Sylvester and the magic pebble*. New York: Simon & Schuster.

Viorst, J. (1972). *Alexander and the terrible, horrible, no good, very bad day*. New York: Atheneum.

Waber, B. (1975). *Ira sleeps over*. Boston: Houghton Mifflin.

Wiesner, D. (1988). *FreeFall*. New York: Lothrop, Lee & Shepard Books.

Wiesner, D. (1992). *Tuesday*. New York: Clarion Books.

Traditional Literature (Fairy Tales, Fables, Myths, and Folktales)

Adams, A. (illus.). (1975). *Hansel and Gretel*. New York: Scribner's.

Asbojornsen, P. C., and Jorgen, E. M. (1957). *The three Billy Goats Gruff*. New York: Harcourt Brace Jovanovich.

Galdone, P. (1972). *The three bears*. New York: Scholastic.

Galdone, P. (1975). *The gingerbread boy*. New York: Seabury Press.

Grimm Brothers. (1968). *Grimm's fairy tales*. Chicago: Follett.

Grimm Brothers. (1968). *Little red riding hood*. New York: Harcourt Brace Jovanovich, Inc.

Havgaard, E. (trans.). (1978). *Hans Christian Andersen: His classic fairy tales*. New York: Doubleday.

Haviland, V. (1980). *The fairy tale treasury*. New York: Dell.

Kent, J. (1974). *Fables and Aesop*. New York: Parents Magazine Press.

McDermott, J. (1972). *Anansi the spider*. New York: Puffin Books.

Perrault, C. (1954). *Cinderella*. New York: Scribner's.

Rockwell, A. (1984). *The three bears and fifteen other stories*. New York: Harper & Row.

Stevens, J. (1971). *The tortoise and the hare*. New York: Holiday House.

Stobbs, W. (1970). *Rumpelstiltskin*. New York: Walck.

Easy-to-Read Books with Limited Vocabulary

Cole, J. (1976). *Fun on wheels*. New York: Scholastic.

Eastman, P. D. (1960). *Are you my mother?* New York: Random House.

Lesieg, T. (1961). *Ten apples up on top*. New York: Random House.

Lobel, A. (1972). *Frog and toad together*. New York: Harper & Row.

Martin, B. (1967). *Brown bear, brown bear, what do you see?* New York: Holt, Rinehart & Winston.

Seuss, Dr. (1957). *The cat in the hat*. New York: Random House.

Seuss, Dr. (1960). *Green eggs and ham*. New York: Random House.

Williams, V. (1990). *More, more, more said the baby*. New York: Scholastic.

Books about Realistic Issues

Ackerman, K. (1994). *By the dawn's early light*. New York: Atheneum.

Alexander, M. (1971). *Nobody asked if I wanted a baby sister*. New York: Dial Press.

Balens, A. (1990). *Jesse's daycare*. Boston: Houghton Mifflin.

Hazen, B. (1983). *Tight times*. New York: The Viking Press.

Hoban, R. (1960). *Bedtime for Frances*. New York: Harper & Row.

Kelley, T. (1994). *I've got chicken pox*. New York: Dutton Children's Books.

Lapsley, S. (1975). *I am adopted.* New York: Bradbury Press.

Limb, S. (1993). *Come back, Grandma.* New York: Knopf.

May, J. (1971). *Why people are different colors.* New York: Holiday House.

Preston, E. (1969). *The temper tantrum book.* New York: Viking.

Sonnenborn, R. (1970). *Friday night is papa night.* New York: Viking.

Viorst, J. (1971). *The tenth good thing about Barney.* New York: New Antheneum Press.

Weber, A. (1969). *Elizabeth gets well.* New York: Thomas Y. Crowell.

Yolen, J. (1991). *All those secrets of the world.* Boston: Little, Brown.

Zolotow, C. (1963). *The quarreling book.* New York: Harper & Row.

Wordless Storybooks

Alexander, M. (1968). *Out! Out! Out!* New York: Dial Press.

Alexander, M. (1970). *Bobo's dream.* New York: Dial Press.

Aruego, J. (1971). *Look what I can do.* New York: Scribner's.

Hutchins, P. (1968). *Rosie's walk.* New York: Macmillan.

Keats, E. J. (1973). *Skates.* New York: Franklin Watts.

Mayer, M. (1967). *A boy, a dog, and a frog.* New York: Dial Press.

Oxenbury, H. (1982). *Good night, good morning.* New York: Dial Press.

Ward, L. (1973). *The silver pony.* Boston: Houghton Mifflin.

Wezel, P. (1964). *The good bird.* New York: Harper & Row.

Poetry Books

Adoff, A. (1973). *Black is brown is tan.* New York: Harper & Row.

Coatsworth, E. (1966). *The sparrow bush.* New York: W. W. Norton.

Cole, W. (1981). *Poem stew.* New York: Lippincott.

Fisher, A. (1963). *Cricket in a thicket.* New York: Scribner's.

Frank, J. (1990). *Snow toward evening: A year in the river valley.* New York: Dial Books.

Goldstein, S. B. (1989). *Bear in mind: A book of bear poems.* New York: Viking.

Hopkins, L. B. (1993). *Extra innings.* San Diego: Harcourt Brace Jovanovich.

Hudson, W. (1993). *Pass it on.* New York: Scholastic Books.

Joseph, L. (1990). *Coconut kind of day: Island poems.* New York: Lothrop, Lee & Shepard Books.

Kuskin, K. (1980). *Dogs and dragons, trees and dreams.* New York: Harper & Row.

Larrick, N. (1968). *On city streets.* New York: M. Evans.

Nicholls, J. (1985). *Magic mirror and other poems for children.* Winchester, MA: Faber & Faber.

O'Neil, M. (1961). *Hailstones and halibut bones.* New York: Doubleday.

Prelutsky, J. (1983). *Random House book of poetry for children.* New York: Random House.

Schwartz, A. (1992). *And the green grass grew all around.* New York: Harper Collins.

Sendak, M. (1962). *Alligators all around us.* New York: Harper & Row.

Silverstein, S. (1974). *Where the sidewalk ends.* New York: Harper & Row.

Stevenson, R. L. (1977). *A child's garden of verses.* New York: Platt & Munk.

Westcott, N. B. (1994). *Never take a pig to lunch and other poems about the fun of eating.* New York: Orchard Books.

Informational Books

Alexander, H. (1990). *Look inside your brain*. New York: Putnam.

Bessar, M. (1967). *The cat book*. New York: Holiday House.

Cole, J. (1983). *Cars and how they go*. New York: Thomas Y. Crowell.

Lewellen, J. (1981). *Moon, sun, and stars*. Chicago, IL: Children's Press.

May, J. (1969). *Living things and their young*. New York: Follett.

Rockwell, A. (1971). *The toolbox*. New York: Macmillan.

Rockwell, A. (1972). *Machines*. New York: Macmillan.

Selsam, M. (1973). *How kittens grow*. New York: Four Winds Press.

Skaar, G. (1966). *All about dogs*. New York: Young Scott Books.

Swallow, S. (1973). *Cars, trucks, and trains*. New York: Grosset & Dunlap.

Yepsen, R. (1983). *Train talk*. New York: Pantheon.

Biography

Aliki. (1977). *The many lives of Benjamin Franklin*. Englewood Cliffs, NJ: Prentice Hall.

Austin, M. C. (ed.). (1960). Easy to read discovery books (titles follow). Champaign, IL: Garrard Publishing Co.
Daniel Boone; Lafayette; Theodore Roosevelt; Abraham Lincoln; George Washington Carver; Clara Barton; Paul Revere; The Wright Brothers.

Bedard, M. (1992). *Emily*. New York: Doubleday Dell Publishing Group.

Graves, C. P. (1966). *John F. Kennedy*. New York: Dell.

Halliburton, W. J. (1984). *The picture life of Jesse Jackson*. New York: Franklin Watts.

Livingston, M. C. (1993). *Abraham Lincoln: A man for all people*. New York: Holiday House.

Montgomery, E. (1971). *Walt Disney: Master of make believe*. Champaign, IL: Garrard Publishing Co.

Quackenbush, R. (1985). *(titles follow)*. Englewood Cliffs, NJ: Prentice Hall.
Ahoy! Ahoy! Are you there? A story of Alexander Graham Bell; Don't you dare shoot that bear! A story of Theodore Roosevelt; Here a plant, there a plant, everywhere a plant, plant! A story of Luther Burbank; Mark Twain? What kind of name is that? A story of Samuel Langhorne Clemens; Quick, Annie give me a catchy line! A story of Samuel F. B. Morse; The Beagle and Mr. Flycatcher: A story of Charles Darwin; What got you started, Mr. Fulton? A story of James Watt and Robert Fulton; What has wild Tom done now!!!? A story of Thomas Alva Edison.

Sutton, F. (1968). *Master of ballyhoo: The story of P. T. Barnum*. New York: Putnam's.

Magazines for Children

Chickadee. Young Naturalist Foundation, 17th and M Streets NW, Washington, DC 20036. (ages 4–8)

Crayola Kids Magazine. Meredith Publishing Service, Box 40025, Des Moines, IA 50340–0425. (ages 3–8)

Cricket. Open Court Publishing Co., Box 100, La Salle, IL 61301. (ages 6–12)

The Dinosaur Times. CSK Publications/B&W Publications, 500 S. Buena Vista Street, Suite 101, Burbank, CA 91521–6018. (all ages)

Ebony, Jr. Johnson Publishing Co., 820 South Michigan Avenue, Chicago, IL 60605. (ages 6–12)

Highlights for Children. 803 Church Street, Honesdale, PA 18431. (ages 2–12)

Let's Find Out. Scholastic Inc., 2931 E. McCarty Street, P. O. Box 3710, Jefferson City, MO 65102–9957. (ages 3–7)

Ranger Rick. National Wildlife Federation, 1412 16th Street NW, Washington, DC 20036. (ages 5–12)

Science Weekly. Claude Mayberry, 2141 Industrial Parkway, Suite 202, Silver Spring, MD 20904. (ages 4–8)

Sesame Street. Children's Television Workshop, One Lincoln Plaza, New York, NY 10023. (ages 3–6)

Stone Soup. Children's Art Foundation, P. O. Box 83, Santa Cruz, CA 95063. (ages 6–12)

Your Big Backyard. National Wildlife Federation, 1412 16th Street NW, Washington, DC 20036. (ages 1–4)

Predictable Books

Repetitive Phrases

Arno, E. (1970). *The gingerbread man.* New York: Scholastic.

Galdone, P. (1970). *The three little pigs.* New York: Seabury Press.

Galdone, P. (1975). *The little red hen.* New York: Scholastic.

Langstaff, J. (1984). *Oh, a-hunting we will go.* New York: Atheneum.

Lobel, A. (1979). *A treeful of pigs.* New York: Greenwillow.

Martin, B. (1967). *Brown bear, brown bear, what do you see?* New York: Holt, Rinehart & Winston.

Piper, W. (1954). *The little engine that could.* New York: Platt & Munk.

Polushkin, M. (1978). *Mother, mother I want another.* New York: Crown.

Raffi. (1989). *Everything grows.* New York: Crown Publishers, Inc.

Sendak, M. (1962). *Chicken soup with rice.* New York: Harper & Row.

Seuling, B. (1976). *Teeny-tiny.* New York: Viking.

Rhyme

Aardema, V. (1981). *Bringing the rain to Kapiti Plain.* New York: Dial Books.

Ahlberg, J. A. (1978). *Each peach pear plum.* New York: Viking.

Bonnie, R. (1961). *I know an old lady.* New York: Scholastic.

Bunting, E. (1994). *Flower garden.* San Diego: Harcourt Brace.

Cameron, P. (1961). *I can't said the ant.* New York: Coward, McCann & Geoghegan.

DeRegniers, B. S. (1968). *Willy O'Dwyer jumped in the fire.* New York: Atheneum.

Emberley, B. (1967). *Drummer Hoff.* Englewood Cliffs, NJ: Prentice Hall.

Fleming, D. (1993). *In the small, small pond.* New York: Henry Holt & Company.

Hoberman, M. A. (1978). *A house is a house for me.* New York: Viking.

Kraus, R. (1970). *Whose mouse are you?* New York: Macmillan.

Lodge, B. (1979). *Rhyming Nell.* New York: Morrow.

Seuss, Dr. (1965). *Fox in socks.* New York: Random House.

Familiar Sequences (days of the week, numbers, letters, months of the year, etc.)

Baum, A., and Baum, J. (1962). *One bright Monday morning.* New York: Random House.

Brown, M. (1957). *The three Billy Goats Gruff.* New York: Harcourt Brace Jovanovich.

Carle, E. (1969). *The very hungry caterpillar.* New York: Philomel.

Carle, E. (1977). *The grouchy ladybug.* New York: Harper Collins.

Keats, E. J. (1971). *Over in the meadow.* New York: Scholastic.

Mack, S. (1974). *10 bears in my bed.* New York: Pantheon.

Roy, R. (1980). *The three ducks went wandering.* New York: Scholastic.

Schulevitz, U. (1967). *One Monday morning.* New York: Scribner's.

Van Allsburg, C. (1987). *The Z was zapped.* Boston: Houghton Mifflin.

Cumulative Patterns (as the story progresses, the previous line is repeated)

Aardema, V. (1975). *Why mosquitos buzz in people's ears.* New York: Dutton.

Emberly, B. (1967). *Drummer Hoff.* Englewood Cliffs, NJ: Prentice Hall.

Guilfoile, E. (1962). *The house that Jack built.* New York: Holt, Rinehart & Winston.

Kent, J. (1971). *The fat cat.* New York: Scholastic.

Lobel, A. (1984). *The rose in my garden.* New York: Greenwillow.

Mayer, M. (1975). *What do you do with a kangaroo?* New York: Scholastic.

McGovern, A. (1967). *Too much noise.* Boston: Houghton Mifflin.

Waber, B. (1966). *"You look ridiculous," said the rhinoceros to the hippopotamus.* Boston: Houghton Mifflin.

Westcott, N. B. (1980). *I know an old lady who swallowed a fly.* Boston: Little, Brown.

Williams, L. (1986). *The little old lady who was not afraid of anything.* New York: Harper Collins.

Stories with Conversation

Freeman, D. (1968). *Corduroy.* New York: Penguin.

Galdone, P. (1972). *The three bears.* New York: Seabury Press.

Hoban, R. (1964). *Bread and jam for Frances.* New York: Harper & Row.

Kellogg, S. (1971). *Can I keep him?* New York: Dial Press.

McGovern, A. (1971). *Stone soup.* New York: Scholastic.

Meddaugh, S. (1992). *Martha speaks.* New York: Houghton Mifflin.

Sharmat, M. (1980). *Gregory, the terrible eater.* New York: Scholastic.

Waber, B. (1966). *"You look ridiculous," said the rhinoceros to the hippopotamus.* Boston: Houghton Mifflin.

Zolotow, C. (1962). *Mr. Rabbit and the lovely present.* New York: Harper & Row.

Books that Foster Critical Discussions

Cannon, J. (1993). *Stellaluna.* Orlando FL: Harcourt Brace.

Galdone, P. (1962). *The hare and the tortoise.* New York: McGraw-Hill.

Lindquist, W. (1970). *Stone soup.* New York: Western Publishing Co., Inc.

Lionni, L. (1973). *Swimmy.* New York: Random House.

Pfister, M. (1992). *The rainbow fish.* New York: North-South Books.

Silverstein, S. (1964). *The giving tree.* New York: Harper & Row.

Viorst, J. (1976). *Alexander and the terrible, horrible, no good, very bad day.* New York: Atheneum.

Werenko, L. (1988). *It Zwibble and the big birthday party.* New York: Scholastic.

Zolotow, C. (1972). *William's doll.* New York: Harper & Row.

Books for Enhancing Listening and Discrimination of Sounds

Brown, M. W. (1939). *The noisy book.* New York: Harper & Row.

Heide, F. (1970). *Sound of sunshine, sound of rain.* New York: Parents' Magazine Press.

Johnston, T. (1973). *Night noises and other mole and troll stories.* New York: Putnam's.

Kaufman, L. (1965). *What's that noise?* New York: Lothrop.

Kuskin, K. (1962). *All sizes of noises.* New York: Harper & Row.

McGovern, A. (1967). *Too much noise.* Boston: Houghton Mifflin.

Perkins, A. (1968). *The ear book.* New York: Random House.

Seuss, Dr. (1970). *Mister Brown can moo: Can you?* New York: Random House.

Showers, P. (1961). *The listening walk.* New York: Thomas Y. Crowell.

Teal, V. (1967). *The little woman wanted noise.* Chicago: Rand McNally.

Books for Building Sound–Symbol Relationships

Consonants

B

Berenstain, S. and J. (1971). *The Berenstain B book*. New York: Random House.

Bottner, B. (1992). *Bootsie Barker bites*. New York: Putnam's.

Calder, L. (1985). *Blast off, barefoot bear!* New York: Tern Enterprises.

Lindenbaum, P. (1992). *Boodil my dog*. New York: Henry Holt & Company.

Moncure, J. (1984). *My "B" sound*. Elgin, IL: Child's World Publishing.

Peet, B. (1977). *Big, bad Bruce*. Boston: Houghton Mifflin.

C (hard)

Berenstain, S. and J. (1972). *C is for clown*. New York: Random House.

Krauss, R. (1945). *The carrot seed*. New York: Scholastic.

Mandel, P. (1994). *Red cat white cat*. New York: Henry Holt & Company.

Rounds, G. (1991). *Cowboys*. New York: Holiday House.

C (soft)

McPhail, D. (1974). *Cereal box*. Boston: Little, Brown.

Wildsmith, B. (1970). *Circus*. New York: Franklin Watts, Inc.

Woodman, J. (1986). *Bossy bear at the circus*. London: Brimax Books.

D

Cole, B. (1994). *Dr. Dog*. New York: Knopf.

Hoff, S. (1994). *Duncan the dancing duck*. New York: Clarion Books.

Lexau, J. (1987). *The dog food caper*. New York: Dial Books.

Moncure, J. (1984). *My "D" sound*. Elgin, IL: Child's World Publishing.

Steig, W. (1982). *Doctor DeSoto*. New York: Farrar, Straus & Giroux.

Zemack, H. and M. (1973). *Duffy and the devil*. New York: Farrar, Straus & Giroux.

F

Littledale, F. (1987). *The farmer in the soup*. New York: Scholastic.

Lobel, A. (1970). *Frog and toad are friends*. New York: Harper & Row.

G (hard)

Buckley, R. (1985). *The greedy python*. New York: Scholastic.

Burningham, J. (1976). *Mr. Grumpy's motor car*. New York: Thomas Y. Crowell.

Galdone, P. (1981). *The three Billy Goats Gruff*. Boston: Houghton Mifflin.

Keats, E. J. (1969). *Goggles*. New York: Collier Books.

Seuss, Dr. (1960). *Green eggs and ham*. New York: Beginner Books.

Sharmat, M. (1984). *Gregory the terrible eater*. New York: Scholastic.

G (soft)

Galdone, P. (1975). *The gingerbread boy*. New York: Clarion Books.

Lionni, L. (1979). *Geraldine, the music mouse*. New York: Random House.

Rey, H. A. (1973). *Curious George*. Boston: Houghton Mifflin. (Other titles in this series include *Curious George rides a bike*, *Curious George goes to the circus*, and *Curious George learns the alphabet*.)

H

Hadithi, M., and Kennaway, A. (1994). *Hungry hyena*. Boston: Little, Brown.

Johnson, C. (1960). *A picture for Harold's room*. New York: Harper & Row.

Kuskin, K. (1979). *Herbert hated being small*. Boston: Houghton Mifflin.

Moncure, J. (1984). *My "H" sound*. Elgin, IL: Child's World Publishing.

Zion, G. (1976). *Harry the dirty dog*. New York: Harper & Row.

J

Cole, J. (1987). *Norma Jean jumping bean*. New York: Random House.

Degan, B. (1983). *Jamberry*. New York: Harper and Row.

Hennessy, B. G. (1990). *Jake baked the cake*. New York: Viking.

Kalan, R. (1981). *Jump frog jump*. New York: Greenwillow Books.

Moncure, J. (1984). *My "J" sound*. Elgin, IL: Child's World Publishing.

Stobbs, W. (1969). *Jack and the beanstalk*. New York: Delacorte.

Whitney, A. (1971). *Just awful*. Reading, MA: Addison-Wesley.

K

Holmelund, M. (1968). *A kiss for little bear*. Harper Trophy.

Maestro, B. and G. (1982). *The key to the kingdom*. New York: Harcourt Brace Jovanovich.

Moncure, J. (1984). *My "K" sound*. Elgin, IL: Child's World Publishing.

Schongut, E. (1983). *Look kitten*. New York: Little Simon.

Wood, A. (1985). *King Bidgood's in the bathtub*. New York: Harcourt Brace Jovanovich.

L

Cosgrove, S. (1985). *Leo the lop*. Los Angeles, CA: Price, Stern & Sloan.

DeRegniers, B. S. (1989). *Laura's story*. New York: Atheneum.

Krauss, R. (1971). *Leo the late bloomer*. New York: Windmill Books, Simon & Schuster.

London, J., and Long, S. (1994). *Liplap's wish*. San Francisco: Chronicle Books.

Moncure, J. (1984). *My "L" sound*. Elgin, IL: Child's World Publishing.

Zolotow, C. (1987). *I like to be little*. New York: Thomas Y. Crowell.

M

Allen, J. (1990). *Mucky moose*. New York: MacMillan Publishing Company.

Bemelmans, L. (1977). *Madeline*. New York: Puffin Books.

Kellogg, S. (1976). *Much bigger than Martin*. New York: Dial Press.

Numeroff, L. J. (1991). *If you give a moose a muffin*. New York: Harper Collins.

Moncure, J. (1984). *My "M" sound*. Elgin, IL: Child's World Publishing.

Wolcott, P. (1974). *Marvelous mud washing machine*. Reading, MA: Addison-Wesley.

N

Brown, M. W. (1939). *The noisy book*. New York: Harper.

Guilfoile, E. (1957). Nobody listens to Andrew. Chicago: Follett.

Masner, J. (1989). *Nicholas Cricket*. New York: Harper and Row.

McGovern, A. (1967). *Too much noise*. Boston: Houghton Mifflin.

Ryland, C. (1986). *Night in the country*. New York: Bradbury Press.

Wezel, P. (1967). *The naughty bird*. Chicago: Follett.

P

Brown, R. (1973). *Pig in the pond*. New York: D. McKay.

DePaola, T. (1978). *The popcorn book*. New York: Holiday House.

Duvoisin, R. (1950). *Petunia*. New York: Knopf.

Keats, E. J. (1972). *The pet show*. New York: Macmillan.

Rockwell, A. (1993). *Mr. Panda's painting*. New York: MacMillan Publishing Company.

Roth, S. (1966). *Pick a peck of puzzles*. New York: Arnold Norton.

Q

Beatty, J. (1967). *The queen wizard*. New York: Macmillan.

Blue, R. (1969). *A quiet place*. New York: Franklin Watts, Inc.

Carle, E. (1990). *The very quiet cricket*. New York: Philomel.

Hurd, T. (1978). *The quiet evening*. New York: Greenwillow Books.

Johnston, T., and DePaola, T. (1985). *The quilt story*. New York: Putnam's.

Zolotow, C. (1963). *The quarreling book*. New York: Harper & Row.

R

DePaola, P. (1992). *Rosie and the yellow ribbon*. Boston: Joy Street Books.

Fisher, A. (1983). *Rabbits, rabbits*. New York: Harper & Row.

Heilbroner, J. (1962). *Robert and rose horse*. New York: Random House.

Kellogg, S. (1981). *A rose for Pinkerton*. New York: Dial Press.

Kent, J. (1982). *Round robin*. Englewood Cliffs, NJ: Prentice Hall.

Sendak, M. (1975). *Really Rosie*. New York: Harper & Row.

Shulevitz, U. (1969). *Rain, rain, rivers*. New York: Farrar, Straus & Giroux.

S

Ayliffe, A. (1992). *Slither, swoop, swing*. New York: Viking.

Brown, M. (1947). *Stone soup*. New York: Scribner's.

Keats, E. J. (1976). *The snowy day*. New York: Puffin Books.

Kessler, E. and L. (1973). *Slush, slush!* New York: Parents Magazine Press.

Lionni, L. (1973). *Swimmy*. New York: Random House.

Stadler, J. (1985). *Snail saves the day*. New York: Thomas Y. Crowell.

T

Birney, B. G. (1994). *Tyrassosaurus Tex*. Boston: Houghton Mifflin Company.

Cosgrove, S. (1984). *Tee-tee*. Vero Beach, FL: Rourke Enterprises, Inc.

Lexau, J. M. (1971). *T for Tommy*. New York: Garrard.

Ness, E. (1965). *Tom tit tot*. New York: Scribner's.

Preston, E. M. (1969). *The temper tantrum book*. New York: Viking.

Seuling, B. (1976). *Teeny-tiny woman*. New York: Viking.

V

Bovetz, M. (1993). *Machines*. Washington: Wright Group.

Carle, E. (1969). *The very hungry caterpillar*. New York: Philomel.

DeArmond, F. U. (1963). *The very, very special day*. New York: Parents' Magazine Press.

Duvoisin, R. (1961). *Veronica*. New York: Knopf.

W

Carlstrom, N. W. (1993). *How does the wind walk?* York: MacMillan Publishing Company.

Keats, E. J. (1964). *Whistle for Willie*. New York: Viking.

Nyblom, H. (1968). *The witch of the woods*. New York: Knopf.

Ross, C. (1993). *The Whirlys and the west wind*. Boston: Houghton Mifflin.

Sendak, M. (1963). *Where the wild things are*. New York: Harper & Row, Publishers.

X

Moncure, J. (1979). *My "X, Y, Z" sound box*. Elgin, IL: Child's World Publishing.

Robbins, J. (1985). *Addie meets Max*. New York: Harper and Row.

Thomas, P. (1979). *There are rocks in my socks said the ox to the fox*. New York: Lee, Lothrop and Shepard.

Y

Marshall, J. (1973). *Yummers*. Boston: Houghton Mifflin.

Seuss, Dr. (1958). *Yertle the turtle and other stories*. New York: Random House.

Z

Modesitt, J., and Johnson, L. S. (1990). *The story of Z*. Boston: Picture Book Studio.

Seuss, Dr. (1950). *If I ran the zoo*. New York: Random House.

Seuss, Dr. (1955). *On beyond zebra*. New York: Random House.

Vowels (long and short)

A

Bayer, J. (1984). *A, my name is Alice*. New York: Dial Press.

Boynton, S. (1983). *A is for angry: An animal and adjective alphabet*. New York: Workman Publishers.

Hiawyn, O. (1982). *Angry Arthur*. New York: Harcourt Brace Jovanovich.

Moncure, J. (1984). *Short a and long a: Play a game*. Elgin, IL: Child's World Publishing.

E

Freschet, B. (1977). *Elephant and friends*. New York: Scribner's.

Kent, J. (1975). *The egg book*. New York: Macmillan.

Milhous, K. (1951). *The egg tree*. New York: Scribner's.

Moncure, J. (1984). *Short e and long e: Play a game*. Elgin, IL: Child's World Publishing.

Rockwell, A. and H. (1985). *The emergency room*. New York: Macmillan.

I

Bonshall, C. (1974). *And I mean it, Stanley*. New York: Harper & Row.

Fischer, A. (1965). *In the woods, in the meadow, in the sky*. New York: Scribner's.

Moncure, J. (1984). *Short i and long i: Play a game*. Elgin, IL: Child's World Publishing.

Oram, H. (1985). *In the attic*. New York: Holt, Rinehart & Winston.

Zolotow, C. (1966). *If it weren't for you*. New York: Harper & Row.

O

Allen, L. J. (1979). *Ottie and the star*. New York: Harper & Row.

Kessler, L. (1976). *Ghosts and crows and things with O's*. New York: Scholastic.

Moncure, J. (1984). *Short o and long o: Play a game*. Elgin, IL: Child's World Publishing.

Thaler, M. (1982). *Owly*. New York: Harper & Row.

U

Moncure, J. (1984). *Short u and long u: Play a game*. Elgin, IL: Child's World Publishing.

Pinkwater, D. (1982). *Umbrellas and parasols*. New York: Dutton.

Yashima, T. (1969). *Umbrella*. New York: Viking.

Digraphs

CH

Archambault, J., and Martin, B. Jr. (1989). *Chicka, chicka boom boom*. New York: Scholastic.

Brown, M. W. (1982). *Little chicken*. New York: Harper & Row.

Hoff, S. (1961). *Little chief*. New York: Harper & Row.

Kwitz, M. (1983). *Little chick's breakfast*. New York: Harper & Row.

Sendak, M. (1962). *Chicken soup with rice*. New York: Harper & Row.

PH

Govan, C. (1968). *Phinny's fine summer*. New York: World Publishing.

SH

Adams, A. (1981). *Shoemaker and the elves*. New York: Macmillan.

Cowley, J. (1990). *Mrs. Wishy Washy*. Bothell, WA: Wright Group.

Cowley, J. (1988). *Shoo*. Bothell, WA: Wright Group.

Kline, S. W. (1984). *SHHH!* New York: Whitman Publishers.

Rogers, P. (1986). *Sheepchase*. New York: Viking.

Shaw, N. (1989). *Sheep on a ship*. Boston: Houghton Mifflin.

TH

Cowley, J. (1987). *One thousand currant buns*. WA: Wright Group.

Loedhas, S. (1962). *Thistle and thyme*. Toronto: Alger.

Word Families

Brown, M. W. (1984). *Goodnight moon*. New York: Harper & Row.

Butler, A., and Neville, P. (1987). *May I stay home today?* Crystal Lake, IL: Rigby.

Cowley, J. (1990). *Dan the flying man*. Bothell, WA: Wright Group.

Patrick, G. (1974). *A bug in a jug*. New York: Scholastic.

Seuss, Dr. (1957). *The cat in the hat*. New York: Random House.

Books for Following Directions

Asche, F. (1976). *Good lemonade*. New York: Franklin Watts, Inc.

Benjamin, C. (1982). *Cartooning for kids*. New York: Thomas Y. Crowell.

Carle, E. (1993). *Draw me a star*. New York: Scholastic.

DePaola, T. (1978). *Pancakes for breakfast*. New York: Harcourt Brace Jovanovich.

Gibbons, G. (1990). *How a house is built*. New York: Scholastic.

Gibbons, G. (1983). *Paper, paper everywhere*. New York: Harcourt Brace Jovanovich.

Hutchins, P. (1968). *Rosie's walk*. New York: Macmillan.

McGovern, A. (1971). *Stone soup*. New York: Scholastic.

Vaughan-Ashton, M. (1984). *Wombat stew*. New York: Scholastic.

Series Books

Allard, H. (1977). *The stupids step out*. Boston: Houghton Mifflin.
The stupids die.
The stupids have a ball.

Bemelmans, L. (1977). *Madeline*. New York: Puffin Books.
Madeline and the gypsies.
Madeline in London.

Freeman, D. (1968). *Corduroy*. New York: Viking.
Corduroy's party.
Corduroy's toys.

Gramathy, H. (1978). *Little Toot*. New York: Putnam's.
Little Toot on the Grand Canal.
Little Toot on the Mississippi.

Hargreaves, R. (1980). *The Mr. Men books*. Los Angeles: Price, Stern & Sloan Publishers.
Mr. Happy, Mr. Noisy, Mr. Impossible.
Mr. Strong, Mr. Small, Mr. Fussy.

Hoban, R. (1976). *Bedtime for Frances*. New York: Harper & Row.
A baby sister for Frances.
Bread and jam for Frances.

Lindgren, B. (1982). *Sam's cookie*. New York: Morrow.
Sam's bath.
Sam's ball.
Sam's teddy bear.

Lobel, A. (1979). *Frog and toad are friends*. New York: Harper & Row.
Frog and toad all year.
Frog and toad together.

Marshall, J. (1972). *George and Martha*. Boston: Houghton Mifflin.
George and Martha encore.
George and Martha rise and shine.

Parish, P. (1970). *Amelia Bedelia*. New York: Scholastic.
Amelia Bedelia goes shopping.
Good work, Amelia Bedelia.

Rey, H. A. (1973). *Curious George*. Boston: Houghton Mifflin.
Curious George flies a kite.
Curious George goes to the circus.

Rylant, C. (1987). *Henry and Mudge, The first book of their adventures*. New York: Bradbury Press.
Henry and Mudge and the bedtime thumps.
Henry and Mudge and the long weekend.

Taylor, M. (1976). *Henry the explorer*. New York: Atheneum.
Henry explores the jungle.
Henry explores the mountains.

Waber, B. (1975). *The house on East 88th Street*. Boston: Houghton Mifflin.
Lyle and the birthday party.
Lyle finds his mother.

Wells, R. (1979). *Max's first words*. New York: Dial Press.
Max's new suit.
Max's ride.

Zion, C. (1976). *Harry the dirty dog*. New York: Harper & Row.
Harry and the lady next door.
Harry by the sea.

Children's Books Related to Themes

All about Me Books

Blaine, M. (1975). *The terrible thing that happened at our house*. New York: Four Winds Press. (realistic literature)

Carlson, N. (1988). *I like me*. New York: Viking Press. (picture book)

Giff, P. (1988). *Ronald Morgan goes to bat*. New York: Viking Press. (picture book)

Hoban, R. (1968). *A birthday for Frances*. New York: Scholastic. (picture book)

Joosse, B. (1989). *Dinah's mad, bad wishes*. New York: Harper & Row. (picture book)

Kalman, B. (1985). *Happy to be me*. New York: Crabtree Publishing Co. (realistic)

Mayer, M. (1988). *Just my friend and me*. Racine, WI: Western Publishing Co., Inc. (picture book)

Parish, P. (1988). *Amelia Bedelia's family album*. New York: Greenwillow Books. (picture book)

Sharmat, M. (1977). *I'm terrific*. New York: Holiday House. (realistic)

Animal Books

Barrett, J. (1970). *Animals should definitely not wear clothing*. New York: Atheneum.

Carle, E. (1989). *Animals animals*. New York: Philomel Books. (poetry)

Crowther, R. (1982). *A jungle jumble*. Kansas City: Hallmark Children's Edition. (wordless moveable book)

Emberly, R. (1986). *Jungle sounds*. Boston: Little, Brown. (audiotape available)

Fox, M. (1988). *Koala Lou*. San Diego: Harcourt Brace Jovanovich.

Mayer, M. (1989). *What do you do with a kangaroo?* New York: Scholastic. (Big Book)

National Wildlife Federation. *Your big backyard*. Washington, DC: National Wildlife Federation. (magazine)

Prelutsky, J. (1983). *Zoo doings*. New York: Greenwillow Books. (poetry)

Tafuri, N. (1988). *Junglewalk*. New York: Greenwillow Books. (wordless)

Dinosaurs

Aliki. (1985). *Dinosaurs are different*. New York: Harper & Row. (informational)

Barton, B. (1989). *Dinosaurs, dinosaurs*. New York: Crowell. (informational)

Brown, M., and Kensky, S. (1982). *Dinosaurs, beware: A safety guide*. Boston: Little, Brown.

DePaola, T. (1990). *Little grunt and the big egg*. New York: Holiday House. (fairytale)

Hennessey, B. G. (1988). *The dinosaur who lived in my backyard*. New York: Viking Press. (picture book)

Hoff, S. (1975). *Dinosaur dos and don'ts*. New York: Windmill Books. (picture book)

Kingdon, J. (1982). *The ABC dinosaur book*. Chicago, IL: Children's Press. (picture book)

Most, B. (1990). *Four & twenty dinosaurs*. New York: Harper & Row. (adapted nursery rhymes)

Prelustky, J. (1988). *Tyrannosaurus was a beast*. New York: Greenwillow Books. (poetry)

Rosenbloom, J. (1987). *The funniest dinosaur book ever*. New York: Sterling.

Rowe, E. (1989). *Giant dinosaurs*. New York: Scholastic. (Big Book)

Ecology

Bash, B. (1989). *Desert giant: The world of the saguaro cactus*. Boston: Little, Brown.

Bloome, E. (1971). *The air we breathe*. Garden City, New York: Doubleday. (informational)

Carle, E. (1987). *The tiny seed*. Saxonville, MA: Picture Book Studio. (picture book)

Cherry, L. (1990). *The great kapok trees: A tale of the amazon rain forest*. San Diego: Harcourt Brace Jovanovich.

Kudlinski, K. (1988). *Rachel Carson, pioneer of ecology*. New York: Viking Kestrel. (biography)

Lionni, L. (1968). *The alphabet tree*. New York: Pantheon Books. (alphabet book)

Peet, B. (1970). *The wump world*. Boston: Houghton Mifflin.

Seuss, Dr. (1971). *The Lorax*. New York: Random House. (picture book)

Tressalt, A. R. (1972). *The dead tree*. New York: Parents' Magazine Press. (picture book)

Udry, J. M. (1956). *A tree is nice*. New York: Harper & Row. (picture book)

Families: Multicultural Books

General Books about Families

Blaine, M. (1975). *The terrible thing that happened at our house*. Illus. J. Walner. New York: Scholastic.

Casey, J. (1991). *Dear Annie*. New York: Greenwillow.

McPhail, D. (1984). *Fix it*. Illus. by author. New York: Dutton Children's Books.

Books about African-American Families

Caines, J. (1982). *Just us women*. Illus. P. Cummings. New York: Harper & Row.

Clifton, L. (1975). *My brother fine with me*. Illus. M. Barnett. New York: Holt.

Mendez, P. (1989). *The Black snowman*. Illus. C. Byard. New York: Scholastic.

Strickland, D., and Strickland, M. (1994). *Families: Poems celebrating the African American experience*. Illus. J. Ward. Honesdale, PA: Boyds Mills Press.

Books about Asian Families

Coutan, H. (1974). *First snow*. Illus. Vo-Dinh. New York: Knopf.

Say, A. (1993). *Grandfather's journey*. Illus. by author. Boston: Houghton Mifflin Co.

Young, A. (1989). *Lon Po Po: A red-riding hood story from China*. Illus. by author. New York: Philomel Books.

Books about Latino Families

Meyer, L. (1993). *Grandma's helper*. Illus. M. Passicot. Glenview, IL: Scott, Foresman and Company.

Mora, P. (1992). *A birthday basket for Tia*. Illus. C. Lang. New York: Macmillan.

Pampa, C. M. (1991). *On the Pampas*. Illus. by the author. New York: Holt.

American Eskimo

Joosse, B. (1991). *Mama, Do you love me?* Illus. by B. Lavallee. New York: Scholastic, Inc.

Ireland

Balian, L. (1980). *Leprechauns never lie*. Illus. by author. Nashville: Abingdon.

DePaola, T. (1989). *Tony's bread*. Illus. by author. New York: Putnam's.

Italy

DePaola, T. (1989). *Tony's bread*. Illus. by author. New York: Putnam's.

Jamaican Family Story

Hoffman, M. (1991). *Amazing Grace*. Illus. C. Binch. New York: Scholastic, Inc.

Jewish Folktale

Gilman, P. *Something from nothing*. Illus. by author. New York: Scholastic, Inc.

Native American Family Folktale

Goble, P. (1980). *The gift of the sacred dog*. Illus. by author. New York: Macmillan.

Russian Family Folktale

Polacco, P. (1990). *Babushka's doll*. Illus. by author. New York: Simon and Schuster.

Five Senses

Adolph, A. (1989). *Chocolate dreams*. New York: Lothrop, Lee & Shephard. (picture book)

Aliki. (1989). *My five senses*. New York: Harper & Row. (informational)

Baum, A. and J. (1962). *One bright Monday morning*. New York: Random House. (picture book)

Gardner, B. (1980). *The turn about, think about, look about book*. New York: Lothrop, Lee & Shepard. (picture book)

Rylant, C. (1988). *All I see*. New York: Orchard Books. (picture book)

Showers, P. (1990). *Ears are for hearing*. New York: Harper & Row. (informational)

Insects and Reptiles

Carle, E. (1984). *The mixed up chameleon*. New York: Crowell. (picture book)

Carle, E. (1986). *The very hungry caterpillar*. New York: Philomel. (Big Book)

Dorros, A. (1987). *Ant cities*. New York: Crowell.

Farber, N. (1979). *Never say ugh to a bug*. New York: Greenwillow. (poetry)

Haberman, M. A. (1976). *Bugs: Poems*. New York: Viking. (poetry)

Mayer, M. (1987). *There's an alligator under my bed*. New York: Dial Books for Young Readers.

National Geographic World. National Geographic Society. Washington, DC. (magazine)

Parker, J. (1988). *I love spiders*. New York: Scholastic. (informational)

Petie, H. (1975). *Billions of bugs*. Englewood Cliffs, NJ: Prentice Hall. (counting/rhymes)

Ryder, J. (1990). *Lizard in the sun*. New York: Morrow Junior Books.

Ocean Life

Anderson, H. C. (1971). *The little mermaid*. New York: Harper & Row. (traditional)

Bowden, J. C. (1979). *Why the tides ebb and flow*. Boston: Houghton Mifflin.

Carle, E. (1987). *A house for a hermit crab*. Saxonville, MA: Picture Book Studio. (informational)

Carle, E. (1989). *Animals animals*. New York: Philomel. (poetry)

Gibbons, G. (1988). *Sunken treasures*. New York: Crowell. (realistic)

Hauser, H. (1984). *Book of marine fishes*. Los Angeles: Petersen Publishing Co. (informational)

Lester, H. (1988). *Tacky the penguin.* Boston: Houghton Mifflin. (picture book)

Peet, B. (1975). *Cyrus the unsinkable sea serpent.* Boston: Houghton Mifflin.

Tokuda, W., and Hall, R. (1986). *Humphrey, the lost whale.* Union City, CA: Heian International. (realistic)

Seasons and Holidays

Autumn

Bridwell, N. (1986). *Clifford's Halloween.* New York: Scholastic. (picture book)

Buscaglia, L. (1982). *The fall of Freddie the leaf.* New York: Holt, Rinehart & Winston. (informational)

Devlin, H., and W. (1971). *Cranberry Thanksgiving.* New York: Parents Magazine Press.

McGovern, A. (1973). *The pilgrim's first Thanksgiving.* New York: Scholastic. (informational)

Nielson-Barsuhn, R. (1985). *In fall.* Chicago: Children's Press. (poetry)

Santrey, L. (1983). *Autumn.* Mahwah, NJ: Troll Associates. (informational/photography)

Stevenson, J. (1986). *Fried feathers for Thanksgiving.* New York: Scholastic. (picture book)

Winter

Brett, J. (1989). *The mitten.* New York: Putnam. (Ukranian folk tale)

Briggs, R. (1985). *The snowman.* Boston: Little, Brown. (wordless picture book)

Frost, R. (1978). *Stopping by woods on a snowy evening.* New York: Dutton. (poetry)

Keats, E. J. (1962). *The snowy day.* New York: Viking. (Big Book)

Kroll, S. (1987). *It's groundhog day!* New York: Scholastic. (picture book)

Prelutsky, J. (1984). *It's snowing! It's snowing!* New York: Greenwillow. (poetry)

Prelutsky, J. (1983). *It's Valentine's Day.* New York: Scholastic. (poetry)

Ziefer, H. (1988). *Snow magic.* New York: Viking Kestrel.

Spring

Allington, R. (1981). *Spring.* Milwaukee: Raintree Children's Books. (informational)

Clifton, L. (1973). *The boy who didn't believe in spring.* New York: Dutton.

Delton, J. (1989). *Spring sprouts.* New York: Young Yealing: Dell. (read aloud)

Holmelund, E. (1989). *It's spring.* New York: Greenwillow. (picture book)

Kalman, B. (1985). *We celebrate spring.* New York: Crabtree Publishing Co. (informational)

Krensky, S. (1990). *Lionel in the spring.* New York: Dial Books for Young Readers. (picture book)

Summer

Garelick, M. (1973). *Down to the beach.* New York: Four Winds Press. (informational)

Kroll, S. (1990). *Gone fishing.* New York: Crown. (picture book)

McCloskey, R. (1976). *Blueberries for Sal.* New York: Puffin Books. (picture book)

Moncure, J. B. (1985). *In summer.* Chicago, IL: Children's Press. (poetry)

Prelutsky, J. (1984). *What I did last summer.* New York: Greenwillow. (poetry)

Robbins, K. (1987). *Beach Days.* New York: Viking Kestrel.

Space

Cole, J. (1990). *The magic school bus lost in the solar system.* New York: Scholastic. (informational)

Keats, E. J. (1981). *Regards to the man in the moon.* New York: Four Winds Press. (picture book)

Krupp, E. C. (1985). *The comet and you.* New York: Macmillan.

Livingston, M. C. (1988). *Space songs.* New York: Holiday House. (poetry)

Muirden, J. (1987). *Going to the moon.* New York: Random House. (informational)

National Air and Space Museum. (1988). *Discovery: A tour of space flight vehicles for children grades pre-school through 3.* Washington, DC: Smithsonian Institution. (informational)

Sadler, M. (1984). *A stair in outer space.* Englewood Cliffs, NJ: Prentice Hall. (picture book)

Schoberle, C. (1986). *Beyond the milky way.* New York: Crown Publishers. (picture book)

Simon, S. (1988). *Galaxies.* New York: Morrow Junior Books.

Children's Literature Related to Cultural Diversity

African-American Books

Cowen-Fletcher, J. (1994). *It takes a village*. New York: Scholastic.

Geraghty, P. (1994). *The hunter*. New York: Crown.

Isadora, R. (1992). *Over the green hills*. New York: Greenwillow.

Mendez, P. (1989). *The black snowman*. New York: Scholastic. (picture book)

San Souci, R. (1989). *The boy and the ghost*. New York: Simon & Schuster. (folklore)

Steptoe, J. (1987). *Mufaro's beautiful daughters*. New York: Lothrop, Lee & Shephard. (folktale)

Asian Books

Birdseye, T. (1990). *A song of stars*. New York: Holiday House. (legend)

Demi. (1991). *The artist and the architect*. New York: Holt.

Mahy, M. (1990). *The seven Chinese brothers*. New York: Scholastic. (legend)

McCoy, K. K. (1993). *A tale of two tengu*. Illinois: Albert Whitman & Company.

Young, E. (1989). *Lon Po Po: A red-riding hood story from China*. New York: Philomel. (folktale)

Latino Books

Dorros, A. (1991). *Tonight is carnival*. New York: Dutton Children's Books.

Ets, M. (1963). *Gilberto and the wind*. New York: Viking.

Everett, L. (1988). *Amigo means friend*. Mahwah, NJ: Troll Associates. (realistic)

Pena, S. (1981). *Kikiriki: Stories and poems in English and Spanish for children*. Houston, TX: Arte Publico. (stories and poems)

Roberts, M. (1986). *Henry Cisneros: Mexican American mayor*. Chicago: Children's Press. (biography)

Native American Books

Bierhorst, J. (1994). *On the road of stars*. New York: MacMillan Publishing Company.

Goble, P. (1990). *Iktomi and the ducks*. New York: Orchard Books. (folk-tale)

Jones, H. (selector). (1971). *The trees stand shining: Poetry of the North American Indians*. New York: Dial. (Indian songs)

Longfellow, H. W. (1983). *Hiawatha*. New York: Dial. (epic poem)

Lyon, G. E., and Catalanotto, P. (1993). *Dreamplace*. New York: Orchard Books.

McDermott, G. (1975). *Arrow to the sun*. New York: Viking Press. (myth)

Children's Literature About Children's Special Needs

Communication Problems (Speech and Language Differences)

Fleischman, P. (1980). *The half-a-moon inn*. New York: Harper & Row.

Flournoy, V. (1985). *The patchwork quilt*. New York: Dial.

Greenfield, E. (1974). *She came bringing me that little baby girl*. Philadelphia, PA: Lippincott.

Hamilton, V. (1985). *The people could fly*. New York: Knopf.

Mathis, S. B. (1975). *The hundred penny box*. New York: Puffin.

Mayer, M. (1976). *Liza Lou and the yellow belly swamp*. New York: Four Winds Press.

Physical Disabilities (visual, hearing, physical)

Visual

Brighton, C. (1984). *My hands, my world*. New York: Macmillan.

Cohen, M. (1983). *See you tomorrow, Charles.* New York: Greenwillow.

Maclachlan, P. (1979). *Through Grandpa's eyes.* New York: Harper & Row.

Yalen, J. (1977). *The seeing stick.* New York: Thomas Y. Crowell.

Hearing

Charlip, R. (1987). *Handtalk birthday: A number and storybook in sign language.* New York: Four Winds Press.

Peterson, J. W. (1984). *I have a sister. My sister is deaf.* New York: Harper & Row.

Riskind, M. (1981). *Apple is my sign.* New York: Harcourt Brace Jovanovich.

Physical

Frevert, P. D. (1983). *It's OK to look at Jamie.* Mankato, MN: Creative Education.

Henriod, L. (1982). *Grandma's wheelchair.* Niles, IL: Whitman.

Honeyman, A. (1980). *Sam and his cart.* St. Paul, MN: EMC.

Rabe, B. (1981). *The balancing girls.* New York: Dutton.

Learning Disabilities

Hermes, P. (1983). *Who will take care of me?* New York: Harcourt Brace Jovanovich.

Hirsch, K. (1977). *My sister.* Minneapolis, MN: Carolrhoda Books.

Ominsky, E. (1977). *Jan O, a special boy.* Englewood Cliffs, NJ: Prentice-Hall.

Sobol, H. (1977). *My brother Stephen is retarded.* New York: Macmillan.

Appendix B

Quality Television Programs with Associated Children's Books

Educational Programs

Sesame Street

Dickson, A. H. (1986). *Grover's bad, awful day.* Racine, WI: Western Publishing Co. in conjunction with Children's Television Workshop.

Hautzey, D. (1986). *It's not fair: A Sesame Street start to read book.* New York: Random House.

Roberts, S. (1981). *Ernie's big mess.* New York: Random House.

Rosenberg-Turow, C. (1985). *Big Bird's day on the farm.* Racine, WI: Western Publishing Co. in conjunction with Children's Television Workshop.

Sommers, T. (1986). *Big Bird goes to the doctor.* Racine, WI: Western Publishing Co. in conjunction with Children's Television Workshop.

Stiles, N., and Wilcox, D. (1974). *Grover and the everything in the whole wide world museum.* New York: Random House.

Mr. Roger's Neighborhood

Rogers, F. (1983). *Mister Rogers' planet purple.* Dallas: Texas Instruments, Inc.

Rogers, F. (1986). *Going to the doctor.* New York: Putnam's.

Rogers, F. (1987). *Making friends.* New York: Putnam's.

Rogers, F. (1988). *No one can ever take your place.* New York: Random House.

Rogers, F. (1988). *When monsters seem real.* New York: Random House.

Rogers, F. (1989). *Going to the dentist.* New York: Putnam's.

Reading Rainbow

Cauley, B. (1979). *The ugly duckling.* New York: Harcourt Brace Jovanovich.

Flack, M. (1961). *The story about Ping.* New York: Viking.

Flourney, V. (1985). *The patchwork quilt.* New York: Dial Press.

Geringer, L. (1985). *A three hat day.* New York: Harper & Row.

Havill, J. (1986). *Jamaica's find.* Boston: Houghton Mifflin.

Lobel, A. (1972). *Frog and toad together.* New York: Harper & Row.

Lyon, D. (1985). *The runaway duck.* New York: Lathrop, Lee & Shepard.

Viorst, J. (1972). *Alexander and the terrible, horrible, no good, very bad day.* New York: Macmillan.

Muppets

Bruce, S. B. (1982). *Gonzo and the giant chicken.* New York: Random House.

Gikow, L. (1985). *Jim Henson presents Goldilocks, Baby Piggy's dream.* New York: Random House.

Kates, L. (1986). *Make believe with the Muppet Babies: A storybook.* New York: Random House.

Muntean, M. (1984). *Muppet Babies through the year.* New York: Random House.

Stevenson, J. (1986). *Bo saves the show.* New York: Random House.

Nickelodeon (cable)

Rey, H. A. (1973). *Curious George*. Boston: Houghton Mifflin.

Rey, H. A. (1977). *Curious George flies a kite*. Boston: Houghton Mifflin.

Rey, H. A. (1985). *Curious George visits the zoo*. Boston: Houghton Mifflin.

Disney (cable)

Chase, A. (1964). *Mary Poppins*. Racine, WI: Western Publishing Co., Inc.

Disney, W. (1950). *Alice in Wonderland*. Racine, WI: Western Publishing Co., Inc.

Gag, W. (1938). *Snow White and the seven dwarfs*. New York: Putnam's.

Knights, H. (1978). *Cinderella*. New York: Random House.

Jim Henson's Mother Goose Stories (The Disney Channel)

(1973). *The Random House book of Mother Goose*. New York: Random House.

Battaglia, A. (1973). *Mother Goose*. New York: Random House.

DePaola, T. (1985). *Tomie dePaola's Mother Goose*. New York: Putnam's.

Storytime (PBS)

Alborough, J. (1993). *Cuddly Dudley*. Cambridge, MA: Candlewick Press.

Brett, J. (1987). *Goldilocks and the three bears*. New York: G. P. Putnam's Sons.

Greenfield, E. (1991). *First pink light*. Black Butterfly Children's Books.

Keats, E. J. (1979). *Maggie and the pirate*. New York: Scholastic, Inc.

The Magic School Bus (PBS)

Cole, J. (1992). *The magic school bus on the ocean floor*. New York: Scholastic.

Cole, J. (1990). *The magic school bus lost in the solar system*. New York: Scholastic.

Cole, J. (1987). *The magic school bus inside the earth*. New York: Scholastic.

Cole, J. (1986). *The magic school bus at the waterworks*. New York: Scholastic.

Madeline (The Family Channel)

Bemelmans, L. (1977). *Madeline*. New York: Puffin Books.

Bemelmans, L. (1977). *Madeline's rescue*. New York: Puffin Books.

Bemelmans, L. (1977). *Madeline and the bad hat*. New York: Puffin Books.

Bemelmans, L. (1977). *Madeline in London*. New York: Puffin Books.

Bemelmans, L. (1977). *Madeline and the gypsies*. New York: Puffin Books.

Charlie Brown

Schulz, C. M. (1976). *It's the Easter beagle, Charlie Brown*. New York: Scholastic.

Schulz, C. M. (1976). *A Charlie Brown Thanksgiving*. New York: Scholastic.

Schulz, C. M. (1976). *Be my valentine, Charlie Brown*. New York: Random House.

Schulz, C. M. (1979). *You're the greatest, Charlie Brown*. New York: Random House.

Schulz, C. M. (1981). *Life is a circus, Charlie Brown*. New York: Random House.

Care Bears (The Disney Channel)

Kahn, P. (1985). *Care Bears try, try again*. New York: Random House.

Katz, B. (1983). *Care Bears book of bedtime poems*. New York: Random House.

Woods, S. B. (1986). *Care Bears cousins mystery adventure*. New York: Random House.

Dumbo's Circus (The Disney Channel)

Razzi, J. (1985). *Dumbo's circus*. New York: Bantam Books.

Walt Disney Productions. (1988). *Dumbo*. Racine, WI: Western Publishing Co., Inc.

Walt Disney Productions. (1987). *Dumbo and the magic feather*. Racine, WI: Western Publishing Co., Inc.

The New Adventures of Winnie the Pooh (The Disney Channel)

Calmenson, S. (1994). *Winnie the Pooh and Tigger too*. New York: Disney Press.

Milne, A. A. (1993). *Pooh and Piglet go hunting*. New York: Dutton.

Milne, A. A. (1993). *Pooh goes visiting*. New York: Dutton.

Milne, A. A. (1957). *The world of Pooh*. New York: Dutton.

Books Featured as Television Specials

Andersen, H. C. (1986). *Ugly duckling*. New York: Knopf.

Andersen, H. C. (1979). *Thumbelina*. New York: Dial Press.

Baum, F. (1984). *The Wizard of Oz*. New York: Random House.

Chase, A. (1957). *How the Grinch stole Christmas*. New York: Random House.

Gag, W. (1938). *Snow White and the seven dwarfs*. New York: G. P. Putnam's Sons.

Gladone, P. (1985). *Rumpelstiltskin*. New York: Clarion Books.

Knights, H. (1978). *Cinderella*. New York: Random House.

Lofting, H. (1920). *The story of Doctor Doolittle*. New York: Lippincott.

Ormerod, J. (1990). *The frog prince*. New York: Lothrop, Lee & Shepard.

Rowland, J. R. (1989). *The elves and the shoemaker*. Chicago: Contemporary Books.

Seuss, Dr. (1971). *The Lorax*. New York: Random House.

Tolkien, J. R. (1984). *The Hobbit*. Boston: Houghton Mifflin.

Wilder, L. I. (1935). *Little house on the prairie*. New York: Harper & Row.

Appendix C

Computer Software Designed to Promote Literacy Development and Creativity

Preschool Parade   **Grade: K–1**

Description: Children work with clowns and animals to learn the alphabet, counting, shapes, and more.

Hardware: MacPlus or higher; 1MB RAM; System 6.07 or later; hard drive; sound card recommended

Availability: Nordic Software

Stickybear's Reading Room   **Grade: PreK–2**

Description: This bilingual program in Spanish and English includes activities in sentence building, word matching, and word finding.

Hardware: System 6.07 with 2MB RAM or System 7 with 4MB RAM; color monitor

Availability: Optimum Resource

Storybook Weaver   **Grade: K–12**

Description: This software allows students to create stories of Arabian Knights, African Tribesmen, and Indian Weavers.

Hardware: System 6.07 or later; 1MB for black and white; 2MB for color; 4MB for System 7

Availability: MECC

Storybook Maker   **Grade: K–3**

Description: Students use this program to create stories, edit work, illustrate, and read.

Hardware: Mac LC or higher; 4MB RAM; (5MB Recommended); System 7; 12" color monitor; CD ROM drive

Availability: Conter Software

Community Exploration   Grade: 1–12 (ESL, Sp. Ed.)

Description: This software increases student vocabulary while presenting interesting locations within the community.

Hardware: 4MB RAM (5MB is recommended for best performance); MAC LC or better; System 7; 12" color monitor; CD ROM drive

Availability: Jostens Home Learning

Reader Rabbit 1   Grade: PreK–1

Description: This software helps to establish letter recognition, spelling patterns, and early vocabulary.

Hardware: Hard drive System 6.0 or later

Availability: The Learning Company

Creative Writer   Grade: 3–9 (Sp. Ed.)

Description: Developed with direct input from teachers, parents, and children, this software was designed for creating stories, poetry, cards, and a lot more.

Hardware: Mac hard drive and 4MB for color or Systems 7.0 or higher; Windows 386 or higher; hard drive, mouse and VGA or better; 4MB preferred

Availability: Microsoft Corp.

Wiggleworks   Grade: K–2

Description: Three stages in this program offer classroom literacy development activities based on a variety of levels. This package offers trade books and software for interactive reading, writing, and letter exploration.

Hardware: Color Mac; 4MB; hard disk; CD ROM drive optional; 7.0 System or higher; microphone, speakers, and printer recommended

Availability: Scholastic Inc.

Storybook Theatre   Grade: 1–4

Description: Students can create animated stories while experimenting with characters, settings, animation, sound effects, and words.

Hardware: Color Mac and hard drive 2MB; System 7.0, 4MB required

Availability: Learningways, Inc.

A Field Trip to the Sky   Grade: 2–10

Description: Students take a trip through the solar system and beyond. Interactive sun and moon labs. Literacy is developed across content areas.

Hardware: Color MAC and CD ROM required; 4MB Windows 3.1 or higher, color monitor, and CD ROM required

Availability: Sunburst Communications

Appendix D

Suggestions for the Instructors: Assignments, In-Class Activities, and the Confusabet Lesson

Literacy Development in the Early Years: Helping Children Read and Write was written for students in graduate and undergraduate classes in courses such as Early Literacy Development and Reading in the Elementary School, or in an Early Childhood Curriculum course that includes literacy development as a major component. The book can also be used for staff development courses for classroom teachers.

The book suggests several activities to do with students. I'd like to highlight a few that I have used successfully in class sessions or as assignments.

At the beginning of each chapter are focus questions that students should read prior to reading the chapter. At the end of every chapter are activities contributed by classroom teachers that relate to the chapter. In addition, there are activities to engage in as well as case studies to work out. Read the cases and the activities; you might find that some of them are appropriate for class interaction in small groups and for discussion.

Activities to participate in as you work your way through the book are as follows:

1. Chapter 2 suggests that each student start his or her own portfolio of class work. Included in the portfolio should be the instructor's assignments. As students do assignments, they collect the work in the portfolio and record grades. Teachers should meet with each student once a semester to conference about his or her progress, and review the portfolios.

2. In Chapter 2 it is suggested that students select a child that they can study as they read the book. The child should be between the ages of 2 and 8 years. The student is to begin a portfolio for the child, and meet with him or her from time to time, to try strategies and assess and describe certain behaviors. Specifically, the students should obtain a sample of writing, drawing, oral language,

and a story retelling from the child. In addition, several of the measures provided in the book can be used to accumulate data about the child. For example:

a. When studying the family, interview the child's parents with the form concerning the home literacy environment found in Chapter 3.

b. When reading Chapter 4 on language development, collect a language sample and analyze it for sentence length and number of different words. To elicit language from a child, ask him or her to tell you about family, pets, TV shows they like, or games they play. Tape record the discussion and transcribe it for analysis.

c. When reading Chapter 6, interview the child using the form in that chapter that evaluates motivation for reading and writing.

d. When reading Chapter 7, have the child retell a story read to them. Tape record the retelling and transcribe it. Analyze it with the retelling instrument in the chapter. Children can also be asked to rewrite the story. The rewriting can be analyzed with the same tool.

e. In Chapter 8, evaluate the child's knowledge about print with the checklist included.

f. In Chapter 9, collect a writing sample from the child to determine the stage of writing, and analyze it for sense of story structure, the mechanics of writing, etc. To elicit a writing sample you might have the child draw a picture and write about it. Talk about ideas to write before writing. For emergent writers, assure them that any way they can write is fine. Show them samples of children's writing from the text for them to see that one letter or scribble writing is fine.

3. At least three or four times during the semester, have the class break up into groups to deal with one of the cases presented at the end of the chapters. Have the students solve the problem presented, and have them relate their findings to the group. Compare the differences in solutions. A case that will generate a good deal of discussion is the one in Chapter 7 about Teachers A, B, and C. Have the students respond to the questions posed about the teachers, and discuss which teacher each would wish to be. The students must select one. Discuss the pros and cons of each of the teachers in the case.

4. Have students keep dialogue journals about readings that have made an impression on them. They can also include incidents in class that were particularly interesting, fun, or of concern. Respond to their journals with comments of your own.

5. Have your students take a vocabulary test, using words from the glossary. Teachers need to be aware of the technical language associated with early literacy when talking with peers, interviewing for a job, and explaining issues to parents.

6. Have students bring five genres of children's literature to class to share in groups. This gives them the opportunity to browse through lots of books and

see the variety of genres available. Set the books up as if they were going into a classroom. This will give a sense of the numbers and types of books that should be in a literacy center.

7. Ask students to draw a floor plan for their ideal classroom using the philosophy and strategies learned. Pay particular attention to the literacy center. Be sure they create plans to support literacy instruction for whole groups, small groups, and one-to-one settings.

8. Ask each student to be involved in a storytelling project. Give students a list of early literacy skills from those outlined on the checklists provided in the book. Have them select a skill they would like to teach. Ask them to find a picture story book that will enable that skill to be taught. For example, if their skill is to teach sequencing, a story such as *The Old Lady Who Swallowed the Fly* provides a sequence of events that are easily followed. The student then selects a technique for storytelling from those described in Chapter 6, such as a chalk talk, roll story, felt story, or other techniques they create themselves. A lesson plan is developed in which the teacher will present the story and teach the skill through the use of the material created. The material is designed for children to use to practice the skill taught. In Chapter 6 the Idea from the Classroom for the Classroom concerning the story *A Bunny Called Nat* illustrates this type of assignment. Students present the storytelling in class.

9. Have the students select a group to work with. Have the group select a topic for a thematic unit. Using the guide for the unit in Chapter 10, divide up the sections and prepare a thematic unit for a classroom of children from ages 2 through 8 years.

10. Have students participate in a teacher researcher project. Each student will select a topic dealing with early literacy, and carry out a mini-study. The study should include a statement of purpose, a short literature review related to the topic, a description of methods and procedures to follow during the study, a discussion of how the data will be analyzed, a report of the results of the data collection, and a discussion concerning the results. This is a large project that is introduced to students early in the semester in order for them to have ample time to carry it out. When writing the literature review, the students should be required to consult a few articles from professional journals. Some topics for study are: literacy and play, computers and early literacy, family literacy, multicultural concerns in early literacy, and early intervention programs.

11. Have students bind their own books based on the directions given in Chapter 9. Have them use the book for their dialogue journal or for writing their storytelling lesson plan.

12. Encourage students to join a professional organization such as the International Reading Association or the National Association of the Education of Young Children.

13. Encourage your students to subscribe to a professional journal and a commercial teacher magazine.

14. Encourage students to read a good book, go to cultural events, or participate in other enriching activities. This will make them more interesting people to be with.

15. For the type of information presented in the course, I think a take-home test is most appropriate. Questions can be selected by the instructor from those asked in the activities at the end of the chapter.

16. One important activity to offer your students is to let them experience what it would be like to be a child learning to read. For this demonstration, I am providing you with materials and a plan for a class experience. This activity should take about 45 minutes of class time and should be done early in the semester when you are teaching theory. The lesson involves learning how to read with an alphabet called the *Confusabet*. Following is a plan for carrying out the Confusabet. Materials needed are provided in this Appendix. You can photocopy them for use in your lesson plan before beginning the lesson or use the pages in the book.

The Confusabet Lesson

Objective: to experience how it feels to learn to read and write for a better understanding of the process and how children feel when they are learning.

Materials

Confusabet Alphabet and translation
Confusabet sight words and their translation
Confusabet worksheets
Confusabet reading book and translation (books must be assembled)

Procedures

1. Prior to beginning the lesson, ask students to think about and write down the following during the experience:
   a. What methods were used to teach reading? Which were good and which were not particularly good?
   b. What emotions did you experience while learning to read and write the Confusabet?
   c. What strategies did you use to teach yourself how to read and write?
2. Hand out or turn to the Confusabet alphabet and pictures that have the names of the Confusabet characters on them.
3. Name the characters and have the students repeat their names.

4. Hand out or turn to worksheet #1. Ask students to find the character's name among other Confusabet words.

5. Hand out or turn to the list of Confusabet words. Provide students with context clues for each word to help them figure out what it says. For example: The color of the traffic light that means you should stop is _____. Have the students fill in the word and point to the Confusabet word that is red. Context clues are provided in the translations at the end of Appendix D.

6. Do this for all words and provide your own context clues.

7. Repeat the words with the students. You may repeat them all together, call on those who raise their hands, and call on students who do not raise their hands.

8. Turn to or hand out worksheet #2 with the Confusabet words just introduced and ask students to underline and name the word in each list that is the same as the first word at the top of the list.

9. Turn to or distribute the Confusabet primer. Call on students to read a line or a page at a time. Try round robin reading as well.

   During the Confusabet lesson, role-play as if you are a teacher of 6-year-olds. Praise students for doing well. Do some positive reinforcing and use some positive teaching techniques. Try techniques that are often used and words that are often said to students that are punitive, such as: "If you don't get this work correct you won't get to take the book home to your parents" or "You weren't listening; that's why you don't know the words" or "If you don't stop talking, you'll be sent to the principal's office."

   During the Confusabet exercise, students will talk to each other naturally to try and work things out. When this happens, say: "Please do your own work and keep your eyes on your own paper" or " Don't help each other; you have to learn to do it yourself" or "It's too noisy in here" and "We can't wait for you even though you haven't finished your work." When students have answers and are very anxious to give them say: "You've already had your turn; give someone else a chance" or "Please settle down; you are disrupting the rest of the class." When students look ahead to preview materials handed out, say, "Please wait for me to tell you when to turn the page" or "Don't go ahead of me, we aren't up to that yet." This type of role-playing allows students to experience even more how children feel in the classroom, where these types of comments often occur.

10. After reading the Confusabet materials, ask students to write their names and then the sentence: "I like to read and write," with Confusabet symbols.

11. At the end of the lesson ask the questions posed at the beginning:
    a. What methods did I use that were good? What methods did I use that were not very good?

    b. What emotions did you experience?
    c. How did you teach yourself to learn to read?
    d. How did you go about learning to write?

Students will express that they experienced fear, anger, and frustration when they were having trouble. They will suggest that they wanted to tune out and not participate. Those who were succeeding will suggest that they were excited, they wanted to continue, and they wanted to share their excitement. Frequently students who are succeeding will be greeted with remarks such as "You've already had a turn, settle down and let me give someone else a chance." When asked how they felt about this response, they will say that their excitement was drained.

When students discuss the strategies they used to learn to read, they will often make comments similar to the following:

1. I used my past experience with knowledge from our real alphabet to help. For example, the Confusabet words have the same number of symbols as our alphabet. They also resemble some of the letters of our alphabet and I was able to make associations.
2. I used the picture clues.
3. I used surrounding words or the context to figure out the word. (contextual and syntactic clues)
4. I memorized symbols from one page to the next to try and remember.
5. Some words were long or had an unusual shape, which helped me to get a word. (configuration)
6. I looked at the first letter of a word to give me help in figuring it out.

When students are asked some of the things they did to help them read they may say:

1. I pointed to the print to help me find my place.
2. I moved my eyes around the page to try and find clues.
3. I called out words one at a time, the way young children do.

What the students realize as a result of participating in the Confusabet experience is that they look to meaning, past experience, associative strategies, and visual clues to figure out the words, more than they do individual skills such as phonics.

The Confusabet lesson presented here is adapted from materials created by Mildred Letton Wittock from the University of Chicago.

Confusabet Alphabet Letters

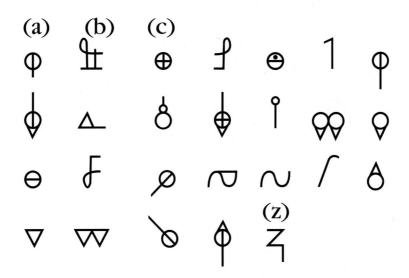

(a) (b) (c)

Confusabet Story Characters

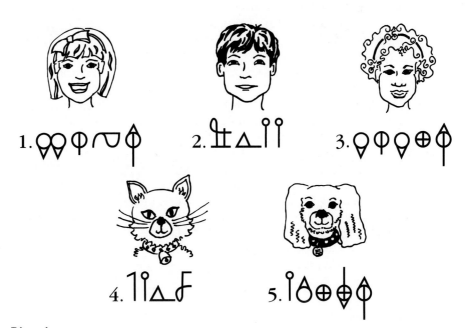

Directions:
Instructor names the characters for the students. Students repeat the names.

Confusabet Vocabulary Words

1. ⣉φ⌒φ 2. ♁△⦚ 3. ♀φ♀⊕φ

4. ⦚△ƒ 5. ⦚♁⊕φφ 6. ⌒⊖⊖

7. ⊕⊖⣉⊖ 8. ▸▴▪ 9. ⌒⊖ƭ

10. φ♁/⊖⣉⊖♁△⦚⊖ 11. ⌒♁♀

12. ⦚♁♀♀φ 13. ♁ƒ 14. ♁♁⣉ƒ

15. φ⊖ 16. ⦚⊖⊖φ 17. φ⊖♁

18. φ/ 19. /φ⊖ 20. △/

21. △⌒ 22. /φ⊖⣉ 23. ⊕φ♀

24. φ♀ƭ 25. ⊖φ 26. ⦚♁♀

Directions:
Instructor gives a context clue for each word to help student to read it. Students repeat the words. Clues are on page 397.

Confusabet Worksheet 1

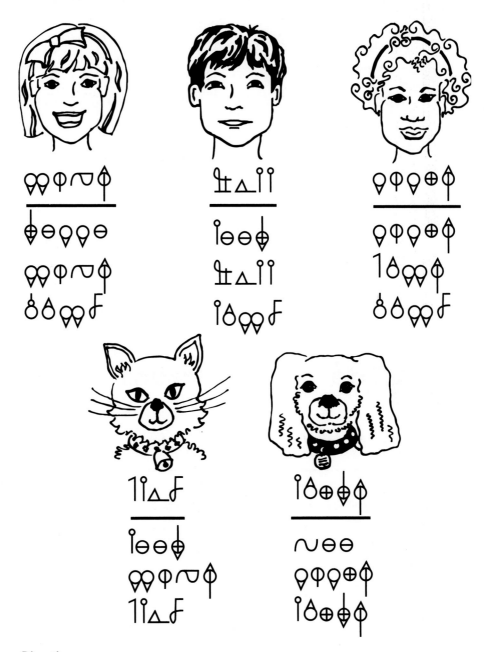

Directions:

Circle the name of the character in the list of words under his or her name, say the name as you circle it.

Confusabet Worksheet 2

Directions:
Circle the underlined word in each column. Say the word as you circle it.

Confusabet Primer

Confusabet Story #1

Confusabet Story #2

Confusabet Story #3

‌1ꟾΔϝ ϙϙ⅃ ꟾઠⴲϕϕ

ⴲϴꟼⵕϴ 1ꟾΔϝ. ⴲϴꟼⵕϴ ꟾઠⴲϕϕ.

ⴲϴꟼⵕϴ ϙϙ⅃ ∿ϴϴ.

ⴲϴꟼⵕϴ ϙϙ⅃ ∿ϴϴ ⌿ϕϴ
ϙઠ⌿ϴꟼϴⵕΔꟾϴ.

ⴲϴꟼⵕϴ ϙϙ⅃ ∿ϴϴ ⌿ϕϴ ∿ϴ⅃
ϙઠ⌿ϴꟼϴⵕΔꟾϴ.

ⴲϴꟼⵕϴ 1ꟾΔϝ. ⴲϴꟼⵕϴ ꟾઠⴲϕϕ.
ꟾϴϴϕ ϙϙ⅃ ∿ϴϴ.

Confusabet Story #4

[Confusabet script text — lines of symbolic characters]

Confusabet Story #5

[Confusabet script text — lines of symbolic characters]

Confusabet Translations

**1. Story Character Names 2. Vocabulary Translations with Context Clue Sentences
3. Story Translations for Primer**

Story Character Names

1. Mary, 2. Bill, 3. Nancy, 4. Flip, 5. Lucky

Vocabulary Translations with Context Clue Sentences

6. see- With my eyes I _____.
7. come- Please _____ over here.
8. (comma) ,   (period) .   ? (question mark)
9. red- The top color light on a traffic signal is _____.
10. automobile- Another name for a car is an _____.
11. run- When I go fast on my feet I _____.
12. funny- A clown is _____.
13. up- When we take off in an airplane we go _____.
14. jump- When I play with a rope I _____ up.
15. go- The green traffic light means for us to _____.
16. look- A word that rhymes with book and means to see is _____.
17. you- Not me but _____.
18. at- Come and look _____ it.
19. the- _____ red automobile.
20. it- Let's get into _____.
21. is- It _____ fun to ride in.
22. them- I'm going over there to be with _____.
23. can- Yes I _____.
24. and- Come _____ play with me.
25. oh- When I am surprised I say _____.
26. fun- When I play with my friend I have _____.

Story Translations for Primer

Primer Title — *Look and See*

Story #1— *Bill*
Look at Bill.
Look at Bill jump.
Look at Bill jump up.
Jump up, jump up.

Story #2— *Nancy and Bill and Mary*
Look Bill, Look Mary.
See Nancy.
Look and see Nancy.
Funny funny Nancy.

Story #3— *Flip and Lucky*
Come Flip Come Lucky
Come and see
Come and see the automobile
Come and see the red automobile
Come Flip, come Lucky, Look and See.

Story #4— *The Red Automobile*
Look at the red automobile.
Come and look at it.
It is fun. Look at it.

Story #5— *(Without pictures)*
Jump up and run Flip.
Jump up and run Bill.
Look Mary. Can you see them?

Glossary

aesthetic talk   A form of conversation revolving around narrative literature in which children interpret and discuss what has been heard or read in relation to themselves.

aliterate   An individual who can read but chooses not to.

alphabetic understanding   Knowing that words are composed of letters.

auditory discrimination   The ability to hear, identify, and differentiate among familiar sounds,   similar sounds, rhyming words, and letter sounds.

authentic assessment   Assessment based on activities that represent and reflect the actual learning and instruction in the classroom.

balanced perspective to literacy instruction   The selection of theory and strategies to match learning styles of children. Constructivist and explicit strategies are both used.

behaviorist approach   A learning theory in which adults provide a model and children learn through imitation encouraged by positive reinforcement.

big books   Oversized books designed to allow children to see the print as it is being read.

buddy reading   The pairing of a child from an upper grade with a younger child for storybook reading.

comprehension   An active process whereby a reader interprets and constructs meaning about the text based on prior knowledge and experience.

conference   Meeting with the teacher or peer to discuss work in progress.

consonant blends   Two or three letters that, when placed together, merge into one sound while retaining representations of each letter sound (e.g., *bl* or *str*).

constructivist theory   A theory that views learning as an active process where children construct knowledge to learn by problem solving, guessing, and approximating.

context clues   The use of syntax and semantic meaning of text to aid in word identification.

contracts   Assignment sheets designating specific activities to be carried out by individual learners based on their needs, interests, and ability levels.

cooperative learning   An instructional strategy in which children come together to learn through debate and discussion.

cryptoanalytic intent   Knowing there is a relationship between printed letters and the spoken sound.

cultural diversity   Reference to the wide variety of backgrounds, languages, customs, and environments represented within the larger society or a given classroom.

decoding   Identifying words by using letter-sound and structural analysis.

digraph   Two letters that, when placed together, make a new sound unlike the sound of either individual letter (e.g., *th* or *ch*).

directed listening/reading and thinking activity (DLTA/DRTA)   A framework which offers directions and strategies for organizing and retrieving information from a text that is read by or to a child. The steps in DLTA or DRTA include preparation for listening/reading with prequestions and discussion, setting a purpose for reading, reading the story, and a follow-up postreading discussion based on the purpose set prior to reading.

early intervention   Programs, for children with special needs or those who are "at risk," in early childhood education intended to prevent potential problems in literacy development. The focus of the programs is on developmentally appropriate instruction using authentic reading and writing experiences.

efferent talk   A formal mode of conversation about expository text used to inform and persuade.

emergent literacy   As coined by Marie Clay, refers to a child's early unconventional attempts at reading, writing, and listening.

engagement perspective   A description of readers who have reached their fullest potential; readers who are strategic, social, knowledgeable, and motivated.

environmental print   Familiar print found in the surroundings such as logos, food labels, and road signs.

explicit instruction   A teacher-directed strategy with emphasis on teaching a task and the specific steps needed to master it.

family literacy Refers to the different ways in which family members initiate and use literacy in their daily living.

functional print Print for a purpose such as informational signs, directions, greeting cards, lists, letters to pen pals, and messages for the notice board.

gifted Demonstrating exceptional ability.

graphemes Letters that make up individual sounds.

inclusion Special help and enrichment are offered in the regular classroom with the help of resource teachers and regular teachers planning together and teaching all children. This is in place of or in addition to pull out programs for special help.

independent reading and writing periods (IRWP) A socially interactive time wherein children select among books and other literacy-related materials.

integrated language arts An approach to literacy instruction that links reading, writing, listening, and language skills.

interdisciplinary literacy instruction Integration of content-area learning with literacy.

intergenerational literacy initiatives Planned, systematic programs specifically designed to improve the literacy development of both adults and children.

invented spelling Improvised spelling for words unknown in conventional spelling wherein one letter often represents an entire syllable.

journal writing Written entries in notebooks by children including: *dialogue,* which is shared with teachers or peers who respond to what they read; *personal,* involving private thoughts related to children's lives or topics of special interest; *reading response,* writing in response to text reading; and *learning log,* a record of information usually involving other content areas.

K-W-L A cognitive strategy that enhances comprehension by assessing with students what they *K*now, what they *W*ant to know, and what they *L*earned before and after reading.

language experience approach (LEA) A reading instruction method aimed at linking oral with written language on the premise that what is thought can be said, what is said can be written, and what is written can be read.

learning centers Spaces in the classroom filled with materials for independent student activity focusing on current topics of study within content areas and including literacy materials as well.

learning disabled Demonstrating significant difficulty in the acquisition and use of reading, writing, listening, speaking, and/or mathematical skills.

literacy center A classroom area composed of a library corner and writing area.

literature-based instruction An approach to teaching reading in which varied genres of children's literature are used as the main source of reading material.

literature circles Discussion groups used to encourage critical discussions about literature among children.

literature genre A specific type of literature such as picture storybook, informational book, or poetry.

mainstreaming Placing children with special needs in regular classroom settings for part or all of the school day to provide social and instructional integration.

mapping and webbing Strategies for understanding text through the use of graphic representations for categorizing and structuring information. Maps deal with more detailed representations.

mental imagery Visualization of readings used to increase comprehension and clarify thought.

metacognition Awareness of one's own mental processes concerning how learning takes place.

morning message A daily message about items of interest to children written by the teacher who points out concepts about print.

narrative writing Writing stories.

nonstandard English A dialectal form of English that differs from the standard form in words, syntax, and language patterns.

parent-involvement programs Programs designed to involve and inform parents about activities that will promote their children's literacy development in school.

partner reading Peers reading together either simultaneously side by side or taking turns reading to each other.

phonemes Sounds made by individual letters and combinations of letters that make a single sound.

phonemic awareness Knowing that words are composed of a sequence of spoken sounds that have no isolated meaning and being able to hear those sounds.

phonics A strategy that involves learning the alphabetic principles of language and knowledge of letter-sound relationships. Children learn to associate letters with the phonemes or basic speech sounds of English, to help them break the alphabetic code and become independent readers in the pronunciation of words.

portfolio assessment A strategy for measuring student progress by collecting samples of their work that is placed into a folder called a portfolio. Materials include: samples of student's written work or drawings, anecdotal records, audiotapes, videotapes, checklists, teacher-made and standardized test results, among others.

process approach to writing Steps involved in the production of text including prewriting, drafting, conferencing, revising, editing, and performing.

pull out programs Students are taken out of their classrooms for special help in literacy instruction or enrichment.

reading readiness Various skills considered prerequisite in learning to read such as auditory discrimination, visual discrimination, and motor skills.

reading recovery An early intervention program devised by Marie Clay in which first graders experiencing difficulties with reading receive intensive, one-on-one instruction using developmentally appropriate integrated Language Arts techniques.

reading and writing workshop A large block of time in which children have the opportunity to read and write with peers, and experience instructional guidance from the teacher.

rich literacy environments Environments rich with materials that encourage reading and writing and support instruction.

scaffolding A strategy in which teachers provide children with modeling and support to help them acquire a skill.

semantics Meaning that language communicates.

shared book experiences Whole- or small-group reading instruction through literature selections, in which Big Books are often used so that children can see the print and pictures. Big Books enable children to listen and participate in actual book readings.

standardized tests An assessment measure, commercially prepared and norm-referenced, that reports results in terms of grade level scores and percentile ranks.

story retellings The recital of familiar stories, in children's own words, in written or oral form to develop and assess comprehension of story.

story structure The elements of a well-constructed story including setting, theme, plot episodes, and resolution.

sustained silent reading (SSR) A time allocated for children to read silently.

syntax The structure of language or rules that govern how words work together in phrases, clauses, and sentences.

telegraphic language A form of speech used by children at about twelve months of age in which content words, such as nouns and verbs, are used, for example "Mommy cookie," but function words, such as conjunctions and articles, are omitted.

thematic unit A topic of study is learned through explorations across all areas of the curriculum.

think, pair, share A discussion strategy that combines think time with cooperative learning. Following teacher-posed questions, the teacher first has children *think* about their answers; then children *pair* with a partner to discuss their responses; and finally, during *share,* the students share responses with the group.

t-unit An independent clause with all its dependent clauses attached that is helpful in measuring a child's language complexity.

very own words Favorite words generated by children, written on index cards, and kept in a container for them to read and write.

visual discrimination The ability to note similarities and differences visually between objects, including the ability to recognize colors, shapes, and letters.

whole language A philosophy from which strategies are drawn for literacy development. Strategies include the use of real literature, with the concurrent instruction of reading, writing, and oral language in meaningful, functional, and cooperative contexts, to help students become motivated to read and write.

word analysis skills Knowledge about print including the use of context and syntax to decipher unknown words; the development of sight vocabulary; and the use of word configuration, structural analysis, and phonics.

writing mechanics Skills related to writing such as spelling, handwriting, punctuation, and spacing.

zone of proximal development Based on Vygotsky's theory, this term refers to the period of time when a child has been guided by an adult and no longer needs the help. The adult retreats and allows the child to work on his or her own.

The Glossary was composed with the help of:

Erica Erlanger, Patricia DeWitt, Katherine Heiss, Pamela Kelliher, Lisa Lozak, Monica Saraiya and Connie Zauderer.

Bibliography

Adams, M. J. (1990). *Beginning to read: Thinking and learning about print.* Urbana: University of Illinois Center for the Study of Reading.

Allen, R. V. (1976). *Language experience in communication.* Boston: Houghton Mifflin.

Altwerger, A., Diehl-Faxon, J., and Dockstader-Anderson, K. (1985). Reading aloud events as meaning construction. *Language Arts, 62,* 476–484.

Anderson, R. C., Fielding, L. G., and Wilson, P. T. (1988). Growth in reading and how children spend their time outside of school. *Reading Research Quarterly, 23,* 285–303.

Anderson, R. C., Hiebert, E. H., Scott, J. A., and Wilkinson, I. A. G. (1985). *Becoming a nation of readers.* Washington, DC: National Institute of Education.

Anderson, A., and Stokes, S. (1984). Social and institutional influences on the development and practice of literacy. In H. Goelman, A. Oberg, and F. Smith (Eds.), *Awakening to literacy.* Exeter, NH: Heinemann Educational Books.

Anderson, R. C., Wilson, P. T., and Fielding, L. G. (1985, December). A new focus on free-reading. Symposium presentation at the National Reading Conference, San Diego.

Andrews, G. (1954). *Creative rhythmic movement for children.* Englewood Cliffs, NJ: Prentice Hall.

Applebee, A. N. and Langer, J. A. (1983). Instructional scaffolding: Reading and writing as natural language activities. *Language Arts, 60,* 168–175.

Applebee, A. N., Langer, J. A., and Mullis, M. (1988). *Who reads best? Factors related to reading achievement in grades 3, 7, and 11.* Princeton, NJ: Educational Testing Service.

Ashton-Warner, S. (1959). *Spinster.* New York: Simon & Schuster.

Ashton-Warner, S. (1963). *Teacher.* New York: Bantam.

Auerbach, E. (1989). Toward a social-contextual approach to family literacy. *Harvard Educational Review, 56,* 165–181.

Baghban, M. (1984). *Our daughter learns to read and write.* Newark, DE: International Reading Association.

Baumann, J. F. (1984). The effectiveness of a direct instruction paradigm for teaching main idea comprehension. *Reading Research Quarterly, 20,* 93–115.

Bauman, J. F. (1992). Effect of think aloud instruction on elementary students' comprehension monitoring abilities. *Journal of Reading Behavior, 24* (2), 143–172.

Bergeron, B. (1990). What does the term whole language mean? A definition from the literature. *Journal of Reading Behavior, 23,* 301–329.

Biehler, R. F. (1976). *Child development: An introduction.* Boston: Houghton Mifflin.

Birnbaum, J., and Emig, J. (1983). Creating minds: Created texts. In R. Parker and F. Davis (eds.), *Developing literacy, Young children's use of language.* Newark, DE: International Reading Association.

Bissex, G. (1980). *GYNS at work: A child learns to write and read.* Cambridge, MA: Harvard University Press.

Blachman, B. A., and James, S. L. (1985). Metalinguistic abilities and reading achievement in first-grade children. In J. Niles and R. Lalik (eds.), *Issues in literacy: A research perspective* (pp. 280–286). Rochester, NY: National Reading Conference.

Bloom, B. (1964). *Stability and change in human characteristics.* New York: John Wiley.

Bloom, B. (1972). *Language development: Form and function in emerging grammars.* Cambridge, MA: MIT Press.

Book Industry Study Group. (1984). *The 1983 consumer research study on reading and book publishing.* New York: Book Industry Study Group.

Brandt, D. (1990). *Literacy as involvement: The acts of writers, readers, and texts.* Carbondale, IL: Southern Illinois University Press.

Britton, J. (1982). The spectator role and the beginnings of writing. In M. Nystrand (Ed.), *What writers know: The language, process and structure of written discourse.* New York: Academic Press.

Brown, A. (1975). Recognition, reconstruction, and recall of narrative sequences of preoperational children. *Child Development, 46,* 155–166.

Brown, C. S., and Lytle, S. (1988). Merging assessment and instruction: Protocols in the classroom. In S. M. Glazer, L. W. Searfoss, and L. M. Gentile (eds.), *Reexamining reading diagnosis: New trends and procedures* (pp. 94–102). Newark, DE: International Reading Association.

Brown, R. (1973). *A first language: The early stages.* Cambridge, MA: Harvard University Press.

Brown, R., and Bellugi, U. (1964). Three processes in the child's acquisition of syntax. *Harvard Educational Review, 34,* 133–151.

Brown, R., Cazden, C., and Bellughi-Klima, U. (1968). The child's grammar from one to three. In J. P. Hill (Ed.), *Minnesota symposium on child development.* Minneapolis: University of Minnesota Press.

Bruner, J. (1975). The ontogenesis of speech acts. *Journal of Child Language, 3,* 1–19.

Bumsted, L. A. (1981). Influencing the frequency of children's cooperative and learning task-related behavior through change in the design and management of the classroom. Master's thesis, Cornell University.

Calkins, L. M. (1983). *Lessons from a child: On the teaching and learning of writing.* Exeter, NH: Heinemann Educational Books.

Calkins, L. M. (1986). *The art of teaching writing.* Exeter, NH: Heinemann Educational Books.

Cambourne, B. (1987). Language, learning and literacy. In A. Butler, and J. Turbill (eds.), *Towards a reading-writing classroom.* Portsmouth, NH: Heinemann.

Cazden, C. (1972). *Child language and education.* New York: Holt, Rinehart & Winston.

Chall, J. S., Conrad, S. S., and Harris-Sharples, S. H. (1983). *Textbooks and challenges: An inquiry into textbook difficulty, reading achievement, and knowledge acquisition.* Final Report to the Spencer Foundation. Chicago, IL.

Chomsky, C. (1965). *Aspects of a theory of syntax.* Cambridge, MA: MIT Press.

Chomsky, C. (1972). Stages in language development and reading. *Harvard Educational Review, 42,* 1–33.

Clark, M. M. (1976). *Young fluent readers.* London: Heinemann Educational Books.

Clark, M. M. (1984). Literacy at home and at school: Insights from a study of young fluent readers. In H. Goelman, A. Oberg, and F. Smith (eds.), *Awakening to literacy.* Exeter, NH: Heinemann Educational Books.

Clay, M. M. (1966). *Emergent reading behavior.* Doctoral dissertation, University of Auckland, New Zealand.

Clay, M. M. (1972). *Reading: The patterning of complex behavior.* Auckland, New Zealand: Heinemann Educational Books.

Clay, M. M. (1975). *What did I write?* Auckland, New Zealand: Heinemann Educational Books.

Clay, M. M. (1979). *The early detection of reading difficulties: A diagnostic survey with recovery procedures.* Auckland, New Zealand: Heinemann Educational Books.

Clay, M. M. (1987). Implementing reading recovery: Systematic adaptations to an educational innovation. *New Zealand Journal of Educational Studies, 22,* 35–38.

Cochran-Smith, M. (1984). *The making of a reader.* Norwood, NJ: Ablex Publishing Corporation.

Cohen, D. (1968). The effects of literature on vocabulary and reading achievement. *Elementary English, 45,* 209–213, 217.

Cohen, M. (1980). *First grade takes a test.* NY: Dell Publishing Co.

Cullinan, B. E. (ed.). (1987). *Children's literature in the reading program.* Newark, DE: International Reading Association.

Cullinan, B. E. (1989). *Literature and the child* (2nd ed.). Orlando, FL: Harcourt Brace Jovanovich.

Cullinan, B. E. (1992). *Invitations to read: More children's literature in the reading program.* Newark, DE: International Reading Association.

Delgado-Gaitan, C. (1992). School matters in the Mexican-American home: Socializing children to education. *American Educational Research Journal, 29,* 459.

Delpit, L. (1995). *Other People's Children.* Presentation at the National Reading Conference, New Orleans, December 1995.

Dewey, J. (1966). *Democracy and education.* New York: First Press (original work published 1916).

Durkin, D. (1966). *Children who read early.* New York: Teachers College Press.

Dyson, A. H. (1985). Individual differences in emerging writing. In M. Farr (ed.), *Advances in writing research: Vol. 1: Children's early writing development.* Norwood, NJ: Ablex Publishing Corp.

Dyson, A. H. (1986). Children's early interpretations of writing: Expanding research perspectives. In D. Yoden and S. Templeton (eds.), *Metalinguistic awareness and beginning literacy.* Exeter, NH: Heinemann Educational Books.

Dyson, A. H. (1993). *Social worlds of children learning to write in an urban primary school.* New York: Teachers College Press.

Ehri, L. C. (1979). Linguistic insight: Threshold of reading acquisition. In T. G. Waller and G. E. MacKinnon (eds.), *Reading research: Advances in theory and practice* (Vol. 1). New York: Academic Press.

Ferreiro, E. (1978). What is written in a written sentence? *Journal of Education, 160,* 24–39.

Ferreiro, E., and Teberosky, A. (1982). *Literacy before schooling.* Exeter, NH: Heinemann Educational Books.

Field, T. (1980). Preschool play: Effects of teacher/child ratios and organization of classroom space. *Child Study Journal, 10,* 191–205.

Flood, J. (1977). Parental styles in reading episodes with young children. *Reading Teacher, 30,* 864–8]67.

Ford, M. E. (1992). *Motivating humans.* Newbury Park, CA: Sage.

Foster, C. R. (1982). Diffusing the issues in bilingualism and bilingual education. *Phi Delta Kappan, 63,* 338–345.

Froebel, F. (1974). *The education of man.* Clifton, NJ: Augustus M. Kelly.

Galda, L., and Cullinan, B. E. (1991). Literature for literacy: What research says about the benefits of using trade books in the classroom. In J. Flood, J. Jensen, D. Lapp, and J. R. Squire (eds.), *Handbook of research on teaching the English language arts.* New York: Macmillan.

Gambrell, L., Pfeiffer, W., and Wilson, R. (1985). The effect of retelling upon comprehension and recall of text information. *Journal of Educational Research, 78,* 216–220.

Gambrell, L. B. (1993). The impact of running start on the reading motivation and behavior of first-grade children (Research report). College Park, MD: University of Maryland, National Reading Research Center.

Gambrell, L. B., and Almasi, J. (1994). Fostering comprehension development through discussion. In L. M. Morrow, J. K. Smith, and L. C. Wilkinson (eds.), *Integrated language arts: Controversy to consensus* (pp. 71–90). Boston: Allyn & Bacon.

Gambrell, L. B., Almasi, J. F., Xie, Q., and Heland, V. (1995). Helping first graders get off to a running start in reading: A home-school-community program that enhances family literacy. In L. Morrow (ed.), *Family literacy connections at school and home.* Newark, DE: International Reading Association.

Gambrell, L. B., and Jawitz, P. B. (1993). Mental imagery, text illustrations, and children's story comprehension and recall. *Reading Research Quarterly, 28,* 264–273.

Genishi, C., and Dyson, A. (1984). *Language assessment in the early years.* Norwood, NJ: Ablex Publishing Corp.

Gesell, A. (1925). *The mental growth of the preschool child.* New York: Macmillan.

Gibson, E., and Levin, H. (1975). *The psychology of reading.* Cambridge, MA: MIT Press.

Gillian, S. (1936). The reading mother. In H. Fellerman (ed.), *Best loved poems of American people.* New York: Doubleday.

Gonzales-Mena, J. (1976). English as a second language for preschool children. *Young Children, 32,* 14–20.

Goodman, K. S. (1967). Reading: A psycholinguistic guessing game. *Journal of the Reading Specialist, 4,* 126–135.

Goodman, Y. (1980). The root of literacy. In M. Douglas (ed.), *Claremont Reading Conference forty-fourth yearbook.* Claremont, CA: Claremont Reading Conference.

Goodman, Y. (1984). The development of initial literacy. In H. Goelman, A. Oberg, and F. Smith (eds.), *Awakening to literacy.* Exeter, NH: Heinemann Educational Books.

Goodman, Y. (1986). Children coming to know literacy. In W. H. Teale and E. Sulzby (eds.), *Emergent literacy: Writing and reading.* Norwood, NJ: Ablex Publishing Corp.

Goodman, Y., and Altwerger, B. (1981). *Print awareness in preschool children: A study of the development of literacy in preschool children* (Occasional Paper 4). Tucson: University of Arizona, College of Education, Arizona Center for Research and Development, Program in Language and Literacy.

Graves, D. H. (1983). *Writing: Teachers and children at work.* Exeter, NH: Heinemann Educational Books.

Graves, D. (1994). *A fresh look at writing.* New Hampshire: Heinemann Educational Books, Inc.

Graves, D., and Hansen, J. (1983). The author's chair. *Language Arts, 60,* 176–183.

Greaney, V. (1980). Factors related to amount and type of leisure reading. *Reading Research Quarterly, 15,* 337–357.

Green, J. (1985). Children's writing in an elementary school postal system. In M. Farr (ed.), *Advances in writing research: Vol. 1. Children's early writing development.* Norwood, NJ: Ablex Publishing Corp.

Gundlach, R., McLane, J., Scott, F., and McNamee, G. (1985). The social foundations of early writing development. In M. Farr (ed.), *Advances in writing research: Vol. 1. Children's early writing development.* Norwood, NJ: Ablex Publishing Corp.

Hall, M. A. (1976). *Teaching reading as a language experience.* Columbus, OH: Chas. E. Merrill.

Halliday, M. A. K. (1975). *Learning how to mean: Exploration in the development of language.* London: Edward Arnold.

Hansen, J. (1987). *When writers read.* Portsmouth, NH: Heinemann Educational Books, Inc.

Hansen, J. S. (1969). The impact of the home literacy environment on reading attitude. *Elementary English, 46,* 17–24.

Harste, J., Woodward, V., and Burke, C. (1984). *Language stories and literacy lessons.* Exeter, NH: Heinemann Educational Books.

Hardy, B. (1968). Toward a poetics of fiction: An approach through narrative. In *The novel: A forum on fiction.* Providence: Brown University Press.

Heath, S. B. (1980). The function and uses of literacy. *Journal of Communication, 30,* 123–133.

Heath, S. B. (1982). What no bedtime story means. *Language in Society, 11,* 49–76.

Heath, S. B. (1993). *Ways with words.* Cambridge, England: Cambridge University Press.

Hiebert, E. H. (1978). Preschool children's understanding of written language. *Child Development, 49,* 1231–1234.

Hiebert, E. H. (1981). Developmental patterns and interrelationships of preschool children's print awareness. *Reading Research Quarterly, 16,* 236–260.

Hiebert, E. H. (1986). Using environmental print in beginning reading instruction. In M. R. Sampson (ed.), *The pursuit of literacy: Early reading and writing.* Dubuque, IA: Kendall/Hunt.

Hiebert, E. H., and Taylor, B. (1994). *Getting reading right from the start.* Newark, DE: International Reading Association.

Hittleman, D. (1983). *Developmental reading: A psycholinguistic perspective.* Chicago: Rand McNally.

Hoffman, J. V., Roser, N. L., and Farest, C. (1988). Literature sharing strategies in classrooms serving students from economically disadvantaged and language different home environments. In J. E. Readance and R. S. Baldwin (eds.), *Dialogues in literacy research.* Thirty-seventh Yearbook of the National Reading Conference. Chicago, IL: National Reading Conference.

Holdaway, D. (1979). *The foundations of literacy.* Sydney: Ashton Scholastic.

Holdaway, D. (1986). The structure of natural learning as a basis for literacy instruction. In M. Sampson (ed.), *The pursuit of literacy: Early reading and writing.* Dubuque, IA: Kendall/Hunt.

Huck, C. (1976). *Children's literature in the elementary school* (3rd ed.). New York: Holt, Rinehart & Winston.

Huck, C. S. (1992). Books for emergent readers. In C. E. Cullinan (ed.), *Invitations to read: More children's literature in the reading program.* Newark, DE: International Reading Association.

Hunt, K. W. (1970). *Syntactic maturity in children and adults.* Monograph of the Society for Research in Child Development (Vol. 25). Chicago: University of Chicago Press.

IRA (International Reading Association). (1985). *Literacy development.* Newark, DE: International Reading Association in early childhood (Pre-K through 3rd grade).

Jagger, A. (1985). Allowing for language differences. In G. S. Pinnell (ed.), *Discovering language with children.* Urbana, IL: National Council of Teachers of English.

Jewell, M., and Zintz, M. (1986). *Learning to read naturally.* Dubuque, IA: Kendall/Hunt.

Johnson, P., and Pearson, P. D. (1982). *Prior knowledge connectivity and the assessment of reading comprehension* (Technical Report 245). Urbana, IL: University of Illinois.

Juel, C. (1989). The role of decoding in early literacy instruction and assessment. In L. Morrow & J. Smith (eds.), *Assessment for instruction in early literacy* (pp. 135–154). Englewood Cliffs, NJ: Prentice Hall.

Juel, C. (1994). Teaching phonics in the context of the integrated language arts. In L. Morrow, J. K. Smith, & L. C. Wilkinson (eds.), *Integrated language arts: Controversy for consensus* (pp. 133–154). Boston: Allyn & Bacon.

Karbon, J. C. (1984). An investigation of the relationship between prior knowledge and vocabulary development using semantic mapping with culturally diverse students. Unpublished doctoral dissertation, University of Wisconsin at Madison.

Lamme, L. (1981). *Learning to love literature: Preschool through grade 3.* Urbana, IL: National Council of Teachers of English.

Leichter, H. P. (1984). Families as environments for literacy. In H. Goelman, A. Oberg, and F. Smith (eds.), *Awakening to literacy.* Exeter, NH: Heinemann Educational Books.

Lennenberg, E. (1967). *Biological foundations of language.* NY: John Wiley.

Lennenberg, E., and Kaplan, E. (1970). Grammatical structures and reading. In H. Levin and J. Williams (eds.), *Basic studies in reading.* New York: Basic Books.

Lenz, L. (1992). Crossroads of literacy and orality: Reading poetry aloud. *Language Arts, 69,* 597–603.

Lepper, M. R. (1988). Motivational considerations in the study of instruction. *Cognition and Instruction, 5,* 289–309.

Leu, D. J., and Kinzer, C. (1991). *Effective reading instruction. K–8* (2nd ed.). New York: Merrill.

Linden, M. and Wittrock, M. C. (1981). The teaching of reading comprehension according to the model of generative learning. *Reading Research Quarterly, 17,* 44–57.

Loughlin, C. E., and Martin, M. D. (1987). *Supporting literacy: Developing effective learning environments.* New York: Teachers College Press.

Maehr, M. L. (1976). Continuing motivations: An analysis of a seldom considered educational outcome. *Review of Educational Research, 46,* 443–462.

Mandler, J., and Johnson, N. (1977). Remembrance of things parsed: Story structure and recall. *Cognitive Psychology, 9,* 111–151.

Martinez, M., and Teale, W. (1988). Reading in a kindergarten classroom library. *Reading Teacher, 41*(6), 568–572.

Martinez, M., and Teale, W. (1987). The ins and outs of a kindergarten writing program. *Reading Teacher, 40,* 444–451.

Mason, J. (1980). When do children begin to read? An exploration of four-year-old children's letter and word reading competencies. *Reading Research Quarterly, 15,* 203–227.

Mason, J. (1982). Acquisition of knowledge about reading. Paper presented at the Annual Meeting of the American Educational Research Association, New York.

Mason, J. (1986). *Reading instruction for today.* Glenview, IL: Scott, Foresman.

Mason, J., and McCormick, C. (1981). *An investigation of pre-reading instruction: A developmental perspective* (Technical Report 224). Urbana: University of Illinois, Center for the Study of Reading.

Mason, J., Stewart, J., and Dunning, D. (1986). *Testing kindergarten children's knowledge about reading* (Technical Report 368). Urbana: University of Illinois, Center for the Study of Reading.

McCormick, C., and Mason, J. (1981). What happens to kindergarten children's knowledge about reading after summer vacation? *Reading Teacher, 35,* 164–172.

McCracken, M., and McCracken, J. (1972). *Reading is the only tiger's tail.* San Rafael, CA: Lewsing Press.

McNeil, D. (1970). *The acquisition of language: The study of developmental psycholinguistics.* New York: Harper & Row Publishers.

Menyuk, P. (1977). *Language and maturation.* Cambridge, MA: MIT Press.

Mitchell, J. N. (1984). Advantages and disadvantages of retelling for reading assessment. Presentation at the International Reading Association Conference, Atlanta, GA.

Montessori, M. (1965). *Spontaneous activity in education.* New York: Schocken Books.

Moore, G. (1986). Effects of the spatial definition of behavior settings on children's behavior: A quasi-experimental field study. *Journal of Environmental Psychology, 6* (3), 205–231.

Morphett, M. V., and Washburne, C. (1931). When should children begin to read? *Elementary School Journal, 31,* 496–508.

Morrow, L. M. (1978). Analysis of syntax in the language of six-, seven-, and eight-year-olds. *Research in the Teaching of English, 12,* 143–148.

Morrow, L. M. (1981). *Supertips for storytelling.* New York: Harcourt Brace Jovanovich, Inc. Instructor Books.

Morrow, L. M. (1982). Relationships between literature programs, library corner designs and children's use of literature. *Journal of Educational Research, 75,* 339–344.

Morrow, L. M. (1983). Home and school correlates of early interest in literature. *Journal of Educational Research, 76,* 221–230.

Morrow, L. M. (1984). Reading stories to young children: Effects of story structure and traditional questioning strategies on comprehension. *Journal of Reading Behavior, 16,* 273–288.

Morrow, L. M. (1985a). *Promoting voluntary reading in school and home.* Bloomington, IN: Phi Delta Kappa Educational Foundation.

Morrow, L. M. (1985b). Retelling stories: A strategy for improving children's comprehension, concept of story structure and oral language complexity. *Elementary School Journal, 85,* 647–661.

Morrow, L. M. (1986). *Promoting responses to literature: Children's sense of story structure.* Paper presented at the National Reading Conference, Austin, TX.

Morrow, L. M. (1987a). The effects of one to one story readings on children's questions and comments. In S. Baldwin and J. Readance (eds.), *Thirty-sixth yearbook of the National Reading Conference.* Rochester, NY.

Morrow, L. M. (1987b). Promoting voluntary reading: The effects of an inner city program in summer day care centers. *The Reading Teacher, 41,* 266–274.

Morrow, L. M. (1988). Young children's responses to one-to-one story readings in school settings. *Reading Research Quarterly, 23*(1), 89–107.

Morrow, L. M. (1990). Preparing the classroom environment to promote literacy during play. *Early Childhood Research Quarterly, 5,* 537–554.

Morrow, L. M. (1992). The impact of a literature-based program on literacy achievement, use of literature, and attitudes of children from minority backgrounds. *Reading Research Quarterly, 27,* 250–275.

Morrow, L. M. (1995). *Family literacy connections at school and home.* Newark, DE: International Reading Association.

Morrow, L. M., and O'Connor, E. (1995). Literacy partnerships for change with "at risk" kindergartners. In R. Allington & Walmsley (eds.), *No quick fix: Rethinking literacy programs in America's elementary schools* (pp. 97–115).

Morrow, L. M., O'Connor, E. M., and Smith, J. (1990). Effects of a story reading program on the literacy development of at-risk kindergarten children. *Journal of Reading Behavior, 20*(2), 104–141.

Morrow, L. M., Paratore, J. R., and Tracey, D. H. (1994). *Family literacy: New perspectives, new opportunities.* International Reading Association, Newark, DE.

Morrow, L. M., and Rand, M. (1991). Promoting literacy during play by designing early childhood classroom environments. *Reading Teacher, 44,* 396–405.

Morrow, L. M., Scoblionko, J., and Shafer, D. (1995). The family reading and writing appreciation program. In L. M. Morrow (Ed.), *Family literacy connections in schools and communities,* pp. 70–86. Newark, DE: International Reading Association.

Morrow, L. M., Sharkey, E., and Firestone, W. (1994). Collaborative strategies in the integrated language arts. In L. M. Morrow, J. K. Smith, and L. C. Wilkinson (eds.), *Integrated language arts: Controversy to consensus* (pp. 155–176). Boston: Allyn & Bacon.

Morrow, L. M., and Smith, J. K. (1990). The effect of group setting on interactive storybook reading. *Reading Research Quarterly, 25,* 213–231.

Morrow, L. M., and Tracey, D. H. (1996). Instructional environments for language and learning. Considerations for young children. In J. Flood, S. B. Heath, and D. Lapp (eds.), *Handbook for literacy educators: Research on teaching the communicative and visual arts.* New York: Macmillan

Morrow, L. M., Tracey, D., and Maxwell, C. M. (1995). *A survey of family literacy in the United States.* Newark, DE: International Reading Association.

Morrow, L. M., and Weinstein, C. S. (1982). Increasing children's use of literature through program and physical design changes. *Elementary School Journal, 83,* 131–137.

Morrow, L. M., and Weinstein, C. S. (1986). Encouraging voluntary reading: The impact of a literature program on children's use of library centers. *Reading Research Quarterly, 21,* 330–346.

Nash, B. (1981). The effects of classroom spatial organization on four- and five-year-old children's learning. *British Journal of Educational Psychology, 51,* 144–155.

National Center for Family Literacy (1993). Parents and children together. In *Creating an upward spiral of success* (pp. 6–8). Louisville, KY: National Center for Family Literacy.

National Reading Research Center (1991). Conceptual framework: The engagement perspective. In National Reading Research Center: A Proposal from the University of Maryland and the University of Georgia (pp. 8–10). Athens, GA and College Park, MD.

Neuman, S., and Roskos, K. (1990). The influence of literacy-enriched play settings on preschoolers' engagement with written language. In J. Zutell and S. McCormick (eds.), *Literacy theory and research: Analyses from multiple paradigms* (pp. 179–187). Thirty-ninth yearbook of the National Reading Conference. Chicago: National Reading Conference.

Neuman, S., and Roskos, K. (1992). Literary objects as cultural tools: Effects on children's literacy behaviors in play. *Reading Research Quarterly, 27* (3), 202–225.

Neuman, S., and Roskos, K. (1993). *Language and literacy learning in the early years: An integrated approach.* Orlando, FL: Harcourt, Brace.

Newman, J. (1984). *The craft of children's writing.* Exeter, NH: Heinemann Educational Books.

Newman, J. (ed.). (1985). *Whole language: Theory in use.* Exeter, NH: Heinemann Educational Books.

Ninio, A. (1980). Picture book reading in mother-infant dyads belonging to two subgroups in Israel. *Child Development, 51,* 587

Ninio, A., and Bruner, J. (1978). The achievement and antecedents of labeling. *Journal of Child Language, 5,* 1–15.

O'Flahavan, J., Gambrell, L. B., Guthrie, J., Stahl, S., and Alverman, D. (1992, April). Poll results guide acti-vities of research center (p. 12). *Reading Today.* Newark, DE: International Reading Association.

Oldfather, P. (1993). What students say about motivating experiences in a whole language classroom. *The Reading Teacher, 46,* 672–681.

Palincsar, A. S., Brown, A. L., and Martin, S. M. (1987). Peer interaction in reading, comprehension instruction. *Journal of Educational Psychology, 23,* 231–253.

Pappas, C., Keifer, B., and Levstik, L. (1995). *An integrated language perspective in the elementary school, Theory into action.* New York: Longman.

Parker, R. (1983). Language development and learning to write. In R. Parker and F. Davis (eds.), *Developing literacy: Young children's use of language*. Newark, DE: International Reading Association.

Paulu, N. (1987). *Dealing with dropouts: The urban superintendent's call to action*. Washington, DC: Office of Educational Research.

Pearson, P. D., Hanson, J., and Gordon, C. (1979). Effects of background knowledge on young children's comprehension of explicit and implicit information. *Journal of Reading Behavior, 11*, 201–209.

Pearson, P. D., and Johnson, D. D. (1978). *Teaching reading comprehension*. New York: Holt, Rinehart & Winston.

Pedersen, P. P. (1994). *A handbook for developing multicultural awareness*. Alexandria, VA: American Counseling Association.

Pellegrini, A., and Galda, L. (1982). The effects of thematic fantasy play training on the development of children's story comprehension. *American Educational Research Journal, 19*, 443–452.

Pflaum, S. (1986). *The development of language and literacy in young children* (3rd ed.). Columbus, OH: Chas. E. Merrill.

Piaget, J., and Inhelder, B. (1969). *The psychology of the child*. New York: Basic Books.

Pinnell, G. S., Freid, M. D., and Estice, R. M. (1990). Reading recovery: Learning how to make a difference. *The Reading Teacher, 43*(4), 282–295.

Pittelman, S. D., Levin, K. M., and Johnson, D. P. (1985). An investigation of two instructional settings in the use of semantic mapping with poor readers (Program Report 85–4). Madison: Wisconsin Center for Educational Research, University of Wisconsin.

Read, C. (1975). Children's categorization of speech sounds in English (National Research Report 17). Urbana, IL: National Council of Teachers of English.

Richards, J. (1979). Adjunct post questions in text: A critical review of methods and processes. *Review of Educational Research, 49*, 181–196.

Rivlin, L., and Weinstein, C. (1984). Educational issues, school settings, and environmental psychology. *Journal of Environmental Psychology, 4*, 347–364.

Robinson, V., Strickland, D., and Cullinan, B. (1977). The child: Ready or not? In L. Ollila (Ed.), *The kindergarten child and reading*. Newark, DE: International Reading Association.

Rosenthal, B. A. (1973). An ecological study of free play in the nursery school. Doctoral dissertation, Wayne State University.

Rosenblatt, L. M. (1988). *Writing and reading: Transactional theory* (Report No. 13). University of California, Berkeley, CA: Center for the Study of Writing.

Roser, N., and Martinez, M. (1985). Roles adults play in preschool responses to literature. *Language Arts, 62*, 485–490.

Routman, R. (1991). *Invitations: Changing as teachers and learners K–12*. NH: Heinemann Educational Books, Inc.

Rousseau, J. (1962). *Emile* (ed. and trans. William Boyd). New York: Columbia University Teachers College. (original work published 1762)

Ruddell, R., and Ruddell, M. R. (1995). *Teaching children to read and write, Becoming an influential teacher*. Boston: Allyn & Bacon.

Rusk, R., and Scotland, J. (1979). *Doctrines of the great educators*. New York: St. Martin's Press.

Saltz, E., and Johnson, J. (1974). Training for thematic-fantasy play in culturally disadvantaged children: Preliminary results. *Journal of Educational Psychology, 66*(4), 623–630.

Schickedanz, J. A. (1986). *More than ABC's: The early stages of reading and writing*. Washington, DC: National Association for the Education of Young Children.

Schickedanz, J. A. (1993). Designing the early childhood classroom environment to facilitate literacy development. In B. Spodek and O. N. Saracho (eds.), *Language and literacy in early childhood education: Yearbook in early childhood education* (Vol. 4). New York: Teachers College Press.

Schickedanz, J. A., York, M. E., Stewart, I. S., and White, A. (1990). *Strategies for teaching young children*. Englewood Cliffs, NJ: Prentice Hall.

Seefeldt, C., and Barbour, N. (1986). *Early childhood education: An introduction*. Columbus, OH: Chas. E. Merrill.

Sharon, S. (1980). Cooperative learning in small groups: Recent methods and effects of achievement, attitudes, and ethnic relations. *Review of Educational Research, 50*, 241–271.

Skinner, B. F. (1957). *Verbal behavior*. Boston: Appleton-Century-Crofts.

Slavin, R. (1977). Student learning teams and scores adjusted for past achievement: A summary of field experience (Rep. No. 227). Baltimore, MD: Johns Hopkins University Center for Social Organization of Schools.

Slavin, R. E., and Madden, N. A. (1989). What works for students at risk: A research synthesis. *Educational Leadership, 46*, 4–13.

Smith, F. (1971). *Understanding reading*. New York: Holt, Rinehart & Winston.

Smith, F. (1972). The learner and his language. In R. Hodges and E. H. Rudorf (eds.), *Language and learning to read*. Boston: Houghton Mifflin.

Smith, F. (1978). *Understanding reading* (2nd ed.). New York: Holt, Rinehart & Winston.

Smith, F. (1983). A metaphor for literacy: Creating words or shunting information? In F. Smith (ed.), *Essays into literacy*. Exeter, NH: Heinemann Educational Books.

Snow, C., and Perlmann, R. (1985). Assessing children's knowledge about bookreading. In L. Galda and A. Pellegrini (eds.), *Play, language, and stories*. Norwood, NJ: Ablex Publishing Corp.

Snow, C. E. (1983). Literacy and language: Relationships during the preschool years. *Harvard Educational Review, 53,* 165–189.

Spaulding, C. I. (1992). The motivation to read and write. In J. W. Irwin and M. A. Doyle (eds.), *Reading/writing connections: Learning from research* Newark, DE: International Reading Association, (pp. 177–201).

Spiegel, D. L. (1981). *Reading for pleasure: Guidelines*. Newark, DE: International Reading Association.

Spielberg, S. (1987). Acceptance speech at the Academy Award Ceremonies. Los Angeles.

Spivak, M. (1973). Archetypal place. *Architectural Forum, 140,* 44–49.

Spodek, B. (1988). Conceptualizing today's kindergarten curriculum. *Elementary School Journal, 89,* 203–212.

Stanovich, K. E. (1986). Mathew effects in reading: Some consequences of individual differences in the acquisition of literacy. *Reading Research Quarterly, 21,* 360–407.

Stauffer, R. G. (1980). *The language-experience approach to the teaching of reading* (2nd ed.). New York: Harper & Row.

Stewart, J., Benjamin, L., and Mason, L. (1987). An early literacy program: Putting research into practice. Paper presented at the University of the Virgin Islands.

Stewig, J. W., and Sebesta, S. (eds.). (1978). *Using literature in the elementary classroom*. Urbana, IL: National Council of Teachers of English.

Sticht, T. G., and McDonald, B. A. (1989). *Making the nation smarter: The intergenerational transfer of cognitive ability*. San Diego, CA: Applied Behavioral and Cognitive Sciences.

Sue, D. W., Arredondo, P., and McDavis, R. J. (1992). *Journal of Counseling and Development, 70,* 447–482.

Sulzby, E. (1985). Children's emergent reading of favorite storybooks. *Reading Research Quarterly, 20,* 458–481.

Sulzby, E. (1986a). Kindergarteners as writers and readers. In M. Farr (ed.), *Advances in writing research: Vol.1. Children's early writing*. Norwood, NJ: Ablex Publishing Corp.

Sulzby, E. (1986b). Children's elicitation and use of metalinguistic knowledge about "word" during literacy interactions. In P. Yaden and S. Templeton (eds.), *Metalinguistic awareness and beginning literacy*. Exeter, NH: Heinemann Educational Books.

Sulzby, E. (1987). Simplified version of Sulzby's (1985) classification scheme for "Children's emergent reading of favorite storybooks."

Sutfin, H. (1980). The effects on children's behavior of a change in the physical design of a kindergarten classroom. Doctoral dissertation, Boston University.

Taylor, B. M., Frye, B. J., and Maruyama, M. (1990). Time spent reading and reading growth. *American Educational Research Journal, 27,* 351–362.

Taylor, B. M., Strait, J., and Medo, M. A. (1994). Early intervention in reading: Supplemental instruction for groups of low-achieving students provided by first-grade teachers. In E. H. Heibert, and B. Taylor (eds.), *Getting ready right from the start* (pp. 107–123). Newark, DE: International Reading Association.

Taylor, D. (1983). *Family literacy*. Exeter, NH: Heinemann Educational Books.

Taylor, D., and Dorsey-Gaines, C. (1988). *Growing up literate*. Portsmouth, NH: Heinemann.

Taylor, D., and Strickland, D. (1986). *Family storybook reading*. Exeter, NH: Heinemann Educational Books.

Teale, W. (1978). Positive environments for learning to read: What studies of early readers tell us. *Language Arts, 55,* 922–932.

Teale, W. (1981). Parents reading to their children: What we know and need to know. *Language Arts, 58,* 902–911.

Teale, W. (1982). Toward a theory of how children learn to read and write naturally. *Language Arts, 59,* 555–570.

Teale, W. (1984). Reading to young children: Its significance for literacy development. In H. Goelman, A. Oberg, and F. Smith (eds.), *Awakening to literacy*. Exeter, NH: Heinemann Educational Books.

Teale, W. (1986). The beginning of reading and writing: Written language development during the preschool and kindergarten years. In M. Sampson (ed.), *The pursuit of literacy: Early reading and writing*. Dubuque, IA: Kendal/Hunt.

Teale, W. (1987). Emergent literacy: Reading and writing development in early childhood. In J.

Readance and R. S. Baldwin (eds.), *Thirty-sixth Yearbook of the National Reading Conference*. Rochester, NY: National Reading Conference.

Teale, W., Hiebert, E., and Chittenden, E. (1987). Assessing young children's literary development. *Reading Teacher, 40*, 772–778.

Temple, C., Nathan, R., Burris, N., and Temple, F. (1988). *The beginnings of writing*. Boston: Allyn and Bacon.

Templeton, S. (1991). *Teaching the integrated language arts*. Boston: Houghton Mifflin.

Thorndyke, R. (1977). Cognitive structures in comprehension and memory of narrative discourse. *Cognitive Psychology, 9*, 77–110.

Tompkins, G. E., and Koskisson, I. K. (1995). *Language arts content and teaching strategies*. Englewood Cliffs, NJ: Prentice Hall.

Torrey, J. (1969). Learning to read without a teacher. *Elementary English, 46*, 556–559.

Turner, J. D. (1992, April). *Identifying motivation for literacy in first grade: An observational study*. Paper presented at the annual meeting of the American Educational Research Association, San Francisco.

Tunmer, W. E., and Nesdale, A. R. (1985). Phonemic segmentation skill and beginning reading. *Journal of Educational Psychology, 77*, 417–427.

Valencia, S. W., Hiebert, E. H., and Afflerbach, P. (eds.). (1994). *Authentic reading assessment: Practices and possibilities*. Newark, DE: International Reading Association.

Veatch, J., Sawicki, F., Elliot, G., Barnett, E., and Blackey, J. (1973). *Key words to reading: The language experience approach begins*. Columbus, OH: Chas. E. Merrill.

Vygotsky, L. S. (1978). *Mind in society: The development of psychological processes*. Cambridge, MA: Harvard University Press.

Vygotsky, L. S. (1981). The genesis of higher mental functions. In J. J. Wertsch (ed.), *The concept of activity*. White Plains, NY: M. E. Sharpe.

Ward, M., and McCormick, S. (1981). Reading instruction for blind and low vision children in the regular classroom. *The Reading Teacher, 34*, 434, 444.

Williams, J. P. (1985). The case for explicit decoding instruction. In J. Osborn, P. T. Wilson, and R. C. Anderson (eds.), *Reading education: Foundations for a literate America*. Lexington, MA: Heath, Lexington Books.

Wittrock, M. C. (1974). Learning as a generative process. *Educational Psychologist, 11*, 87–95.

Wittrock, M. C. (1986). Students' thought processes. In M. C. Wittrock (ed.), *Handbook of research on teaching* (pp. 297–314). New York: Macmillan.

Yaden, D. (1985). Preschoolers' spontaneous inquiries about print and books. Paper presented at the Annual Meeting of the National Reading Conference, San Diego.

Yager, S., Johnson, D. W., and Johnson, R. T. (1985). Oral discussion, group to individual transfer, and achievement in cooperative learning groups. *Journal of Educational Psychology, 77*, 60–66.

Children's Literature Bibliography

Aliki. (1974). *Go tell Aunt Rhody*. New York: Macmillan.

Base, G. (1987). *Animalia*. New York: Harry N. Abrams.

Bemelmans, L. (1939). *Madeline*. New York: Viking.

Bemelmans, L. (1953). *Madeline's rescue*. New York: Viking.

Berenstain, S. J. (1987). *The Berenstain bears and too much birthday*. New York: Random House.

Brenner, B. (1972). *The three little pigs*. New York: Random House.

Brown, M. (1939). *The noisy book*. New York: Harper.

Brown, M. (1947). *Goodnight moon*. New York: Harper Collins.

Brown, M. (1957). *The three billy goats gruff*. New York: Harcourt Brace.

Burton, V. L. (1943). *Katy and the big snow*. Boston: Houghton Mifflin.

Carle, E. (1969). *The very hungry caterpillar*. New York: Philomel.

Cole, J. (1987). *The magic school bus inside the earth*. New York: Scholastic.

DePaola, T. (1973). *Charlie needs a clock*. Englewood Cliffs, NJ: Prentice Hall.

DePaola, T. (1978). *The popcorn book*. New York: Holiday House.

Duvoisin, R. (1950). *Petunia*. New York: Alfred A. Knopf.

Eastman, P. D. (1960). *Are you my mother?* New York: Random House.

Emberley, B. (1967). *Drummer Hoff*. Englewood Cliffs, NJ: Prentice Hall.

Flack, M. (1932). *Ask Mr. Bear*. New York: Collier Books.

Fujikawa, A. (1980). *Jenny learns a lesson*. New York: Grosset & Dunlap.

Galdone, P. (1973). *The little red hen*. Boston: Houghton Mifflin.

Hazen, B. S. (1983). *Tight times*. New Jersey: Picture Puffins.

Hennessy, B. G. (1991). *The missing tarts*. New York: Puffin Books.

Hoban, R. (1964). *Bread and jam for Frances*. New York: Harper & Row.

Holdsworth, W. (1968). *The gingerbread boy*. New York: Farrar, Straus & Giroux.

Hurd, E. (1980). *Under the lemon tree*. Boston: Little, Brown.

Hutchins, P. (1968). *Rosie's walk*. New York: Collier Books.

Izawa, T. (1968a). *Goldilocks and the three bears*. New York: Grosset Dunlap.

Izawa, T. (1968b). *The little red hen*. New York: Grosset & Dunlap.

Johnson, C. (1955). *Harold and the purple crayon*. New York: Harper & Row.

Kasza, K. (1988). *The pig's picnic*. New York: Putnam.

Keats, E. (1962). *The snowy day*. New York: Viking.

Keats, E. (1966). *Jenny's hat*. New York: Harper & Row.

Keats, E. J. (1967). *Peter's chair*. New York: Harper & Row, Publishers.

Keats, E. J. (1971). *Over in the meadow*. New York: Scholastic.

Keats, E. (1974). *Pet show*. New York: Aladdin Books.

Lenski, L. (1965). *The little farm*. New York: Henry Z. Walek.

LeSieg, T. (1961). *Ten apples up on top*. New York: Random House.

Lionni, L. (1963). *Swimmy*. New York: Pantheon.

Livingston, M. C. (1993). *Abraham Lincoln: A man for all people*. New York: Holiday House.

McCloskey, R. (1948). *Blueberries for Sal*. New York: Viking.

McGovern, A. (1967). *Too much noise*. Boston: Houghton Mifflin.

McNulty, F. (1979). *How to dig a hole to the other side of the world*. New York: Harper and Row.

Piper, W. (1954). *The little engine that could*. New York: Platt and Munk.

Potter, B. (1902). *The tale of Peter Rabbit*. New York: Scholastic Book Services.

Quakenbush, R. (1972). *Old MacDonald had a farm*. New York: Lippincott.

Quackenbush, R. (1973). *Go tell Aunt Rhody*. New York: Lippincott.

Rey, H. A. (1941). *Curious George*. Boston: Houghton Mifflin.

Sendak, M. (1962). *Chicken soup with rice*. New York: Harper & Row, Publishers.

Sendak, M. (1963). *Where the wild things are*. New York: Harper & Row, Publishers.

Seuss, Dr. (1940). *Horton hatches the egg*. New York: Random House.

Seuss, Dr. (1957a). *How the Grinch stole Christmas*. New York: Random House.

Seuss, Dr. (1957b). *The cat in the hat*. New York: Random House.

Seuss, Dr. (1960). *Green eggs and ham*. New York: Random House.

Seuss, Dr. (1970). *Mister Brown can moo: Can you?* New York: Random House.

Slobodkina, E. (1947). *Caps for sale*. Reading, MA: Addison-Wesley.

Viorst, J. (1972). *Alexander and the terrible, horrible, no good, very bad day*. New York: Atheneum.

Westcott, N. B. (1980). *I know an old lady*. Boston: Little, Brown.

White, E. B. (1952). *Charlotte's web*. New York: Scholastic.

Zolotow, C. (1962). *Mr. Rabbit and the lovely present*. New York: Harper & Row.

Index